The 70-270 Cram Sheet

This Cram Sheet contains distilled, key facts about Windows XP Professional. Review this information as the last thing you do before you enter the testing center; pay special attention to those areas where you think you need the most review. You can transfer any of these facts from your head onto a blank sheet of paper immediately before you begin the exam.

INSTALLATION AND DEPLOYMENT

1. Know the differences between ACPI and APM when installing the OS, as well as the ramifications if the wrong one is in place after installation.

2. Know all the following processes for unattended and Remote Installation Service (RIS) installations:
   - ➤ winnt.sif—Used to automate CD-ROM-based installs.
   - ➤ sysprep.inf—The answer file for System Preparation (Sysprep) installs.
   - ➤ winnt.exe with the /u, /s, and /udf switches—Used for unattended installations.
   - ➤ winnt32.exe and unattend.txt— Automate an upgrade to Windows XP.
   - ➤ Requirements for RIS are Active Directory, DNS, and DHCP.

3. winnt32.exe with the checkupgradeonly switch is used to verify hardware and software compatibility before installation.

4. rbfg.exe is used to create remote boot disks for RIS clients if computers don't have network adapters with Pre-boot Execution Environment (PXE) boot ROM.

5. riprep.exe is used to create images of Windows XP Professional and applications for an RIS server.

6. risetup.exe is used to configure RIS.

7. update.exe /integrate:fullpath is used to apply a service pack to a distribution share in slipstream mode.

8. Know how to convert to an NTFS file system after installation, as well as how to stop the conversion after it has been initialized.

9. Remember that you can roll back to the old OS after Windows XP is installed in some circumstances, but never when upgrading from Windows 2000.

10. Know the details surrounding dynamic update for installation as well as the critical switches: dudisable, dushare, and duprepare.

11. Understand the sysprep tool and the essential switches that are available: clean, factory, nosidgen, and reseal.

12. Know the two important commands used with the User State Migration tool: scanstate and loadstate.

13. Know the different updates that are available:
    - ➤ Dynamic Update
    - ➤ Automatic Updates
    - ➤ Windows Update—

14. Know that SUS can deploy service packs, as well as other critical security updates.

CONFIGURING AND MANAGING RESOURCES

15. The default permissions for new shares is Everyone, Allow, Read. If share permissions conflict with NTFS permissions, the *most restrictive* permissions take precedence.

16. When you combine NTFS permissions based on users and their group memberships, the *least restrictive* permissions take precedence. However, Deny entries always override Allow entries.

17. By default, NTFS permissions are inherited from the parent folder. Permissions that are not inherited are referred to as *explicit.* Explicit permissions always override inherited permissions.

18. To change NTFS permissions on a file or folder, you must be the owner or have the Change Permissions permission, which itself is part of Full Control. NTFS permissions are retained from the source folder whenever you move subfolders or files to another folder on the same NTFS volume. NTFS permissions are inherited from the destination folder in all other move and copy operations.

19. NTFS for Windows XP supports both file compression and data encryption. Encryption is implemented via the Encrypting File System (EFS). You can compress or encrypt a file, but not both.

20. Windows XP Professional and Windows 2000 computers can connect to print devices that are attached to Windows XP, Windows 2000, and Windows Server 2003 print servers through a web browser. This feature uses the Internet Printing Protocol (IPP). IIS must be running on the machine you want to connect to. You can enter one of the following URLs into your web browser:

   ➤ http://print_server_name/printers

   ➤ http://print_server_name/
      printer_share_name

21. USB drives can be write-protected by modifying the StoreageDevicePolicies Registry key and WriteProtect Registry value.

SECURITY ACCOUNTS AND POLICIES

22. The Administrator account can be disabled with a GPO. This requires that a new user account be created with administrative privileges before the original Administrator account is disabled.

23. Local user and group accounts can be granted privileges and permissions to resources on the same system only. They cannot access resources on other systems.

24. Local user accounts can belong to local groups on the same system only. Domain user accounts can belong to global groups, universal groups, domain local groups, and machine local groups.

25. Renaming an account maintains all group memberships, permissions, and privileges of the account. Copying a user account maintains group memberships, permissions, and privileges assigned to its groups, but doing so does not retain permissions associated with the original user account. Deleting and re-creating an account with the same name loses all group memberships and permissions.

26. The most powerful group on a system is its local Administrators group. The Power Users group is an excellent group for most users who need to control the computer's resources, but not the computer's administration.

27. Organizational Units (OUs) in Active Directory create a hierarchical structure of containers for other objects, such as users, groups, and computers. Objects inherit attributes of their parent objects.

28. The Resulting Set of Policies (RSoP) is the final set of policies that is applied to the user and computer. The gpresult tool can help determine this RSoP, as can the RSoP MMC snap-in. The gpupdate tool can help "refresh" the policies to ensure the correct policies are applied.

29. The Group Policy Management Console is used from a Windows XP client to help administer GPOs stored in Active Directory.

30. There are more than 600 new GPOs added with SP2. The majority of these new GPO settings control Windows Firewall and Internet Explorer.

31. The Security Center is the new command central for administering security on the Windows XP client. You can configure Windows Firewall, virus protection, Automatic Updates, and Internet Explorer security through the interface.

MANAGING USER AND DESKTOP SETTINGS

32. Know the purpose and configuration of all the accessibility features: StickyKeys, FilterKeys Narrator, Magnifier, and On-Screen Keyboard.

33. Use the MSCONFIG utility to change system startup settings, enable and disable services, and modify BOOT.ini file settings.

34. The Regional and Language Options applet in Control Panel specifies user and input locales. It can also be used to add new input languages. Use this applet to pair input locales with a specific keyboard layout when a user needs to work with different languages.

35. Transfer data files and program settings from pre-Windows XP computers using either the User State Migration Tool (USMT) or the File Settings and Transfer (FAST) Wizard.

36. Applications can be deployed to users via a Group Policy. Applications can be either published or assigned. Install published applications via the Add and Remove Programs applet. Assigned applications have shortcuts in the Start menu, which will launch the installation program for an assigned application upon first use.

37. Typically, only applications compiled as an .msi file can be deployed via a Group Policy. However, non-.msi applications can use a ZAP file to tell Group Policy how to install the application.

38. To enable roaming profiles, enter the UNC path to the user's profile in the user's account properties.

39. To configure mandatory profiles, rename ntuser.dat to ntuser.man.

40. The Offline Files feature caches copies of network files locally. It is enabled by default on the client. On the server side, Manual Caching of Documents is the default setting for shared folders. You can choose to Encrypt Offline Files to Secure Data from the Offline Files tab of the Folder Options dialog box.

41. Dualview is an advanced display option that enables a mobile computer to extend the Windows XP desktop onto both its built-in LCD display and an external monitor. It also supports desktop PCs that have one video adapter installed with two video output ports. You enable Dualview via the Display applet in Control panel.

42. Use the Program Compatibility Wizard to run legacy applications in Compatibility Mode for Windows 95, Windows 98/Me, Windows NT 4 SP5, or Windows 2000. No other modes are available.

HARDWARE AND DEVICE DRIVERS

43. Windows XP can control whether users can install signed or unsigned drivers, or both, for a chosen device. The selection for this is called Driver

EXAM CRAM™ 2

Windows XP Professional

Derek Melber

Dan Balter

MCSA/MCSE 70-270 Exam Cram 2: Windows XP Professional

Copyright © 2005 by Que Publishing

International Standard Book Number: 0-7897-3360-9

Library of Congress Catalog Card Number: 2004118403

Printed in the United States of America

First Printing: June 2005

08 07 06 05   4 3 2 1

Trademarks

All terms mentioned in this book that are known to be trademarks or service marks have been appropriately capitalized. Que Publishing cannot attest to the accuracy of this information. Use of a term in this book should not be regarded as affecting the validity of any trademark or service mark.

Warning and Disclaimer

Every effort has been made to make this book as complete and as accurate as possible, but no warranty or fitness is implied. The information provided is on an "as is" basis. The authors and the publisher shall have neither liability nor responsibility to any person or entity with respect to any loss or damages arising from the information contained in this book or from the use of the CD or programs accompanying it. Windows is a registered trademark of Microsoft Corporation.

Bulk Sales

Que Publishing offers excellent discounts on this book when ordered in quantity for bulk purchases or special sales. For more information, please contact

> **U.S. Corporate and Government Sales**
> 1-800-382-3419
> corpsales@pearsontechgroup.com

For sales outside the U.S., please contact

> **International Sales**
> international@pearsoned.com

Publisher
Paul Boger

Executive Editor
Jeff Riley

Acquisitions Editor
Jeff Riley

Development Editor
Steve Rowe

Managing Editor
Charlotte Clapp

Project Editor
Seth Kerney

Copy Editor
Barbara Hacha

Indexer
John Sleeva

Proofreader
Juli Cook

Technical Editor
Bert Smith

Publishing Coordinator
Pamalee Nelson

Multimedia Developer
Dan Scherf

Interior Designer
Gary Adair

Cover Designer
Anne Jones

Page Layout
TnT Design

Que
CERTIFICATION

Que Certification • 800 East 96th Street • Indianapolis, Indiana 46240

A Note from Series Editor Ed Tittel

You know better than to trust your certification preparation to just anybody. That's why you, and more than 2 million others, have purchased an Exam Cram book. As Series Editor for the new and improved Exam Cram 2 Series, I have worked with the staff at Que Certification to ensure you won't be disappointed. That's why we've taken the world's best-selling certification product—a two-time finalist for "Best Study Guide" in CertCities' reader polls—and made it even better.

As a two-time finalist for the "Favorite Study Guide Author" award as selected by CertCities readers, I know the value of good books. You'll be impressed with Que Certification's stringent review process, which ensures the books are high quality, relevant, and technically accurate.

Exam Cram 2 books also feature a preview edition of MeasureUp's powerful, full-featured test engine, which is trusted by certification students throughout the world.

As a 20-year-plus veteran of the computing industry and the original creator and editor of the Exam Cram Series, I've brought my IT experience to bear on these books. During my tenure at Novell from 1989 to 1994, I worked with and around its excellent education and certification department. At Novell, I witnessed the growth and development of the first really big, successful IT certification program—one that was to shape the industry forever afterward. This experience helped push my writing and teaching activities heavily in the certification direction. Since then, I've worked on nearly 100 certification related books, and I write about certification topics for numerous Web sites and for *Certification* magazine.

In 1996, while studying for various MCP exams, I became frustrated with the huge, unwieldy study guides that were the only preparation tools available. As an experienced IT professional and former instructor, I wanted "nothing but the facts" necessary to prepare for the exams. From this impetus, Exam Cram emerged: short, focused books that explain exam topics, detail exam skills and activities, and get IT professionals ready to take and pass their exams.

In 1997 when Exam Cram debuted, it quickly became the best-selling computer book series since "*...For Dummies*," and the best-selling certification book series ever. By maintaining an intense focus on subject matter, tracking errata and updates quickly, and following the certification market closely, Exam Cram established the dominant position in cert prep books.

You will not be disappointed in your decision to purchase this book. If you are, please contact me at etittel@jump.net. All suggestions, ideas, input, or constructive criticism are welcome!

Ed Tittel

I dedicate this book to my wife, whom I love unconditionally.

—Derek Melber

I dedicate this second-edition book to my loving family—
Alison, Alexis, and Brendan.

—Dan Balter

About the Authors

Dan Balter is the Chief Technology Officer for InfoTechnology Partners, Inc., a Microsoft Certified Partner company. He works as an IT consultant and trainer for both corporate and government clients and has worked with several network operating systems throughout his 22-year career. Dan prides himself on tackling complex, technical topics and making them understandable for people. Dan is a Microsoft Certified Desktop Support Technician (MCDST), a Microsoft Certified Systems Administrator (MCSA) on Windows 2000 and Windows Server 2003, and a Microsoft Certified Systems Engineer (MCSE) on Windows NT 4.0, Windows 2000, and Windows Server 2003. He specializes in Microsoft networking technologies, firewalls, VPNs, and other security solutions in addition to designing and implementing messaging and business solutions for small- to medium-sized organizations.

Dan is the author of *Exam Cram 2: Managing and Maintaining a Windows Server 2003 Environment* and a coauthor for the best-selling books *Exam Cram 2: Supporting Users and Troubleshooting a Windows XP Operating System* and *Exam Cram 2: Windows 2000 Professional*, all published by Que Certification. A graduate of USC's School of Business in 1983, Dan has authored and been featured in more than 300 video- and CD-ROM-based computer training courses, including instructional titles on installing, configuring, and administering Windows 95, Windows 98, Windows NT, Windows 2000, Windows XP, and Windows Server 2003. He is also a featured video trainer for courses on Microsoft Exchange Server, Microsoft Outlook, and Intuit's QuickBooks small business accounting software. Dan is also a partner in BlastThroughLearning.com, a self-paced multimedia computer training provider.

Dan and his family live in the Santa Rosa Valley area in Southern California, near the city of Camarillo. Dan lives with his lovely wife, Alison, their 9-year-old daughter, Alexis, their 6-year-old son, Brendan, and their golden retriever, Brandy. When he's not writing, researching, or consulting, Dan enjoys traveling and going on Disney cruises with his family, swimming, playing racquetball and basketball, rooting for the Los Angeles Galaxy soccer team and the L.A. Lakers, going for long walks, listening to music, and exploring new age spirituality. Dan can be contacted via email at Dan@InfoTech-Partners.com.

Derek Melber is an independent technical trainer, consultant, and author who specializes in Microsoft products and technologies. Derek has written many books on Windows Active Directory, Group Policy Objects, Active Directory security, Windows security, and other Windows topics.

Derek also runs a website, www.auditingwindows.com, which is dedicated to Windows Security and Auditing. There you will find the only books on Auditing Windows Security. The site is full of great information, links, and custom training options.

If Group Policy is your quest, pick up Derek's latest administrators book, which is the Group Policy Guide. This is one of the books in the Windows Server 2003 Resource Kit.

You might run into Derek at a conference where he is speaking. Derek speaks at TechMentor, IIA, MISTI, and other specialized conferences throughout the USA and Canada. He focuses on Active Directory, Group Policy Objects, security, and auditing security.

Derek provides custom and off-the-shelf training on all the topics on which he speaks and writes. To get more information, please email him at derekm@braincore.net.

Acknowledgments

Dan Balter: Without a doubt, my beautiful wife and my two incredible kids give me the encouragement, support, and the strength that I need to carry on and always see things through to their completion, just like the second edition of this book! Alison is much more than just my wife; she's my mentor, my inspiration, and my lifetime partner! My daughter, Alexis, is almost 9 years old now—she never fails to amaze me with her creativity, her love, her warmth, her intelligence, and her willingness to learn. My son, Brendan, is just about 6 years old now, and he is a constant source of happiness, fun, affection, brilliance, and incessant energy! So, first and foremost, I am indebted to my family for their unfailing love and support.

I owe a lot of gratitude to my coauthor, Derek Melber. Derek is a great guy and a consummate professional. He did a superb job on the second edition revisions to this book and he was willing to put up with me missing all our deadlines while he finished early!

I also want to offer my heartfelt appreciation to my top notch technical staff: Tim Leonard and Matt Singleton. Tim has been a full-time consultant at my company, InfoTechnology Partners, Inc, for about a year and a half. He has quickly become an invaluable resource, and he is very much responsible for the rapid growth of our company without sacrificing our first-class customer service! In 2004, Matt traveled all the way to California from his native Houston, Texas, just to come onboard with us! Matt has been a terrific addition to our firm and his extensive knowledge of Cisco networking and VoIP technology is an incredible added bonus!

Over the past several years, my good friend, Alan Sugano, has supplied me with a lot of his technical wisdom, offered me his wide array of experiences in the IT world, and has given me an incredible amount of moral support. Alan, I appreciate your friendship very, very much! To the Thousand Oaks Chapter of BNI, thank you all for all your support. To Forrest Andrews, www.LaserCartridgeSupply.com, I appreciate you always hanging in there with me—you're a terrific friend!

Because I enjoy a very active business and personal life, I count my blessings every day for the outstanding individuals who assist my wife and me with an ever-growing list of things that must be attended to. To our nanny, Sonia Aguilar, her husband Hugo, and their kids Claudia, Gaby, and Huguito—thank you so much for taking such great care of our kids. We are very fortunate to have you all in our lives! To Gaby Hyar, muchas gracias a ti para todo que haces para nosotros! Tu eres la mejor! To Anne Ward, our office manager, thank you for taking such good care of our business matters, and oftentimes, our personal matters! To Dan Holme, thank you for your fantastic insight, your knowledge, your advice, and your support—I truly enjoy our business relationship and our friendship!

To Greggory Peck, thanks for partnering with us on Blast Through Learning (www.BlastThroughLearning.com) and thank you for being an incredible friend! A ton of appreciation goes out to Scott McIntyre, Dave Henson, and Jeremy Moskowitz—I really appreciate all of your friendships; you guys all provide me with a lot of inspiration to always keep learning and to be the best author, trainer, and consultant that I can be! To Ron Sharpshair, thank you for all your guidance, wisdom, and advice that helps to make me a stronger and better person each and every day! To Carrie Sharpshair, president of www.CasualCuisine.com, thanks for your incredible gourmet meals, which helped me to write this second edition book! Also, to Reverend Mary Lacalle and everyone associated with www.UnityCenterChurch.com, thank you for always being a guiding light, for assisting me in staying on the spiritual path, and for allowing me to have the opportunity to make a difference within our own small community and within the world.

A world of thanks and love go to Herb and Maureen Balter, my mom and dad, for being the terrific parents and grandparents that you are! To my brother and my sister-in-law, Gary and Linda Balter, thanks for all your love and support! To my in-laws, Charlotte and Bob Roman, your love and caring is never ending and very much appreciated! To my *medical staff* and great friends, Dr. Steven Perry, D.C. and Dr. Anita Srinivasa, M.D., your friendship means the world to me and to my family. Thank you for all that you've done and for all that you continue to do for us!

Finally, to Jeff Riley and Steve Rowe at Que Certification, once again, you guys had more patience with me than I think I ever deserved while I struggled to complete this second edition. Thank you so much for continuing to believe in me! To everyone else at Pearson Education, thank you for the mutually beneficial ongoing relationship that my wife and I have developed with you over the last several years. To Kim Spilker at Pearson Education, I like your spunk. You can take Alison and me to dinner anytime, just try not to embarrass me in front of a hundred authors and publishers next time!

Derek Melber: I must first acknowledge the woman that I love above all others—my wife, Yvette. To her I give my unconditional love and dedication for a lifetime. I also want to thank my two beautiful daughters, Alexa and Ashelley. They must get their beauty from their mother!

To Dan Balter, my coauthor, I want to provide my thanks for working with me, again, and for being there for me. You are a great guy, with so many gifts. It is an honor to work with you again!

I also want to thank Jeff Riley and Steve Rowe for their patience and dedication to this book. They are true warriors in their fields.

Finally, I want to thank all of the students, attendees, readers, and IT professionals that have supported me for so many years. Without you, your questions, support, answers, guidance, and input, I would not be able to write books and perform training. Thank you.

We Want to Hear from You!

As the reader of this book, *you* are our most important critic and commentator. We value your opinion and want to know what we're doing right, what we could do better, what areas you'd like to see us publish in, and any other words of wisdom you're willing to pass our way.

As the executive editor of Que Certification, I welcome your comments. You can email or write me directly to let me know what you did or didn't like about this book—as well as what we can do to make our books better.

Please note that I cannot help you with technical problems related to the topic of this book. We do have a User Services group, however, where I will forward specific technical questions related to the book.

When you write, please be sure to include this book's title and author as well as your name, email address, and phone number. I will carefully review your comments and share them with the author and editors who worked on the book.

Email: feedback@quepublishing.com

Mail: Jeff Riley
            Executive Editor
            Que Publishing
            800 East 96th Street
            Indianapolis, IN 46240 USA

For more information about this book or another Que Certification title, visit our website at www.examcram2.com. Type the ISBN (excluding hyphens) or the title of a book in the Search field to find the page you're looking for.

Contents at a Glance

Introduction   xxi

1 Installing and Deploying Windows XP Professional   1

2 Establishing, Configuring, and Managing Resources   39

3 Setting Up, Managing, and Troubleshooting Security Accounts and Policies   95

4 Implementing and Managing User and Desktop Settings   125

5 Installing, Configuring, and Troubleshooting Hardware Devices and Drivers   175

6 Implementing, Managing, and Troubleshooting Disk Storage   217

7 Implementing, Managing, and Troubleshooting Network Protocols and Services   259

8 System Monitoring, Performance Optimization, and Recovery Features   291

9 Installing, Administering, and Troubleshooting Remote Access Services   329

10 Practice Exam I   363

11 Answers to Practice Exam I   379

12 Practice Exam II   395

13 Answers to Practice Exam II   413

A What's on the CD-ROM   431

Glossary   437

Index   463

Table of Contents

Introduction xxi

Chapter 1
Installing and Deploying Windows XP Professional 1

Hardware Requirements   2
    Setup Disks   3
Upgrading to Windows XP Professional   3
    Preupgrade Checklist   3
    File System Considerations   5
    Windows XP Uninstall Feature for Windows 98 and Windows
    ME Upgrades   5
Installation Options for Windows XP Professional   6
    Installation Methods   6
Joining a Workgroup   19
Joining a Domain   20
Using the USMT to Migrate User Settings and Files   21
    Files and Settings Transfer (FAST) Wizard   22
    USMT from the Command Line   23
Deploying Service Packs (SPs) Using Group Policy and
Slipstreaming   25
    Group Policy Deployments of SPs   25
    Using Software Update Services (SUS)   25
    Slipstreaming SPs   25
    Unattended SP2 Installs from the Command Line   26
    Applying SPs Manually   26
    Removing SPs   27
    Installing Hotfixes   27
Automatic Updates   28
Dynamic Update   29
    Creating a Network Share for Dynamic Update   30

Product Activation   30

Troubleshooting Failed Installations   31

Exam Prep Questions   33

    Answers to Exam Prep Questions   36

Need to Know More?   38

Chapter 2
Establishing, Configuring, and Managing Resources 39

Managing Access to Shared Folders   40

    Creating Shared Folders from My Computer or Windows
Explorer   41

    Creating Shared Folders from the Shared Folders MMC
Snap-in   41

    Using Automatically Generated Hidden Shares   42

    Connecting to Shared Resources on a Windows Network   43

    Controlling Access to Shared Folders   45

Monitoring, Managing, and Troubleshooting Access to Files and
Folders   48

    NTFS Security: Users and Groups   49

    NTFS Security: Basic and Advanced Permissions   52

    Controlling Access to Files and Folders by Using
Permissions   60

    Optimizing Access to Files and Folders   64

    Controlling Write Access to USB Storage Devices
Under SP2   67

    Auditing System and Network Events   68

Managing and Troubleshooting Web Server Resources   72

    IIS Console: Administering the Default Web and
FTP Sites   74

    Web Folders and the WebDAV Protocol   76

    Troubleshooting Internet Information Services   78

Managing Local and Network Print Devices   79

    Connecting to Local and Network Printers   80

    Managing Printers and Print Jobs   82

    Configuring Print Server and Printer Properties   83

    Using the Internet Printing Protocol (IPP)   86

Exam Prep Questions   87

    Answers to Exam Prep Questions   91

Need to Know More?   93

Chapter 3
**Setting Up, Managing, and Troubleshooting Security Accounts
and Policies** **95**

Built-in User and Group Accounts   96
    Creating Local User and Group Accounts   98
    Configuring Account Properties   99
    Renaming Accounts   101
    Disabling or Enabling User Accounts   101
    Deleting Accounts   102
    Using the User Accounts Tool   102
    Passwords   103
    Fast User Switching   104
    Authentication   105
Managing Domain User Accounts   106
    Creating Domain User Accounts   106
    Creating Template User Accounts   106
    Disabling and Deleting User Accounts   107
Understanding and Implementing Group Policy   107
    Local Group Policy   107
    Group Policy Objects (GPO)   108
    User Rights Assignment   109
    Security Options   110
    Account Policies   110
    Audit Policies   111
    SP2 GPO Changes   112
Resultant Set of Policy (RSoP)   112
    Group Policy Result   113
    Group Policy Update   114
    RSoP Snap-in   114
Security Configuration and Analysis   115
    Security Templates   116
Software Restriction Policies   117
    Two Types of Software Restriction Policies   118
    Software Identification Rules   118
    Integration with Microsoft Passport via the Internet   119
Data Execution Prevention   119
Windows Security Center   120
Exam Prep Questions   121
    Answers to Exam Prep Questions   123
Need to Know More?   124

Chapter 4
Implementing and Managing User and Desktop Settings 125

Configuring and Managing User Profiles   126
    User Profiles   126
    Roaming User Profiles   128
    Managing User Profiles Behavior Through Group Policy   129
    Fast User Switching   130
Using Offline Files   130
    Setting Up Offline Files and Folders   131
    Making Files and Folders Available Offline   133
    Synchronizing Offline Files and Folders   135
    Accessing Offline Files and Folders   137
    Managing Offline Files and Folders   137
Configuring and Troubleshooting Desktop Settings   137
    Keyboard Applet   138
    Display Applet   138
    Mouse Applet   139
    Sounds and Audio Devices Applet   139
    Scanners and Cameras Applet   139
    Speech Applet   140
    Taskbar and Start Menu Applet   140
    Wireless Network Setup Wizard   143
Troubleshooting and System Settings   143
    The MSCONFIG.EXE Utility   143
    Application Program Compatibility Support   145
Windows Installer Service   148
    Installing Packages   149
    Publishing MSI Packages   150
Multiple-Language Support and Regional Options   153
    Windows XP Multilingual User Interface Pack   153
    Language Options   154
    Regional Options: Locales   154
File Settings and Transfer Wizard   157
    Transferring Settings from One Computer to Another   158
Accessibility Options   160
    Accessibility Options Applet   160
    Accessibility Wizard   163
    Additional Accessibility Features   163
Advanced Video Display Options   164
    ClearType Display Support   164
    Dualview Multiple Display Support   165

Fax Features   165
    The Fax Console: Managing Faxes, Settings, and
    Options   166
Scheduled Tasks   168
    Creating a Task   168
Exam Prep Questions   171
    Answers to Exam Prep Questions   173
Need to Know More?   174

Chapter 5
Installing, Configuring, and Troubleshooting Hardware Devices
and Drivers...175

Implementing, Managing, and Troubleshooting Hardware   176
    Universal Plug and Play—Extending the PnP Standard   177
    Installing, Configuring, and Managing Hardware   178
    Device Driver Updates   180
    Updating Your System Files Manually from the Windows
    Update Website   183
    The Driver Rollback Feature   184
    Managing and Troubleshooting Device Conflicts   184
    Managing and Troubleshooting Driver Signing   185
    Using Cameras and Scanning Devices   188
    Using Modems for Dial-up Connections   189
    Configuring and Managing CD and DVD Media
    Devices   191
    Installing, Configuring, and Troubleshooting USB
    Devices   192
    Using Network Adapters   194
    Using Infrared Data Association (IrDA) Devices   194
    Wireless Networking Support   195
    Installing, Configuring, and Supporting Video Display
    Adapters   197
    Configuring Multiple-Monitor Support   197
    Removable Storage Support   200
    Managing Tape Devices   201
    Upgrading a System from One to Two Processors   201
    Mobile Computing   203
    Managing Hardware Profiles   204
    Power Management Support   206
    Managing Card Services   209
Exam Prep Questions   210
    Answers to Exam Prep Questions   212
Need to Know More?   214

Chapter 6
Implementing, Managing, and Troubleshooting Disk Storage 217

Disk Storage Management   218
    Basic Disks   218
    Dynamic Disks   219
    Comparing Basic Disks to Dynamic Disks   220
    Upgrading Disks   221
    Moving Disks to Another Computer   224
    Reactivating a Missing or Offline Disk   225
Basic Partitions   225
    Partitions and Logical Drives on Basic Disks   226
Dynamic Volumes   227
    Simple Volumes   228
    Spanned Volumes   228
    Striped Volumes   229
    Mirrored Volumes and RAID-5 Volumes   230
    Limitations of Dynamic Disks and Dynamic Volumes   230
Troubleshooting Disks and Volumes   232
    Diagnosing Problems   232
    Monitoring Disk Performance   233
    Detecting and Repairing Disk Errors   234
    The Disk Defragmenter Tool   234
    Understanding Why Files Are Not Moved to the Beginning of
    NTFS Partitions and Volumes   235
    Using the Disk Cleanup Wizard   235
File Systems Supported in Windows XP   236
    FAT and FAT32   236
    The Windows XP NTFS File System   237
    Converting from One File System to Another   237
Assigning, Changing, or Removing Drive Letters   239
Mounted Drives   240
    Creating a Mounted Drive   240
Support for FAT32 on DVD-RAM Disks   241
Disk Quotas   241
Data Compression   243
    Moving and Copying Compressed Files and Folders   244
Data Encryption   245
    Keeping Data Private with the Encrypting File System
    (EFS)   245
Data Protection from Removable USB Storage Media   251
    Making USB Storage Drives Read-only   251

Exam Prep Questions   253
    Answers to Exam Prep Questions   256
Need to Know More?   258

Chapter 7
Implementing, Managing, and Troubleshooting Network
Protocols and Services **259**

Configuring and Troubleshooting TCP/IP   260
    Deciphering the TCP/IP Protocol Suite for
    Windows XP   260
    Understanding TCP/IP Computer Addresses   263
    Understanding Classful IP Addressing   264
    Understanding Variable-Length Subnet Masks   264
    Understanding Classless Interdomain Routing   265
    Configuring TCP/IP   266
    Troubleshooting TCP/IP   268
Working with TCP/IP Profiles   271
Connecting to Novell NetWare Networks and Unix-Based Computer
Systems   272
    Novell NetWare Connectivity   272
    Unix Connectivity   274
Network Bridging   274
Windows Messenger   275
Remote Desktop   277
    Configuring Remote Desktop   277
    Connecting with Remote Desktop   278
    Remote Desktop Web Connection   279
Understanding Remote Assistance   280
Exam Prep Questions   284
    Answers to Exam Prep Questions   287
Need to Know More?   290

Chapter 8
System Monitoring, Performance Optimization, and
Recovery Features **291**

Backing Up and Restoring Data   292
    Using Windows Backup   292
    Required Permissions for Backing Up Files   293
    Backup Types   293
    Configuring File and Folder Backup Jobs   295
    Backing Up the System State   295
    Scheduling Backup Jobs   296

Volume Shadow Copy Technology   298
Restoring Files and Folders   298
Troubleshooting and Repairing Windows XP Professional
Systems   299
Safe Mode and Other Advanced Startup Options   299
System Recovery Settings   302
The Recovery Console   304
System Restore   307
Automated System Recovery   309
Performance Optimizing and Troubleshooting   310
System Monitor   310
Performance Logs and Alerts   312
Managing Performance   314
Task Manager   320
Monitoring Event Logs   321
Proactively Managing Security Threats   322
Exam Prep Questions   324
Answers to Exam Prep Questions   326
Need to Know More?   328

Chapter 9
Installing, Administering, and Troubleshooting Remote
Access Services **329**
Authentication Protocols   330
Extensible Authentication Protocol (EAP)   331
IP Security (IPSec)   331
Layer 2 Tunneling Protocol (L2TP)   332
Remote Authentication Dial-in User Service (RADIUS)   332
Bandwidth Allocation Protocol (BAP)   332
Encryption   333
Connecting to Remote Access Servers   334
Setting Up and Configuring VPN Connections   336
Configuring Windows Firewall   337
The Windows Security Center   343
Configuring Windows Firewall Exceptions   345
WF Logging   347
Configuring and Troubleshooting ICS   348
Configuring ICS   348
Troubleshooting ICS   349
Managing Enhanced Network Security Under SP2   350
Understanding Restrictions to TCP/IP Raw Sockets   351
Understanding TCP/IP Outbound Connection Limits   351
Managing Changes to RPCs, DTC, COM, and DCOM   352

Exam Prep Questions   356
Answers to Exam Prep Questions   359
Need to Know More?   362

Chapter 10
Practice Exam I...**363**

Chapter 11
Answers to Practice Exam I **379**

Chapter 12
Practice Exam II...**395**

Chapter 13
Answers to Practice Exam II **413**

Appendix A
CD Contents and Installation Instructions **431**

Multiple Test Modes   431
Study Mode   431
Certification Mode   431
Custom Mode   432
Adaptive Mode   432
Missed Question Mode   432
Non-Duplicate Mode   432
Question Types   432
Random Questions and Order of Answers   433
Detailed Explanations of Correct and Incorrect Answers   433
Attention to Exam Objectives   433
Installing the CD   433
Creating a Shortcut to the MeasureUp Practice Tests   435
Technical Support   435

Glossary...**437**

Index..**463**

Introduction

Welcome to *MCSA/MCSE 70-270 Exam Cram 2: Windows XP Professional!* Whether this is your first or your fifteenth Exam Cram 2 book, you'll find information here that will help ensure your success as you pursue knowledge, experience, and certification. This book aims to help you get ready to take—and pass—Microsoft Certification Exam 70-270, "Installing, Configuring, and Administering Microsoft Windows XP Professional." This Introduction explains Microsoft's certification programs in general and talks about how the Exam Cram 2 series can help you prepare for Microsoft's Windows 2003 certification exams.

Exam Cram 2 books help you understand and appreciate the subjects and materials you need to pass Microsoft certification exams. *Exam Cram 2* books are aimed strictly at test preparation and review. They do not teach you everything you need to know about a topic. Instead, we (the authors) present and dissect the questions and problems we've found that you're likely to encounter on a test. We've worked to bring together as much information as possible about Microsoft certification exams.

Nevertheless, to completely prepare yourself for any Microsoft test, we recommend that you begin by taking the Self-Assessment included in this book immediately following this Introduction. This tool will help you evaluate your knowledge base against the requirements for an MCSE under both ideal and real circumstances.

Based on what you learn from that exercise, you might decide to begin your studies with some classroom training or some background reading. On the other hand, you might decide to pick up and read one of the many study guides available from Microsoft or third-party vendors on certain topics, including Que Publishing's *Exam Prep* series. We also recommend that you supplement your study program with visits to www.examcram2.com to receive additional practice questions, get advice, and track the Windows 2003 MCSE program.

We also strongly recommend that you install, configure, and fool around with the software you'll be tested on, because nothing beats hands-on experience and familiarity when it comes to understanding the questions you're likely to encounter on a certification test. Book learning is essential, but hands-on experience is the best teacher of all!

Taking a Certification Exam

After you've prepared for your exam, you need to register with a testing center. Each computer-based MCP exam costs $125, and if you don't pass, you may retest for an additional $125 for each additional try. In the United States and Canada, tests are administered by Pearson VUE and Thomson Prometric. Here's how you can contact them:

➤ VUE—You can sign up for a test or get the phone numbers for local testing centers through the web page at www.vue.com/ms/.

➤ Prometric—You can sign up for a test through the company's website at www.prometric.com. Or you can register by phone at 800-755-3926 (within the United States and Canada) or at 410-843-8000 (outside the United States and Canada).

To sign up for a test, you must possess a valid credit card, or you can contact either company for mailing instructions to send in a check (in the U.S.). Only when payment is verified, or your check has cleared, can you actually register for a test.

To schedule an exam, call the number or visit either of the web pages at least one day in advance. To cancel or reschedule an exam, you must call before 7 p.m. Pacific standard time the day before the scheduled test time (or you may be charged, even if you don't appear to take the test). When you want to schedule a test, have the following information ready:

➤ Your name, organization, and mailing address.

➤ Your Microsoft Test ID. (Inside the United States, this means your Social Security number; citizens of other nations should call ahead to find out what type of identification number is required to register for a test.)

➤ The name and number of the exam you want to take.

➤ A method of payment. (As we've already mentioned, a credit card is the most convenient method, but alternative means can be arranged in advance, if necessary.)

After you sign up for a test, you'll be informed as to when and where the test is scheduled. Try to arrive at least 15 minutes early. You must supply two forms of identification—one of which must be a photo ID—to be admitted into the testing room.

All exams are completely closed-book. In fact, you will not be permitted to take anything with you into the testing area, but you will be furnished with a blank sheet of paper and a pen or, in some cases, an erasable plastic sheet and an erasable pen. We suggest that you immediately write down on that sheet of paper all the information you've memorized for the test. In *Exam Cram 2* books, this information appears on a tear-out sheet inside the front cover of each book. You will have some time to compose yourself, record this information, and take a sample orientation exam before you begin the real thing. We suggest you take the orientation test before taking your first exam, but because they're all more or less identical in layout, behavior, and controls, you probably won't need to do this more than once.

When you complete a Microsoft certification exam, the software will tell you whether you've passed or failed. If you need to retake an exam, you'll have to schedule a new test with Prometric or VUE and pay $125.

 The first time you fail a test, you can retake it the next day. However, if you fail a second time, you must wait 14 days before retaking that test. The 14-day waiting period remains in effect for all retakes after the second failure.

How to Prepare for an Exam

Preparing for any Windows MCSE test requires that you obtain and study materials designed to provide comprehensive information about the product and its capabilities that will appear on the specific exam for which you are preparing. The following list of materials will help you study and prepare:

➤ The Windows XP Professional product CD includes comprehensive online documentation and related materials; it should be a primary resource when you are preparing for the test.

➤ The exam-preparation materials, practice tests, and self-assessment exams can be found on the Microsoft Training and Services page at www.microsoft.com/learning/. The Testing Innovations link offers examples of the new question types found on the Windows 2003 MCSE exams. Find the materials, download them, and use them!

➤ The exam-preparation advice, practice tests, questions of the day, and discussion groups can be found at www.examcram2.com.

In addition, you'll probably find any or all of the following materials useful in your quest for Windows XP Professional expertise:

➤ Study guides—Several publishers—including Que Publishing—offer Windows XP Professional titles. Que Certification includes the following:

➤ The *Exam Cram 2* series—These books give you information about the material you need to know to pass the tests.

➤ The *Exam Prep* series—These books provide a greater level of detail than the *Exam Cram 2* books and are designed to teach you everything you need to know from an exam perspective. Each book comes with a CD that contains interactive practice exams in a variety of testing formats.

Together, the two series make a perfect pair.

➤ Multimedia—The MeasureUp Practice Tests CD that comes with each *Exam Cram* and *Exam Prep* features a powerful, state-of-the-art test engine that prepares you for the actual exam. MeasureUp Practice Tests are developed by certified IT professionals and are trusted by certification students around the world. For more information, visit www.measureup.com.

➤ Classroom training—CTECs, online partners, and third-party training companies (such as Wave Technologies, Learning Tree, Data-Tech, and others) all offer classroom training on Windows XP Professional. These companies aim to help you prepare to pass Exam 70-270. Although such training runs upward of $350 per day in class, most of the individuals lucky enough to partake find it to be quite worthwhile.

➤ Other publications—There's no shortage of materials available about Windows XP Professional. The resource sections at the end of each chapter should give you an idea of where we think you should look for further discussion.

By far, this set of required and recommended materials represents a nonpareil collection of sources and resources for Windows XP Professional and related topics. We anticipate you'll find that this book belongs in this company.

About This Book

Each topical *Exam Cram 2* chapter follows a regular structure, along with graphical cues about important or useful information. Here's the structure of a typical chapter:

➤ Opening hotlists—Each chapter begins with a list of the terms, tools, and techniques you must learn and understand before you can be fully conversant with that chapter's subject matter. We follow the hotlists with one or two introductory paragraphs to set the stage for the rest of the chapter.

➤ Topical coverage—After the opening hotlists, each chapter covers a series of topics related to the chapter's subject title. Throughout this section, we highlight topics or concepts likely to appear on a test using a special Exam Alert layout, like this:

This is what an Exam Alert looks like. Normally, an Exam Alert stresses concepts, terms, software, or activities that are likely to relate to one or more certification test questions. For that reason, we think any information found offset in Exam Alert format is worthy of unusual attentiveness on your part. Indeed, most of the information that appears on the Cram Sheet appears as Exam Alerts within the text.

Pay close attention to material flagged as an Exam Alert; although all the information in this book pertains to what you need to know to pass the exam, we flag certain items that are really important. You'll find what appears in the meat of each chapter to be worth knowing, too, when preparing for the test. Because this book's material is very condensed, we recommend that you use this book along with other resources to achieve the maximum benefit.

In addition to the Exam Alerts, we have provided tips that will help you build a better foundation for Windows XP Professional knowledge. Although the information may not be on the exam, it is certainly related and will help you become a better test taker.

This is how tips are formatted. Keep your eyes open for these, and you'll become a Windows XP Professional guru in no time!

➤ Exam Prep Questions—Although we talk about test questions and topics throughout the book, a section at the end of each chapter presents a series of mock test questions and explanations of both correct and incorrect answers.

➤ Details and resources—Every chapter ends with a section titled "Need to Know More?" This section provides direct pointers to Microsoft and third-party resources offering more details on the chapter's subject. In addition, this section tries to rank or at least rate the quality and thoroughness of the topic's coverage by each resource. If you find a resource you like in this collection, use it, but don't feel compelled to use all the resources. On the other hand, we recommend only resources we use on a regular basis, so none of our recommendations will be a waste of your time or money (but purchasing them all at once probably represents an expense that many network administrators and would-be MCPs and MCSEs might find hard to justify).

The bulk of the book follows this chapter structure slavishly, but there are a few other elements we'd like to point out. Chapters 10 and 12, "Practice Exam I" and "Practice Exam II," include sample tests that provide a good review of the material presented throughout the book to ensure you're ready for the exam. Chapters 11 and 13 are the answer keys to these questions.

Finally, the tear-out Cram Sheet attached next to the inside front cover of this *Exam Cram 2* book represents a condensed and compiled collection of facts and tips we think you should memorize before taking the test. Because you can dump this information out of your head onto a piece of paper before taking the exam, you can master this information by brute force—you need to remember it only long enough to write it down when you walk into the test room. You might even want to look at it in the car or in the lobby of the testing center just before you walk in to take the test.

How to Use This Book

We've structured the topics in this book to build on one another. Therefore, some topics in later chapters make more sense after you've read earlier chapters. That's why we suggest you read this book from front to back for your initial test preparation. If you need to brush up on a topic or you have to bone up for a second try, use the index or table of contents to go straight to the topics and questions you need to study. Beyond helping you prepare for the test, we think you'll find this book useful as a tightly focused reference to some of the most important aspects of Windows XP Professional.

Given all the book's elements and its specialized focus, we've tried to create a tool that will help you prepare for—and pass—Microsoft Exam 70-270.

Thanks, and enjoy the book!

Installing and Deploying Windows XP Professional

Terms you'll need to understand:

✓ FAT, FAT32, and NTFS
✓ Unattended installation
✓ Setup Manager
✓ Answer file
✓ System Preparation Tool (**Sysprep.exe**)
✓ Remote Installation Services (RIS)
✓ **Risetup.exe**
✓ **Riprep.exe**
✓ Automatic Updates
✓ Dynamic Updates
✓ Windows Update
✓ Software Update Services (SUS)
✓ User State Migration Tool (USMT)
✓ FAST Wizard

Techniques you'll need to master:

✓ Understanding installation advantages and disadvantages of using FAT, FAT32, and NTFS
✓ Creating an answer file using Setup Manager
✓ Creating an image using Sysprep
✓ Configuring the RIS server
✓ Creating an image for the RIS server using Riprep
✓ Scanning and loading user data using the USMT
✓ Troubleshooting installation failures

Planning for the installation of Windows XP is an essential part of getting the job done right. If you attempt to install XP without taking a look at your current environment and hardware, the installation will most likely fail and it will be hard to determine why. With this in mind, let's take a look at some of the requirements and items to consider during the planning phase of your installation.

Hardware Requirements

The following are the *minimum* hardware requirements for installing Windows XP Professional:

➤ 233MHz Pentium or higher central processing unit (CPU)

➤ 64MB of memory (Microsoft recommends 128MB)

➤ A 1.5GB hard drive with a minimum of 650MB of free space

➤ Super VGA (8005600) or higher-resolution video adapter and monitor

➤ Keyboard

➤ Mouse

➤ CD-ROM or DVD drive

Windows XP SP2 requires a minimum of 1.6GB of hard drive space during installation. After installation, SP2 might require as much as 1.5GB of hard disk space, depending on which options are configured.

Another important aspect to consider before installing Windows XP Professional is the BIOS version and features of your system. It is best to install the latest BIOS from your hardware vendor before tackling the XP Professional installation. Features such as Plug and Play and Advanced Configuration and Power Interface (ACPI) are important for the full functionality of XP.

ACPI allows the OS to control power management and drives the core Plug and Play functions in Windows XP. If you install Windows XP on a system that does not support ACPI, you must upgrade the system to support ACPI; otherwise, you will most likely see a Blue Screen of Death (BSOD). This is because the Hardware Abstraction Layer (HAL) for ACPI is not the same as that of Advanced Power Management (APM), which is used if ACPI is not supported.

After you've verified that the computer meets these minimum hardware requirements, you should check to see whether devices such as the video adapter and the network adapter are compatible. To do this, check the Hardware Compatibility List (HCL), which every Windows XP CD-ROM contains. However, this file becomes out of date rather quickly because of all the new additions to the HCL that occur after the burning of your CD. To view the most current HCL, visit www.microsoft.com/hcl.

Setup Disks

Microsoft believes that the hardware that is required to run Windows XP Professional needs to be bigger and better than the hardware required by any previous OS. With newer hardware, you will get all the great new features, such as Plug and Play, ACPI, bootable CD-ROMs, and so on. Because of these robust features, Microsoft has removed the need or capability to create or use the setup disk sets that were available with Windows NT and 2000 Professional.

Upgrading to Windows XP Professional

Windows NT 4 supported upgrades only from previous Windows NT operating systems, whereas Windows 2000 would upgrade from almost anything. Windows XP, on the other hand, allows for many upgrade paths, but has some limitations. The following is a list of Windows operating systems that you can directly upgrade to Windows XP Professional:

➤ Windows 2000

➤ Windows NT 4 (Service Pack 6)

➤ Windows 98 (all editions)

➤ Windows ME

All other OS versions must first get to one of these levels before an upgrade to XP can be performed.

The easiest operating system to upgrade from is Windows 2000. This operating system shares a lot of features with Windows XP, including its Registry. You can upgrade Windows 98 and NT quite smoothly as well, but you need to take some precautions, which are detailed in the next section.

Preupgrade Checklist

Before you upgrade to Windows XP Professional, you need to check the current operating system configuration for any of the following areas that could cause conflicts during and after the upgrade process:

➤ Hardware and software compatibility—The Windows XP Professional CD-ROM contains a utility called `Chkupgrd.exe`, which scans the current OS and hardware to see whether any known items are incompatible with Windows XP Professional. You can run the utility using various methods. One of the most common methods is to place the Windows XP CD-ROM in the computer and click the Upgrade option. The utility runs before the upgrade to alert you about any incompatibilities. However, if you are not prepared to perform an upgrade on the computer, you can run the utility by placing the Windows XP Professional CD-ROM in the computer, selecting Start, Run, and then typing `D:\I386\winnt32.exe /checkupgradeonly` (where `D:` is the drive letter your CD-ROM drive uses). The utility scans the system and creates a text file of the results, which you can save to the computer or print. The `Chkupgrd.exe` tool is also referred to as the Readiness Analyzer.

If you are attempting to install Windows XP Professional on a system that has third-party SCSI or RAID controllers, you will need to select F6 during the initial blue screen of the setup process. If you miss this selection and setup proceeds, you will most likely end up with an error specifying that the boot device is not accessible, and you will need to start the installation again.

➤ Update packs—Because of major differences between the Windows XP Registry and those of Windows 95 and 98, some applications may not work after the upgrade. Software vendors may supply an update pack (also called migration dynamic link libraries, or DLLs) that you can use during the upgrade process. Obtain an upgrade pack and place it on the local hard drive. During the upgrade process, the installer asks whether any upgrade packs should be used. Select Yes and then type in the file path to the upgrade pack to continue the installation process.

➤ File system selection—Windows XP has three options from which to choose for a file system: the old standby, FAT; the newer option, FAT32; and the best option for the systems that support it, NT File System (NTFS). NTFS is the best option because it supports security, compression, disk quotas, encryption, mount points, and remote storage.

➤ Disk utilities—Windows XP Professional uses a new version of NTFS that causes conflicts with antivirus software and disk defragmenting software. You should uninstall such applications before you upgrade.

➤ Drive compression—Before upgrading, you should uncompress any drives that you have compressed with DriveSpace or DoubleSpace. These Windows 95 and 98 drive compression utilities are incompatible with Windows XP.

➤ BIOS—Ensure that you have the latest BIOS that will support Windows XP.

➤ Backup—The only true way to recover from a failed installation or OS is with a good backup.

➤ Compression—Windows XP supports compression when NTFS is installed. However, Windows XP does not support any other third-party compression utilities in an upgrade scenario. Always uncompress files before upgrading to ensure a clean and successful path.

➤ Virus scan software—It is always best to disable, and in some instances uninstall, virus scan software before an upgrade. These programs may have files open and limit the access to system resources during an upgrade.

➤ Incompatible software—This is a rather vague item, but it is better to be safe than sorry in an upgrade. Programs such as third-party protocols and clients, virus scanners, and ACPI/APM tools can cause serious problems with an upgrade. Always try to eliminate these programs from interfering with your upgrade.

File System Considerations

During the upgrade to Windows XP, Microsoft makes some assumptions about which file system you are running, based on your current OS. If you are running Windows 9*x*, Microsoft assumes you are running FAT32 or, in some instances, FAT. If you are running Windows NT or 2000, Microsoft assumes you are running NTFS.

If you are upgrading from Windows NT or 2000, you will keep the existing file system, NTFS, as you move into Windows XP. If you are upgrading from Windows 98, you will have more choices. Remember, you are running FAT32, so for security reasons, you probably want to run NTFS in XP. However, for compatibility reasons and functionality, you might want to stick with your FAT32 file system, at least for a little while. One main reason is the new uninstall feature, discussed next.

 If you want to take advantage of both the uninstall feature and NTFS, do your file system configuration in phases. First, keep FAT32 until your XP Professional box has proved itself to be stable. Then, convert your system to NTFS using the **convert** command to get the benefits of the better security, compression, and encryption features.

Windows XP Uninstall Feature for Windows 98 and Windows ME Upgrades

Microsoft has built in an uninstall feature to Windows XP Professional, but it has serious limitations. The main reason that the option was built in was to accommodate those who want to move from Windows 98 to Windows XP Professional.

Of course, many of these installations will be for those who work in a small office or home environment. Those who work in a medium to large corporate environment will be better off installing Windows XP Professional fresh, to eliminate some of the potential Registry, security, and folder structure differences that occur with an upgrade.

Some of the limitations that come with the uninstall feature include the following:

➤ You cannot uninstall if you have converted the file system from FAT to NTFS.

➤ You do not have the uninstall option if you have upgraded from Windows NT or Windows 2000.

➤ Applications that have been removed while XP is running will behave strangely. For example, although the Start menu icons will be present, the executables will have been removed.

➤ Applications that were added while XP is running will behave strangely. This occurs because the restored image does not have the correct Registry values for these applications.

To successfully remove Windows XP Professional, you need to go to the Add/Remove Programs applet in the Control Panel. Then select the Add/Remove button associated with the Windows XP option that is under the list of installed software. This enables you to uninstall Windows XP and return to the version of Windows 98/ME that you were running previously.

Installation Options for Windows XP Professional

Microsoft understands that different installation needs exist and thus supplies many methods. Windows XP keeps that tradition by offering multiple options for fresh installations.

Installation Methods

Windows XP Professional has many installation methods, listed next. Some of these methods are manual in nature, requiring human intervention during the installation process. Other methods require only minimal initial human intervention and are considered to be automated installation methods:

➤ Manual CD method

➤ Network attended installations

➤ Network unattended installations using an answer file

➤ Sysprep installation

➤ Sysprep unattended installation using an answer file

➤ Remote Installation Services (RIS), using a CD image

➤ RIS—CD image unattended installation using an answer file

➤ RIS—Riprep image

➤ RIS—Riprep image unattended installation using an answer file

CD-ROM Installation

The easiest method for installing Windows XP Professional is simply to put the Windows XP Professional CD-ROM into the CD-ROM drive and boot the computer. The computer boots from the CD-ROM and starts the first phase of the installation, copying the installation files to the local hard drive. Then the computer reboots and starts the graphical user interface (GUI) phase of the installation. You can install Windows XP Professional in this fashion if your computer's BIOS supports the option to boot from a CD-ROM drive and the system has El-Torito No Emulation support for bootable CD-ROMs. The El-Torito No Emulation is the standard for bootable CD-ROM support.

This form of installation is an attended installation of Windows XP Professional that requires someone to sit in front of the target computer and answer all the installation prompts, such as the End User License Agreement (EULA). Before you start the installation process, you need to ensure that the computer meets the minimum hardware requirements of Windows XP Professional. Unlike Windows NT, Windows XP supports only Intel-based computers.

Installing Over a Network

Another installation method is to place the contents of the Windows XP Professional CD-ROM in a folder on a network server and then share the folder. This network server is called a *distribution server*. Establish a network connection to the distribution server to start the installation. If Windows 95, 98, Windows NT 4.0 Workstation, or Windows 2000 Professional is on the target computer, connect to the share point and execute winnt32.exe to start the installation process. The same method holds true for a target computer running Windows 2000 Server or Windows Server 2003; however, you cannot perform an upgrade installation for Windows XP from any server operating system—you can perform only a clean (new) installation. If DOS is on the target computer, use a network boot disk to connect to the source files and use winnt.exe to start the installation. You use winnt32.exe in a 32-bit environment, whereas you use winnt.exe in a 16-bit/DOS environment.

Automating the Installation of Windows XP Professional

Performing an attended installation option means that someone must be in front of the computer to answer all the installation prompts. If you need to install hundreds, maybe thousands, of computers, this is a very inefficient method. This section discusses how to use Setup Manager, the System Preparation (Sysprep) tool, and Remote Installation Service (RIS) for automating the installation process.

Creating Unattended Answer Files and Uniqueness Database Files by Using Setup Manager

The Setup Manager utility answers the installation prompts and saves the answer results in an answer file called Unattend.txt. Windows XP can then use Unattend.txt during the installation to configure the screen resolution and other typical hardware and OS settings. This tool is much improved in Windows XP and adds more options and greater flexibility than its predecessor. Setup Manager can now do the following:

➤ Agree to the EULA

➤ Input the Product ID for installation

➤ Create a distribution share point

➤ Create a listing of unique computer names for a Uniqueness Database File (UDF)

➤ Add third-party Plug and Play drivers and other resources

➤ Add printers, scripts, batch files, and other commands to the distribution share

You must extract Setup Manager from a CAB file on the Windows XP Professional CD-ROM to create Unattend.txt. To extract Setup Manager, perform the following steps:

1. Insert the Windows XP Professional CD-ROM into the computer and select the Deploy.cab file, located in the Support\Tools folder.

2. Double-click the Deploy.cab file to view the contents.

3. Right-click Setupmgr.exe and select Extract. Choose a location from the Explorer menu to extract the file.

You can now create the answer file. Double-click the `Setupmgr.exe` icon to launch the wizard. The `Setupmgr.exe` utility is a multipurpose tool because you can use it to create answer files for several types of unattended installations. We will concentrate on a Windows XP unattended installation. Perform the following steps to create an answer file:

1. Double-click the `Setupmgr.exe` icon to start the utility.

2. Click Next to pass the welcome page.

3. Select the Create A New Answer File option button (it is selected by default) and click Next.

4. The next page displays which product the answer file installs. The three choices are Windows XP Unattended Installation, Sysprep Install, and RIS. Select the Windows XP Unattended Installation option button and click Next.

5. Choose the Windows XP Professional option button and click Next.

6. The next page displays several options regarding user interaction. Typically, no user interaction is required. If, however, you want the installation to stop so you can enter the computer name, select Hide Pages. This option hides all pages in which answers were provided, but stops at any areas that you have left blank. Select the Fully Automated option button and click Next.

7. Next, you will determine whether you will use this answer file with the CD or a distribution folder. For the purposes of this example, select Yes, Create or Modify a Distribution Folder.

8. The next window asks where the installation files will be obtained— copied from the CD or from the file system. Select Copy the Files from CD.

9. After selecting the source, you need to determine the destination folder. The next page offers suggested locations and folder names for the distribution share point. If you have already created the distribution share, select Modify an Existing Distribution Folder. If you select this option, just the answer file is created. Accept the default by clicking the Next button.

10. Select the check box to agree to the EULA and click Next.

11. Type in a name and an organization and click Next.

12. Select display settings such as Color, Screen Area, and Refresh Frequency. Unless all computers have identical video cards with identical monitors, you should set these fields to Use Windows Default. Click Next to continue.

13. The Time Zone page appears next. Choose the correct time zone the computer is located in and click Next.

14. Input the Product ID that matches the CD-ROM contents that you will be using for the installation.

15. Type in the computer names or import a comma-delimited file that contains all computer names that should be used for the installation of new computers. Optionally, you can select the Automatically Generate Computer Names Based on Organization Name check box. Checking this results in a combination of the organization name that you typed into the dialog box and a unique alphanumeric combination (for example, coriol-1AD2RT). The computer name needs to be 15 characters or fewer. Use either method and click Next.

16. Enter a password that the local administrator of the computer will use. You also have an option to encrypt the administrator password, which will be stored in the answer file. This is a good option to ensure security of the installed system.

 The password can be up to 127 characters long.

Enter a password and click Next.

17. This page provides two options for Network Settings: Typical and Custom. If you select Typical, Microsoft Client, File, and Print Sharing, as well as the Transmission Control Protocol/Internet Protocol (TCP/IP) are installed. Additionally, the client will be configured as a Dynamic Host Configuration Protocol (DHCP) client. If you need to enter a static IP address or add or subtract network services, use the Custom option. Select Typical or Custom and click Next.

18. The Workgroup or a Domain page appears next. If the computer is to join a domain during the installation, you must type in the name of the domain as well as enter a username and password of a user who has the right to add workstations to a domain. Fill in the appropriate fields and click Next.

19. You've reached the end of creating a basic answer file. If you need to add other drivers or scripts, select the Yes, Edit the Additional Settings option button. For the purposes of this discussion, select No, Do Not Edit the Additional Settings, and click Next.

20. The files are copied to the distribution share; the last page displayed is a summary page of the files that you created. Click Finish.

Piecing Together an Unattended Network Install

Now that you have created the answer file and the distribution share, let's put it all together to see how to launch an unattended installation of Windows XP Professional. To master this task, you must understand a few switches that are involved. The winnt.exe command has multiple switches to control its functionality. The following is a list of switches that relate to unattended installations:

➤ /u:answer <file>—Used for an unattended installation from a DOS-based client (which will use the winnt.exe command). The file contains answers to the installation prompts.

➤ /s:sourcepath—Points to the location of the Windows XP installation files.

➤ /udf:id—Used in conjunction with a UDF file, which overrides the values of the answer file. You typically use this file to provide unique configuration parameters during the installation process. The ID designates which settings contained in the UDF file should be used.

If you are upgrading or installing from a Windows 98/ME or Windows NT/2000 client, you need to use the winnt32.exe command to perform the installation. For this case, some different switches are available. The following are the more important switches that differ from those in the preceding list:

➤ /unattend—Used with winnt32.exe to create an unattended upgrade or install to Windows XP from a Windows 98/ME or Windows NT/2000 client.

➤ /makelocalsource—Copies the contents of the CD-based installation to the local hard drive for future reference when the CD is not available.

➤ /dudisable—Turns off the Dynamic Updates function on the client that is being installed.

➤ /duprepare:pathname—Prepares a folder for the distribution of Windows Update files and device drivers. This folder will then be used by subsequent installations to obtain these files.

➤ /dushare:pathname—Specifies the shared folder where the installation will point during the dynamic update portion of installation.

These switches are new to Windows XP and are emphasized for installations. Be sure you can distinguish among them if you need to use them during an installation.

You use these switches in combination to launch an unattended installation of Windows XP Professional using Setup Manager. To launch an unattended installation, follow these steps:

1. Use a network boot disk to connect the target computer to the network.

2. Next, use the net use command to map to the distribution share point using an available drive letter.

3. Switch the command prompt to the mapped drive letter (such as I) and use the following as an example to launch an unattended installation for a computer called computer1:

```
I:\WINNT.EXE /s:I:\i386 /u:unattend.txt
    /udf:computer1,unattend.udb
```

Investigate all the options that are available with the Setup Manager by running through the file-creation process several times while choosing different options each time to see how the results vary. Remember that you also can use this Setup Manager utility to create answer files for System Preparation tool and RIS installations, both of which are discussed in this chapter.

The Setup Manager can also create an answer file that is used with a CD-based installation. To complete this, you will save the answer file as winnt.sif and place it on a floppy disk for access during the installation process.

Creating and Deploying a Windows XP Image Using the System Preparation Tool

The System Preparation tool (Sysprep) prepares a master image of a computer that contains Windows XP Professional and any software applications that users might need. The concept is to use Sysprep in conjunction with third-party disk-imaging software. Disk-imaging software makes an exact mirror image of whatever is on the computer, including all the unique parameters of Windows XP. Each Windows XP computer has its own unique Security Identifier (SID) and its own unique computer name. Multiple computers on the network can't duplicate these settings. If you were to apply an image that contained these unique settings to several computers, they would all have the same computer name and the same SID. Sysprep removes all the unique parameters from a Windows XP computer before the computer is imaged. It is a very easy tool to use, but you must follow several specific steps to use it. The first step is to create a folder called sysprep in %systemdrive% (for example, C:\sysprep).

When cloning, the hardware needs to be similar, which would include the number of processors, HD controller, HAL, and power management. The other components will be automatically recognized by Plug and Play during the configuration phase of the installation.

To use Sysprep, you must extract it from the Deploy.cab file and place it in the sysprep folder. Perform the following steps to extract Sysprep.exe and a helper file called Setupcl.exe:

1. Insert the Windows XP Professional CD-ROM into the computer and select the Deploy.cab file, located in the Support\Tools folder.

2. Double-click the Deploy.cab file to view the contents.

3. Right-click Sysprep.exe and select Extract. Use the Explorer menu to extract the file to the sysprep folder that you created. Right-click Setupcl.exe and extract it to the sysprep folder.

The next step is to install and configure all applications that must be in the disk image. After you have accomplished this, run sysprep.exe in the sysprep folder. Using the sysprep.exe command removes all unique parameters from the computer and then shuts down the computer. Reboot the computer with a disk image boot disk and create an image of the computer.

After you have applied an image to a computer, a Mini-Setup Wizard runs. It prompts you to put back the unique parameters that you took out. The SID is generated automatically at this point. However, you'll have to input the following settings:

➤ Computer Name

➤ User Name

➤ Regional Settings

➤ Company Name

➤ Network Settings

➤ Time Zone

➤ Place Computer in a Workgroup or Join a Domain

As you can see, you need to enter a fair amount of information for every computer you apply the image to. You can use Setup Manager, discussed earlier in this chapter, to create an answer file called Sysprep.inf. This file provides the preceding settings to the Mini-Setup Wizard to answer all the installation prompts. The end result is an unattended installation of the image.

You must place **Sysprep.inf** in the sysprep folder or on a floppy disk, which is the default location where the Mini-Setup Wizard looks for the answer file (it checks the sysprep folder first) after you have applied the image. Another point to note is that you should apply the image to computers with similar hardware. When you apply the image, **Sysprep.exe** triggers Plug and Play to resolve the differences in hardware. However, if the hard disk controller or the HAL on the image is different from its counterpart on the computer to which you are applying the image, the image installation will fail (for example, if you create the image on a computer that contains a HAL for a computer with multiple processors, but you are applying the image to a uniprocessor computer).

Windows XP has incorporated another new feature that is great for OEMs and might just be great for you, too: new switches that control the installation of a system that will be used for redistribution. These options, listed next, allow for a cleaner and more efficient manipulation of the images that are created with Sysprep:

➤ Audit—Reboots the computer into factory mode, not generating a new SID or running any applications located in the Run Once portion of the setup files.

➤ Clean—Clears the critical devices database that is used by the SysprepMassStorage section in the Sysprep.inf file.

➤ Factory—Boots the system into a special mode that will allow for automated customization of a preinstallation on the factory floor. This will be done by using a Bill of Materials file to automate software installations and updates to software, drivers, the file system, and the Registry.

The **Factory.exe** file must be located in the **%systemdrive%\sysprep** folder to utilize the factory switch.

➤ Nosidgen—Runs Sysprep without generating a new SID for the computer. This is an excellent option if you are preinstalling domain controllers.

➤ Reseal—This option is run after the OEM has run Sysprep in factory mode and configured the system to be delivered to the customer.

Deploying Windows XP Professional by Using Remote Installation Services (RIS)

You can use RIS to deploy Windows XP Professional over a network from a remote installation server. RIS integrates a few of the installation methods discussed thus far into one tight bundle. You can use it to install Windows XP Professional to a computer with a blank hard drive or to reinstall Windows XP Professional to repair a corrupted system.

The main goal of RIS is to reduce total cost of ownership (TCO) by having one central location for either the end users or administrators to install Windows XP Professional. To install Windows XP Professional using RIS, a user presses the F12 key during the boot process to find a RIS server and start the installation. Three steps are involved in making RIS work:

1. Configure the client.

2. Configure network servers for RIS.

3. Create a Windows XP Professional image.

The next few sections uncover the details of these areas.

Configuring Network Services and Hard Drive Space Requirements

Before you can install and configure RIS, several prerequisites must be in place on the network. The following is a list of the RIS requirements you must meet before you install it:

➤ DHCP server—The client will obtain an IP address from a DHCP server during the boot process. You cannot use RIS until a DHCP server is available. A Windows XP DHCP server cannot give IP addresses to clients unless it is authorized to do so. Authorization is done through the DHCP Manager snap-in.

➤ Domain Name Service (DNS)—After the network adapter has an IP address, it needs to find a RIS server. The client finds RIS by querying a DNS server to find where an Active Directory server or domain controller (DC) is located.

➤ Active Directory—Active Directory informs the client where a RIS server can be found.

➤ Nonsystem partition—RIS demands its own partition. You cannot install RIS on a system or boot partition, which is usually the C partition.

> The reason for the separate partition is the Single Instance Storage (SIS) groveler service, which will create pointers to existing duplicate files, thereby saving disk space. The service won't use system files that are active.

It is recommended that you reserve at least 2GB for a RIS partition.

Installing and Configuring the RIS Service

You can install the RIS service on a domain controller or on a member server running Windows 2000 Server or Windows Server 2003 after you have met all the prerequisites. After you have installed the service, you must configure it. Perform the following steps to install the RIS service:

1. Log on to the server as Administrator.

2. Open the Control Panel (select Start, Settings, Control Panel) and double-click Add/Remove Programs.

3. Click the Add/Remove Windows Components button and select the Remote Installation Services check box.

4. Insert the Windows 2000 Server CD-ROM. The service is copied to the server and you are prompted to reboot the server after the service has been installed.

Now that you have installed RIS, you must run `risetup.exe` to copy the initial CD-based image of Windows XP Professional on the RIS server and configure the RIS server to respond to clients' requests. The initial image is a copy of the I386 folder found on the Windows XP Professional CD-ROM. Perform the following steps to configure RIS:

1. Select Start, Run, type "`risetup.exe` " into the Run dialog box, and click OK.

2. The Remote Installation Services Setup Wizard presents a welcome page that reminds you of some of the RIS prerequisites. Click the Next button.

3. By default, the wizard offers to create the RIS folder structure and files on the C partition (even though the wizard itself reminds you that this can't be done). Choose a drive letter for a nonsystem partition to place the files into and then click the Next button.

4. The next dialog box asks whether the RIS server should respond immediately to client requests before you have even finished the configuration. Leave the check box deselected. You can select it after you have configured the RIS server in Active Directory Users and Computers.

5. The next dialog box asks where the system should look for the Windows XP Professional installation files. Type the drive letter for the CD-ROM drive and the path to the installation files (for example, `D:\I386`). Click Next.

6. The next dialog box suggests a folder name for the initial image. Each image that is created has its own folder. Use the default name provided or type in a different name, and then click Next.

7. The next dialog box asks you to provide a descriptive name for this image. Use the default or type in a different name. Click the Next button to get to the finish line.

8. You're finished. The final dialog box summarizes the parameters that you selected. Click the Finish button. `Risetup.exe` now copies the contents of the I386 folder to the folder structure that you just created and completes the installation process.

When the installation is finished, you need to configure the RIS server to respond to RIS clients. You have to log on as a domain administrator to complete this final step. Launch the Active Directory Users and Computers Console by selecting Start, Programs, Administrative Tools, Active Directory Users and Computers. Next, right-click the RIS Server Computer object and select Properties. Click the Remote Install tab from the Properties page. On this tab, select the Respond to Client Computers Requesting Service option, shown in Figure 1.1.

Creating Additional Images

The Risetup.exe Wizard created the first image of Windows XP Professional for you. However, that image provides only an attended installation of the OS. You can create additional images in a few ways:

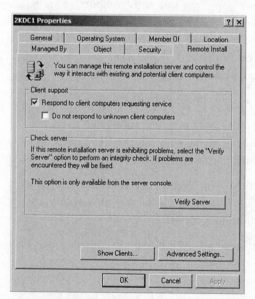

Figure 1.1 The Remote Install tab.

➤ Use Setup Manager to create an answer file for your CD-based image. This allows for custom and unattended installations. The answer file will be attached to the CD-based image by using the Remote Install tab from the RIS server properties page. Here, you will add another image by attaching the answer file to the existing image.

When locking down the security to images, it is best to control the ACL to the answer file, not the image folder. This will still allow users or administrators access to the installation files, but not the answer file that controls the listing of the additional images.

➤ Install another CD-based image to the RIS server. This is important if you will be supporting multiple OSs, such as Windows 2000 and XP Professional.

➤ Create additional images that contain the OS as well as any necessary applications and configuration. RIS installs a utility called `Riprep.exe` that you can use to create images of the OS and any installed applications.

The functionality of `Riprep.exe` is similar to that of a third-party disk-imaging application. The major benefit of using a Riprep image is that you can include software in the image, instead of having to wait for SMS or GPO software deployment to install the applications. However, `Riprep.exe` has some limitations. It can make an image only of the C partition of a computer. If a computer contains C and D partitions, only the C partition will be part of the image. Also, when you apply the image to a computer via RIS, any existing partitions are deleted. The entire hard drive is repartitioned as a single partition and then is formatted with NTFS. If you can work within those limits, you can easily configure and deploy `Riprep.exe` images. Perform the following steps to create a `Riprep.exe` image:

1. Connect the computer that you are imaging to the network.

2. Install Windows XP Professional and any applications that users may need. Connect to the REMINST share point on the RIS server. Run `riprep.exe` from `\RIS Server\REMINST\Admin\I386\riprep.exe`.

3. The Remote Installation Preparation Wizard is launched. It asks you on which RIS server the image should be placed and the name of the folder to which the image should be copied.

4. The last task is to provide a user-friendly name for the image (such as Marketing or Sales).

After you complete these steps, `Riprep.exe` copies the image to the designated RIS server. However, `Riprep.exe` acts a lot like `Sysprep.exe`. In addition to creating an image, `Riprep.exe` removes the unique attributes, such as the SIDs and the computer name. When the RIS client downloads the image, the Mini-Setup Wizard asks you to put back what was taken out. The creation of the Riprep image contains an answer file, which is located in the `i386\Templates` folder of the image on the RIS server. This answer file, `Risetup.sif`, can be modified to automate and customize the installation of the Risetup image.

Because the Riprep process takes everything from the disk and puts it into the image, you could store virtually anything in the image for future reference. You could place the critical drivers for printers, NICs, and video adapters from the XP Professional CD. You could place custom settings in the image as well, such as critical help files for a business application, custom drivers, and business files.

Configuring Clients

The client computer can connect to a RIS server in two ways. The first method is to install a peripheral connection interface (PCI) network adapter that contains a Preboot Execution Environment (PXE) boot ROM. You then have to configure the computer's BIOS to boot from the PXE network adapter. When the computer boots from the PXE network adapter, it attempts to get an IP address from a DHCP server. After the network adapter has an IP address, the user is prompted to press the F12 key to locate a RIS server.

The second method is when the network adapter does not have the PXE boot ROM on board. In this case, you can use a RIS boot disk, which supports multiple network adapter manufacturers' NICs, such as 3Com and Intel. Use the `rbfg.exe` utility to create a RIS boot disk. After you have installed RIS, you can find the utility in `RemoteInstall\Admin\i386\rbfg.exe`.

Downloading an Image

After you have configured a RIS server with several images, users can boot their computers from the network adapter and press F12 to find a RIS server. The server then displays a welcome screen; press Enter to bypass this screen. Next, users must log on to the domain.

 The person installing the system must have the ability to add computers to the domain. Within Active Directory, this is done by giving the user the permission to add child objects to the domain, typically at the OU level.

After the users are logged on, they see a list of images to choose from. The users select an image from the list, and RIS reformats the entire drive and downloads the image to the target computer. After about 30 to 40 minutes, users have a clean installation of the operating system and applications.

Joining a Workgroup

When you are installing your Windows XP Professional client, you will be asked whether you want to be a member of a workgroup or domain. This is a very important issue, but one that can be addressed easily to help you decide. A workgroup is a great option for a small company or a home office environment. In a workgroup, the usernames are kept locally, in a decentralized manner. If, for example, Derek needs to gain access to Dan's PC, Dan will need to add Derek to his list of users, which is located on his local PC. Of course, you can see that this arrangement can get out of hand very quickly and become too much overhead for even a small environment.

Joining a Domain

For most environments that will be using Windows XP Professional, it will be better to have the computer join a domain. Unlike the workgroup option, the domain option keeps the list of users centrally, on the domain controllers. This allows for easier tracking and access to resources because a single username exists for each user in the entire domain. The domains that you can join include Windows NT and Windows 2000 and Server 2003 Active Directory domains. To join a domain, you still need to have the credentials that you did in previous Microsoft OSs:

➤ Local administrator privileges to the Windows XP Professional computer

➤ Username and password of a domain type administrator with permission to Create Computer Accounts in the OU or domain

➤ Account operators

➤ Domain Admins

➤ Enterprise Admins

If you want to add the computer to the domain after the installation, you would use the interface that is shown in Figure 1.2. If you want to join the domain during the installation of the OS, you need to supply the credentials for the domain administrative account that meets the criteria in the preceding list. Both attended and unattended installations can have the computer join the domain during the installation.

Figure 1.2 Interface to change between a workgroup and a domain.

To join a domain, right-click My Computer and select Properties. Then select the Computer Name tab. Here you can select either the manual option—the Change button—or the automated wizard option—the Network ID button. Figure 1.2 illustrates the interface.

Using the USMT to Migrate User Settings and Files

If you have decided to perform a fresh installation of Windows XP Professional, you have made a good choice. However, you have also decided that the settings that were on the computer OS before will be lost, or have you? Windows 2000 launched with a tool that allowed administrators to copy user settings before the old OS was removed. These settings were then reapplied to the new OS after installation. The tool was the User State Migration Tool (USMT).

Microsoft has included this tool with XP directly so that user settings can be gracefully migrated from one system to another. The idea is to allow for fresh installations, but also to achieve a lower TCO. The following is a sampling of the different settings, folders, and file types that are transferred by default (the settings are for both the OS and certain Microsoft applications):

Accessibility options:

➤ Fonts

➤ Network printers and mapped network driver

Browser and mail settings:

➤ Folder and taskbar options

Mouse and keyboard options:

➤ Regional settings

➤ Microsoft Office, Outlook, Word, Excel, PowerPoint settings

➤ Stored mail and contacts

Folders:

➤ My Documents, My Pictures

➤ Desktop

➤ Favorites

File types:

➤ CH3, CSV, DIF, DOC, DOT, DQY, IQY, MEW, OQY, POT, PPA,
PPS, PPT, PRE, RQY, RTF, SCD, SH3, TXT, WPD, WPS, WQ1,
WRI, XLS

Files and Settings Transfer (FAST) Wizard

The FAST Wizard is designed to accommodate the transfer of settings from a single computer or an upgrade to the same system. The data that is going to be saved can be stored on the local system, a server, or removable media. After the user data has been saved to a UNC file, it can then be backed up or burned to a CD-ROM for more permanent storage.

To get the transfer of the user data to work, you need to mine the information from the existing, or old, system. If this is a pre-XP box, you need to obtain a Wizard Disk, or use the Windows XP Professional CD to access the Fastwiz.exe tool. To create the Wizard Disk, you need to run the Files and Settings Transfer Wizard, located under Start, All Programs, Accessories, System Tools. Figure 1.3 shows the portion of the tool that creates the Wizard Disk.

Figure 1.3 The FAST Wizard interface that allows for the creation of the Wizard Disk.

To start the process of saving data, you need to be logged on as the user that will be migrated. During the archiving of the old system, you will have an opportunity to customize exactly which portion of the system, files, and settings you want saved. Figure 1.4 shows the interface for customizing the settings, files and folders, and file types.

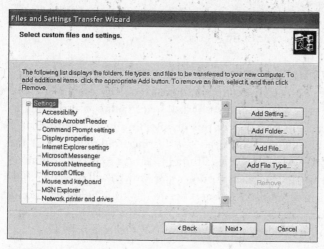

Figure 1.4   Customization of the FAST Wizard files and settings.

After you have the old system archived, you can install the new Windows XP Professional computer. After the computer is installed, start up the FAST Wizard and download the information to the new XP system.

If you want to run the FAST Wizard for multiple users, you must perform these steps multiple times.

USMT from the Command Line

If you work for a large corporation, you will certainly need a more robust tool than the FAST Wizard. That is where the USMT command-line options come into play. These options are fully customizable to migrate multiple user settings. However, you will need to have the following requirements in place to use this option:

➤ A server to which both source and target computers can gain access.

➤ Adequate space for migrating all users' data.

➤ Source computers containing the users' accounts to be transferred.

➤ A target computer running Windows XP Professional that does not contain a profile for the user whose state you will be transferring.

➤ An account with administrative privilege on the target computer. The account cannot have the same name as the migrating user account.

➤ The account name and password of the users whose settings and files are to be transferred.

After you have acquired all this information, you are ready to start the migration. The migration will occur in three phases.

Phase I: Prepare the Server

The server share needs to be created to house the users' data. A standard configuration needs to have a large amount of disk space with a shared folder to house the users' data. For purposes of this discussion, suppose that folder is named USMT_DATA. Then, you need two distinct folders to house the USMT migration files and executables. It might be best to make two different folders so that you can keep each portion separate. You will need one folder to house the scanning portion and another folder to handle the loading portion of the process. In the scanning folder, copy the following files from the ValueAdd\MSFT\USMT folder on the Windows XP Professional CD:

➤ Scanstate.exe

➤ *.dll

➤ *.inf

In the loading folder, copy the following files from the same location:

➤ Loadstate.exe

➤ *.dll

➤ MigUser.inf

Phase II: Scan the Source Computer

Next, you need to scan the user state on the source computer. This is an easy phase that consists of multiple steps. First, map a drive to the scanning folder that you have on the server. Then run the following command while you're logged in as the user to be migrated:

```
Scanstate /I .\migapp.inf /I .\migsys.inf /I .\migfiles.inf
/I .\sysfiles.inf \\<server>\USMT_DATA
```

 The INF files in the command are fully customizable to incorporate different applications, files, and settings.

Phase III: Load the Target Computer

Finally, you are ready to load the target computer. To successfully install the user settings, you need to be logged in with administrative rights and confirm that the users whose data you are migrating do not have an existing account on the target computer. When all these items are taken care of, you can map a drive to the loading folder that you have on the server and run the following command:

```
Loadstate /I .\miguser.inf \\<server>\\UMT_DATA
```

Deploying Service Packs (SPs) Using Group Policy and Slipstreaming

Installing SPs in Windows NT was a very time-consuming process. First, you had to install the OS, and then you had to apply the SP. Windows XP allows you to incorporate an SP with the installation files. Combining the latest SP with the Windows XP installation files enables you to install them as one. In Windows NT, however, if you installed a new service after applying an SP, you had to reapply the SP for the new service to gain any benefits the SP might have to offer. Additionally, you had to reinstall some services after you applied an SP. Thankfully, you don't have to contend with these situations in Windows XP.

Group Policy Deployments of SPs

One great feature of Windows 2000, Windows Server 2003, and Windows XP is the capability to control the computing environment via Group Policy. One control method is the deployment of software through Group Policy Objects (GPOs). A new option is provided for deploying service packs through MSI files and GPOs. This option works best when you assign the service pack to computers in the environment. This way, you get a consistent installation of the SP regardless of which user logs on to the computer.

Using Software Update Services (SUS)

**New
SP2**

SUS is an amazing and extremely valuable service for any enterprise. Between the first release of Windows XP and the release of SP2, Microsoft has updated SUS capabilities to include the installation of service packs. This option requires that an SUS server be installed on a Windows 2000 Server or Server 2003 computer. Then the GPOs control how the Windows XP clients behave to get the updates and service packs installed.

Slipstreaming SPs

The process of combining the Windows XP installation files with an SP is called *slipstreaming*. You apply an SP to a distribution share of the installation files by executing update.exe /integrate:fullpath.

There was an old method for slipstreaming service packs, which was to use the **/s** switch. This has been replaced with the **/integrate:fullpath** switch.

If you install Windows XP using the slipstreamed distribution, the installations contain the SP. Using this method can save you a lot of time and helps you to avoid having to apply an SP after each installation.

Unattended SP2 Installs from the Command Line

There are two ways to install Windows XP SP2 from a command line. The two methods are similar, but they use different files: Update.msi or Xpsp2.exe. In both cases, common command-line switches can be used to control the behavior of the installation. Following are some of the more common switches that you might use:

➤ /quiet (does not show a display and asks no questions)

➤ /n (does not create a backup to remove the SP)

➤ /f (force apps closed to reboot)

➤ /forcerestart

➤ /norestart

➤ /uninstall

➤ /integrate:fullpath (used for slipstreaming)

Most new service packs, updates, and hotfixes come with an **update.msi** installation file, which supports all these switches. This also means that you can slipstream these different files into a shared copy of Windows XP or a RIS image of Windows XP.

The new **update.msi** also supports "out of order" installation of patches and service packs. This allows you to install the updates in any order, and the Installer component of Windows XP will handle any conflicts and out-of-date updates that might be included in a service pack that is already applied.

Applying SPs Manually

If you didn't have the opportunity or capability to create a slipstreamed distribution share, you can apply an SP by running update.exe on the local machine. If you install any new services after applying the SP, Windows XP gets any files it needs for those services from the installation files or the SP.

This process updates a service or an application without requiring you to continually reapply the SP whenever you add something new.

Removing SPs

There are two primary methods for uninstalling a service pack. The first is the old-standby method, which is to go to the Add or Remove Programs in Control Panel. This option allows you to uninstall the service pack while the system is still operational. Another option to remove a service pack is to use the spuninst.exe program, which is located under the %systemroot%\$NTServicePackUninstall$\spuninst folder. This folder is created when you install the service pack (unless you also use the /n switch).

 The **spuninst.exe** program can also be run from the Recovery Console in case the system is not stable enough to boot successfully.

Installing Hotfixes

A few common ways exist to deploy hotfixes to Windows XP Professional clients. The first way is to deploy the hotfixes during the installation of the OS itself. To accomplish this form of installation, you need to create and configure the following items:

1. Create a distribution folder. This will be named i386 and will contain a folder named OEM. The installation process will refer to this folder for the inclusion of additional files and content.

2. Create an answer file. This will instruct the installation on how to interact with the distribution folder that you have created in the first step.

3. Create a Cmdlines.txt file. This file will contain specific lines of code that install each hotfix separately.

4. Copy files to the distribution folder. After all the files are created, you will then copy three items (the answer file, the Cmdlines.txt file, and the hotfix executables) to the distribution folder.

5. Start the installation. The final step is to install the OS, which will in turn install the hotfixes from the entries that were placed in the Cmdlines.txt file. The two installation commands for XP are winnt.exe and winnt32.exe.

Another option to install hotfixes with ease is to use the Qchain.exe tool from Microsoft. This tool allows multiple hotfixes to be installed without a reboot. Of course, if you attempt to install hotfixes normally, without a reboot, you could cause serious damage to your system, even corruption and complete failure.

Hotfixes can also be distributed using SUS, SMS, GPOs, and the update.msi method, if the hotfix comes with this file. The distribution of hotfixes is similar to service packs now, so the options are also similar.

Automatic Updates

Automatic Updates is the new look and feel for the Critical Update Notification feature that was available in the Windows 9x series and Windows 2000. This feature automatically contacts the Windows Update site at Microsoft to detect any critical updates for the system. This is an excellent service that is built in; but for some environments, usually corporations, the service can be a problem, creating a situation where administrators do not know which updates have been installed on the client computers. However, by selecting Control Panel, System, and then selecting the Automatic Updates tab, the administrator can control how these critical updates are handled, as shown in Figure 1.5. The four configurations are as follows:

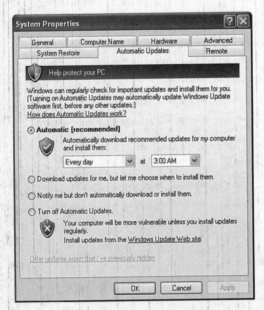

Figure 1.5 The Automatic Updates tab of the System Properties dialog box.

➤ Automatic (recommended)—This option will allow the computer to automatically download the updates and install them at a set interval.

➤ Download Updates for Me, but Let Me Choose When to Install Them—Downloads the updates in the background and then prompts the user for the installation of the updates.

➤ Notify Me but Don't Automatically Download or Install Them—First prompts the user to download the updates and then prompts the user for the installation of the updates after they are downloaded.

➤ Turn Off Automatic Updates—Disables the automatic update feature, forcing manual installation of the updates or the use of Start, Windows Update to obtain the new updates.

 The automatic updates client that was installed with SP1 or later on Windows XP clients includes the functionality for supporting SUS.

Dynamic Update

Dynamic Update allows Windows XP Professional Setup to function with the built-in Windows Update feature. Dynamic Update will allow the download of critical fixes and drivers needed during the setup process. This feature is designed to help reduce difficulties during setup. One way that difficulties are minimized is to make the device drivers that are not included on the Windows XP Professional CD-ROM available through Dynamic Update. Dynamic Update cannot overwrite any device drivers that are located on the OS CD-ROM by default. It allows only for new device drivers. If a new device driver is available from Microsoft, it can be obtained after the installation by using the Windows Update feature.

Two types of files are downloaded by Dynamic Update:

➤ Replacement files—Files that are typically DLLs that replace the errant files located on the CD-ROM. These replacement files are flagged to replace files that need critical fixes or updates.

➤ Device drivers—These files are new device drivers that were not available on the CD-ROM. Any updates to existing device drivers are not available through Dynamic Update.

For clients to take advantage of Dynamic Update, the following criteria must be met:

➤ A connection to the location of the files and drivers must exist. This can be either the Internet or a network share containing the updates, which were downloaded by a network administrator earlier.

➤ The client needs to be running Internet Explorer 4.1 or later versions of the following two files: `Winenet.dll` and `Shlwapi.dll`.

During a manual installation, the user is prompted to connect to the Internet and download the updates from the Microsoft website. In an unattended installation, Dynamic Update is enabled by default, which will have the installation attempt to connect to the Internet or shared folder. If Dynamic Update needs to be disabled for an unattended installation, the `DUDisable=yes` switch must be used. This will typically be located in the answer file that is generated.

Creating a Network Share for Dynamic Update

Many compelling reasons exist to not want users accessing the Internet to download Windows Updates during the installation of the OS or even after the OS is installed. One method to eliminate this access is to create a network share that contains the files and drivers that the administrator feels are important for the company environment.

To create the shared folder, the administrator first needs to access the corporate site for the Windows Update and download the essential files for the computers in the enterprise, including updates and device drivers. This establishes a controlled environment for these updates and device drivers, ensuring that users cannot simply connect and download files that could cause compatibility issues. After the files have been downloaded to the correct share point on the server, the `DUPrepare:pathname` switch needs to be used against the path to prepare it for delivery to the clients. To point the installation, either attended or unattended, to this new share point, add the `DUShare:pathname` switch to the installation command or the answer file.

Product Activation

Product activation is an attempt to reduce the piracy of the Windows XP Professional product. Every system that is installed needs to be activated within 30 days, or the system will no longer function until it is activated.

Those enterprises, both large and small, that have an open license agreement for Windows XP do not have to activate the installations of XP Professional. This is to allow for the diverse methods of installation and optimize the installation process.

The activation of your OS is based on the Product ID as well as hardware that is located within the system. For those of you who change hardware on your systems, this can cause some issues. However, if you significantly overhaul your hardware, you will need to reactivate your system. Activation can be done over the Internet or via a phone call to Microsoft. In either case, the process is rather painless and takes only a few minutes.

In the latest release from Microsoft, Windows Product Activation (WPA) will be tied solely to the BIOS. This means that any hardware device can be swapped and the product will not need to be reactivated. However, if the motherboard manufacturer changes, the system will require a reactivation. This precludes a BIOS change on the same motherboard. If you upgrade your system, the same rules apply, which means that if you significantly overhaul your hardware, you will need to reactivate.

Troubleshooting Failed Installations

Windows XP Professional should install on most new computers without too much difficulty. However, there are some common reasons why it may not install properly. The following is a list of typical installation problems:

➤ Media errors—These are problems you encounter with the distribution CD-ROM. Make sure the problem exists with the media itself, not access to the media. If you place the Windows XP Professional CD-ROM in a shared drive for installation, too many people could be using the drive at one time. This may generate some errors. However, if only one person is connected to the shared drive and errors persist, get a replacement for the distribution CD-ROM. In addition, always restart failed installations caused by media errors.

➤ Incompatible CD-ROM drive—Many specifications exist for CD-ROM drives. You can install Windows XP from most drives, but there are always exceptions. If the CD-ROM drive is not compliant, replace it or place the distribution files on the network. Also, as mentioned earlier in this chapter, the Windows XP CD-ROM is bootable and can be installed from El-Torito-compatible drives. If the CD-ROM can't boot, ensure that the drive is compliant and that the boot order in the BIOS has been set to the CD-ROM drive. Ensure that the level of BIOS that you are running supports bootable CD-ROMs. Also, the controller card for the CD-ROM drive could be failing, or the drive itself could be bad.

➤ Installation halts or errors—If a STOP error occurs during the installation, it is typically the result of incorrect or incompatible drivers. Obtain the correct and current drivers and restart the installation process. Also, the installation may stop just after the copy or text phase, with a warning that the master boot record has a virus. This warning typically results when the BIOS has the virus warning option enabled. Turn this option off and restart the installation. As a final measure, ensure that all devices are on the HCL.

➤ Lack of drive space—Windows XP needs much more free space compared to its predecessors. Ensure that at least 650MB of free space is available.

➤ Dependency failures—For the installation to be completed successfully, all services must be able to start when needed. Some services depend on others to complete a task. For example, if the drivers for the network adapter could not load, that will affect all services that depend on the network adapter's successful installation. As a result, the computer won't be able to join the domain.

➤ Problems joining the domain—If the network adapter has initialized but the computer still can't join the domain, verify that the DNS server is online and that you are using the correct IP address of the DNS server. Also, verify that you typed the domain name correctly. If problems persist, install the computer to a workgroup to complete the installation.

Exam Prep Questions

1. You are the network administrator for the East branch of the ACME publishing company. You have a Windows 2000 domain that contains Windows 95, Windows 98, Windows NT 4, and Windows 2000 clients. Your network has four locations, each configured as an Active Directory site.

   You want to upgrade all the clients to Windows XP to take advantage of the Remote Assistance capability. You upgrade the Windows 98, NT, and 2000 clients, but are having trouble upgrading the Windows 95 clients. What should you do to the Windows 95 clients?

   ○ A. Run the Readiness Analyzer

   ○ B. Run `winnt32 /checkupgradeonly`

   ○ C. Run `winnt /checkupgradeonly`

   ○ D. Upgrade them to Windows 98

2. You are the network administrator at the AllMine talent company. You are looking to upgrade your Windows NT domain to Windows 2000. You want to take advantage of the new Group Policy Objects that can control desktop settings, security, and software installation. You want to use the DFS service to create a load-balanced and fault-tolerant environment for the software deployment and maintenance via Group Policy.

   To prepare your environment for the Windows 2000 domain, you want to install Windows XP on all the clients before the Windows 2000 domain is installed. You want to create the most efficient installation for your 10,000 client computers. You currently use a third-party cloning and distribution package and need to continue to use this package for the distribution of Windows XP Professional. You want the installation to be completely automated.

   Which options should you use? (Check all correct answers.)

   ❑ A. Create an answer file using Setup Manager.

   ❑ B. Create a uniqueness database file using Setup Manager.

   ❑ C. Use the CD-based image using RIS.

   ❑ D. Create an image using Riprep.

   ❑ E. Create an image using Sysprep.

3. As the administrator for the CertCore consulting group, you are responsible for 50 consultants and 100 office personnel. CertCore has four offices within the major metropolitan area that the consultants work from. Domain controllers are in each of the four locations.

   At this time, the budget is insufficient to have a quality lab, so the consultants are using their own desktop systems to troubleshoot client issues. You need to find a technology that will enable the consultants in the company to quickly reinstall their Windows XP Professional desktop in case they corrupt their system while troubleshooting client issues. The consultants need to have the capability to boot their system without any floppy disk. After the installation, the computer account needs to be located in the same OU that it was before, to obtain the correct Group Policies. Finally, the installation needs to include a core set of applications that can then be controlled after the OS is installed via Group Policy.

How should you proceed?

- ○ A. Save the contents of the i386 folder from the Windows XP Professional CD to the network, giving the consultants permissions to the winnt32 command.
- ○ B. Install a RIS server, which contains the CD-based image for Windows XP Professional.
- ○ C. Create a Riprep image.
- ○ D. Create a Sysprep image.

4. You are in charge of the deployment of Windows XP for all 25,000 users at ACME computer sales. The current network consists of Windows 2000 Professional systems and a Windows 2000 domain. Most of the users are located at the main production plant, but others are located at sales offices throughout the United States.

You do not want to upgrade the systems, because most of them were upgraded from Windows NT 4 Workstation in the last rollout. However, you want to save as much of the user-based settings and files as possible to minimize both calls to the Help Desk and user complaints. You decide to use the File and Settings Transfer Wizard to migrate the user settings and files. What will you need to do to get the settings from the Windows 2000 Professional systems?

- ○ A. Run the scanstate command from the Windows 2000 domain controller.
- ○ B. Run the loadstate command from the client computer.
- ○ C. Create a Wizard Disk to run on the Windows 2000 Professional computers.
- ○ D. Run the FAST Wizard from the Windows XP client to save the user settings.

5. You are the chief technology officer for the ACME web development company. Your company develops high-end websites and web applets for e-commerce companies. You have more than 1,000 developers in the company who code in different languages, including C#, ASP, VB, and XML. Each developer computer is running Windows XP Professional, and the user is not a Power User or Administrator on the local system.

The current infrastructure is a Windows 2000 domain running Active Directory. You had to implement Active Directory to control each type of developer through Group Policy and to delegate control to the head developer in each discipline. Each type of developer, user account, and computer account is located in a separate OU. You have had issues

with some service packs overwriting critical system files that were
needed to develop and test certain applications that were developed.
You need to develop a strategy to roll out future service packs to each
discipline only after the service pack has been tested and has shown
that it does not cause any damage to the developer computer.

What should you do?

- ○ A. Create a logon script that runs a batch file to install the service pack
  when the computer is rebooted.
- ○ B. Save the service pack to a network share and allow the developer access
  to the share to install the service pack at the developer's own leisure.
- ○ C. Use the QCHAIN command to install the service pack through a logon
  script, based on the group that the developer is a member of.
- ○ D. Configure a Group Policy at each developer OU that will apply the
  service pack after it has been tested for that type of developer.

6. As the administrator for Que Publishing, you are planning to install
   1,000 Windows XP Professional computers in the next month. You are
   currently running Windows 95 on these clients and will use a network
   unattended installation to install the new OS.

   Security is an important facet for your industry because the users need
   to use the Internet so much to do research. You are aware of at least
   four security hotfixes that you want installed during the installation of
   the initial OS. You want to use the new Dynamic Update feature to
   install these updates, as well as some of the other updates that you have
   tested to be safe and stable for your environment. However, you do not
   want the client to access the Internet during the installation to receive
   these updates.

   What should you do? (Check all correct answers.)

- ❑ A. Create a Group Policy to point the client to the share that contains the
  hotfixes and updates.
- ❑ B. Create a share on the network and download the hotfixes and updates
  to it.
- ❑ C. When installing the client, be sure to use the dushare switch with the
  installation command.
- ❑ D. When installing the client, be sure to use the duprepare switch with the
  installation command.

7. You are in charge of the web developers in your company. Your compa-
   ny creates e-commerce web sites and applications for small businesses.
   The developers' computers run Windows XP Professional and Internet
   Information Services (IIS).

   The company has 150 developers. The developers need to have stable
   environments to work in to ensure that they are productive. During the
   installation process of Windows XP Professional, the OS is installed,
   service packs are applied, applications are installed, and any Microsoft
   hotfixes or updates are installed. However, sometimes additional hotfixes
   and updates need to be applied to support security and functionality of

the development environment. The developer must automatically be made aware of any update and then must be in control of the update being downloaded and installed.

Which option should you configure?

- O A. Windows Update.
- O B. Automatic Updates.
- O C. Dynamic Update.
- O D. Configure a server and share with the contents of the updates and use the dushare command on the client.

8. You are the network administrator in charge of the Windows XP Professional rollout for your company. You have been planning for your 1,500-user rollout for the past three months. You have a Windows 2000 Active Directory–based domain and only two locations.

   You have eight phases to your overall deployment plan, which will last for two months. You are halfway through the phases when trouble hits. You have users complaining that they can no longer access their Windows XP Professional computer.

   What should you do?

   - O A. Have the users restart their computers and press F12.
   - O B. Activate the Windows XP Professional computers.
   - O C. Boot the computers to the Recovery Console.
   - O D. Boot the computers and press F8.

Answers to Exam Prep Questions

1. Answer D is correct. It is not possible to upgrade Windows 95 clients directly to Windows XP Professional. You must first upgrade them to Windows 98, and then you can make the upgrade to Windows XP. Answer A is incorrect because this is a tool that is used to determine whether your system will be compatible with Windows XP. Answers B and C are incorrect because the /checkupgradeonly switch determines whether the existing system is compatible with Windows XP. In addition, the /checkupgradeonly switch is not compatible with the winnt command.

2. Answers A and E are correct. To optimize the installation of Windows XP Professional using a third-party cloning and distribution package, you need to use Sysprep.exe. Sysprep allows for the creation of images that use a minisetup program to make the system unique on the network. In addition to using the Sysprep tool, you need to make an answer file to answer the minisetup questions automatically. This will make the installation automated. Answer B is incorrect because the uniqueness database file is used for network installations, not for Sysprep installations. Answers C and D are incorrect because they are referring to the use of RIS. RIS is not used with third-party cloning tools.

3. Answer C is correct. Riprep is a tool that is used with RIS servers. Riprep enables not only the core OS to be imaged, but also the applications that are currently installed. The image is stored on the RIS server and is made available to clients that have a PXE boot ROM NIC or can support a PXE boot ROM floppy disk. The system that is created can have the applications installed via Group Policy software deployment. Then when the Riprep image is created, the applications and software are both included and the software will be maintained and controlled via Group Policy. Answer A is incorrect because the i386 folder from the CD will not give the application requirements in the image, nor the capability to boot without a floppy, in the case that the existing OS is corrupt. Answer B is incorrect because a CD-based image through RIS will not include the applications that are required in the scenario. Answer D is incorrect because Sysprep is not capable of producing an image that will work without some form of third-party client, which would require an OS running or a boot disk.

4. Answer C is correct. To save the settings and files from a Windows 2000 Professional system, you need to have a wizard disk or the Fastwiz.exe tool from the Windows XP Professional CD-ROM. This will start the FAST Wizard and allow the user settings to be saved to the hard disk, removable media, or network share. Answers A and B are incorrect because they would be used in the command-line method, not with the FAST Wizard. Answer D is incorrect because you can't run the FAST Wizard on a client to save files from another system.

5. Answer D is correct. For this deployment, it will be ideal to create a Group Policy that will apply the service pack through the use of MSI packages. After the service pack has been thoroughly tested for a developer type, it can be quickly installed through the use of software deployment using Group Policy. Answer A is incorrect because the capability to control the installation is too limiting through a batch file. Also, it would be extremely difficult to control the batch file application to computers, whereas through GPOs it would be very easy. Answer B is incorrect because there would be no control over who actually had the service pack. There could also be a problem if the developer uses someone else's machine and incorrectly installs the service pack there. Answer C is incorrect because this tool is used to install hotfixes without rebooting, not service packs.

6. Answers B and C are correct. First, you need to create a share that contains the hotfixes and updates. You need to connect to the corporate site located on the Windows Update site to select which files you want to include in your share. Then the client needs to be redirected to the correct share by using the dushare switch during the installation. Answer A is incorrect because GPOs can't be used to install from the Dynamic Update share; this is available at installation only. Answer D is incorrect

because the duprepare switch prepares the Dynamic Update share, which is not used on the client portion of the installation.

7. Answer B is correct. When a user needs to be automatically updated about new hotfixes and updates, the Automatic Updates option must be configured. This tool can be set up to trigger when there is an update to then allow the user to download and install the update. This option also has settings that can download the updates but then prompt for installation and, of course, completely disable the automatic updates. If you disable the automatic updates, you will need to manually use the Windows Update feature. Answer A is incorrect because this option is a manual process. Answer C is incorrect because this option is available only during the installation of the product. Answer D is incorrect because the dushare switch is used with Dynamic Update and is available only during the installation of the product.

8. Answer B is correct. If you are installing your Windows XP Professional computers from a nonvolume license CD, you need to activate your computers. This requires that the computer communicate with the clearinghouse located on the Internet or via a phone call to the clearinghouse to activate the installation of XP. By default, you have 30 days to use the product before it will become inoperable from not having been activated on your system. Answer A is incorrect because this is used for a RIS installation. You have a good installation; you just need to activate what is installed. Answer C is incorrect because the Recovery Console won't be available without activating the system. Answer D is incorrect because the F8 menu option won't be available until you activate the product.

Need to Know More?

Microsoft Corporation. *Microsoft Windows XP Professional Resource Kit*, 2nd ed. Redmond, WA: Microsoft Press, 2003. ISBN 0735619743. This book reviews the core aspects of installation preparations and the installation options.

Bott, Ed, and Carl Siechert. *Microsoft Windows XP Inside Out*, 2nd ed. Redmond, WA: Microsoft Learning, 2004. ISBN 073562044X. This book covers several aspects of installing, maintaining, and troubleshooting Windows XP systems.

Search the TechNet CD (or its online version through www.microsoft.com) and the Windows 2000 Professional Resource Kit CD using the keywords "sysprep", "RIS", "Remote Installation Services", "Windows Product Activation (WPA)", "Setup Manager", and "Automatic Updates".

Establishing, Configuring, and Managing Resources

Terms you'll need to understand:

✓ Shared folders
✓ Hidden shares
✓ Simple file sharing
✓ Offline files/client-side caching
✓ Share permissions
✓ NT File System (NTFS)
✓ NTFS permissions
✓ User rights
✓ Built-in security principals
✓ Access control list (ACL)
✓ Access control entry (ACE)
✓ Taking ownership of objects
✓ Auditing
✓ Internet Information Server (IIS)
✓ Internet Printing Protocol (IPP)

Techniques you'll need to master:

✓ Creating network shares
✓ Configuring share permissions
✓ Configuring options for offline files
✓ Setting basic and advanced NTFS permissions
✓ Viewing effective permissions
✓ Learning how to turn on auditing
✓ Installing and managing Internet Information Services
✓ Connecting to printers over the Internet

Why do we have computer networks, anyway? The answer is that they empower us to collaborate on projects and share information with others, whether they're around the corner or across the globe. If you're working on a Windows XP Professional system that is connected to a network, you can share one or more of that system's folders with other computers and users on that network. Drive volumes and folders are not automatically shared for all users in Windows XP Professional. Members of the Administrators group and the Power Users group, discussed later in this chapter, are the only users who retain the rights to create shared network folders.

Managing Access to Shared Folders

Windows XP Professional implements a new feature called Simple File Sharing, which is enabled by default when the computer is a standalone or a member of a network workgroup. Simple File Sharing is disabled when the computer is a member of a Windows domain. Simple File Sharing creates a Shared Documents folder, inside of which it creates two subfolders—Shared Pictures and Shared Music. Remote users who access a shared folder over the network always authenticate as the Guest user account when Simple File Sharing is enabled. The properties sheet for a shared folder under Simple File Sharing configures both share permissions and NTFS permissions (if the shared folder is stored on an NTFS volume) simultaneously—you are not allowed to configure the two permissions separately. For example, you cannot make a shared folder private, under Simple File Sharing, unless the folder resides on an NTFS volume.

To turn off Simple File Sharing for a standalone system or for a computer that is a member of a workgroup, perform the following steps:

1. Open a window in either My Computer or Windows Explorer.

2. Click Tools, Folder Options from the menu.

3. Click the View tab.

4. Clear the Use Simple File Sharing (Recommended) check box under the Advanced Settings section.

5. Click OK.

NOTE

The Shared Documents, Shared Pictures, and Shared Music folders are not available if the Windows XP Professional computer is a member of a Windows domain.

Creating Shared Folders from My Computer or Windows Explorer

To share a folder with the network with Simple File Sharing disabled, you can use My Computer or Windows Explorer and follow these steps:

1. Open a window in either My Computer or Windows Explorer.

2. Right-click the folder that you want to share and then select Sharing and Security from the pop-up menu.

3. Click the Share This Folder button.

4. Type in a share name or accept the default name. Windows XP uses the actual folder name as the default Share Name.

5. Type in a comment, if you desire. Comments appear in the Browse list when users search for network resources. Comments can help users locate the proper network shares.

6. Specify the User Limit: Maximum Allowed or Allow This Number Of Users. Windows XP Professional permits a maximum of 10 concurrent network connections per share. Specify the Allow This Number Of Users option only if you need to limit the number of concurrent users for this share to fewer than 10.

7. Click OK to create the shared folder. The folder now becomes available to others on your network.

NOTE

To remove a network share, right-click the shared folder and choose the Sharing and Security option. Click the Do Not Share This Folder option button and click OK. The folder will no longer be shared with the network.

The Security tab of an NTFS folder's properties dialog box is not displayed when Simple File Sharing is enabled and the computer is not a member of a Windows domain. To display the Security tab so that you can view and work with NTFS permissions for folders and files, open a window in My Computer or Windows Explorer and select Tools, Folder Options. Click the View tab and clear the check box titled Use Simple File Sharing (Recommended).

Creating Shared Folders from the Shared Folders MMC Snap-in

To share a folder with the network with Simple File Sharing disabled, you can use the Shared Folders MMC snap-in from a custom console, or you can use the Shared Folders snap-in as part of the Computer Management Console by following these steps:

1. Right-click the My Computer icon and select Manage, or open an empty Microsoft Management Console window and add the Shared Folders snap-in for the local computer.

2. Expand the Shared Folders node and click Shares.

3. Right-click the Shares subnode and select New File Share.

4. Type the path and folder name into the Folder to Share box, or click Browse to locate it.

5. Type a name for the share into the Share Name box, and optionally, type in a Share Description.

6. Click Next.

7. Select one of the basic share permissions listed, or click Customize Share and Folder Permissions to define your own share permissions. The default selection is All Users Have Full Control. *Remember, these are share permissions that apply only to users accessing this share remotely over the network—not to NTFS security permissions!*

8. Click Finish and then click Yes or No when prompted to create another shared folder.

Generally, if you are working with shared folders residing on NTFS volumes, it is a good idea to leave all share permissions at their default setting: Everyone–Full Control. Use NTFS security permissions to specify access control levels for both users and groups. By having only one set of permissions to manage, security access levels are less confusing, and you avoid possible conflicts with share permissions. In addition, NTFS security permissions apply to both remote network users and local users, so users cannot circumvent security permissions by logging on to the local computer.

To remove a shared folder from the Shared Folders snap-in, right-click the shared folder and select Stop Sharing. Click Yes and the folder will no longer be shared on the network.

Using Automatically Generated Hidden Shares

Windows XP Professional automatically creates shared folders by default each and every time the computer is started. These default shares are often referred to as *hidden* or *administrative* shares because a dollar sign ($) is appended to their share names, which prevents the shared folder from being displayed on the network Browse list. Users cannot easily discover that these shares exist. When users browse through the My Network Places window, for example, they cannot see that such hidden shares even exist; Microsoft Windows Networking does not allow hidden shares to be displayed. The default hidden network shares include the following:

➤ C$, D$, E$, and so on—One share gets created for the root of each available hard drive volume on the system.

➤ ADMIN$—This shares the `%systemroot%` folder with the network (for example, `C:\Windows`).

➤ IPC$—This share is used for interprocess communications (IPCs). IPCs support communications between objects on different computers over a network by manipulating the low-level details of network transport protocols. IPCs enable the use of distributed application programs that combine multiple processes working together to accomplish a single task.

➤ print$—This share holds the printer drivers for the printers installed on the local machine. When a remote computer connects to a printer over the network, the appropriate printer driver is downloaded to the remote PC.

Although you can temporarily disable hidden shares, you cannot delete them without modifying the Registry (which is not recommended), because they get re-created each time the computer restarts. You can connect to a hidden share, but only if you provide a user account with administrative privileges along with the appropriate password for that user account. Administrators can create their own custom administrative (hidden) shares by adding a dollar sign to the share name of any shared folder. Administrators can view all the hidden shares that exist on a Windows XP Professional system from the Shared Folders MMC snap-in.

Connecting to Shared Resources on a Windows Network

Users and network administrators have several options available to them for connecting to shared network resources, including the following:

➤ Type in a Universal Naming Convention (UNC) path from the Start, Run dialog box in the format `\\servername\sharename`.

➤ Navigate to the share from the My Network Places window.

➤ Employ the `net use` command from a command prompt window.

If you want to connect to a shared folder named "samples" that resides on a Windows computer named SALES7, click Start, Run, type **SALES7**\ **samples**, and click OK. At this point, you are connected to that shared resource, provided that you possess the proper user ID, password, and security permissions needed to access the shared folder.

Connecting to Network Resources with the My Network Places Window

You can connect to a network share from My Network Places. To use the My Network Places window, perform the following steps:

1. Click Start, My Network Places.

2. In the Network Tasks section on the right, click the Add a Network Place link, which reveals the Add Network Place Wizard.

3. Click Next, click Choose Another Network Location, and then click Next again.

4. Enter the Internet or Network Address, or click Browse to locate the network share by viewing the available network resources. You can connect to one of the following types of resources:

   ➤ A shared folder using the following syntax: **server****share**

   ➤ A web folder using the following syntax: **http://webserver/share**

   ➤ An FTP site using the following syntax: **ftp://ftp.domain.name**

5. Click Next to enter a name for the network place or accept the default name.

6. Click Next again to view a summary of the Network Place that you are adding.

7. Click Finish to establish the connection to the shared folder, provided that you have the proper permissions. A list of network resources to which you have already connected is then displayed within the My Network Places window.

For Command-Line Junkies: The Net Share and Net Use Commands

You can create and delete shared folders from the command line instead of using the GUI. Windows XP offers several Net commands that you use from the command line. You can view all the available Net commands by typing **Net /?** at a command prompt window. To create a new shared folder, type

`Net Share share_name=x:\folder_name`, where share_name represents the name you want to assign to the shared folder, `x:` represents the drive letter where the folder resides, and `folder_name` represents the actual name of the folder. For help with the various options and syntax of the `Net Share` command, type `Net Share /?` at the command prompt.

You also have the option of connecting to network shares via the `Net Use` command. For help with the various options and syntax of the `Net Use` command, type `net use /?` at the command prompt. To connect to a remote resource from the command line, follow these steps:

1. Open a command prompt window (click Start, (All) Programs, Accessories, Command Prompt, or click Start, Run, type **cmd**, and click OK).

2. At the command prompt, type `net use X: \\servername\sharename` and press Enter, where `X:` is a drive letter that you designate (for example, `net use M: \\sales7\samples`). If you possess the appropriate permissions for that network share, you should see the message The Command Completed Successfully displayed in your command prompt window.

Controlling Access to Shared Folders

When you, as a network administrator, grant access to shared resources over the network, the shared data files become very vulnerable to unintentional, as well as intentional, destruction or deletion by others. This is why network administrators must be vigilant in controlling data access security permissions. If access permissions to shared folders are too lenient, shared data may become compromised. On the other hand, if access permissions are set too stringently, users who need to access and manipulate the data may not be able to do their jobs. Managing access control for shared resources can be quite challenging.

Shared Folder Properties: Configuring Offline Files

By right-clicking a shared folder and selecting Sharing, you can modify some of the shared folder's properties. You can specify whether network users can cache shared data files on their local workstations. The Offline Files feature is also referred to as Client-Side Caching (CSC). To configure offline access settings for the shared folder, click the Caching button to display the Cache Settings dialog box. The default is to allow caching of files whenever you create a new shared folder. To disable this feature, you must clear the Allow Caching of Files in This Shared Folder check box in the Cache Settings dialog box. If you allow caching of files for a shared folder, you must choose from three options in the Caching Settings dialog box:

➤ Automatic Caching Of Documents—This option relies on the workstation and server computers to automatically download and make available offline any opened files from the shared folder. Older copies of files are automatically deleted to make room for newer and more recently accessed files. To ensure proper file sharing, the server version of the file is always opened.

➤ Automatic Caching of Programs and Documents—This setting is recommended for folders that contain read-only data or for application programs that have been configured to be run from the network. This option is not designed for sharing data files, and file sharing in this mode is not guaranteed. Older copies of files are automatically deleted to make room for newer and more recently accessed files.

➤ Manual Caching of Documents—This is the default caching setting. This setting requires network users to manually specify any files that they want available when working offline. This setting is recommended for folders that contain user documents. To ensure proper file sharing, the server version of the file is always opened.

Click OK in the Caching Settings dialog box after making any configuration changes for offline access to the shared folder.

You configure the computer's Offline Files feature from the Folder Options dialog box as shown in Figure 2.1. You can navigate to the Folder Options dialog box by opening either My Computer or the Windows Explorer, clicking the Tools menu, and then selecting Folder Options. The Folder Options dialog box allows you to enable or disable Offline Files, specify synchronization options, turn on or off encryption for offline files, and set the disk space allocation for offline files in addition to adjusting several other settings.

The default cache size is configured as 10 percent of the client computer's available disk space. You can change this setting by selecting Tools, Folder Options from the menu bar of any My Computer or Windows Explorer window. The Offline Files tab of the Folder Options dialog box displays the system's offline files settings, as shown in Figure 2.1.

The default location on Windows XP computers for storage of offline files is **%systemroot%\CSC** (for example, **C:\Windows\CSC**). You can use the **Cachemov.exe** tool from the Windows 2000 Professional Resource Kit or from the Windows 2000 Server Resource Kit to relocate the CSC folder onto a different drive letter. The **Cachemov.exe** utility moves the CSC folder to the *root* of the drive volume that is specified. After the CSC folder has been moved from its default location, all subsequent moves place it in the *root* of the drive letter. **Cachemov.exe** never returns the folder to its original default location.

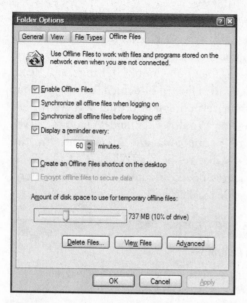

Figure 2.1   The Offline Files tab of the Folder Options dialog box.

Shared Folder Permissions

In addition to the Caching button, located at the bottom of the Sharing tab of a shared folder's Properties dialog box, is the Permissions button. The caption next to this button reads To Set Permissions for Users Who Access This Folder over the Network, Click Permissions. However, these "share" permissions are intended solely for backward-compatibility purposes; you should avoid changing the default settings on share permissions (Everyone:Allow Full Control) unless a share resides on a file allocation table (FAT) or FAT32 drive, which provides no file system security. In most circumstances, you should store all data and applications on NTFS-formatted drives. In fact, as a general rule, you should format (or convert) all system drive letters as NTFS. With the availability of third-party tools, as well as the native Windows XP Recovery Console, which permits command-line access to NTFS drives (even if the system won't boot), it's difficult to argue against NTFS for all drives in Windows XP.

Microsoft has positioned the NTFS file system as the preferred file system for Windows XP by making features such as security permissions, auditing, data compression, data encryption, reparse points, multiple named data streams, and Volume Shadow Copy Service available only on NTFS-formatted drive letters.

Network share permissions have their roots in the days of Windows for Workgroups 3.11, before Windows NT and NTFS. Share permissions provided a way for administrators to control access to files for network users. Only three share permissions are available: Full Control, Change, and Read. These three permissions can be explicitly allowed or denied. Under previous versions of Windows, the default share permission setting was Allow:Full Control for the Everyone group. For Windows XP and Windows Server 2003, however, the default share permissions are Allow:Read for the Everyone group! For shared folders that reside on FAT or FAT32 drives, share permissions do offer some degree of access control for network users. However, they provide no security for local access.

Table 2.1 Network Share Permissions	
Permission Name	**Level of Access Control**
Read	View filenames and subfolder names; view data stored within files; execute application program files.
Change	Includes all Read permissions; change data within files; delete files and subfolders.
Full Control	Includes all Read and Change permissions; modify NTFS permissions on files and folders.

Share permissions apply only to access over the network; these permissions have absolutely nothing to do with the underlying file system, which is why NTFS permissions are preferred. If you have a mixture of share permissions and NTFS permissions on the same folder, troubleshooting access control issues becomes more difficult. Use either share permissions or NTFS permissions, not both. You'll find that it is much easier to troubleshoot access control issues if you set all share permissions to Allow:Change for the Everyone group and use NTFS file system-level permissions only to configure all necessary access control settings. In addition, NTFS security permissions provide you with much more granular control than share permissions.

Monitoring, Managing, and Troubleshooting Access to Files and Folders

The NTFS file system for Windows XP Professional offers several accessibility features that help administrators maintain and safeguard applications and data. Although you can somewhat control access to shared network folders by managing share permissions, Windows XP NTFS provides a very robust access control solution. In addition to offering administrators more granularity of security access control over files and folders than network share permissions, NTFS permissions reside at the file system level, which allows administrators to manage only one set of access control settings for both network users and local users. For troubleshooting resource access, you can enable auditing for folders and files residing on NTFS volumes.

NTFS Security: Users and Groups

You can apply NTFS security permissions to resources such as files, folders, and printers for specific users or groups of users. Windows XP Professional installs four local users by default: Administrator, HelpAssistant, SUPPORT_xxxxxxxx (the x's represent a unique number for your Windows XP system), and Guest. The Guest user account and the SUPPORT_xxxxxxxx account are disabled by default. The Administrator user account is all powerful on the local machine and cannot be deleted, although it can be renamed.

Nine local groups are installed automatically: Administrators, Backup Operators, Guests, HelpServicesGroup, Network Configuration Operators, Power Users, Remote Desktop Users, Replicator, and Users. The Power Users group is not present in any edition of Windows 2000 Server or Windows Server 2003; it exists only as a Local group in Windows XP Professional. The Administrators account is all powerful because it is a member of the Administrators group, and you cannot remove the Administrator user account from membership in the Administrators group. However, you can rename the Administrator account. Table 2.2 outlines the Local groups that are installed by default when you first install Windows XP Professional.

Table 2.2 Local Groups Installed by Default in Windows XP Professional	
Local Group	**Role**
Administrators	Group members possess full administrative control for managing the local system, local users, and Local groups.
Backup Operators	Group members have the rights to back up and restore files and folders on the local system.
Guests	Group members can't make permanent alterations to their desktop settings. The default Guest account is automatically a member of this group. By default, group members possess no specific rights or permissions on objects. If the local computer joins a Windows domain, the Global Domain Guests group automatically becomes a member of the Local Guests group.

(continued)

Table 2.2 Local Groups Installed by Default in Windows XP Professional *(continued)*	
Local Group	**Role**
HelpServicesGroup	Members of this group can log on to the system and use helper applications to diagnose system problems. This group is used in conjunction with the HelpAssistant and SUPPORT_xxxxxxxx user accounts.
Network Configuration Operators	Members in this group can have some administrative privileges to manage configuration of networking features.
Power Users	Group members can add new local user accounts and change existing local user accounts. Members can also create shared folders and shared printers on the network. Power Users retain administrative powers with some restrictions. Thus, Power Users can run legacy applications in addition to certified applications.
Remote Desktop Users	Members in this group are granted the right to log on using the Remote Desktop or Terminal Services client software.
Replicator	This group supports file replication within a Windows domain.
Users	Group members can perform tasks only after an administrator has specifically granted them rights to do so. They can access resources on only those objects for which an administrator has granted them permissions. When user accounts get created, each new user automatically becomes a member of the Local Users group. If the local computer becomes a member of a Windows domain, the Global Domain Users group automatically becomes a member of the Local Users group.

Special Built-in Security Principals

Special built-in security principal entities apply to any user account that happens to be using a Windows XP computer in a particular manner at a given time. For example, when a user logs on to a Remote Desktop session, the security principal Terminal Server User gets applied to the user account for the duration of the Remote Desktop session until the user logs off. When a user logs on to a computer remotely over the network, that user's account gets the Network security principal applied to it until the user disconnects from that network connection. Table 2.3 outlines the various user-related built-in security principals for Windows XP Professional. Figure 2.2 displays both user-related and computer-, process-, and service-related built-in security principals for a Windows XP domain member computer.

Table 2.3   Built-in Security Principals Installed by Default Under Windows XP Professional

Built-in Security Principal	Role
Everyone	Includes all users who access the computer. The best practice is to avoid using this group. If you enable the Guest account, any user can become authorized to access the system, and the user inherits the rights and permissions assigned to the Everyone group.
Authenticated Users	These users have valid user accounts on the local system, or they possess a valid user account within the domain of which the system is a member. It is preferable that you use this group over the Everyone group for preventing anonymous access to resources. The Guest account is never considered an Authenticated User.
Creator Owner	A user who creates or takes ownership of a resource. Whenever a member of the Administrators group creates an object, the Administrators group is listed as the owner of that resource in lieu of the actual name of the user who created it.
Creator Group	A placeholder for an access control entry (ACE) that can be inherited.
Network	Any user accounts from a remote computer that access the local computer via a current network connection.
Interactive	Any user accounts that are logged on locally.
Anonymous Logon	Any user accounts that Windows XP did not validate or authorize. Users cannot log on to the system as an Interactive user and an Anonymous Logon User at the same time.
Dialup	Any user accounts that are currently connected via dial-up networking.
Remote Interactive Logon	Any user who logs on to the computer using a Remote Desktop (Terminal Services) client connection.
Terminal Server User	Any user who accesses the computer using a Remote Desktop (Terminal Services) client connection.

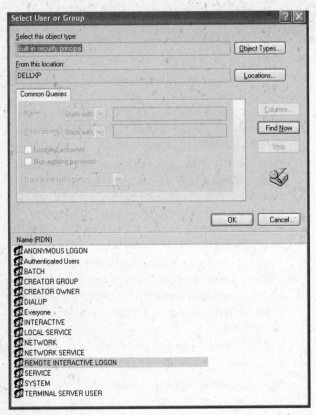

Figure 2.2 Windows XP built-in security principals can be displayed from the Select User or Group dialog box.

NTFS Security: Basic and Advanced Permissions

NTFS security permissions can be assigned both to users and groups and are applied to resources such as folders, files, printers, and other objects. NTFS permissions are broken down into access control list (ACL) settings and access control entries (ACEs). The ACL shows "who" (user or group) is granted access to an object. ACEs detail the specific permission entries (read, write, and so on) for each specific object (folder or file, for example). NTFS permissions for Windows XP can be very complex and granular when you use advanced permissions. Basic permissions are much more simple; they enable you to allow or deny access to resources based on six fundamental levels: Read, Read and Execute, List Folder Contents (applies to folders only), Write, Modify, and Full Control. Advanced (or special) permissions enable you to fine-tune permission settings for allowing or denying such activities as reading or writing extended object attributes.

Basic NTFS Permissions

Basic permissions are composed of predefined advanced NTFS permissions and are applied per user and per group. Individual file permissions differ slightly from the permissions that apply to folders. Table 2.4 highlights the basic NTFS security permissions that are available for files and folders.

Table 2.4	Basic NTFS Security Permissions for Files and Folders
Permission	**Description**
Full Control	Allows/denies full access to objects within the folder. Includes the capability to read, write, delete, modify, change permissions, and take ownership of the folder.
Modify	Allows/denies the capability to read, write, delete, modify, and read permissions for the folder.
Read & Execute	Allows/denies specified users and groups the capability to traverse the folder, execute files within the folder, list its contents, read its contents, read its attributes and extended attributes, and read its permissions.
List Folder Contents (applies only to Folders)	Allows/denies essentially the same permissions as Read & Execute. Allows/denies the capability to display files and subfolders, but this permission does not affect a user's capability to run (execute) an application program as the Read & Execute permission does.
Read	Allows/denies the same permissions as List Folder Contents except for Traverse Folder and Execute File.
Write	Allows/denies the capability to create files and write data, create folders and append data, and write attributes and extended attributes.

The List Folder Contents permission is inherited by folders, but not by files, and it should appear only when you view folder permissions. Read & Execute is inherited by both files and folders and is always present when you view file or folder permissions. By default, NTFS security permissions are inherited from an object's parent. An administrator can manually override the default inheritance and can explicitly configure permission settings.

Advanced NTFS Permissions

NTFS advanced permissions are the building blocks for basic permissions. In Windows XP, advanced permissions allow administrators to have very granular control over exactly what types of access users can have over files and folders. Advanced permissions are somewhat hidden from view. They allow administrators to fine-tune ACE (security) settings. The Security tab in a file or folder's Properties dialog box notifies you when advanced permissions are present. Click the Advanced button to view, add, modify, or remove advanced permissions. At the bottom of the Security tab, Windows XP displays a notification just to the right of the Advanced button that says For Special Permissions or for Advanced Settings, Click Advanced.

After you click Advanced, you see the Advanced Security Settings dialog box, which shows each access control setting that has been applied per user and per group. To view individual advanced permission entries, click one of the users or groups listed and then click the Edit button. The Permission Entry dialog box, shown in Figure 2.3, appears. It gives administrators very fine control over the capability of individual users and groups to manipulate data and program files that are stored on NTFS drive volumes. Table 2.5 shows the list of advanced NTFS permissions available under Windows XP.

From this dialog box, you can perform the following:

➤ Change the Name so that this permission entry applies to some other user or group.

➤ Modify the Apply Onto drop-down list to specify exactly where these advanced permissions should apply.

➤ Alter the actual permission entries themselves by marking or clearing the Allow or Deny check box for each permission that you want to affect.

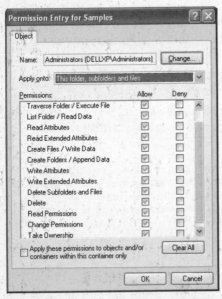

Figure 2.3 The Permission Entry dialog box for the Samples NTFS folder.

Table 2.5	Advanced NTFS Security Permissions for Both Files and Folders
Permission	**Description**
Full Control	Grants the Allow setting for all basic and advanced NTFS security permissions, including the entries for Change Permissions and Take Ownership.

(continued)

Table 2.5 Advanced NTFS Security Permissions for Both Files and Folders *(continued)*

Permission	Description
Traverse Folder/ Execute File	Allows or denies moving through folders to reach other files or folders, even if the user has no permissions for the traversed folders (applies to folders only). Traverse Folder takes effect only when the group or user is not granted the Bypass Traverse Checking user right in the Group Policy snap-in. (By default, the Everyone group is given the Bypass Traverse Checking user right). The Execute File permission allows or denies running application program files.
List Folder/ Read Data	Allows or denies viewing file names and subfolder names within the folder and allows or denies viewing data in files.
Read Attributes	Allows or denies viewing the attributes, such as read-only, hidden, and archive, of a file or folder.
Read Extended Attributes	Allows or denies viewing the extended attributes of a file or folder. Some extended attributes are defined by application programs and can vary by application.
Create Files/ Write Data	Allows or denies creating files within a folder, and allows or denies making changes to a file and overwriting the existing data.
Create Folders/ Append Data	Allows or denies creating folders within a folder, and allows or denies making changes to the end of a file, but not changing, deleting, or overwriting existing data.
Write Attributes	Allows or denies changing the attributes, such as read-only or hidden, of a file or folder.
Write Extended Attributes	Allows or denies changing the extended attributes of a file or folder. Extended attributes are defined by programs and may vary by program. Some extended attributes are defined by application programs and can vary by application.
Delete Subfolders and Files	Allows or denies deleting subfolders and files, even if the Delete permission has not been granted on the subfolder or file.
Delete	Allows or denies deleting the file or folder. If you don't have the Delete permission on a file or folder, you can still delete it if you have been granted Delete Subfolders And Files permission on the parent folder.
Read Permissions	Allows or denies reading the permissions that exist on a file or folder.
Change Permissions	Allows or denies changing permissions, such as Full Control, Read, and Modify, on the file or folder.
Take Ownership	Allows or denies taking ownership of a file or folder. The owner of a file or folder can always change permissions on it, even if other permissions have been assigned to safeguard the file or folder.

To change NTFS security permissions, you must be the owner of the file or folder whose permissions you want to modify, or the owner must grant you permission to make modifications to the object's security settings. Groups or users who are granted Full Control on a folder can delete files and subfolders within that folder regardless of the permissions protecting those files and subfolders. If the permission check boxes on the Security tab of an object's properties sheet are shaded, the file or folder has inherited the permissions from the parent folder. By clearing the Inherit from Parent the Permission Entries That Apply to Child Objects check box, you can copy those inherited permissions and turn them into explicit permissions, or you can remove them entirely and manually establish new explicit permissions. This check box is located at the bottom of the Advanced Security Settings dialog box.

NTFS security permissions are *cumulative*. Users obtain permissions by having them assigned directly to their user accounts, in addition to obtaining permissions via group memberships. Users retain all permissions as they are assigned. If a user named Dan has the Allow:Read permission for the Graphics folder, and if Dan is a member of the Users group, which has been assigned Allow:Write permission for the same folder, Dan has both the Allow:Read and Allow:Write permissions. Permissions continue to accumulate. But remember: *Deny entries always override Allow entries for the same permission type (Read, Modify, Write, and so on).*

Default NTFS Security Permissions

Under Windows XP, by default, all NTFS-formatted drive volumes are assigned Allow Read and Execute as special permissions for the Everyone group for the root of each drive volume. Folders and subfolders within each drive volume do not automatically inherit this default permission setting. These defaults are different from the defaults for previous versions of Windows. When you install Windows XP Professional on an NTFS volume, the `%systemroot%` folder (for example, `C:\Windows`) is automatically assigned special default security permissions for the following groups: Administrators, System, and Creator Owner.

If you upgrade from Windows NT 4 Workstation to Windows XP Professional, all existing users become members of the local Power Users group under Windows XP. This default upgrade behavior ensures that existing users can run noncertified applications under Windows XP, because Windows XP permissions for members of the Users group are more restrictive than under Windows NT 4.

More stringent NTFS security permissions now get applied to the root of all NTFS drive volumes whenever you upgrade to Windows XP, format a drive volume as NTFS under Windows XP, or use the `convert.exe` command on a drive volume under Windows XP. The new default NTFS security permissions are outlined here and illustrated in Figure 2.4:

Figure 2.4   The Advanced Security Settings dialog box showing the default NTFS permissions for the root of a drive volume converted to NTFS.

➤ System—Full Control with inherited permissions from parent folder

➤ Administrators—Full Control with inherited permissions from parent folder

➤ Creator Owner—Full Control with inherited permissions from parent folder

➤ Everyone—Read and Execute with no inherited permissions from parent folder

➤ Users—Read and Execute with inherited permissions from parent folder

You should not change the default security settings for the **%systemroot%** folder and its subfolders. Modifying the default permissions for the Windows XP Professional system files can have very adverse effects on the system. In addition to not changing its default permissions, you should never attempt to compress or encrypt the **%systemroot%** folder or any of its subfolders. Compression or encryption placed on the system folders can render Windows XP Professional unstable or possibly unbootable.

NTFS Permission Conflicts

Obviously, a user may be a member of several groups. You can apply NTFS permissions to both users and groups for access control over resources such as files and folders. For security permissions assigned to a user that conflict with other security permissions that have been granted to groups, of which the user is also a member, the most liberal permissions take precedence for that user. The one overriding exception is any explicit Deny permission entry. Deny permissions always take precedence over Allow permissions.

 Just as Deny permissions always take precedence over Allow permissions, explicit permissions always override inherited permissions.

NTFS Permissions Versus Share Permissions

Because share permissions apply to network access only, they can complicate and possibly confuse access control settings when you apply them on top of NTFS security permissions, which take effect at the file system level. If share permissions and NTFS permissions conflict, the permissions that both sets (share permissions and NTFS permissions) have in common apply.

As an example, suppose that for the shared folder named C:\Samples, you have set the share permissions for the Users group to Allow:Read. At the same time, suppose that you also have NTFS permissions set on that folder, and you have applied the Allow:Modify NTFS permission for the Users group on that folder. Now you have conflicting permissions—Allow:Read at the share level and Allow:Modify at the NTFS level. The net result is that members of the Users group are granted the capability only to read the files within that folder when accessing it over the network; they cannot make any changes to those files, because only the permissions that both the share and NTFS have in common get enforced. The NTFS Modify permission includes the capability to read from and write data to files; the share Read permission only includes the capability to read data from files. Therefore, the only permission entry that both sets of permissions have in common is Read.

As you can see, conflicting permissions may make it difficult to decipher which permissions users are granted when they are accessing files over the network. Therefore, the best practice is to place all shared network data and applications on NTFS drive volumes and set the appropriate security permissions for users and groups at the NTFS level. Remember that under Windows XP, the default share permission is Allow:Read for the Everyone group. You must change this default setting if you want users to be able to make any changes to data files that are stored within each shared folder. By setting share permissions on each share to Allow:Change for the Everyone group, NTFS security permissions can then flow through and apply equally to both local users and network users, and administrators have to manage only one set of permissions.

Keep in mind that only the security permissions that both a shared folder and NTFS have in common get applied to files and subfolders. Windows XP and Window Server 2003 automatically set default share permissions to *Everyone:Allow:Read*. This is quite different from the default behavior in Windows 2000 and Window NT 4.0 where the default share permissions were Everyone:Allow:Full Control.

Users and Groups: Local Accounts Versus Domain Accounts

In Windows networking environments, user accounts and group accounts always participate in one of two security contexts: workgroup security (also known as *peer-to-peer networking*) and domain security. Workgroup security is the default security context for individual and networked Windows 2000 Professional and Windows XP Professional computers that are not members of a Windows domain. Workgroups are logical groupings of computers that do not share a centrally managed user and group database. Local users and groups are managed from each computer's Local Users and Groups folder within the Computer Management Console. You must maintain users and groups separately on each computer. No centralized management scheme exists within a workgroup environment; duplicate user and group accounts must exist on each computer to grant and control access permissions on each workstation's individual resources. User and group accounts are stored within a local database on each Windows XP Professional computer.

In a Windows domain network environment, on the other hand, the domain acts as a central administration point for managing users, groups, and security permissions. A domain is simply a logical grouping of computers that share a centrally managed database. Duplicate user and group accounts are unnecessary and unwarranted within the domain security context. Users log on to the domain from any domain member computer, and their Domain group memberships, along with their user rights, follow them wherever they travel throughout the domain.

A Windows Active Directory domain maintains a domainwide database of users and groups that is referred to as the *directory*. The Active Directory database is physically stored on domain controller computers. The Active Directory database can contain much detailed information about its users. The Active Directory database is replicated and synchronized with all the other domain controllers within a domain. Under Windows Active Directory domains, group memberships travel with users throughout the entire forest.

Windows XP User Permissions Versus User Rights

In Windows XP, users are granted two types of access control settings:

➤ Permissions—Windows XP permissions pertain to what the user can do to objects (for example, permissions for reading, creating, modifying, or deleting files, folders, or printers). Windows XP objects include a wide variety of items in addition to files, folders, and printers, including processes, threads, ports, devices, and Registry keys.

> Rights—Windows XP user rights determine what privileges the user has to interact with the operating system (for example, shut down the system, install software, log on locally, log on over the network, and so on). Administrators for Windows XP Professional computers can modify the default rights for users through the Local Security Settings snap-in of the Microsoft Management Console (MMC).

 All you need to remember is that users and groups have *rights* assigned to them; objects (files, folders, printers, and so on) have *permissions* assigned to them.

Controlling Access to Files and Folders by Using Permissions

Users gain access to NTFS files and folders by virtue of being granted explicit or implicit (inherited) permissions for those resources directly to their user account or through access permissions granted to groups to which the users belong. To assign Read-Only security permissions to a user or a group for a specific folder, follow these steps:

1. Right-click the folder on which you want to apply permissions and select either the Sharing and Security option or the Properties option.

2. Click the Security tab.

3. If the permissions check boxes for the user or group are grayed out, those permissions are being inherited from a parent folder. To set your own permissions and not allow permissions to be inherited, click the user and/or group that you want to work with and click the Advanced button. Clear the check box labeled Inherit from Parent the Permission Entries That Apply to Child Objects. Include These with Entries Explicitly Defined Here. As soon as you clear that check box, a Security message box will appear, shown in Figure 2.5.

4. For permissions that are not being inherited, skip this step. Click Copy to copy the permissions that were being applied to the file or folder through inheritance and make the permission explicit, click Remove to completely remove all the permissions that were being applied through inheritance, or click Cancel to leave the inherited permissions in place. Click OK to close the Advanced Security Settings dialog box and return to the Security tab of the object's properties sheet.

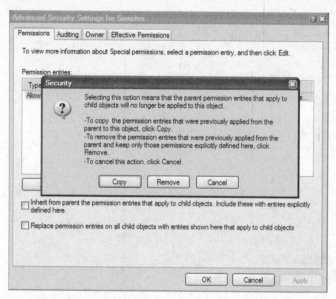

Figure 2.5   The Security message box for disallowing inherited NTFS permissions.

5. If the user(s) or group(s) to which you want to assign permissions do not currently appear, click the Add button.

6. From the Select Users or Groups dialog box, shown in Figure 2.6, type the group or user to which you want to assign permissions in the Enter the Object Names to Select text box. Click the Check Names button to verify that you have entered the correct names for the users or groups. Optionally, you can click the Advanced button to generate a list of users and groups from which to choose, as shown in Figure 2.7. Click the Find Now button to generate the list of users and groups. Select the users and/or groups you want to apply permissions to. Click OK for the advanced Select Users or Groups dialog box.

Figure 2.6   The Select Users or Groups basic dialog box.

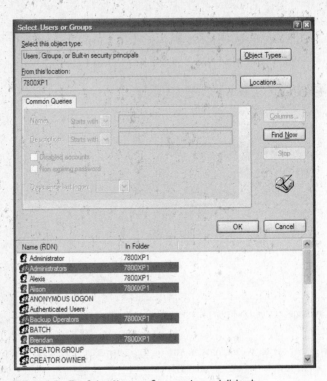

Figure 2.7 The Select Users or Groups advanced dialog box.

7. Click OK for the basic Select Users or Groups dialog box.

8. Verify that the Allow check boxes are marked for the Read & Execute, List Folder Contents, and Read permissions, as shown in Figure 2.8.

9. Click OK to accept your settings.

Denying Access to a Resource

Deny permissions always override Allow permissions, so you can be assured that after you establish Deny permissions for a particular user or group on a resource, no other combination of Allow permissions through group memberships can circumvent the Deny permission. To assign Deny security permissions to a user or a group for a specific folder, follow these steps:

1. Right-click the folder on which you want to apply permissions and select Properties.

2. Click the Security tab.

Figure 2.8   The Security tab of an NTFS folder showing permissions for users and groups.

3. If permissions are being inherited for the user and/or group that you want to work with, click the Advanced button and clear the check box labeled Inherit from Parent the Permission Entries That Apply to Child Objects. Include These with Entries Explicitly Defined Here. Click Copy or Remove for the inherited permission entries, and click OK for the Advanced Security Settings dialog box.

4. If the user(s) or group(s) to which you want to assign permissions do not currently appear, click the Add button.

5. Type in the group(s) or user(s) that you want to assign permissions to from the Select Users or Groups dialog box.

6. Click OK.

7. Click the Deny check box for each permission entry that you wish to explicitly disallow.

8. Click OK to accept your settings.

If you deny the Read permission for a group on a particular folder, any member of that group is denied the capability to read the contents of that folder. When you assign Deny permissions for a user or a group on a file or folder, as soon as you click OK in the Properties dialog box, a Security message box, shown in Figure 2.9, appears. It reminds you that Deny permissions take precedence over Allow permissions.

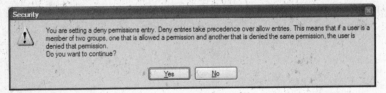

Figure 2.9 A Security message box requests confirmation that you want to set a Deny permissions entry.

Click Yes in the Security message box to have the new Deny permissions take effect. When users who are members of a group that is assigned Deny permissions for reading a folder attempt to gain access to that folder, they are greeted by an Access Is Denied message box, shown in Figure 2.10.

Figure 2.10 The Access Is Denied message box.

Optimizing Access to Files and Folders

The best practice is to always assign NTFS security permissions to groups rather than to individual users. You should place users into appropriate groups and set NTFS permissions on those groups. In this manner, permissions are easier to assign and maintain.

NTFS Permissions: Moving and Copying Files and Folders

Moving or copying files and folders from an NTFS drive volume to network drives or other media that are non-NTFS volumes results in the loss of all NTFS security permission settings for the objects moved or copied. The result of moving or copying NTFS files and folders to different NTFS folders varies depending on whether the objects are being moved or copied, and depending on the destination drive volume. Table 2.6 shows the different effects on NTFS permissions when copying files and folders versus moving files and folders.

Files *moved* within the same NTFS drive letter *retain* their permissions. For all other transfers, the files *inherit* their permissions from the destination folder.

Table 2.6   NTFS Permissions That Are Retained or Inherited When You Move and Copy Files and Folders

Type of Transfer	Effective Permissions after Move or Copy
Moving within the same NTFS volume	Files and folders that are moved retain their permissions from the source folder.
Moving to a different NTFS volume	Files and folders that are moved inherit their permissions from the destination folder.
Copying within the same NTFS volume	Files and folders that are copied inherit their permissions from the destination folder.
Copying to a different NTFS volume	Files and folders that are copied inherit their permissions from the destination folder.

The standard Windows XP Xcopy.exe command-line utility offers /O and /X options that retain an object's NTFS permissions, in addition to inheriting the destination folder's permissions. The /X switch also retains any auditing settings (which are discussed later in this chapter). To retain only an object's source permissions without inheriting any permissions from the destination folder, use the Scopy.exe tool or the Robocopy.exe tool from the Windows 2000 Professional Resource Kit or the Windows 2000 Server Resource Kit.

Viewing Effective Permissions

Prior to Windows XP, there was no simple way to determine quickly which effective permissions a user actually had by evaluating implicit permissions against explicit permissions, and by comparing a user's own assigned permissions to his or her inherited permissions from his or her group memberships. Now, under Windows XP, an easy method exists for determining effective NTFS permissions right from the Advanced Security Settings dialog box. To display effective permissions for a user or a group, perform the following steps:

1. Right-click an NTFS folder and select Sharing and Security.

2. Click the Security tab and then click the Advanced button.

3. From the Advanced Security Settings dialog box, click the Effective Permissions tab.

4. Click the Select button to choose a user or a group for which you want to display effective permissions. Type in the user, group, or security principal name and click OK.

5. View the effective permissions for the user, group, or security principal that you selected, as shown in Figure 2.11.

Figure 2.11 The Effective Permissions tab displays effective NTFS security permissions for users and groups for specific folders and files.

Taking Ownership of Files and Folders

A user who has ownership of a file or folder can transfer ownership of it to a different user or to a group. Administrators can grant users the capability to take ownership of specified files and folders. In addition, administrators have the authority to take ownership of any file or folder for themselves. Object ownership cannot be assigned to others; a user must have permission to take ownership of an object.

Changing ownership of files and folders can become necessary when someone who is responsible for certain files and folders leaves an organization without granting any other users permissions to them. To take ownership of a folder as an administrator, follow these steps:

1. Log on to the system as the administrator or an equivalent user.

2. Right-click the folder from Windows Explorer or My Computer and select Properties.

3. Click the Security tab.

4. Click the Advanced button.

5. Click the Owner tab in the Advanced Security Settings dialog box.

6. Click the name of the person in the Change Owner To section to change the folder's ownership.

7. If you also want the ownership to change for the subfolders and files, mark the Replace Owner on Subcontainers and Objects check box.

8. Click OK for the Advanced Security Settings dialog box.

9. Click OK for the Properties dialog box.

Controlling Write Access to USB Storage Devices Under SP2

Keychain drives, jump drives, pen drives—however you care to refer to them—these small and portable USB 2.0 storage devices are everywhere these days. Until Windows XP SP2, an IT manager had a difficult decision: disable the mass storage device driver for storage devices that connect via USB or allow the default settings and hope that no authorized user steals any company data. No middle ground exists in this debate because disabling the storage driver over USB connections turns off support for *all* USB storage devices.

Making USB Storage Drives Read-Only

Because SP2 is focused on enhancing and improving computer security, Microsoft created a new storage device policy named WriteProtect to prevent users from moving or copying data onto USB-connected drives. Even under SP2, this new Registry setting does not exist by default; you must manually create the appropriate Registry entries if you want to take advantage of this new security feature. The new WriteProtect policy is a per-computer setting, not a per-user setting. To turn on the USB storage WriteProtect feature, perform the following steps using the Windows XP Registry Editor:

 As mentioned earlier in the chapter and throughout this book—editing the Windows XP Registry is a risky procedure that can render a computer unstable or unbootable. Be sure to have a good, recent, reliable backup before editing the Registry. It is also a good idea to create a Restore Point using the System Restore feature *before* editing the Registry.

1. Click, Start, Run, type **regedit**, and click OK.

2. Navigate to the HKEY_LOCAL_MACHINE\SYSTEM\CurrentControlSet\ Control key.

3. Right-click the Control subkey as described in step 2 and select New, Key.

4. Type the name for the new subkey—**StorageDevicePolicies**.

5. Right-click the new subkey, StorageDevicePolicies, that you just created and click New, DWORD value.

6. Type the name of the new value, **WriteProtect**, and then click some-where other than on this new value name to save the name you entered.

7. Double-click the new WriteProtect value name so that you can enter the decimal value data of 1 to enable this new setting. The value data of 0 turns off the WriteProtect setting for USB storage devices.

8. Exit the Windows XP Registry Editor.

How Upgrading to Windows XP Affects File-Sharing Behavior

Windows NT 4 Workstation computers and Windows 2000 Professional computers, whether members of a workgroup or a domain, maintain their workgroup or domain membership, respectively, and retain the classic file sharing and security user interface when they are upgraded to Windows XP Professional. Simple File Sharing is disabled. NTFS security permissions and shared folder permissions are not changed after the upgrade.

Windows 98 and Windows ME computers that have "per share" sharing per-missions as members of a workgroup always have Simple File Sharing enabled by default after they are upgraded to Windows XP Professional. Shared folders that have passwords assigned to them are removed; shared folders that have blank passwords remain shared after the upgrade. Windows 98 and Windows ME systems that are logged on to a Windows domain with share-level access enabled are joined to that domain when they are upgrad-ed using the Windows XP Setup program, and Simple File Sharing is dis-abled after the upgrade.

Auditing System and Network Events

Windows XP Professional enables administrators to audit both user and sys-tem events, enabling various auditing policies. When auditing is enabled for specific events, the occurrence of the events triggers a log entry in the Windows XP Professional Security Log. You view the security log with the Event Viewer snap-in of the MMC. By default, auditing is turned off. Before you enable auditing, you should formulate an audit policy to determine which workstations will employ auditing and which events will be audited on those systems. When planning the events to audit, you also need to decide whether you will audit successes and/or failures for each event.

Auditing for the local Windows XP system is enabled through the Local Security Settings snap-in of the MMC, shown in Figure 2.12. You must initially turn on auditing from the Local Security Settings Console for each type of event that you want to monitor.

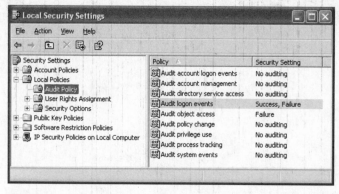

Figure 2.12 The Local Security Settings Console.

You can audit several types of events, such as the following:

➤ File and folder access

➤ Logons and logoffs

➤ System shutdowns and restarts

➤ Changes to user and group accounts

➤ Changes attempted on Active Directory objects if the Windows XP Professional computer is a member of a Windows Active Directory domain

When you track successful events, you can gauge how often different resources are used. This information can be useful when you are planning for future resource allocation. By tracking failed events, you can become aware of possible security intrusions. Unsuccessful logon attempts, attempts to change security permissions, or efforts to take ownership of files or folders may all point to someone trying to gain unauthorized access to the system or to the network. If such attempts occur at odd hours, these events take on an even more suspicious tone. You must be a member of the Administrators group to turn on audit policies; if your computer is connected to a network, network policy settings may prohibit you from configuring audit settings. To enable auditing on a Windows XP Professional system, follow these steps:

1. Launch the Local Security Policy MMC snap-in from the Start, (All) Programs, Administrative Tools folder.

2. At the Local Security Settings Console, expand the Local Policies folder and then click Audit Policy.

3. Double-click the audit policy setting that you want to enable; the dialog box for the audit event will display, as shown in Figure 2.13. To enable auditing of object access, double-click the Audit Object Access policy.

Figure 2.13 The Audit Object Access Properties dialog box.

4. Click the Success check box, the Failure check box, or both check boxes.

5. Click OK.

6. Close the Local Security Settings Console.

After you have turned on audit tracking for object access events, you need to specify which files, folders, or other objects you want to audit. You should be fairly selective about which ones you choose to audit. If you have enabled auditing for successes as well as failures, the system's Security Event log may become filled very quickly if you are auditing heavily used files and folders. You can audit object access only for files and folders that are stored on NTFS volumes. To enable audit logging for specific files, folders, or other objects (such as printers), follow these steps:

1. Log on to the system as the administrator or an equivalent user.

2. Right-click the object from Windows Explorer, My Computer, or Printers and Faxes, and select Properties.

3. Click the Security tab.

4. Click the Advanced button.

5. Click the Auditing tab in the Advanced Security Settings dialog box.

6. Click the Add button.

7. Type in the user or group that you want to track for accessing the object and then click OK. The Auditing Entry dialog box, shown in Figure 2.14, appears.

Figure 2.14 The Auditing Entry dialog box.

8. Select each access event that you want to track by marking each event's associated Successful check box, Failed check box, or both check boxes.

9. By default, audit settings apply to the current folder, subfolders, and files. You can change this behavior by clicking the Apply Onto drop-down list.

10. Click OK for the Auditing Entry dialog box.

11. Click OK for the Advanced Security Settings dialog box.

12. Click OK for the object's Properties dialog box.

After you have properly set up auditing, all events that meet your auditing criteria are logged into the system's Event Viewer Security Log. You access the Event Viewer Console from Start, Administrative Tools, Event Viewer or by right-clicking the My Computer desktop icon and selecting Manage. You'll find the Event Viewer beneath the System Tools folder in the Computer Management Console. By selecting the Security Log, you can view all the auditing events that the system has recorded based on the parameters you have set. If a user deletes an object, for example, that event is listed with all the pertinent information in the security log, shown in Figure 2.15. Double-clicking an event in the log displays the detailed information.

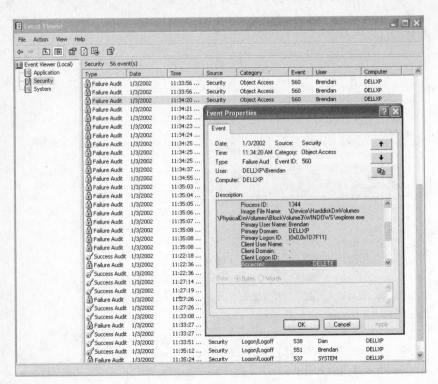

Figure 2.15 An Event Properties window from the Event Viewer security log.

Auditing *successful* actions is a good way to do some capacity planning and performance analysis. Auditing *failed* actions can identify potential security problems. Use Windows Explorer to identify files and folders to audit. Use Regedit to identify Registry keys to audit.

Managing and Troubleshooting Web Server Resources

Unlike Windows 2000 Server and Windows Server 2003, Windows XP Professional is designed for the desktop; therefore, Internet Information Services (IIS) is *not* installed by default. IIS version 5.1 ships with Windows XP Professional. You must manually install IIS by going to the Control Panel, double-clicking the Add or Remove Programs icon, and clicking the Add/Remove Windows Components button. Mark the check box for Internet Information Services (IIS). After you select Internet Information Services (IIS), you can click the Details button to add or remove selective IIS components before you proceed with the installation. Click Next to have the Windows Components Wizard install the web server resources for you. If you upgrade your computer from Windows NT 4 Workstation (or from

Windows 2000 Professional) to Windows XP Professional, IIS 5.1 is installed automatically, provided that you had installed Peer Web Services (or IIS 5) on your previous version of Windows.

Before you can install IIS, your computer must have the Transmission Control Protocol/Internet Protocol (TCP/IP) and its related connectivity utilities installed. In addition, Microsoft recommends that you have a Domain Name System (DNS) server available on your network for hostname to IP address resolution. For very small networks, you may use a HOSTS file or a LMHOSTS file in lieu of a DNS server. A HOSTS file maps DNS host computer names to IP addresses. A LMHOSTS file maps NetBIOS computer names to IP addresses. Windows XP Professional looks for these two text files in the `%systemroot%\system32\drivers\etc` folder. Sample HOSTS and LMHOSTS files are also installed by default into this folder.

After you have installed IIS, you manage the services from the Internet Information Services snap-in of the MMC. You can launch the IIS Console by clicking Start, (All) Programs, Administrative Tools, Internet Information Services. From the IIS Console, you can administer the default FTP site (not installed by default), default website, and the default Simple Mail Transfer Protocol (SMTP) virtual server for the Windows XP Professional computer, as shown in Figure 2.16.

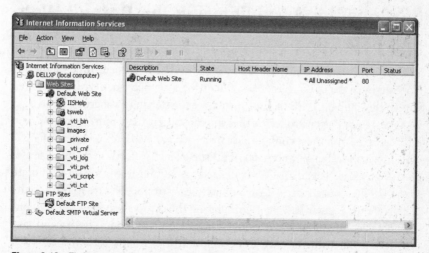

Figure 2.16 The Internet Information Services Console.

Additional HTML-based documentation on IIS administration is available by pointing to `http://localhost/` in your web browser, as shown in Figure 2.17.

Figure 2.17 The Getting Started web page for IIS HTML-based help documentation.

IIS Console: Administering the Default Web and FTP Sites

You can view and modify the settings for each IIS service through the IIS Console by right-clicking the root folder for a service (such as Default Web Site) in the left pane of the console window and selecting Properties. Unlike IIS 5, there are no Master Properties that you can modify that control both web and FTP settings. You must configure each site separately. IIS stores its configuration information for its website(s), FTP site(s), and so forth in its metabase. If the IIS metabase gets damaged or deleted, an administrator must reconfigure all the IIS sites and services. To avoid such a catastrophe, be sure to back up the metabase on a regular basis by right-clicking the computer name root container and selecting All Tasks, Backup/Restore Configuration. The backup gets stored as a file with the .md0 extension, and the default backup location is %systemroot%\system32\inetsrv\metaback. You should copy the metabase backups to removable media or to another computer over the network to preserve the backups in case of a hard-drive failure on the IIS computer.

Administering the Default Website

At any time, an administrator can modify the settings for the default website by right-clicking the site name and selecting Properties from the Internet Information Services (IIS) MMC snap-in. The Default Web Site Properties window, shown in Figure 2.18, enables you to work with settings for the home directory, directory security, HTTP, ISAPI filters, and other configurations. You can change the settings for a virtual directory by right-clicking the directory name and selecting Properties. The Properties dialog box for a virtual directory, shown in Figure 2.19, enables you to configure settings for the virtual directory, for its web documents, for directory security, for HTTP headers, and for working with custom error messages. You can create a new virtual directory for the default website by right-clicking <Default Web Site> from the IIS MMC snap-in and selecting New, Virtual Directory. When the Virtual Directory Creation Wizard launches, you assign a name to the new virtual directory. You must also designate the path for the physical folder where the web files are stored for the new virtual directory. After you have entered this information, you can complete the wizard, thereby setting up a new virtual directory that users can access via the `http://computer_name/virtual_directory_name` Uniform Resource Locator (URL), also known simply as a web address.

Figure 2.18   The Home Directory tab for the IIS Default Web Site Properties dialog box.

Figure 2.19 The Properties dialog box for a virtual directory under IIS.

Administering the Default FTP Site

An administrator can modify the settings for the default FTP site by right-clicking the site name and selecting Properties. You can change the settings for a virtual directory by right-clicking the directory name and selecting Properties. You can create a new virtual directory for the default FTP site by right-clicking <Default FTP Site> and selecting New, Virtual Directory. When the Virtual Directory Creation Wizard launches, you assign a name to the new virtual directory. You must also designate the path for the physical folder where the FTP files will be stored for the new virtual directory. After you have entered this information, you can complete the wizard, thereby setting up a new virtual directory that users can access via the FTP address `ftp://computer_name/virtual_directory_name`.

Web Folders and the WebDAV Protocol

You can share folders with other computers by making them available as Web Folders instead of, or in addition to, sharing them as network shared folders. To share a folder on a Windows XP Professional system as a Web Folder, right-click the folder, select Properties, and click the Web Sharing tab. Click the Add button to assign an Alias name for the Web Folder, specify the permissions for the Web Folder, and click OK to create the Web Folder on the default website. The WebDAV (Web Distributed Authoring and Versioning) protocol acts as a redirector that enables users to open and save documents via Hypertext Transport Protocol (HTTP) port 80. As long as the web server host computer is running IIS 5 or later, and as long as an application program supports saving and retrieving documents via HTTP, you can take advantage of WebDAV. To use WebDAV, type the URL path plus the document name into the Open or Save As dialog box for an application.

Users can encrypt files stored in Web Folders; however, when the data files are transmitted across the network wire, they are *not* encrypted. Encrypted files are always encrypted and decrypted on the local computer before being sent over the network. Network protocols such as Single Socket Layer/Transport Layer Security (SSL/TLS) or Internet Protocol security (IPSec) must be used to encrypt data that travels over the network. The WebDAV protocol, however, encrypts files locally and transmits them over the network as encrypted data.

Service Pack 2 Locks Down WebDAV

Before Windows XP Service Pack 2, users could use the WebDAV protocol to access web servers as a file sharing system over HTTP (port 80) on their organization's intranet or to access web servers on the public Internet using basic authentication. Basic authentication sends users' logon credentials (usernames and passwords) in clear text over the network; this is a security vulnerability. SP2, by default, does not allow users to log on to WebDAV servers using basic authentication over an unencrypted connection.

SP2 provides two Registry settings that you can add and configure if you need to change this default behavior. To enable basic authentication for WebDAV, perform the following steps:

 Modifying the Registry in any way may make your computer unstable or completely unuseable. Always have a recent, reliable backup before making any changes. Any configuration changes to the Registry are done solely at your own risk.

1. Use the Windows XP Registry editor (`regedit.exe`) and navigate to `HKEY_LOCAL_MACHINE\System\CurrentControlSet\Services\WebClient \Parameters`.

2. Right-click the Parameters subkey and create a new DWORD value (unless this value already exists) named **UseBasicAuth**.

3. Double-click the `UseBasicAuth` value, click the Decimal option button, and type in 1 for the value data. This turns on basic authentication for WebDAV, just as it had been set by default prior to SP2.

4. Click OK to close the DWORD Value dialog box.

The other Registry setting that you can add deals with disabling basic authentication over a clear text connection (channel). To disable basic authentication over a clear channel, perform the following steps:

1. Use the Windows XP Registry editor (regedit.exe) and navigate to HKEY_CURRENT_USER\Software\Microsoft\Windows\CurrentVersion\ Internet Settings.

2. Right-click the Internet Settings subkey and create a new DWORD value (unless this value already exists) named **DisableBasicOverClearChannel**.

3. Double-click the DisableBasicOverClearChannel value, click the Decimal option button, and type in 1 for the value data. This turns off basic authentication over a non-encrypted connection (channel).

4. Click OK to close the DWORD Value dialog box.

Troubleshooting Internet Information Services

If users are experiencing problems connecting to the default website, to the default FTP site, or to a new virtual directory that you have created, you can follow the steps listed in the next few sections to attempt to rectify the problem(s).

Internet Website

To isolate problems that may be preventing users from connecting to the Internet website:

➤ Check that the web server contains HTML files in the drive_letter:\inetpub\ wwwroot folder.

➤ Attempt to connect to the web server's home directory using a browser on a computer that has a live connection to the Internet. Your website must have a public IP address that is registered with the InterNIC, and that public IP address must be registered with the Internet's DNS servers. For example, if your registered domain name is QuePublishing.com and you want to view a virtual directory on that website named "aboutus," you would type **www.QuePublishing.com/ aboutus** into the Address line of your web browser. The web page that you requested should appear within your web browser's window.

Intranet Website

To isolate problems that may be preventing users from connecting to an intranet website:

➤ Check that the webserver and the client computers have active network connections.

➤ Verify that a Windows Internet Naming Service (WINS) and/or DNS server is available and functioning on your network for computer name to IP address name resolution.

➤ Go to a client computer, launch a web browser, and type in a valid URL for the web server computer. Intranet URLs can take the format of `http://computer_name/home_page_name.htm` or `http://computer_name/virtual_directory_alias_name`. Examples of this syntax are `http://computer1/myhomepage.htm` and `http://computer1/myvirtualdirectory`.

Managing Local and Network Print Devices

You manage print devices in Windows XP Professional from the Printers and Faxes folder, which is accessible from the Control Panel, or by clicking Start, Printers and Faxes. When working with printing in Windows XP, you need to fully understand the following printing terminology as defined by Microsoft:

➤ Printer—A software interface between the operating system and a print device. It defines ports through which print jobs get routed. Printer names direct print jobs to one or more print devices.

➤ Print device—A piece of equipment (hardware) that physically produces printed documents. A print device may be physically attached to a computer or remotely connected via a network interface.

➤ Printer port—A software interface through which print jobs get directed to either a locally attached print device or a network-connected print device. Windows XP supports local line printer terminal (LPT), COM (serial), and Universal Serial Bus (USB) ports. It also supports network-connected printer port devices such as the Intel NetPort and the Hewlett-Packard (HP) JetDirect.

➤ Print server—A computer that serves as the host for printers that are associated with print devices.

➤ Printer driver—Software specific to each print device (designed to run in Windows XP) that translates printing commands into printer language codes for each print device. PCL5 and PostScript are examples of two types of printer languages.

➤ Print job—The actual document to be printed along with the necessary print-processing command.

➤ Print resolution—What determines the quality and smoothness of the text or images that the print device will render. This specification is expressed in dots per inch (dpi). Higher dpi numbers generally result in better print quality.

➤ Print spooler—The process (service) that runs in the background of Windows XP that initiates, processes, and distributes print jobs. The spooler saves print jobs into a temporary physical file on disk. Print jobs are then despooled and transferred to the appropriate print device.

➤ Print queue—A logical "waiting area" where print jobs are temporarily stored until the print device is available and ready to process each job according to the job's priority level and according to its order within the queue. The default priority is 1, and the priority range is between 1 (lowest) and 99 (highest). Higher priority print jobs print before lower priority jobs.

➤ Printer pooling—A logical configuration in which two or more identical print devices appear as a single printer. To configure Printer Pooling, you must mark the Enable Printer Pooling check box on the Ports tab of a printer's properties sheet. After you enable printer pooling, on the same Ports tab, you can then specify the multiple printer ports to which print jobs are sent.

Connecting to Local and Network Printers

After you add a local printer to a Windows XP Professional computer, you have the option of sharing it with other users on the network. To add a local printer to your system, perform these steps:

1. Log on as an administrator or a member of the Administrators group.

2. Click Start, Printers and Faxes to open the Printers and Faxes window.

3. Click the Add a Printer link from the Printer Tasks pane. The Add Printer Wizard appears. Click Next to continue.

4. Click the Local Printer button. If the printer that you are adding is not Plug and Play compatible, you may clear the Automatically Detect and

Install My Plug and Play Printer check box. If the printer is Plug and Play compliant, Windows XP Professional automatically installs and properly configures it for you.

5. If the printer is not Plug and Play, the Select a Printer Port dialog box appears. Click the port you want to use from the Use the Following Port drop-down list, or click the Create a New Port button and choose the type of port to create from the drop-down list.

6. Click Next.

7. Select the printer Manufacturer and Model. Click the Have Disk button if you have a DVD-ROM, CD-ROM, or disk with the proper printer drivers from the manufacturer. Click the Windows Update button to download the latest drivers available from Microsoft's website. You should strive to use only drivers that have been digitally signed by Microsoft for compatibility.

8. Click Next.

9. Enter a name for the printer. The name should not exceed 31 characters, and best practice dictates that the printer name should not contain any spaces or special characters. Specify whether this printer will be designated as the system's default printer.

10. Click Next.

11. In the Printer Sharing dialog box, click the Share Name button if you want to share this printer with the network. Enter a share name for the printer; it's a good idea to limit the share name to 14 or fewer characters, and to place no spaces within the share name.

12. Click Next.

13. Enter an optional Location name and Comment.

14. Click Next.

15. Click Yes and then click Next when prompted to print a test page; it's always a good idea to make sure that the printer has been set up and is working properly.

16. Click Finish to exit the Add Printer Wizard.

To connect to a network printer, you also use the Add Printer Wizard from the Printers folder. Follow these steps:

1. Log on as an administrator or a member of the Administrators group.

2. Click Start, Printers and Faxes to open the Printers and Faxes window.

3. Click the Add a Printer link from the Printer Tasks pane. The Add Printer Wizard appears. Click Next to continue.

4. Click the option button labeled A Network Printer, or a Printer Attached to Another Computer.

5. Click Next.

6. Follow one of these options:

   ➤ Select Browse for a Printer and then click Next.

   ➤ Select Connect to This Printer, type in the UNC path for the printer, and then click Next.

   ➤ Select Connect to a Printer on the Internet or on a Home or Office Network, type in the URL address for the printer, and then click Next.

7. If you choose to browse for a printer, locate the printer from the Browse for Printer dialog box and then click Next.

8. Click Yes or No when you are prompted to make the printer the system's default, and then click Next.

9. Click Finish to exit the Add Printer Wizard.

Connecting to Network Printers via the Command Line

As mentioned earlier in this chapter, you can use the net use command to connect to network drive shares. You can also use this command to connect to remote printers from a command prompt window. The syntax is as follows:

```
net use lptx: \\print_server_name\printer_share_name
```

Printer ports LPT1, LPT2, and LPT3 are represented by LPTx. The net use command is the only way to connect client computers that are running MS-DOS to network printers.

Managing Printers and Print Jobs

From the Printers and Faxes folder, you manage print jobs by double-clicking the printer icon that you want to work with. After you have opened the printer's print queue window, you can pause printing or cancel all documents from the Printer menu. You can also take the printer offline from the Printer menu. If you select an individual print job that is listed, you can Pause, Resume, Start, or Cancel that job by selecting one of these options from the Documents menu. The print queue window itself displays the document name, the status, the document owner, the number of pages for each print job, the size of the job, the time and date that the job was submitted, and the port used.

Members of the Administrators group and members of the Power Users group have permissions to manage print jobs that are listed in the print queue. At the time that users print one or more documents, they get the built-in security principal Creator Owner applied to their user accounts so that they are granted permission to manage documents as well. Users may manage only their own print jobs unless they are members of the Administrators group or the Power Users group (if the computer is stand-alone or a member of a workgroup) or members of the Print Operators group or the Server Operators group (if the Windows XP print server is a member of a Windows domain). Users can also manage other users' print jobs if they have been granted the Allow Manage Documents permission.

NOTE Windows XP has dropped support for the Data Link Control (DLC) protocol, which is used by some older Hewlett-Packard (HP) Jet Direct cards and Jet Direct print server devices. These older devices should be upgraded to newer HP network interface cards and print devices that support TCP/IP and the standard port monitor.

Configuring Print Server and Printer Properties

A Windows XP Professional computer becomes a print server when you physically connect a printer to the system and then share that printer with the network. You can easily configure many of the properties of your Windows XP Professional system as a print server by selecting File, Server Properties from the Printers and Faxes window. You can configure many print server settings, such as changing the location of the Spool folder, from the Print Server Properties dialog box. Using this dialog box means that you don't have to edit the Registry directly to make changes to your Windows XP print server configuration settings.

By right-clicking one of the available printer icons in the Printers and Faxes folder and choosing Properties, you can configure that printer's settings and options. The printer Properties dialog box contains six tabs (seven tabs for a color printer): General, Sharing, Ports, Advanced, Security, Device Settings, and Color Management (for a color printer).

The General Tab

From the General tab, you can work with the following settings:

➤ Add or modify printer location and comment information.

➤ Set printing preferences such as portrait or landscape orientation.

➤ Select paper source and quality.

➤ Print a test page.

The Sharing Tab

The Sharing tab displays the following options:

➤ Share the printer, change the network share name, or stop sharing the printer.

➤ Install additional printer drivers for client computers that use different operating systems or different Windows NT CPU platforms.

 Windows XP print server computers automatically download the correct printer drivers for client computers that run Windows 95, Windows 98/Me, Windows NT, Windows 2000, and Windows XP and that connect to the print server, as long as the correct drivers have been installed on the print server computer.

 A client computer based on Windows NT 4.0, Windows 2000, or Windows XP checks the printer driver each time it reconnects to the network. A Windows NT 3.x client checks each time the spooler service on the client is started. If the driver is not current, a copy of the new driver is downloaded automatically. The printer driver for a Windows 95-based or Windows 98-based client is not automatically kept current. If you update the driver on the print server, you must *manually* install the driver on Windows 95-based and Windows 98-based clients.

The Ports Tab

On the Ports tab, you have the following configuration options:

➤ Select a port to print to.

➤ Add, configure, and delete ports.

➤ Enable bidirectional printing support.

➤ Enable printer pooling, which enables you to select two or more identical print devices that are configured as one logical printer; print jobs are directed to the first available print device.

The Advanced Tab

On the Advanced tab, you work with scheduling and spooling settings such as these:

➤ Set time availability limits.

➤ Set print job priority.

➤ Change the printer driver or add a new driver.

➤ Spool print jobs and start printing immediately, or start printing after the last page has spooled.

➤ Print directly to the printer; do not spool print jobs.

➤ Hold mismatched documents.

➤ Print spooled documents first.

➤ Retain documents after they have been printed.

➤ Enable advanced printing features (such as metafile spooling) and enable advanced options (such as Page Order, Booklet Printing, and Pages per Sheet); advanced options vary depending on printer capabilities.

➤ Set printing defaults.

➤ Select a different print processor: RAW, EMF, or Text.

➤ Specify a separator page.

The Security Tab

You can configure the following security settings with the Security tab:

➤ Set permissions for users and groups (similar to NTFS file and folder permissions): Allow or Deny Print, Manage Printers, and Manage Documents.

➤ Set up printer auditing (similar to NTFS file and folder access auditing) via the Auditing tab by clicking the Advanced button.

➤ Take ownership of the printer (similar to taking ownership of NTFS files and folders) via the Owner tab by clicking the Advanced button.

➤ View the effective permissions for the printer (similar to viewing the effective permissions for NTFS files and folders) via the Effective Permissions tab by clicking the Advanced button.

For a Windows XP computer that is not a domain member, the default security permissions for printers are as follows: Administrators—Allow Print, Allow Manage Printers, and Allow Manage Documents; Creator Owner—Allow Manage Documents; Everyone—Allow Print; Power Users—Allow Print, Allow Manage Printers, and Allow Manage Documents.

For a Windows XP computer that is joined to a domain, the default security permissions for printers are as follows: Administrators—Allow Print, Allow Manage Printers, and Allow Manage Documents; Creator Owner—Allow Manage Documents; Everyone—Allow Print; Print Operators and Server Operators—Allow Print, Allow Manage Printers, and Allow Manage Documents.

The Device Settings Tab

The Device Settings tab enables you to configure printer-specific settings. The available settings on this tab vary depending on the manufacturer and the model of the printer that you are working with. For example, many printers enable you to configure paper tray assignments, font cartridge settings, and any installable options such as printer memory settings.

Using the Internet Printing Protocol (IPP)

Windows XP Professional computers can connect to printers that are attached to Windows XP, Windows 2000, or Windows Server 2003 print servers by using a web browser and a URL instead of connecting via the GUI or via the command line using a UNC path. IPP works over a corporate intranet or through an Internet connection. IPP gives users the capability to print over an Internet connection. IIS version 5 or later must be running on the print server computer. You can enter one of two available URLs into your web browser:

➤ `http://print_server_name/printers`—This address connects you to the web page for the Printers and Faxes folder on the Windows XP print server computer (however, fax devices are not displayed in the browser window).

➤ `http://print_server_name/printer_share_name`—This address connects you to the web page for the print queue folder for the printer that you specify, as shown in Figure 2.20.

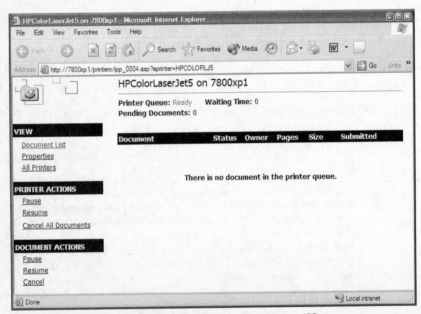

Figure 2.20   The web browser interface for a network printer that uses IPP.

Exam Prep Questions

1. Gregory has just installed Windows XP Professional on a new computer that is a member of a workgroup named Sales. When he goes to create a network shared folder by right-clicking a folder and selecting Sharing and Security, the Properties dialog box for the folder displays only four tabs: General, Sharing, Web Sharing, and Customize. The Sharing tab is divided into two sections: Local Sharing and Network Sharing and Security. No Security tab exists for NTFS permissions, nor does any way exist to set Share permissions. Even when Gregory right-clicks a folder and selects Properties, he still gets the same tabbed dialog box with the same four tabs. The folder resides on an NTFS drive volume. How can Gregory fix this problem?

   - ○ A. Go to Control Panel, Administrative Tools, Local Security Policy, and enable the policy for Network Access: Sharing and Security Model for Local Accounts.

   - ○ B. Open My Computer or Windows Explorer, click Tools, Folder Options, click the View tab, and clear the check box for Use Simple File Sharing.

   - ○ C. Open the Computer Management Console, expand Services and Applications, and click the Services node. Right-click the Workstation service and select Start. Double-click the Workstation service and set the Startup Type to Automatic.

   - ○ D. Open Control Panel and double-click Network Connections. Right-click the Local Area Connection and select Properties. Mark the check box for File and Printer Sharing for Microsoft Networks and click OK.

2. Which of the following methods enable you to create shared network folders? (Check all correct answers.)

   - ❏ A. Right-click a folder in either My Computer or Windows Explorer, select Sharing and Security, click the option button Share This Folder, and click OK.

   - ❏ B. Right-click a folder in either My Computer or Windows Explorer, select Properties, click the Sharing tab, click the option button Share This Folder, and click OK.

   - ❏ C. Open the Computer Management Console, expand Shared Folders, right-click the Shares node, and click New File Share. Follow the onscreen instructions for the Create Shared Folder Wizard.

   - ❏ D. Open a command prompt window. Type **Net Share share_name=x:\ folder_name**, where share_name represents the name you want to assign to the shared folder, x: represents the drive letter where the folder resides, and folder_name represents the actual name of the folder.

3. What is the default setting for offline files under Windows XP Professional when acting as a "server" for other client computers?

- ○ A. Manual caching of documents.
- ○ B. Automatic caching of documents.
- ○ C. Caching is disabled.
- ○ D. Automatic caching of programs and documents.

4. Which of the following Local groups are installed automatically by Windows XP Professional? (Check all correct answers.)

- ❑ A. Network Configuration Operators
- ❑ B. Replicator
- ❑ C. Authenticated Users
- ❑ D. HelpServicesGroup
- ❑ E. Remote Desktop Users
- ❑ F. Creator Group

5. How can you determine the effective NTFS permissions on a file or a folder for a user or a group with the least amount of administrative effort?

- ○ A. Log on as the specific user and test the user's permissions by attempting to read, write, modify, delete, change permissions, and take ownership of specific files and folders.
- ○ B. Log on as an administrative user, right-click a folder or file in question, choose Properties, click Security, click the Advanced button, and click the Effective Permissions tab. Select a user or group to view the effective permissions for that user or group on the specific file or folder.
- ○ C. Open the Computer Management Console, click Shared Folders, and then click Effective Permissions.
- ○ D. Open the Control Panel and double-click Component Services. Right-click the NTFS Permissions node and select Effective Permissions.

6. If you use Windows Explorer to move seven subfolders containing 152 files from e:\docs to e:\letters on Server3, what will happen to their NTFS permissions?

- ○ A. The folders and files moved will retain their same NTFS permissions.
- ○ B. The folders and files moved will inherit their NTFS permissions from the target (destination) folder.
- ○ C. The folders and files moved will have their NTFS permissions reset to the default settings for drive volumes, such as Allow Everyone Read and Execute, and Administrators Full Control.
- ○ D. You will be prompted by a message box asking whether you want the folders and files moved to retain their permissions or inherit their permissions from the target (destination) folder.

7. As a network administrator, how can you ensure that members of the Interns group are allowed to print documents only on Printer4, and that they can print only those documents during nonbusiness hours? In addition, how can you make sure that their print jobs have a higher priority than other print jobs from members of other groups?

○ A. Configure the printer properties for Printer4 on each computer for each member of all the other network groups. In the Printers and Faxes window, right-click Printer4, select Properties, click the Advanced tab, click the Available From button, and specify the business hours that the printer will be unavailable for the Interns group. Decrement the Priority counter so that each member of the other groups will have a lower printing priority for Printer4 than members from the Interns groups.

○ B. For each user in the Interns group, open the Printers and Faxes window, right-click Printer4, select Properties, and click the Security tab. Grant the permissions Allow Print, Allow Manage Printers, and Allow Manage Documents to the Interns group.

○ C. Configure the printer properties for Printer4 on each computer for each member of the Interns group. In the Printers and Faxes window, right-click Printer4, select Properties, click the Advanced tab, click the Available From button, and specify the nonbusiness hours that the printer will be available. Increment the Priority counter so that each member of the Interns group will have a higher printing priority for Printer4 than members from other groups.

○ D. For each user in the Interns group, open the Printers and Faxes window, right-click Printer4, select Properties, and click the Security tab. Click the Advanced button, click the Owner tab, and change the owner to the Interns group.

8. Which of the following statements are true about using the Internet Printing Protocol (IPP)? (Check all correct answers.)

❏ A. The print server computer must be running IIS 4 or later.

❏ B. The print server computer may be running Windows 2000 Professional.

❏ C. You can view all available printers and faxes by typing the following URL into a web browser: `http://print_server_name/printers`.

❏ D. You can connect to specific printer by typing the following URL into a web browser: `http://print_server_name/printer_share_name`.

9. You are the network administrator for a private investigation firm. All workstation computers have either Windows XP or Windows XP SP1 installed. Recently, several small, portable USB 2.0 storage devices have been found around the office containing confidential client files. You need to make sure that no private client data gets copied and falls into the wrong hands. However, many of the company's investigators use portable USB storage devices for legitimate purposes. How can you lock down security on portable storage devices without upsetting the users who rely on it for legitimate reasons? Choose two correct answers.

❏ A. Install Windows XP SP2 on all workstations.

❏ B. Assign Read-only NTFS permissions on all client data files.

❏ C. Disable the USB Mass Storage device driver on all workstations except for those users' computers who really need to use USB storage.

❏ D. Configure the `WriteProtect` value setting in the Registry and set its value data to 0.

❏ E. Configure the `StorageDevicePolicies` value setting in the Registry and set its value data to 1.

❏ F. Configure the `WriteProtect` value setting in the Registry and set its value data to 1.

10. You are the network administrator for Widgets 'R' Us, a privately held manufacturing company. All the workstation computers have Windows XP SP2 installed. Many users take advantage of WebDAV functionality to access and share files over the company's extensive intranet, which spans the globe by connecting all the offices via encrypted virtual private network (VPN) tunnels. Secure Socket Layer (SSL) connections also are used to link users to various internal company web servers. The company's programmers have written several mission-critical applications that rely on WebDAV and basic authentication credentials. Management wants users to continue to use WebDAV, but they do not want anyone to use WebDAV over unencrypted connections, such as port 80, to publicly available websites on the Internet. How can you support basic authentication for WebDAV-enabled applications without supporting clear text logons to public websites? Choose two correct answers.

❏ A. Create a new DWORD value in the Windows XP SP2 Registry under `HKEY_LOCAL_MACHINE\System\CurrentControlSet\Services\WebClient\Parameters`. Name the new DWORD value DisableBasicOverClearChannel and set its value data to 1.

❏ B. Create a new DWORD value in the Windows XP SP2 Registry under `HKEY_LOCAL_MACHINE\System\CurrentControlSet\Services\WebClient\Parameters`. Name the new DWORD value UseBasicAuth and set its value data to 0.

❏ C. Create a new DWORD value in the Windows XP SP2 Registry under `HKEY_CURRENT_USER\Software\Microsoft\Windows\CurrentVersion\Internet Settings`. Name the new DWORD value UseBasicAuth and set its value data to 1.

❏ D. Create a new DWORD value in the Windows XP SP2 Registry under `HKEY_CURRENT_USER\Software\Microsoft\Windows\CurrentVersion\Internet Settings`. Name the new DWORD value DisableBasicOverClearChannel and set its value data to 0.

❏ E. Create a new DWORD value in the Windows XP SP2 Registry under `HKEY_CURRENT_USER\Software\Microsoft\Windows\CurrentVersion\Internet Settings`. Name the new DWORD value DisableBasicOverClearChannel and set its value data to 1.

❏ F. Create a new DWORD value in the Windows XP SP2 Registry under `HKEY_LOCAL_MACHINE\System\CurrentControlSet\Services\WebClient\Parameters`. Name the new DWORD value UseBasicAuth and set its value data to 1.

Answers to Exam Prep Questions

1. Answer B is correct. Simple File Sharing is enabled by default for standalone and workgroup-member computers. Simple File Sharing is disabled by default for domain-member computers. The Folder Options menu is the only way to enable or disable Simple File Sharing. Answer A is incorrect because the policy for Network Access: Sharing and Security Model for Local Accounts does not deal with Simple File Sharing. Answer C is incorrect because the Workstation service is enabled by default. Answer D is incorrect because File and Printer Sharing for Microsoft Networks is enabled by default.

2. Answers A, B, C, and D are all correct. These methods are valid ways to create shared network folders.

3. Answer A is correct because manual caching of documents is the default setting for Windows XP Professional. Answer B is incorrect because automatic caching of documents is not the default setting; however, it is an option. Answer C is incorrect because the caching of offline files is enabled by default. Answer D is incorrect because automatic caching of programs and documents is not the default setting; however, it is an option.

4. Answers A, B, D, and E are all correct. Answer C is incorrect because Authenticated Users is considered to be a built-in security principal, not a Local group. Answer F is incorrect because Creator Group is also considered to be a built-in security principal, not a Local group.

5. Answer B is correct. The Effective Permissions tab is a new feature in Windows XP Professional. Answer A is incorrect because it requires more administrative effort than using the Effective Permissions tab. Answer C is incorrect because no Effective Permissions tab exists for the Shared Folders snap-in. Answer D is incorrect because no Effective Permissions feature exists in the Component Services snap-in.

6. Answer A is correct. Folders and files that are moved within the same NTFS drive volume always retain their permissions from the source folder. Answer B is incorrect because folders and files moved to a different NTFS drive volume inherit their permissions from the target (destination) folder. Answer C is incorrect because folders and files that are moved never have their NTFS permissions reset to drive volume defaults. Answer D is incorrect because Windows Explorer does not prompt the user about retaining or inheriting NTFS permissions when moving or copying files.

7. Answer C is correct. If you set up each computer for each user who belongs to the Interns group, you can specify during which time period the printer is available, and you can specify a higher priority than the default, which is 1. The highest priority setting is 99. Answer A is

incorrect because you do not need to configure computers for the users in groups other than the Interns group, and you cannot specify a priority setting lower than 1 (the default). Answer B is incorrect because printer permissions do not modify printer availability or printer priority settings. Answer D is incorrect because the printer ownership setting does not modify printer availability or printer priority settings.

8. Answers B and D are correct. IPP is supported on Windows 2000 (all editions) and later Microsoft operating systems. You can connect directly to the printer website by typing the URL `http://print_server_name/printer_share_name` into a web browser. Answer A is incorrect because a print server computer must be running IIS 5 or later to support IPP. Answer C is incorrect because IPP displays only print devices, not fax devices. However, the URL is correct.

9. Answers A and F are correct. You must first install SP2 on all workstations so that you can configure the `WriteProtect` value setting in the Registry and set its value data to 1, which enables WriteProtect for USB storage devices. Users may still use USB storage devices for reading files and for copying files obtained at other locations to the local computer and to the network. Answer B is incorrect because assigning NTFS Read-only permissions would still allow users to copy client data to their USB devices. Answer C is incorrect because disabling the USB Mass Storage driver only for certain users' computers would not be very secure because other users could use the computers that still had the driver installed to copy confidential information. Answer D is incorrect because the value data setting of 0 disables the USB WriteProtect feature. Answer E is incorrect because StorageDevicePolicies is the registry subkey, not a value, that you must first create before you create the WriteProtect value setting to enable the WriteProtect feature.

10. Answers E and F are correct. Under SP2, when you create the DWORD value DisableBasicOverClearChannel and set it equal to 1 for the Registry path `HKEY_CURRENT_USER\Software\Microsoft\Windows\CurrentVersion\Internet Settings`, you turn OFF basic authentication over unencrypted connections. When you create the DWORD value UseBasicAuth and set it equal to 1 for the Registry path `HKEY_LOCAL_MACHINE\System\CurrentControlSet\Services\WebClient\Parameters`, you turn ON basic authentication for the WebDAV protocol under SP2. This combination allows basic authentication for WebDAV, but *only over a secure channel*. Answer A is incorrect because the DWORD value DisableBasicOverClearChannel does not belong under the `HKEY_LOCAL_MACHINE\System\CurrentControlSet\Services\WebClient\Parameters` Registry key. Answer B is incorrect because by setting the UseBasicAuth value data to 0, you turn off basic authentication for WebDAV, which already is the default setting under

SP2. Answer C is incorrect because the DWORD value UseBasicAuth does not belong under the HKEY_CURRENT_USER\Software\Microsoft\ Windows\CurrentVersion\Internet Settings Registry key. Answer D is incorrect because by setting the DisableBasicOverClearChannel value data to 0, you turn ON basic authentication over unencrypted connections, which already is the default setting under SP2.

Need to Know More?

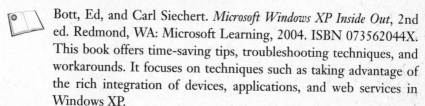

Bott, Ed, and Carl Siechert. *Microsoft Windows XP Inside Out*, 2nd ed. Redmond, WA: Microsoft Learning, 2004. ISBN 073562044X. This book offers time-saving tips, troubleshooting techniques, and workarounds. It focuses on techniques such as taking advantage of the rich integration of devices, applications, and web services in Windows XP.

Microsoft Corporation. *Microsoft Windows XP Professional Resource Kit*, 2nd ed. Redmond, WA: Microsoft Press, 2003. ISBN 0735619743. This all-in-one reference is a compilation of technical documentation and valuable insider information that computer-support professionals and administrators can reference to install, customize, and support Windows XP.

Minasi, Mark. *Mastering Windows XP Professional*. Alameda, CA: Sybex, Inc., 2001. ISBN 0782129811. This book provides in-depth coverage of installing, configuring, and administering Windows XP Professional.

Search the Microsoft TechNet CD (or its online version through www.microsoft.com) using keywords such as "Shared Folders", "Share Permissions", "NTFS Permissions", "User Rights", "Effective Permissions", "Internet Information Services", "Offline Files", "Access Control List", "Built-in Security Principals", "WebDAV", "Basic Authentication", "SP2", and "Service Pack 2".

3

Setting Up, Managing, and Troubleshooting Security Accounts and Policies

Terms you'll need to understand:

✓ Local user account
✓ Local group
✓ Complex password
✓ Domain user account
✓ Global, Universal, and Domain Local groups
✓ Security Identifier (SID)
✓ Authentication
✓ Security Center
✓ Local Group Policy
✓ Group Policy Object (GPO)
✓ Resulting Set of Policies (RSoP)
✓ Software Restriction Policy
✓ Microsoft Passport

Techniques you'll need to master:

✓ Adding and configuring new local user accounts
✓ Adding users and groups from a Domain to a Local group
✓ Properly renaming user accounts to maintain resource access
✓ Configuring the Local Security Policy and the Local Group Policy
✓ Understanding the order in which Group Policies apply to a user and computer when the computer is a member of the domain
✓ Analyzing and configuring computers with the security templates
✓ Using and configuring a Microsoft Passport

The Local Users and Groups snap-in enables you to manage local users and groups. You can get to the snap-in by choosing Start, Control Panel, Performance and Maintenance Category, Administrative Tools, Computer Management, and then by expanding the tree pane of the Computer Management Console until you see the snap-in. In this snap-in, you can create, modify, duplicate, and delete users (in the Users folder) and groups (in the Groups folder).

Built-in User and Group Accounts

The three primary built-in user accounts are Administrator, Guest, and HelpAssistant. The Administrator account is a critical account for your computer and has some essential characteristics, including the following:

➤ Cannot be deleted.

➤ Can be disabled. Be sure to create another user account with administrator privileges before disabling the default Administrator account.

➤ Through its membership in the Administrators group, has all privileges required to perform system administration duties.

➤ Can be renamed.

The Guest account is on your system for rare and infrequent use and should be kept securely disabled. This account also has some distinct characteristics, including the following:

➤ Is disabled by default. Only an administrator can enable the account. If it is enabled, it should be given a password, and User Cannot Change Password should be set if multiple users will log on with the account.

➤ Cannot be deleted.

➤ Can be locked out.

➤ Does not save user preferences or settings.

The HelpAssistant account is on your system for use when the Remote Desktop Assistance functions are used. This account's characteristics include the following:

➤ Disabled by default.

➤ Is automatically enabled when an invitation is created for Remote Assistance.

➤ Can be deleted.

➤ Can be renamed.

Built-in Local groups have assigned to them specific privileges (also called user rights) that enable them to perform specific sets of tasks on a system. The default local group accounts on a Windows XP Professional system are the following:

➤ Administrators—Users in this group have all built-in system privileges assigned. They can create and modify user and group accounts, manage security policies, create printers, and manage permissions to resources on the system. The local Administrator account is the default member and cannot be removed. Other accounts can be added and removed. When a system joins a domain, the Domain Admins group is added to this group, but it can be removed.

➤ Backup Operators—Users in this group can back up and restore files and folders regardless of security permissions assigned to those resources. They can log on and shut down a system, but cannot change security settings.

➤ Power Users—Users in this group can share resources and create user and group accounts. They cannot modify user accounts they did not create, nor can they modify the Administrators or Backup Operators groups. They cannot take ownership of files, back up or restore directories, load or unload device drivers, or manage the security and auditing logs. They can run all Windows XP-compatible applications, as well as legacy applications, some of which members of the Users group cannot execute.

 If you want certain users to have broad system administration capabilities, but do not want them to be able to access all system resources, consider putting them in Backup Operators and Power Users rather than Administrators.

➤ Users—Users in this group can log on, shut down a system, use local and network printers, create local groups, and manage the groups they create. They cannot create a local printer or share a folder. Some down-level applications do not run for members of the Users group because security settings are tighter for the Users group in Windows XP than in Windows NT 4. By default, all local user accounts you create are added to the Users group. In addition, when a system joins a domain, the Domain Users group is made a member of that system's local Users group.

➤ Guests—Users in this group have limited privileges but can log on to a system and shut it down. Members cannot make permanent changes to their desktop or profile. By default, the Built-in Local Guest account is a member. When a system joins a domain, the Domain Guests group is added to the Local Guests group.

➤ Network Configuration Operators—Users in this group have administrative privileges to manage the configuration of networking features.

➤ Remote Desktop Users—Users in this group have the added privilege of logging on through Terminal Services, which in Windows XP is established through a Remote Desktop connection.

Built-in System groups also exist, which you do not see in the user interface while managing other group accounts. Membership of system groups changes based on how the computer is accessed, not on who accesses the computer. Built-in System groups include the following:

➤ Everyone—Includes all users who access the computer, including the Guest account.

➤ Authenticated Users—Includes all users with a valid user account in the local security database or (in the case of domain members) in Active Directory's directory services. You use the Authenticated Users group rather than the Everyone group to assign privileges and group permissions, because doing so prevents anonymous access to resources.

➤ Creator Owner—Contains the user account that created or took ownership of a resource. If the user is a member of the Administrators group, the group is the owner of the resource.

➤ Network—Contains any user with a connection from a remote system.

➤ Interactive—Contains the user account for the user logged on locally at the system.

➤ Anonymous Logon—Includes any user account that Windows XP did not authenticate.

➤ Dial-up—Contains all users who currently use a dial-up connection.

Creating Local User and Group Accounts

To create a local user or group account, right-click the appropriate folder (Users or Groups) and choose New User (or New Group), enter the appropriate attributes, and then click Create.

User account names:

➤ Must be unique.

➤ Are recognized only up to 20 characters, although the name itself can be longer.

➤ Cannot contain the following characters: " / \ [ ] ; : | = + * ? < >

➤ Are not case sensitive, although the user account's name property displays the case as entered.

User account passwords:

➤ Are recommended.

➤ Are case sensitive.

➤ Can be up to 127 characters, although down-level operating systems such as Windows NT 4 and Windows 9x support only 14-character passwords.

➤ Should be a minimum of seven to eight characters.

➤ Should be difficult to guess and, preferably, should mix uppercase and lowercase letters, numerals, and nonalphanumeric characters.

➤ Can be set by the administrator (who can then determine whether users must, can, or cannot change their password) or the user (if the administrator has not specified otherwise).

Select the option User Must Change Password at Next Logon to ensure that the user is the only one who knows the account's password. Select User Cannot Change Password when more than one person (such as Guest) uses the account.

The User Cannot Change Password option is not available when User Must Change Password at Next Logon is selected.

The Password Never Expires option is helpful when a program or a service uses an account. To avoid having to reconfigure the service with a new password, you can set the service account to retain its password indefinitely.

Configuring Account Properties

The information you can specify when creating an account is limited in Windows XP. Therefore, after creating an account, you often need to go to the account's Properties dialog box, which you can access by right-clicking the account and choosing Properties. After the creation of a user, you can specify the groups the user belongs to and the profile settings for the user, as shown in Figure 3.1.

Figure 3.1 The Properties dialog box of a typical user.

Managing Local Group Membership

To manage the membership of a Local group, right-click the group and choose Properties. To remove a member, select the account and click Remove. To add a member, click Add and select or enter the name of the account, as shown in Figure 3.2.

In a workgroup, Local groups can contain only accounts defined in the same machine's local security database. When a system belongs to a domain, its Local groups can also include domain accounts, including user accounts, Universal groups, and Global groups from the enterprise's Active Directory, as well as Domain Local groups from within the system's domain.

Figure 3.2 Interface for adding a user or group to a Local group.

NOTE

Universal groups and Domain Local groups are available to add as members only when the domain is in native mode, meaning that it can contain only Windows 2000 and Windows Server 2003 domain controllers—no Windows NT 4.0 backup domain controllers are allowed under native mode.

Renaming Accounts

To rename an account, right-click the account and choose Rename. Type the new name and press Enter. Each user and group account is represented in the local security database by a long, unique string called a *Security Identifier (SID)*, which is generated when the account is created. The SID is assigned permissions and privileges. The user or group name is just a user-friendly interface name for humans to interact with the computer. Therefore, when you rename an account, the account's SID remains the same and the account retains all its group memberships, permissions, and privileges.

Two situations mandate renaming an account. The first occurs when one user stops using a system and a new user requires the same access as the first. Rather than creating a new local user account for the new user, rename the old user account. The account's SID remains the same, so its group memberships, privileges, and permissions are retained. You should also specify a new password in the account's Properties dialog box and select the User Must Change Password at Next Logon option.

One thing to keep in mind is that the user's Home Directory name will not change along with renaming the user. The administrator will need to change the reference in the user properties and within the directory structure where the folder resides.

The second situation that warrants renaming a user account is the security practice of renaming the built-in Administrator and Guest accounts. You cannot delete these accounts, nor can you remove the Administrator account from the Local Administrators group, so renaming the accounts is a recommended practice for hindering malicious access to a system.

A Group Policy exists to modify the Administrator and Guest name and status (enabled or disabled). You can either create this at the local computer level or at the site, domain, or organizational unit (OU) level within Active Directory.

Disabling or Enabling User Accounts

To disable or enable a user account, open its Properties dialog box and select or clear the Account Is Disabled check box. If an account is disabled, a user cannot log on to the system using that account. Only Administrators can enable the Guest account.

Deleting Accounts

You can delete a local user or group account (but not built-in accounts such as Administrator, Guest, or Backup Operators) by right-clicking the account and choosing Delete. When you delete a group, you delete the group account only, not the members of the group. A group is a membership list, not a container.

 When you delete an account, you are deleting its SID. Therefore, if you delete an account by accident and re-create the account, even with the same name, it will not have the same permissions, privileges, or group memberships. You will have to re-create all those settings. For that reason, and to facilitate auditing, it is recommended that you disable, not delete, any user that leaves an organization.

Using the User Accounts Tool

Another tool for administering local user accounts is the User Accounts tool in Control Panel, shown in Figure 3.3. This tool enables you to create and remove user accounts, as well as specify specific configurations for those users. It is wizard driven and is useful for novice administrators and home users.

The User Account tool changes functions as the computer joins a domain from a workgroup. These changes are to control the access to the computer from other domain users. The following is a list of configurations that can be completed after the computer has become a member of a domain:

➤ Manage the users that can access the local computer.

➤ Modify the type of access a user has on the computer. This would include Standard user, Limited user, or a custom type of user, such as an Administrator.

➤ Manage passwords that are stored on the local computer.

➤ Manage .NET Passport.

➤ Access advanced user and computer settings.

➤ Change the local administrator password.

➤ Modify the secure logon preferences—basically, whether a user is required to press Ctrl+Alt+Delete to log on.

For machines that do not participate in a domain in Windows XP, two categories of user accounts exist: Limited and Administrator. By default, the person installing the operating system is an administrator. An account that is an administrator can perform any and all functions on the computer. By contrast, an account designated as Limited cannot create shares or install software. Table 3.1 lists several of the differences between the accounts.

Figure 3.3 User Accounts tool for administering local users.

Table 3.1 Different Functionality Among Windows XP Accounts		
Function	**Limited**	**Administrator**
Create shares		X
Create printers		X
Install software		X
Create other accounts		X
Change network settings		X
Change passwords	X	X
Change account picture	X	X
Set up .NET Passport	X	X
Access programs	X	X
Change background	X	X
Request Remote Assistance	X	X

Passwords

Passwords are not required, but are highly recommended. If your system has accounts that don't require any form of password, virtually anyone will be able to access your files and folders, even if you don't want them to. It is always recommended to have a password; even a simple password is better than no password at all.

Forgotten Passwords

If you forget your password, you can recover your settings and user account with the Forgotten Password Wizard. The wizard enables you to create a Password Reset Disk to help you open your account and create a new password. The Password Reset Wizard also enables you to change your password.

To protect user accounts in the event that the user forgets the password, every local user can make a Password Reset Disk and keep it in a safe place. Then, if the user forgets his or her password, the password can be reset using the Password Reset Disk, enabling the user to access the local user account again.

If you already made a Password Reset Disk for your local user account through the Forgotten Password Wizard, you can use it to access the computer, even if you have forgotten your password.

Fast User Switching

Fast User Switching is a special feature of Windows XP Professional. Don't be fooled with this option, though, because it is available only when the computer is in a workgroup. The option is removed as soon as the computer is joined to a domain. Fast User Switching makes it possible for users to switch quickly between other users without actually logging off from the computer. Multiple users can share a computer and use it simultaneously, switching back and forth without closing the programs they are running. To switch to another user, click Start, click Log Off, click Switch User, and then click the user account you would like to switch to. The following caveats apply when using Fast User Switching:

➤ It will not appear if it has not been turned on in User Accounts in Control Panel.

➤ It is not available on computers that are members of a network domain.

➤ It can be turned on or off only by users who have administrative privileges on the computer.

➤ It cannot be turned off while multiple users are logged on to the computer.

➤ When it is not turned on, programs shut down when a user logs off, and the computer runs faster for the next user who logs on.

Authentication

When a user wants to access resources on a machine, that user's identity must first be verified through a process called *authentication*. For example, when a user logs on, the security subsystem evaluates the user's username and password. If they match, the user is authenticated. The process of logging on to a machine where you are physically sitting is called an *interactive logon*. Authentication also happens when you access resources on a remote system. For example, when you open a shared folder on a server, you are being authenticated as well, only this time, the process is called a *remote* or *network logon*, because you are not physically at the server.

The Security Dialog Box

The Security dialog box allows for interactive logon to a Windows XP system. You can access the Security dialog box shortly after a system has started, and at any time after logon, by pressing Ctrl+Alt+Delete. If you are not currently logged on, you can enter a username and password. If the system belongs to a domain, you need to be certain that the domain in which your account exists is selected in the Log On To text box. You can either select the domain from the drop-down list or enter your User Principal Name (UPN) in the Username text box. The UPN is an attribute of an Active Directory user object and, by default, is of the form `username@domain.name`, where `domain.name` is the Windows 2000 domain for which your user account resides (for example, braincore.net). The suffix following the @ symbol indicates the domain against which to authenticate the user.

If you are currently logged on to a system, pressing Ctrl+Alt+Delete takes you to the Windows XP Security dialog box, at which point you can do the following:

➤ Log off the system, which closes all programs and ends the instance of the session.

➤ Lock the system, which allows programs to continue running but prevents access to the system. When a system is locked, you can unlock it by pressing Ctrl+Alt+Delete and entering the username and password of the user who locked the system, or an administrator's username and password.

➤ Shut down the system.

➤ Change your password.

➤ Access Task Manager.

Managing Domain User Accounts

Domain user accounts are managed with the Active Directory Users and Computers snap-in. To access it, choose Start, Settings, Control Panel, Administrative Tools, Active Directory Users and Computers. When you open the tool, you connect to an available domain controller. To specify which domain controller or domain you want to modify, right-click the Active Directory Users and Computers node and choose Connect to Domain or Connect to Domain Controller.

Unlike the local security database, which is a static list of users and groups, Active Directory has containers and OUs, which help organize database objects such as users, computers, printers, and other OUs. Therefore, to manage domain user accounts in Windows 2000 or Server 2003, you need to access the correct container or OU that houses your user object.

 The Active Directory Users and Computers tool is not installed by default. You need to install the Admin Pack (**adminpk.msi**) from a Windows Server 2003 domain controller before you can use Active Directory Users and Computers on a Windows XP client computer.

Creating Domain User Accounts

You create domain user accounts by right-clicking the container or OU that will contain the user account and then selecting New, User. A wizard prompts you for basic account properties, including the following:

➤ First name and last name

➤ Full name (by default, the combination of the first and last names)

➤ User logon name and User Principal Name (UPN) suffix

➤ User logon name (pre-Windows 2000)

➤ Password

Creating Template User Accounts

When you expect to create multiple user objects with similar properties, you can create a "template" account that, when copied, initiates the new accounts with predefined attributes. One thing to keep in mind when working with templates is to disable the template account. This will ensure that a real user can't access the network as the template user. Of course, when you copy the template account to create a new user, make sure you enable the new account.

Disabling and Deleting User Accounts

The process for disabling and deleting domain user accounts is the same as for local user accounts, except that you use the Active Directory Users and Computers snap-in to perform the tasks. The check box for disabling an account is on the user's Property sheet, or you can disable the account by right-clicking the user object and selecting the Disable Account menu option.

Understanding and Implementing Group Policy

One of the most powerful aspects of Windows XP Professional and Windows 2000 Active Directory is the implementation of Group Policy. Group Policy is the capability to control finite details of a computer or user quickly and easily. These policies can either be configured at the local level or within the Active Directory structure. Regardless of the location of implementation, these settings are extremely powerful and can change the way normal control and administration is done within a company.

Local Group Policy

Actually, you can administer Local Policies from two locations: a Local Group Policy and a Local Security Policy. The Local Group Policy can be accessed by opening the Group Policy snap-in within a Microsoft Management Console and then selecting the Local Computer option. You can configure security-related settings using the Local Security Policy. Choose Start, Administrative Tools, Local Security Policy. Each of the nodes in the Local Security Policy Console is a security area or scope, within which you will find dozens of security-related settings. The Local Security Policy is nothing more than a subset of the Local Group Policy. So, when you open the Local Group Policy, you are also accessing the Local Security Policy.

 The Local Group Policy can also be accessed by typing **gpedit.msc** at the command prompt.

Managing Local Group Policies

The Local Group Policy and the Local Security Policy tools are most helpful on standalone systems and laptops that roam away from the network environment. The Local Group Policy controls the configuration of the local computer and user. The policy-based settings will apply to a computer at startup and to a user at logon. Also, these policy settings are applied at a refresh interval, which does not require a reboot or logging off. The default refresh interval for all Group Policy Object settings on a Windows XP client is 90 minutes.

In a workgroup environment, you will need to access each computer and make the desired settings on each computer individually. Methods exist to make this more efficient by using security templates, but the process is still a manual one that requires decentralized administration of the policy settings. The solution to this decentralized administration is to implement Active Directory and apply the desired settings to a grouping of computers or users by using Group Policy Objects within Active Directory.

Group Policy Objects (GPO)

Group Policy Objects (GPOs) within Active Directory take the concept of policy-enforced configurations and apply it to multiple computers or users. Unlike Local Group Policy, GPOs provide a centralized enumeration of configuration settings. You can apply, or link, GPOs to the following:

➤ A site—This is an Active Directory object that represents a portion of your network topology with good connectivity—a local area network (LAN), for example.

➤ A domain—This causes the configuration specified by the policy to be applied to every user or computer in the domain.

➤ An OU—This applies policies to users or computers in the OU or any child OUs.

To access Group Policy, you must go to the properties of a site, domain, or OU (SDOU), and click the Group Policy tab. Therefore, to work with group policy for a site, you use the Active Directory Sites and Services Console, whereas to work with group policy for a domain or OU, you use Active Directory Users and Computers.

 Microsoft has released a Group Policy Management Console (GPMC), which allows for easier and more efficient control over GPOs. This is a free download from Microsoft and can run only on Windows XP and Windows Server 2003. After it is installed, it is accessed from the Administrative Tools menu or the MMC as a snap-in.

An individual machine can have only one Local Group Policy, whereas an SDOU can have multiple GPOs linked to them. In the Group Policy Properties dialog box, you can create a new GPO by clicking New, or link an existing GPO to the SDOU by clicking Add. If you select a group policy and click Edit, you expose the GPO in the Group Policy Editor. The GPMC removes much of the complexity of creating and linking GPOs to Active Directory objects. The GPMC displays the domain, OUs, and sites clearly, which can all be right-clicked to expose options for creating and linking GPOs to these nodes.

Application of Group Policy Objects

GPOs are divided into the Computer Configuration and User Configuration nodes. The computer settings apply to every computer in the site, domain, or OU to which the policy is linked, and, by default, to all child OUs. Computer settings take effect at startup and at every refresh interval, which by default is 90 minutes. User settings affect every user in the site, domain, or OU and its children at logon, and after each refresh interval.

 When configuring GPOs, ensure that the computers and/or users lie within the path of the GPO SDOU to receive the policy settings. For example, if you want to control a web server named IIS_Apps, you would need to move this computer object to the proper OU to have the GPO for that OU apply to the IIS_Apps computer.

When a computer starts, its current settings are modified first by any configuration specified by the Local Group Policy. Then the configurations for the SDOU GPOs are applied. The SDOU policies are applied in order: first, the policies linked to the computer's site, then the policies for its domain, and finally the policies for each OU in the branch that leads to the object's OU. The policy settings from the Local Group Policy and the SDOU will append to each other if no conflict exists. If a conflict occurs in a specific configuration setting, the last setting applied has control. Therefore, the policies that are "closest" to the computer—the policies linked to its OU, for example—take precedence if a conflict arises. The same application of policies applies to a user at logon: local policy, site policy, domain policy, and OU policy.

User Rights Assignment

User rights, also called privileges, enable a user or group to perform system functions such as changing the system time, backing up or restoring files, and formatting a disk volume. Some rights are assigned to Built-in groups. For example, all members of the Administrators group can format a disk volume. You cannot deny that right to the members of the Administrators group, nor can you assign that right to a user or group you create. Other rights are assignable. For example, the right to back up files and folders is given by default to all members of the Administrators and Backup Operators, but you can remove the right for those groups or assign the right to other users or groups. You can modify the rights that are visible in the Local Security Policy Console. You do not see the "hard wired" rights in this interface.

User rights, because they are system oriented, override object permissions when the two are in conflict with each other. For example, a user may be denied permission to read a folder on a disk volume. However, if the user has been given the privilege to back up files and folders, a backup of the folder succeeds, even though the user is denied permission to the folder.

Security Options

In the Security Options node are a number of useful security settings. This node highlights one of the advantages of policies, because while many of these settings are accessible elsewhere in the user interface (for example, you can specify driver signing in the System applet), a policy enables you to configure all those settings, from all the tools and applets, into a centralized location.

Some particularly useful options to be familiar with are the following:

➤ Clear the Virtual Memory Pagefile When the System Shuts Down—By default, the pagefile is not cleared and could allow unauthorized access to sensitive information that remains in the pagefile.

➤ Do Not Display Last Username in Logon Screen—This option forces users to enter both their username and password at logon. By default, the policy is disabled and the name of the previously logged-on user is displayed.

➤ Number of Previous Logons to Cache—This policy limits the number of cached profiles that are on a system. Not only will this clean up the hard drive space on a system, but if no cached profiles exist, users will be forced to access a domain controller when logging on to the domain, instead of using cached credentials.

Account Policies

Account policies control the password requirements and how the system responds to invalid logon attempts. The policies you can specify include the following:

➤ Maximum Password Age—Specifies the period of time after which a password must be changed.

➤ Minimum Password Length—Specifies the number of characters in a password. Passwords can contain up to 127 characters; however, most passwords should not exceed 14 characters.

➤ Passwords Must Meet Complexity Requirements—This policy, if in effect, does not allow a password change unless the new password contains at least three of four character types: uppercase (A through Z), lowercase (a through z), numeric (0 through 9), and nonalphanumeric (such as !). All passwords must also be at least six characters long to meet complexity requirements.

➤ Enforce Password History—The system can remember a specified number of previous passwords. When a user attempts to change his or her password, the new password is compared against the history; if the new password is unique, the change is allowed.

➤ Minimum Password Age—Specifies the number of days that a new password must be used before it can be changed again.

➤ Account Lockout Threshold—Specifies the number of denied logon attempts after which an account is locked out. For example, if this is set to 3, a lockout occurs if a user enters the wrong password three times; any further logon attempt will be denied. If this is set to 0, there is no lockout threshold.

➤ Reset Account Lockout Counter After—Specifies the number of minutes after which the counter that applies to the lockout threshold is reset. For example, if the counter is reset after 5 minutes and the account lockout threshold is 3, a user can log on twice with the incorrect password. After 5 minutes, the counter is reset, so the user can log on twice more. A third invalid logon during a 5-minute period locks out the account.

➤ Account Lockout Duration—Specifies how long logon attempts are denied after a lockout. During this period, a logon with the locked out username is not authenticated.

Audit Policies

Audit policies specify what types of events are entered into the Security Log. The most important policies to understand include those in the following list:

➤ Logon Events—Authentication of users logging on or off locally and making connections to the computer from remote systems.

➤ Account Management—Any change to account properties, including password changes and additions, deletions, or modifications to users or groups.

➤ Object Access—Access to objects on which auditing has been specified. Auditing object access, for example, enables auditing of files and folders on an NT File System (NTFS) volume, but you must also configure auditing on those files and folders. Refer to Chapter 2, "Establishing, Configuring, and Managing Resources," for a detailed discussion of auditing.

➤ Privilege Use—Use of any user rights, now called privileges. For example, this policy audits a user who changes the system time, because changing the system time is a privilege.

For each policy, you can specify to audit successes, failures, or both. As events are logged, they appear in the Security Log, which, by default, can be viewed only by administrators. Other logs can be viewed by anyone.

SP2 GPO Changes

Service Pack 2 is known as the "security pack" because of all the security changes it provides. A large amount of those security changes and features can be controlled with GPOs. Microsoft has added more than 600 (no, this is not a typing error) settings to a default GPO. The new settings help control Windows Firewall, Windows Update, Internet communications, and more. The majority of these changes have taken place in the Administrative Templates section of both the User Configuration and Computer Configurations sections.

With so many new GPO settings, you must become familiar with all the new areas and changes that have occurred due to SP2. These changes are available only on Windows XP clients, until the changes are migrated over to the Windows 2000 and Server 2003 domain controllers.

To get the full list of new Administrative Template updates that SP2 provides, go to www.microsoft.com and type the term **policysettings** into the Search box. The results of this search will take you to the site where you can download the Excel spreadsheet that contains all the settings.

Resultant Set of Policy (RSoP)

As you become more familiar with Group Policy, both at the local and Active Directory levels, you will quickly see that they can be very complex. The complexity results not only from the numerous settings that are available within a single Group Policy, but also from the fact that many policies can be applied, and at many different areas within the enterprise. When these settings finally apply to the computer and user on a Windows XP Professional computer, it can be very difficult, because of the array of settings from all the GPOs, to determine the final policies that are applied. Microsoft has gone to great lengths with Windows XP Professional to help decipher the complexity of GPOs and security settings that are possible. Microsoft has done this with three fantastic tools: Group Policy Result (gpresult), Group Policy Update (gpupdate), and the RSoP snap-in.

Group Policy Result

The first tool, Group Policy Result, is a command-line tool. This tool gives you the Resulting Set of Policy (RSoP) that applies to your computer and user accounts. The tool is extremely simple to run and is easy to read when it spits the results back to you. All you need to do is start a command prompt and type **gpresult**, as shown in Figure 3.4.

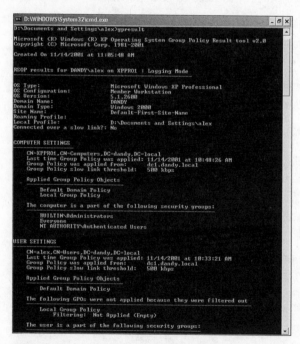

Figure 3.4 Group Policy Result output for the RSoP.

You can also add the **/v** switch to the gpresult command, which provides verbose information about the applied GPOs. Another switch, **/z**, provides "super verbose" output with regard to the GPOs that are applied.

Group Policy Update

It is well known that Group Policies automatically refresh by default. So, when you configure any new setting in the Local or Active Directory Group Policies, the settings will automatically refresh for both the computer and user. For some situations, this is not sufficient, though. You might be testing out new policies and want to see the results immediately, or want to force a new security policy to a department of users immediately. If you need to force a policy immediately, you need only to run the Group Policy Update command-line tool, gpupdate. This tool will investigate the Local and Active Directory–based Group Policies and apply them immediately to both the computer and user accounts. You do not need to run any switches with the tool, but if you want better control, you can use the primary switches listed next:

➤ U: (Computer, User)—Allows explicit refreshing of either the computer or user portions of the policies that need to be applied.

➤ /force—Reapplies all settings in the policies, whereas if no switches are used, only the changed policies apply.

➤ /logoff—Some user-based Group Policy settings exist (such as Folder Redirection) that do not apply until the user logs off and back on. With this switch, the user will be logged off automatically after the other policies refresh.

➤ /boot—Like the user settings, some computer settings require a reboot (such as software deployment). With this switch, the computer will automatically reboot after the other policies refresh.

RSoP Snap-in

The final tool for determining the RSoP is the new RSoP snap-in. This tool enables you to investigate the policies in a GUI interface, which can then be saved to a file or website for archiving. To open this tool, open up a new MMC and add the RSoP snap-in. When you open the tool, you will have the following options for your Windows XP Professional computer:

➤ Computer Scope—You have the choice of selecting either your computer or another computer on the network (as long as you have administrative credentials on the remote computer). You are also able to eliminate the computer portion of the RSoP, if you want to see only user-based settings.

➤ User Scope—You can select the currently logged on user or another user who can access the local computer. Again, you must have the correct privileges to view another user's RSoP. You can also eliminate the user portion of the RSoP, if you want to see only the computer-based settings.

When the tool is run and finishes, it gives you the results in the MMC that you initially opened. Figure 3.5 shows the resulting RSoP format, which is the same format as the original Group Policy Editor.

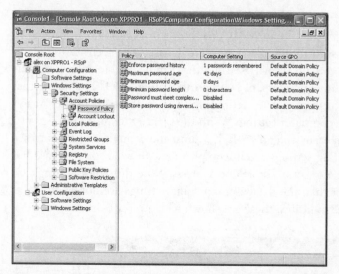

Figure 3.5 RSoP snap-in results for both the local computer and currently logged-on user.

There are two different modes of the RSoP: logging and planning. The logging mode is native to Windows XP and produces the results mentioned previously. The planning mode is available after you install the Administrative Pack and have the administrative privileges to investigate and plan how GPOs will behave when objects are moved within Active Directory.

The RSoP can also be run within the GPMC. There are two options: Logging and Planning.

Security Configuration and Analysis

It was back in the late days of Windows NT 4 that Microsoft introduced the security templates and the capability to lock down the security of a system with a centralized group of settings. The tool has evolved over time and has now come to be known as the Security Configuration and Analysis tool. The tool is a snap-in that is used on a computer-by-computer basis. The tool allows for security analysis and configuration.

The **secedit** command can also be used to analyze and configure security settings to a computer.

After the tool is opened in an MMC, as shown in Figure 3.6, you need to open one of the security templates into a database. The security templates are text files that contain security settings that can be used to analyze a computer, be applied to computers, or be imported into a GPO. The idea is that you bring the security template settings into the database for further analysis of the existing computer settings. With the security template settings in a database, you can easily run an analysis against the computer settings to see whether the existing settings are in compliance with what the database has recorded. Figure 3.6 is a result of one analysis. Note that some settings are equal to or better than the database, but some settings are not as secure as what the database indicates; these are shown with a red x by them.

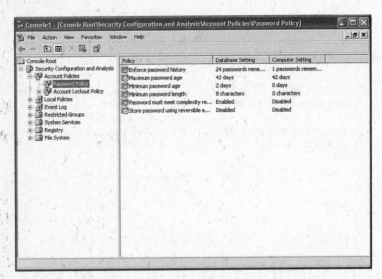

Figure 3.6 Security Configuration and Analysis tool.

Security Templates

Multiple security templates are available and can be used to analyze your computers' security settings. Some are related to the security levels of the system, and others are related to the compatibility of a system with legacy applications. Following is a listing of the different types of security templates:

➤ Securews.inf—This template is designed to boost the security of a Windows XP system with regard to Auditing, Account Policy, and some well-known Registry subkeys.

➤ Hisecws.inf—The settings in this security template will significantly increase the security of the system. You should use this template with caution; the settings might cause the computer to drop communication with the network because of the lack of security on other computers on the network.

➤ Compatws.inf—This template is designed to reduce the security settings on your computer, basically the Users group, so that they can run legacy applications more easily.

Security templates can be modified, copied, and created from scratch. The goal is to make all the necessary security settings in each template and then apply them to the appropriate computers. Security templates can be applied to computers in any one of three ways:

➤ Using the Security Configuration and Analysis MMC snap-in

➤ Using the Secedit command-line tool

➤ Importing security templates into a GPO

Software Restriction Policies

A Software Restriction Policy can help to control users' running of untrusted applications and code. It is clear that most viruses are introduced into the computing environment when users run unauthorized applications and open email attachments. With software restrictions, these undesired applications and code can be eliminated. The following is a listing of some of the controls these policies provide:

➤ Untrusted code is prevented from sending email, accessing files, or performing other normal computing functions until verified as safe.

➤ Protection is provided against infected email attachments. This includes file attachments that are saved to a temporary folder as well as embedded objects and scripts.

➤ ActiveX controls downloaded from the Web are monitored, and neutralized if necessary.

➤ Software restriction policies can be used on a standalone computer by configuring the Local Security Policy.

Two Types of Software Restriction Policies

Software restriction policies can be applied at two security levels:

➤ Unrestricted—Let only trusted code run. If all trusted code can be identified, the administrator can effectively lock down the system. The following are examples of where to apply a "let only trusted code run" policy:

  ➤ Application station

  ➤ Task station

  ➤ Kiosk

➤ Disallowed—Prevent unwanted code from running. In some cases, an administrator cannot predict the entire list of software that users will need to run. In these cases, the administrator can only react and identify undesirable code as it is encountered. Companies with loosely managed clients fall into this model. The following scenarios are examples of this case:

  ➤ Lightly managed personal computers

  ➤ Moderately managed personal computers

Software Identification Rules

An administrator identifies software through one of the following rules:

➤ Hash rule—A Software Restriction Policy's MMC snap-in allows an administrator to browse to a file and identify that program by calculating its hash. A hash is a digital fingerprint that uniquely identifies a program or file. A file can be renamed or moved to another folder or computer and it will still have the same hash.

➤ Path rule—A path rule can identify software by a full pathname, such as C:\Program Files\Microsoft Office\Office\excel.exe or by the pathname leading to the containing folder, such as C:\Windows\System32. (This would refer to all programs in that directory and its subdirectories.) Path rules can also use environment variables, such as %userprofile%\Local Settings\Temp.

➤ Certificate rule—A certificate rule identifies software by the publisher certificate used to digitally sign the software. For example, an administrator can configure a certificate rule that allows only software signed by Microsoft or its IT organization to be installed.

➤ Zone rule—A zone rule identifies software that comes from the Internet, local intranet, trusted sites, or restricted sites zones.

Integration with Microsoft Passport via the Internet

A .NET Passport (also referred to as a Microsoft Passport) provides you with personalized access to Passport-enabled services and websites by using your email address. Passport implements a single sign-in service that enables you to create a single username and password. You can obtain a .NET Passport through the .NET Passport Wizard in User Accounts, shown in Figure 3.7. The .NET Passport Wizard helps you to obtain a .NET Passport or sign in with a Passport you already have. You will be required to configure a .NET Passport when you attempt to use the Windows Messenger application.

Those companies that don't have access to the Internet or don't allow users to use a Microsoft Passport for Windows Messenger, but still want users to take advantage of the Windows Messenger capabilities, can take advantage of the Windows Messenger functionality that is built in to Exchange 2000. With Exchange 2000, users can use their Active Directory credentials to open a Windows Messenger session and talk to other users on the network who also have an Exchange 2000 Windows Messenger account.

Figure 3.7   Microsoft .NET Passport Wizard.

Data Execution Prevention

Data Execution Prevention (DEP) is a new feature for Windows XP Professional that helps prevent code from running in areas of memory where such code should not be running. This helps prevent attackers from placing code in memory to cause default heaps, various stack overflows, and memory pools. This technology does have limitations, though. The hardware that is running on your computer *must* support this technology, which might be some time in coming depending on how often you change the hardware on your client computers.

Windows Security Center

The Security Center is command central for all things security according to Microsoft. Within this tool you will have the capability to configure Windows Firewall, Automatic Updates, Virus Protection, and Internet Explorer security settings. Even though it would be nice if the Security Center also provided immediate access to the Local Group Policy and Local Security Policy, it does not at this time.

To access the Security Center, go to Start, Control Panel, Security Center. When you open up the Security Center, you will see an interface that looks like Figure 3.8.

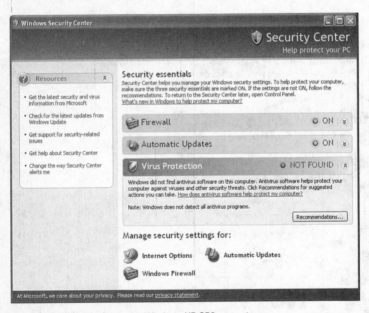

Figure 3.8   Security Center for Windows XP SP2 computers.

The Windows Security Center may not be available if your computer has joined the domain. The Security Center is always available for Windows XP clients that are in a workgroup, but not in a domain. To enable the Security Center for a domain, you will need to enable the setting in a GPO. The setting is located at Computer Configuration, Administrative Templates, Windows Components, Security Center. Here you will find a setting that is named Turn on Security Center (Domain PCs only). Enabling this will allow the XP clients to see the Security Center.

One more feature that the Security Center provides is integration with a virus-checking program. If there isn't an antivirus application installed, the Security Center provides an interface for you to install one, either for a trial period or for purchase. You can also disable the Security Center from monitoring for any antivirus applications if you want to monitor that manually.

Exam Prep Questions

1. You are the administrator for a large company. You have a group of Windows XP Professional computers in a workgroup and want to enable your users to create user and group accounts without giving them excessive rights. How should you configure the users' accounts?

   ○ A. Assign your users to the Local Administrators group on the local machine.

   ○ B. Assign your users to the Server Operators group on the local machine.

   ○ C. Assign your users to the Domain Administrators group in the domain.

   ○ D. Assign your users to the Power Users group on the local machine.

2. Bob took over Mary's duties when Mary retired. You created Bob's user account and put him in the same groups as Mary and changed the ACLS on the resources to allow Bob access. You then deleted Mary's account. Later, Bob comes to you and reports that he can't get access to some resources that he needs that Mary had access to. You give him access, and later he reports the same problem on different resources. How should you have configured Bob's account to avoid the problems you are now facing, without giving Bob unnecessary access?

   ○ A. You should have renamed Mary's account to Bob.

   ○ B. You should have made Bob an administrator in the domain.

   ○ C. You should have made Bob a Server Operator.

   ○ D. You should have changed the DACLS on all resources in the domain to give Bob access.

3. You successfully set the Local Security Policy to enable you to shut down your Windows XP Professional computer without logging on. After joining your computer to the domain, you attempt to shut down your computer without logging on, but the option is not available. Why is the option not available?

   ○ A. The Shutdown Without Logging On option is not available to computers that have joined a domain.

   ○ B. The option in the Local Group Policy no longer applies because the computer is in the domain.

   ○ C. The user needs to be placed in the Local Administrators group for the Local Group Policy to apply.

   ○ D. The Domain Group Policy to Shutdown Without Logging On option is set to disabled.

4. You have enabled auditing on your company's laptops. You want to configure your remote users' laptops to shut down if they are unable to log security events and log all attempts to change Local Group Policies. How should you configure the systems? (Check all correct answers.)

❑ A. Use Security Options in the Local Security settings to set the option to shut down the system if it's unable to log security audits.

❑ B. Configure the Audit Policy Change setting to monitor failed changes.

❑ C. Configure the Audit Policy Change setting to monitor successful changes.

❑ D. Configure the Audit Object Access setting to monitor successful changes.

5. You have 250 Windows XP Professional computers in various OUs in your domain. You want to find out which computer GPOs are being applied to your computers, specifically policies that have been applied in multiple places with a precedence of 1 or higher. What would be the correct syntax to determine this?

○ A. `gpresult /scope user /z`

○ B. `gpresult /scope computer /z`

○ C. `gpresult /scope user /v`

○ D. `gpresult /scope computer /v`

6. You make changes to the local policy on a Windows XP Professional workstation named WKSTN1. You want to refresh only the policy settings that have changed for the computer. What command will you run to accomplish this?

○ A. `gpupdate /target:computer`

○ B. `gpupdate /target:computer /force`

○ C. `gpresult /scope computer`

○ D. `gpresult /scope computer /z`

7. You have made changes to group policy and need to import the new template. What are some different ways to apply these new security template settings to the computers in the enterprise? (Check all correct answers.)

❑ A. Use the `secedit` command.

❑ B. Use an Active Directory–based Group Policy Object.

❑ C. Use the Local Group Policy.

❑ D. Use the `gpupdate` command.

8. You are the administrator of a multidivisional company's network and some of your users are using network applications from a server that may not be approved for their division. All applications are in the same folder. Which software restriction rule would you apply?

○ A. Hash rule

○ B. Certificate rule

○ C. Zone rule

○ D. Path rule

Answers to Exam Prep Questions

1. Answer D is correct. Power Users have the right to create user and group accounts, but they do not have total control over the computer, as an administrator does. Answer A is incorrect because making the users administrators would give them excessive rights. Answer B is incorrect because the Server Operators group does not exist on a Windows XP Professional machine, nor is this group given any privileges on the local system after joining the domain. Answer C is incorrect because, like answer A, it would give the users excessive rights; also, because the machines are in a workgroup, putting them in the Domain Administrators group would have no effect on their capabilities to create users and groups on the local machine.

2. Answer A is correct. Renaming the account would have ensured that Bob had all the access to resources that Mary had. Answer B is incorrect because you would have given Bob more access than was necessary, and it does not ensure that Bob has access to all resources that Mary had. Answer C is incorrect because making Bob a Server Operator does not ensure that Bob has access to all resources that Mary had. Answer D is incorrect because that would have given Bob unnecessary access.

3. Answer D is correct. Local Group Policies are the first to apply of all policies and are overridden by conflicting policy settings that are located at the Active Directory levels. Answer A is incorrect because the option is available at all GPO levels. Answer B is incorrect because Local Group Policies still apply when computers join domains, although they have lower priority. Answer C is incorrect because users don't need to be placed in the Local Administrators group to apply policies after a computer has joined the domain.

4. Answers A, B, and C are correct. You will need to set the option in the Local Security settings to shut down the system if the computer is unable to log security audits, as well as set the Audit Policy Change policy for both success and failure. Answer D is incorrect because auditing object access logs users' access to resources, but not changes to policies.

5. Answer B is correct. The Group Policy Result tool will display the Resultant Set of Policy (RSoP) for a target user and computer. The /Scope switch specifies whether the user or the computer settings need to be displayed. The /z switch specifies that the super-verbose information is to be displayed, which enables you to see whether a setting was set in multiple places. Answer A is incorrect because the scope specified in the syntax is user and you wanted to see computer settings. Answer C is incorrect because the switch /v is used, which will not let you see whether a setting was set in multiple places. This requires super-verbose mode. Answer D is incorrect because of the switch used, as well.

6. Answer A is correct. The Group Policy Update tool refreshes Group Policy settings and has a number of different switches. The /target: switch has two options: Computer or User. By default, both User and Computer policy settings are refreshed if no switch is specified.

Therefore, because you want to refresh only the settings for the computer, you need to specify the option Computer. Answer B is incorrect because the /force switch reapplies all policy settings and you want only the settings that have changed to be refreshed. Answers C and D are incorrect because the gpresult command gives only the Resulting Set of Policies; it does not refresh them in any manner.

7. Answers A, B, and C are correct. The secedit command as well as the Group Policy options at the local and Active Directory level can apply the security templates to a computer. The secedit command is manual, whereas the other two options are more automated because they will automatically refresh for the computer. Answer D is incorrect because gpupdate will update an existing Group Policy, but not apply the security templates themselves.

8. Answer D is correct. A path rule can identify software by a full pathname, such as C:\Program Files\Microsoft Office\Office\excel.exe, or by the pathname leading to the containing folder, such as C:\Windows\System32. Answer A is incorrect because a hash is a digital fingerprint that uniquely identifies a program or file. You would have to identify all the applications' hash. Answer B is incorrect because a certificate rule identifies software by the publisher certificate used to digitally sign the software. The applications may be by different publishers, and you don't want to restrict users' ability to run approved applications. Answer C is incorrect because a zone rule identifies software that comes from the Internet, local intranet, trusted sites, or restricted sites zones. These applications are from a local file server.

Need to Know More?

 Microsoft Corporation. *Microsoft Windows XP Professional Resource Kit*, 2nd ed. Redmond, WA: Microsoft Press, 2003. ISBN 0735619743 This all-in-one reference is a compilation of technical documentation and valuable insider information that computer-support professionals and administrators can reference to install, customize, and support Windows XP.

 Mark Minasi. *Mastering Windows XP Professional*. Alameda, CA: Sybex, Inc., 2001. ISBN 0-78212-981-1. This text gives you all the insider information for the creation of users and groups—and how they interact with a domain. The book also gives a good description of how Group Policies should be used for your XP Professional computer.

Search the TechNet CD (or its online version through www.microsoft.com) and the Windows 2000 Professional Resource Kit CD using the keywords "local user", "SID", "Group Policy Objects", "Local Security Policy", "SDOU", "GPRESULT", "GPUPDATE", and "Microsoft Passport".

4

Implementing and Managing User and Desktop Settings

Terms you'll need to understand:

✓ User profiles
✓ Fast user switching
✓ Offline Files and Folders
✓ MSCONFIG utility
✓ Windows Installer Service
✓ MSI and MST files
✓ ZAP files
✓ Publish and Assign Software
✓ Multilingual User Interface Pack

✓ File Settings and Transfer Wizard
✓ StickyKeys
✓ MouseKeys
✓ Narrator
✓ ClearType
✓ Dualview
✓ Utility Manager
✓ Fax Console
✓ Scheduled Tasks

Techniques you'll need to master:

✓ Configuring Offline Files and Folders options
✓ Implementing Windows Installer Packages
✓ Understanding the functionality of various Control Panel applets
✓ Configuring system startup settings
✓ Implementing software Group Policies
✓ Configuring support for multiple languages
✓ Transferring files and settings between computers

✓ Configuring accessibility options
✓ Setting up Dualview and ClearType display options
✓ Implementing and configuring the Fax service
✓ Configuring and managing tasks with Task Scheduler

Windows XP Professional supports the mobile user community more than ever before. Microsoft addressed several complaints that many users had with Windows NT Workstation 4 under Windows 2000 Professional. Windows XP Professional enhances the mobile user's experience even further. Mobile users of Windows NT Workstation 4 had a difficult job of keeping files on a network file server synchronized with copies they kept on their mobile computer. Windows XP Professional goes a long way toward fixing this problem and others, such as Dynamic Link Library (DLL) conflicts, application repair, and software updates. Also, the user environment has been enhanced and made even more robust in Windows XP Professional by using various control applets.

Configuring and Managing User Profiles

A *user profile* is the look and feel of the user's desktop environment. A profile is a combination of folders, data, shortcuts, application settings, and personal data. For example, users can configure their computer with the screen saver they prefer along with their favorite desktop wallpaper. These settings are independent of other users' settings for a specific local computer. When users log on to their computer for the very first time, a new profile is created for those users from a default user profile. So, when Joe logs on, a profile is created just for Joe. This type of profile is known as a *local profile* and is stored on the computer on which it was created. If Joe logged on to a different computer, his profile would not follow him to the computer he just logged on to. However, you can have a user's profile follow the user around the network if you so choose. This type of profile is called a *roaming user profile*. These profiles are stored on a network server. A local copy of the roaming profile is also found on the client computer.

User Profiles

User profiles in Windows XP employ a similar folder structure as introduced under Windows 2000. This structure is different from the one used with Windows NT 4. One of the folders found within a user's profile is called Local Settings. The Local Settings folder is local to the machine it resides on and does not roam from workstation to workstation when roaming profiles are enabled. Also, a folder called My Documents is contained within a profile. This folder resides in the default location where users' files are saved to disk. The My Documents folder does have the capability to follow users around the network (roam) as they log on to different workstations.

Local Profiles

Windows XP Professional and Windows 2000 Professional local profiles are found in a different location from those in Windows NT 4 Workstation—possibly. If you perform a clean install of Windows XP Professional, a user profile is stored in the root of the system volume in a folder called Documents and Settings\user_logon_name (for example, C:\Documents and Settings\ Joe_User). If, however, you upgrade a Windows NT 4 Workstation to Windows XP Professional, the local profile is stored in the same location as it always was: %SystemRoot%\Profiles\user_logon_name.

Logon Scripts, Home Folders

When a user logs on to a Windows NT domain or to a Windows Active Directory domain from Windows XP Professional, a *logon script* may execute and a *home folder* may be assigned to the user. Logon scripts are often used to map network drives or to execute a batch file. To configure a logon script for a user, perform the following steps on a Windows 2000 Server or on a Windows Server 2003 Active Directory domain controller:

1. Place the logon script in %SystemRoot%\sysvol\<domain name>\ scripts (this is the location for logon scripts for Windows servers acting as domain controllers).

2. Run the Active Directory Users and Computers MMC snap-in, right-click the name of the user, and select Properties. Go to the Profile tab and type the name of the logon script into the Logon Script box.

A home folder is a central location on a network server where users can store their files. All users can have their own home folders to store data. This way, if their workstation fails, they don't lose all their data. Home folders also provide one central location in which users can back up all their data. To create a home folder, perform the following steps on a Windows 2000 Server or on a Windows Server 2003 server:

1. Create a shared folder on the network server to enable home folders.

2. Run the Active Directory Users and Computers MMC snap-in, right-click the name of the user, and select Properties. Go to the Profile tab and click the Connect option button.

3. Click the drop-down arrow and choose an available drive letter.

4. Type in the Uniform Naming Convention (UNC) path to the user's home folder (for example, \\server1\homedir\dan).

Microsoft suggests that users store their data in My Documents. You can then enable a Group Policy under Active Directory to redirect My Documents from the local computer to the user's home folder. The Group Policy also activates offline caching of My Documents to the user's local computer. Group Policy as well as Offline Files and Folders are covered later in this chapter.

Roaming User Profiles

If you have users who move from computer to computer, you can configure their profiles to move with them. A roaming profile is stored on a network server so that the profile is accessible regardless of which computer a user logs on to anywhere within the domain. You can put the profile on the server in two ways. You can copy a profile that is stored locally on a client computer to the profile server the next time the user logs on to the computer. Or you can create on a client computer a profile that you will use as a company standard and then manually copy it to the profile server.

 Roaming user profiles behave differently in Windows XP and Windows 2000 than in Windows NT 4 Workstation. When a user logs on to a computer for the first time, the roaming profile is copied to the client computer. From that point forward, whenever a user logs on to a computer, the locally cached copy of the profile is compared to the roaming user profile. If the local profile and the roaming profile are the same, the local copy is used. Windows XP copies only files that have changed, not the entire profile, as was the case in Windows NT 4.

Use the following steps to configure a roaming profile:

1. Create a shared folder on a server for the profiles.

2. On a Windows XP Professional computer, open the Control Panel, select Performance and Maintenance, and then open the System icon to view the System Properties dialog box.

3. Click the Advanced tab.

4. From the User Profiles section, click the Settings button.

5. Select the user's profile you want to use as a roaming profile and select Copy To. Then type in the UNC path to the shared folder that was created (for example, \\server1\profiles\Dan or \\server1\profiles\%username%).

 The user's profile must be one that was generated from logging on with a domain user account. Local user accounts can't be used as roaming profiles.

6. In the Active Directory Users and Computers MMC, select the account properties for the user. Then select the Profile tab and enter the UNC path to the profile server in the Profile Path field.

7. The first time that the roaming user successfully logs on and then subsequently logs off from a Windows XP workstation, the user's profile is uploaded to the profile server and stored. The next time that the user logs on to the network, the roaming profile is compared with the user's local profile and the most recent profile is used (see Figure 4.1).

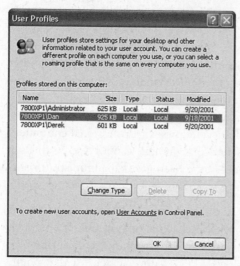

Figure 4.1   The User Profiles dialog box.

 In Windows XP, if you create a roaming profile on an NTFS drive volume by using the **%username%** variable, the user and the built-in local Administrators group are assigned Full Control permission of that directory.

 Local or roaming profiles are protected from permanent change by renaming NTUSER.DAT to NTUSER.MAN. By renaming the file, you have effectively made the profile read-only, meaning that Windows XP does not save any changes made to the profile when the user logs off. NTUSER.DAT is found in the root of a profile and is hidden by default. This file is responsible for the user portion of the Registry and contains all the user settings.

Managing User Profiles Behavior Through Group Policy

Windows XP offers several useful Group Policy settings for working with User Profiles. When you load the Group Policy snap-in for the MMC, expand Computer Configuration, Administrative Templates, System, and then click User Profiles. The settings for User Profiles include Delete Cached Copies of Roaming Profiles so that they won't be stored on the local computer. The Log Users Off When Roaming Profile Fails setting prohibits users from logging on unless their roaming profile is available. Another setting, Prevent Roaming Profile Changes from Propagating to the Server, will not allow any changes to roaming profiles centrally stored on a server. This setting is an excellent option for computers that have multiple users sharing the same profile.

Fast User Switching

Fast User Switching is a new feature in Windows XP. This feature supports switching between multiple users on the same Windows XP computer *without* requiring each user to exit from their applications when they log off. In a standalone or workgroup environment, Windows XP Professional implements Fast User Switching by default. Windows XP Professional computers that are members of a Windows network domain cannot use Fast User Switching. Only users whose accounts have been granted administrator status may enable or disable this feature.

When Fast User Switching is turned on, users may click Start, Log Off and they are presented with two options: Switch User or Log Off. If you click Switch User, any applications that are currently running remain running, and you are returned to the Windows XP Welcome Screen. At that point, another user may log on to the system to work. Multiple users can log on to the computer, one at a time. The application programs that were running when each user is "switched out" continue to execute while another user works on the computer. To enable or disable Fast User Switching, click Start, Control Panel, User Accounts, and select the option Change the Way Users Log On or Off. You must enable Use the Welcome Screen if you want to turn on Fast User Switching.

Using Offline Files

Windows XP offers an improved Offline Files feature as compared to Windows 2000. Also known as *Client-Side Caching (CSC)*, Offline Files under Windows XP addresses several file access problems that plagued Windows NT, such as if the file server is down and users need to access files on the file server, or when users are not connected to the network and they cannot get access to the files they may need. By using Offline Files, users can select files on a network file server and mark them for offline usage. This means that users now have a cached copy of the file on their local computer and can work on the file just as if they were connected to the network. Any offline files that have been changed on a local computer are synchronized with the network file server when the users reconnect to the network.

Setting Up Offline Files and Folders

In Windows XP, the Offline Files feature cannot be turned on if Fast User Switching is enabled, as shown in Figure 4.2. You must go to User Accounts in the Windows XP Control Panel and choose the option Change the Way Users Log On or Off. After Fast User Switching has been disabled, two steps are involved in configuring Offline Files. The first is to configure the share point for offline usage. The second is to cache the files to the client computer.

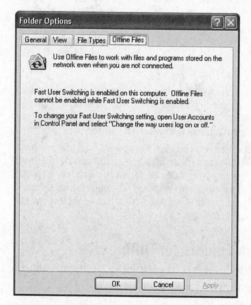

Figure 4.2   The Folder Options dialog box.

Configuring Share Points on a Windows 2000 Server or on a Windows Server 2003 Server

Use the following steps to configure a network shared folder for Offline Files:

1. Share the folder(s) that you want to make available offline.

2. From the Sharing tab, select the Caching button.

3. Select the Allow Caching of Files in This Shared Folder option (this option is selected by default).

4. Select one of the following three options from the Settings drop-down list and then click OK:

   ➤ Manual Caching for Documents—Requires users to select the files they want available for offline usage. This is the default setting.

   ➤ Automatic Caching for Documents—Caches all files that users have opened to their local disk for offline usage. Any older files that are out of synchronization are automatically deleted and replaced by a newer version of the same file.

   ➤ Automatic Caching for Programs—Provides the same capabilities as Automatic Caching for Documents but also caches applications that are run from the network.

5. Click OK to close the Sharing dialog box and to accept the options that you selected.

By default, Windows XP does not allow you to cache files with the **.slm**, **.ldb**, **.mdw**, **.mdb**, **.mde**, **.pst**, and **.db** extensions. However, you can override this setting through a Group Policy. Create a Group Policy for **Computer Configuration\ Administrative templates\Network\Offline Files\Files not cached**.

This policy is meant to exclude files with specific file extensions from being cached. However, if the policy is enabled and no file extensions are added, all file types can be made available offline. This setting overrides the default configuration; it allows files with the previously listed extensions to be cached. You must log off and then log back on for the new settings to take effect. Microsoft recommends that you do not modify the default settings for Offline Files.

Configuring Shared Network Folders for Offline Use

Use the following steps under Windows XP to configure a network-shared folder for making files available offline for remote users:

1. From the My Computer window, select Tools, Folder Options, and click the Offline Files tab to enable Offline Files.

2. Mark the Enable Offline Files check box.

3. Select or deselect any of the other options as you deem appropriate.

4. For increased security of offline data, mark the Encrypt Offline Files to Secure Data check box as shown in Figure 4.3. This is a new feature of Windows XP. Enabling Offline Files encryption is considered a best practice by Microsoft.

5. Share each folder that you want to make available offline.

Figure 4.3   The Folder Options dialog box displaying the Offline Files options.

6. From the Sharing tab, select the Caching button.

7. Select the Allow Caching of Files in This Shared Folder option (this option is selected by default).

8. Select one of the three options from the Settings drop-down list, as outlined previously, and then click OK.

The Offline Files feature cannot be turned on if Fast User Switching is enabled, as shown previously in Figure 4.2. You must go to User Accounts in the Windows XP Control Panel and choose the option Change the Way Users Log On or Off.

Making Files and Folders Available Offline

By default, a Windows XP Professional computer is configured for offline file and folder usage. Use the following steps to make a file or folder available offline:

1. Connect to a share point on a domain or workgroup file server. Right-click a file that you want to use offline and select Make Available Offline (see Figure 4.4).

2. A wizard appears if you are using this feature for the first time, asking whether offline files should be synchronized during logon and logoff. Click Next to accept the default. (Additional options are available after the wizard is finished.)

Figure 4.4 The right-click menu for a file displays the Make Available Offline option when Offline File Caching is enabled.

3. If you want the operating system to remind you that you are not connected to the network, click the Finish button to accept the default option, Enable Reminders. If you accept this option, a computer icon appears in the system tray. Whenever you are disconnected from the network, a balloon appears, notifying you that offline files are available.

After you have completed these steps, a small double-arrow icon appears on the file or folder that you have selected for offline usage. This is a graphical indicator to inform users that the file is located on the network and that a local cached copy of the file is located on their computer.

 Windows NT 4 Workstation does not support offline file caching. However, a Windows XP Professional client can make files available for offline usage from a Windows NT 4 share. When using a Windows XP computer, you can make network files available offline from any remote computer that supports Server Message Block (SMB)-based file sharing, such as Windows 9x, Windows NT 4, Windows 2000, Windows Server 2003, and Windows XP computers.

To view offline files after you are disconnected from the network, open My Network Places or go directly to the drive letter that you typically use to access the files. Yes, that is correct. Offline files maintain their original location even though the computer is offline. Go to My Network Places and select the file server that contains the files. You can see only the files that you made available while offline. Users don't see the "network" while they are offline (see Figure 4.5).

 Under the Windows 2000 Server and Windows Server 2003 family of network operating systems, the Offline Files feature is not available if the server has Terminal Services installed. This holds true whether you are working directly from the console of the Terminal Server or through a Terminal Services session. However, clients can still connect to any Terminal Server and make the files stored on that server available offline from their local workstations.

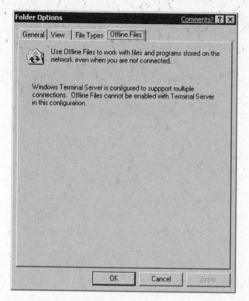

Figure 4.5   The Offline Files tab of the Folder Options dialog box from a Windows Terminal Server computer.

Synchronizing Offline Files and Folders

After you have worked on one or more offline files while you have been away or disconnected from your network, you can reestablish a network connection and log on to the network. Any changes that you made to the file(s) while you were offline are then synchronized with the original file(s) on the network. One caveat: If you have logged on to the network from a slow dial-up connection, it could take a long time to synchronize your offline files while you are logging on.

Several options are available to customize the synchronization process to deal with this type of problem. To customize the process when offline files are synchronized, open a Windows Explorer window and select Tools, Synchronize from the toolbar menu. The first dialog box displays the files and folders that are available offline. To configure synchronization, click the Setup button, which opens the Synchronization Settings dialog box, shown in Figure 4.6.

This dialog box offers three tabs that help you determine when you should synchronize offline files: Logon/Logoff, On Idle, and Scheduled. However, you can also select over what network connection synchronization takes place. For example, to have synchronization occur only when you are connected to the network (versus when you have a slow dial-up connection), select LAN Connection in the When I Am Using This Network Connection drop-down list.

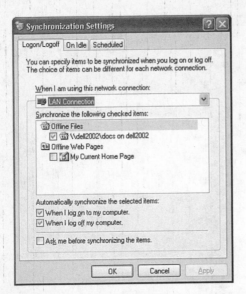

Figure 4.6 The Synchronization Settings dialog box.

Synchronization Details

Now that you have configured synchronization, you are probably wondering what actually happens during this process. Well, that depends. The following are several synchronization scenarios:

➤ An offline file has been deleted and the original network version of the file has not changed. If this happens, Windows XP Professional removes the file from the network file server during synchronization.

➤ A network file has been deleted and the offline version of the file has not changed. If this happens, Windows XP Professional presents a dialog box of this state and gives you the option to either remove the file from the local computer during synchronization or keep the local version.

➤ The offline file has changed and the network version has changed. If this happens, you are presented with a dialog box during the synchronization; it asks you what should be done. The options are to keep the network version, to keep the local version, and to keep both and rename the local version.

➤ Only files that have changed are synchronized. If no changes have occurred, the locally cached copied is used before the network version of the offline file.

Accessing Offline Files and Folders

To access offline files, use My Network Places; however, that is not where the files are actually kept. Offline files are kept in %SystemRoot%\CSC (CSC is hidden by default). This directory contains a database of the offline files. You cannot view or edit individual files from this location. However, if the CSC directory gets quite large and if you use offline files frequently, it is advisable to move this directory from the system partition to a different partition or drive. However, you can't move this directory using Windows Explorer. To move the CSC directory from one partition to another, use the Windows 2000 Resource Kit utility named Cachemov.exe. You may also use the Cachemov.exe tool from the Windows 2000 or Windows Server 2003 Resource Kits as an alternative.

Managing Offline Files and Folders

To manage offline files, open a Windows Explorer window and select Tools, Folder Options, and then select the Offline Files tab. The key options for managing offline folders are the following: turn off the Offline Files feature, delete offline files, and view all the offline files in one window. You can also use a sliding bar to control the amount of disk space made available for files that have been automatically cached to the local drive. The default disk space made available for automatically cached files is 10 percent.

Configuring and Troubleshooting Desktop Settings

The Windows XP Professional desktop combines the best features of Windows 98, Windows ME, and Windows 2000. In general, a regular local or domain user account can configure very few changes on a Windows XP Professional computer. The options that users can configure to customize their desktop are the following Control Panel applets and customization options (see Figure 4.7):

- ➤ Keyboard
- ➤ Display
- ➤ Mouse
- ➤ Sounds and Audio Devices
- ➤ Scanners and Cameras
- ➤ Speech
- ➤ Taskbar and Start Menu
- ➤ Wireless Network Setup Wizard

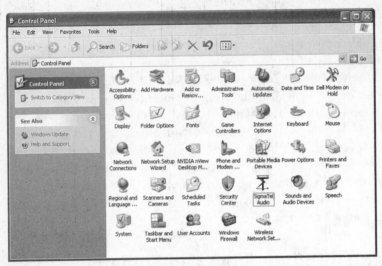

Figure 4.7   The Windows XP Professional Control Panel.

Keyboard Applet

The Keyboard applet adjusts the cursor blink rate, the speed at which a character repeats when you hold down a key, the time lapse before a character repeats, and the input locale for different language groups of keyboard hardware. For example, you can use several language locales with a U.S. keyboard layout so that you can add foreign accent marks to documents that are written in French, Spanish, Italian, and so on. The Regional applet can also be used to configure Input Locales.

Display Applet

The Display applet has changed a bit from Windows 2000. You can now choose from five tabs to affect various aspects of the display:

➤ Themes—Enables the user to choose from various Windows XP desktop themes to customize the graphical user experience. Themes comprise a background for the desktop plus a set of sounds, icons, and associated other elements that serve to personalize a Windows XP computer.

➤ Desktop—Enables the user to select a background wallpaper or a background color for the Windows XP desktop. By clicking the Customize Desktop button, you can choose which icons are displayed on the desktop (the default is Recycle Bin only), modify the graphic for each icon, and run or schedule the Desktop Cleanup Wizard to move unused desktop items to a folder that you select.

➤ Screen Saver—Selects a screen saver but is also a shortcut to the Power Options applet. The Power button on the Screen Saver tab enables you to adjust power schemes and configure Standby and Hibernate modes.

➤ Appearance—Adjusts the window and button styles along with the color and font schemes that are displayed in all dialog boxes and windows. The Effects button gives the user the capability to turn on or off various effects such as menu and tooltip transitions, menu shadowing, and showing window contents while dragging. The Advanced button enables you to highly customize the color and fonts for the Windows XP environment.

➤ Settings—Enables the user to set the screen resolution and the color quality for the display adapter. If you encounter problems with the video display, you can click the Troubleshoot button to invoke the Video Display Troubleshooter. If Windows XP doesn't detect a Plug and Play monitor, it assigns default color depths and resolutions. By clicking the Advanced button, you can adjust several properties for the video display and the display adapter, such as whether to apply new settings without restarting, adjusting the display mode, changing the refresh rate, altering hardware acceleration, and working with color management.

Mouse Applet

The Mouse applet adjusts for left-handed or right-handed use. It also adjusts the double-click speed and the rate at which the cursor moves across the screen.

Sounds and Audio Devices Applet

The Sounds and Audio Devices applet controls sounds for startup, logoff, and other Windows events. It also controls what WAV files are used for critical error alerts and general alerts. You can modify the default devices for voice playback and voice recording as well as work with the properties of various sound and audio hardware that may be installed on a particular PC.

Scanners and Cameras Applet

The Scanners and Cameras applet enables you to manage scanned and photographic images. It also can help you to install a digital camera, a scanner, or another image device that Windows XP Plug and Play may have been unable to detect. To install an image device, you must be an administrative user.

Speech Applet

The Speech applet invokes the Speech Properties dialog box in which you can control the text-to-speech voice selection, preview the voice selection, and specify the voice speed. You can also click the Audio Output button to specify the preferred audio output device and volume level.

Taskbar and Start Menu Applet

The Taskbar and Start Menu applet gives you control over the appearance and behavior of both the taskbar and the Windows XP Start menu. Launching the Taskbar and Start Menu icon from the Control Panel invokes the Taskbar and Start Menu Properties dialog box, illustrated in Figure 4.8. You can also access the Taskbar and Start Menu Properties dialog box by right-clicking a blank area on the taskbar and selecting Properties or by right-clicking a blank area on the Start menu itself and selecting Properties.

Figure 4.8 The Taskbar and Start Menu Properties dialog box.

Windows XP follows in the footsteps of Windows 2000 by making it much easier to arrange and customize the Start menu items than under previous versions of Windows. You can very easily sort menu items by dragging and dropping them. You can drag a menu item from one submenu to another.

Also, you can open pop-up menus by right-clicking them. Windows XP automatically adjusts menu items as well. Windows XP does not attempt to clean up the Start menu by displaying only those items that are used most frequently, as is the case with Windows 2000. However, if you select Classic Start Menu, Use Personalized Menus is enabled by default and items on the Start menu that are not used often are hidden. You can turn off this feature quite easily: Right-click a blank area on the Start menu and select the Properties option. Doing so displays the Start Menu tab of the Taskbar and Start Menu Properties dialog box. Click the Customize button for the Classic Start Menu option to display the Customize Classic Start Menu dialog box. Deselect the option for Use Personalized Menus.

 All questions on the exam will assume that the new Windows XP desktop and environment is being used.

You can find even more customization options when you click the Customize button for either the Start menu or the Classic Start menu on the Start Menu tab of the Taskbar and Start Menu Properties dialog box, as shown in Figure 4.9. On the Advanced tab of the Customize Start Menu dialog box, available options include having submenus open when you pause the mouse pointer over a parent menu item and having newly installed programs highlighted on the Start menu.

The following is a list of the Start menu features and items that you can customize from the Advanced tab of the Customize Start Menu dialog box:

➤ Control Panel

➤ Drag and Drop

➤ Favorites menu

➤ Help and Support

➤ My Computer

➤ My Documents

➤ My Music

➤ My Network Places

➤ My Pictures

➤ Network Connections

➤ Printers and Faxes

➤ Run command

➤ Scroll Programs

➤ Search

➤ System Administrative Tools

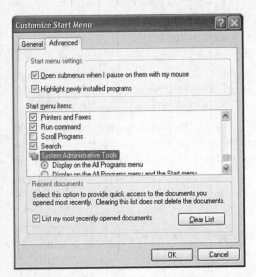

Figure 4.9 The Advanced tab of the Customize Start Menu dialog box.

Other Taskbar Options

The taskbar serves as a multipurpose tool to help make navigating the interface more efficient. The taskbar in Windows XP, similar to that in Windows 2000, offers several customization options. One of the new options for the taskbar is the Group Similar Taskbar Buttons check box, located on the Taskbar tab of the Taskbar and Start Menu Properties dialog box. This option keeps similar opened documents and files together on the taskbar while you are working on them. In addition, if the taskbar becomes too crowded with buttons, this option will automatically group all the same applications into a single button on the taskbar. When you click a grouped taskbar button, you can choose from a pop-up list of all the currently open documents for that group. When you right-click a blank area on the taskbar, you can view many customization choices. One of the available selections is Lock the Taskbar. If you select Lock The Taskbar, you cannot move or size it—it remains stationary.

The Toolbars option enables you to add one or more toolbars to the taskbar for quick access to frequently used features or applications. The available toolbars are the following:

➤ Address—Adds an Address box for entering URLs on the taskbar.

➤ Links—Adds the default Links for Internet Explorer 6 that ship with Windows XP as well as any custom links that you create.

➤ Desktop—Adds icons such as My Documents, My Computer, and My Network Places to the taskbar that by default appear on the desktop under Windows 2000 and Windows 9x.

➤ Quick Launch—Adds three icons (by default) that contain shortcuts to programs that you use most frequently. Under Windows XP, the default Quick Launch toolbar places the Show Desktop (minimizes all windows, even modal dialog boxes), Internet Explorer, and Windows Media shortcuts onto the Quick Launch Pad. You can add or remove shortcuts simply by dragging and dropping them on or off the Quick Launch toolbar.

➤ New Toolbar—Enables you to add your own items to a custom toolbar for placement on the taskbar.

Wireless Network Setup Wizard

The Wireless Network Setup Wizard applet enables you to quickly configure your wireless network. You have the ability to configure the network name (SSID) and control network keys for either WEP or WPA.

Troubleshooting and System Settings

Windows XP sports several new and enhanced troubleshooting and system configuration utilities. By combining the best of Windows 9x and Windows NT/2000, Microsoft now integrates into one product tools that had been available only under Windows 9x and other utilities that had been available only under Windows NT/2000.

The **MSCONFIG.EXE** Utility

The MSCONFIG.EXE tool has been available under Windows 98 and Windows ME, but never under Windows NT/2000. MSCONFIG can be a very useful tool because it combines several important configuration settings into one central utility. By default, no preconfigured icon exists for this tool. You can launch it from a command window or from the Start, Run box by typing **MSCONFIG** and clicking OK. The file itself is located in %SystemRoot%\windows\pchealth\helpctr\binaries. A user does not need administrative privileges to run this program. The System Configuration Utility is divided into six tabs (as shown in Figure 4.10):

➤ General—Enables you to work with system startup settings, the
`Boot.ini` file, and the System Restore feature, and enables you to
expand Windows XP setup files from compressed cabinet files.

➤ SYSTEM.INI—Enables you to directly edit the `System.ini` file instead
of using Notepad or the SYSEDIT utility.

➤ WIN.INI—Enables you to directly edit the `Win.ini` file instead of using
Notepad or the SYSEDIT utility.

➤ BOOT.INI—Enables you to manipulate the system's `Boot.ini` file, but
does not allow you to actually edit the line-item entries. You can change
the default operating system, modify the Timeout setting, verify all boot
paths, and select from several predefined boot options, such as
`/SAFEBOOT`, `/NOGUIBOOT`, `/BOOTLOG`, `/BASEVIDEO` (standard VGA), and `/SOS`
(display system device drivers as they load into memory). You also have
the capability to set advanced options such as `/MAXMEM`, `/NUMPROC`,
`/PCILOCK`, and `/DEBUG` (see Figure 4.11).

Figure 4.10 The General tab of the MSCONFIG utility.

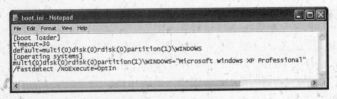

Figure 4.11 The BOOT.INI file.

➤ Services—Displays a listing of all installed services and their current status (stopped or running) on the Windows XP computer. You can enable
or disable each service for the next time the computer is restarted.

➤ Startup—Lists the programs and utilities that are configured to run at system startup. You can enable or disable each startup item to take effect at the next system restart.

There are four new boot.ini switches that are related to the DEP feature. As you can see in Figure 4.11, one of them is already configured by default with the installation of SP2. The switches include the following:

➤ OptIn—This is configured by default and is enabled on computers that have processors that can implement hardware-enforced DEP. The protection is for some system binaries and programs that "opt-in."

➤ OptOut—This is enabled by default for all applications and is typically not disabled.

➤ AlwaysOn—This setting can provide protection for the entire system.

➤ AlwaysOff—This setting will disable DEP for the entire system.

Application Program Compatibility Support

Applications that worked under earlier versions of Windows may fail to operate properly under Windows XP for any one of a variety of reasons: A program may expect older formats of Windows data, or it may expect user information, such as that in personal and temporary folders, to be in specific locations or formats. These types of compatibility issues mostly concern applications developed for Windows 95, 98, or ME, but some applications written for Windows NT 4 or Windows 2000 may also be affected.

To better support legacy applications, Microsoft has built application compatibility support directly into Windows XP. The OS uses a set of legacy application database files both to alert users about compatibility issues when a legacy program is being installed and to support the proper functionality of legacy applications when they are used. The Windows XP compatibility database files are as follows:

➤ MigDB.inf—Used to support migration from Windows 95–, Windows 98–, and Windows Me–based systems. This file contains matching information and flags applications that are incompatible or that require user intervention prior to system upgrade.

➤ NTCompat.inf—Contains the same kinds of information as MigDB, but is used to support upgrades from Windows NT 4 and Windows 2000 systems (see Figure 4.12).

Figure 4.12   The Program Compatibility Wizard.

➤ SysMain.sdb—Contains both matching information and compatibility fixes. It is found in the %Windir%\AppPatch folder.

➤ AppHelp.sdb—Stores only the Help messages that prompt users for patches, provides them with a URL from which to download non-Microsoft patches, or tells them where to find further information. This file is also found in the %Windir%\AppPatch folder.

A compatibility check is performed during the installation of Windows XP Professional. This check serves to warn the user of any serious compatibility problems *before* the setup routine is complete. Problematic applications are listed along with hardware compatibility information in the upgrade report generated by the setup program. Windows XP compatibility support consists of three modes:

➤ End-user modes—Accessible via the Compatibility tab on the Properties dialog box for an application program shortcut or from the Program Compatibility Wizard. You can access the Program Compatibility Wizard by clicking Start, All Programs, Accessories, Program Compatibility Wizard. Users can access six basic modes through the GUI: Windows 95, Windows 98/Windows Me, Windows NT 4 with Service Pack 5, Windows 2000, Run in 256 Colors, and Run in 640×480 Screen Resolution (see Figure 4.13).

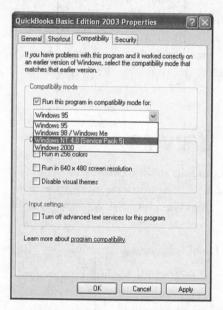

Figure 4.13 The Compatibility tab for a program shortcut's Properties dialog box.

➤ System modes—These include all the end-user modes listed plus a few other options that independent software vendors (ISVs), system administrators, and other IT professionals can use to control the behavior of their applications. These include the Limited User Account security mode and the Profiles mode. The Limited User Account mode is used when an application must operate under a limited security context for a particular user. The Profiles mode can be used to assist an application in determining how to interact with Windows XP user profiles. They can all be accessed and set using either the QFixApp or CompatAdmin tool, both of which are available from Microsoft.

➤ Custom modes—These modes can be created by a system administrator for a particular application or set of applications using the CompatAdmin tool. After they are created, custom modes can apply only to the specific application that the user is installing and can use any specific fix in that package.

Configuring Application Compatibility Settings

You can work with application compatibility settings from the GUI in one of two ways: use the Compatibility tab on the properties sheet for a program's executable file or its shortcut icon or run the Program Compatibility Wizard. Click Start, All Programs, Accessories, Program Compatibility Wizard to launch this tool. The wizard leads you through all the option settings for running an older application under Windows XP. The wizard even prompts you to test the application so that you can verify that it runs correctly. When you complete the wizard, it saves the compatibility settings as part of the program's properties, which you can access by right-clicking the program's executable file, selecting Properties, and clicking the Compatibility tab.

Windows Installer Service

Microsoft created a new method for installing applications under Windows 2000 called *Windows Installer Service Packages*. This software installation service is integrated into Windows XP. Windows Installer Service actually installs packages on a computer.

Windows Installer Service has two essential functions:

➤ It is an operating system service that is responsible for installing, removing, and updating software by asking the Windows Installer Service Package for instructions on how the application should be installed, removed, modified, or repaired.

➤ To create a standard for installing, removing, or modifying applications, you use an application programming interface (API) to communicate with Windows Installer Service about how a package should be modified after an application is installed.

After an application has been installed, Windows Installer Service checks the state of the application while it is being launched. This service provides self-healing capabilities to applications if they were installed as a Windows Installer Service Package. The service is always checking to see if the application needs to be repaired.

The self-healing capability of MSI packages can only replace missing files; it can't repair corrupt files. The only way to fix corrupt files is to manually replace the files or reinstall the application.

The service also helps to resolve DLL conflicts. Windows XP has devised a way to allow an application to alter the location from which DLLs are loaded, instead of having all DLLs located in the system32 directory. This helps to protect DLLs from being overwritten and from other conflicts.

Key parts of an application have a protected tag on them. A Windows Installer Service Package lists critical files that you would need to replace if they were deleted or missing. For example, executables are listed as critical files. If, for example, App1.exe was deleted, Windows Installer Service would locate App1.exe from a network server or ask the user to insert the CD-ROM that contains App1.exe. After locating App1.exe, it would be installed and the application would launch.

Windows Installer Service does a much better job of removing applications compared to previous versions of Windows. During the installation of an application, Windows Installer Service sits in the background looking at everything that is installed, where everything is installed, and what has been changed during the installation. When it comes time to uninstall an application, Windows Installer Service knows exactly where every last component of the application is, thereby successfully uninstalling the application.

If during the installation of an application something happens and the install fails, Windows Installer Service can restart the installation from the point of failure. That may not always be the best solution, though. Windows Installer Service can also roll back everything that was installed up to the point of failure, enabling the user to start the install from scratch.

Installing Packages

A Windows Installer Package (MSI file) contains all the information necessary to tell Windows Installer Service how the application should be installed. To take advantage of the features that Windows Installer Service offers, you must install an application as an MSI file. Applications such as Microsoft Office 2000 and Office XP have their own MSI files. Software developers must design their applications to use this new service. However, existing applications can still gain some of the functionality that MSI files have to offer.

An application can repackage existing applications using third-party tools such as WinInstall LE, which is available on the Windows 2000 Professional CD-ROM but does not ship on the Windows XP Professional CD-ROM. The full-featured version, WinInstall, is published by Veritas Software. This application tracks the installation process and notes all the files that were installed, their locations, and modifications they made to the Registry. You can then customize this information and turn it into an MSI file.

A Microsoft Transform file (MST) can be used to modify and customize a MSI file installation using tools such as those found in the Microsoft Office Resource Kit. MST files contain the customizations; MSI files themselves should never be altered. An MSP file is a Microsoft Windows Installer Patch file used for deploying bug fixes or service releases of a software product.

Patch files cannot remove components or features, change product codes, or remove or change the names of shortcuts, files, or Registry keys. Application assignment scripts (AAS files) contain instructions associated with the publication or assignment of a Windows Installer Package.

You may be wondering what to do if you don't have an MSI file or if you can't repackage the file. Non-Windows Installer–based applications such as Install.exe and Setup.exe must use a ZAP file to publish a package. A ZAP file is just a text file with a .zap extension. The file provides information about how to install a program and the application's properties. ZAP files can only be published, not assigned. ZAP files cannot utilize the advanced features of using MSI files. ZAP file installations cannot use elevated installation privileges, take advantage of the unsuccessful installation rollback feature, or implement the Install on First Use Feature. The following is a basic example of how to create a ZAP file:

```
[application]
FriendlyName= "WinZip Version 7.0"
SetupCommand= \\server1\apps\winzip\WinZip70.EXE
DisplayVersion = 7.0
[ext]
ZIP =
```

Publishing MSI Packages

You typically install MSI files over the network or locally on the client computer. A common method for installing MSI files in a Windows Active Directory domain environment is to publish or assign applications to users through Active Directory. Users (and computers) in Active Directory can be grouped into organizational units (OUs). You can create a Group Policy Object (GPO) and link it to an OU that either publishes or assigns MSI files. If targeted to user accounts, any user accounts in the OU would then receive the software when users log on to their Windows XP Professional computers.

Using Group Policy to Publish or Assign Windows Installer Packages

Network administrators use GPOs to publish or assign application programs. When you *publish* a software application using a GPO, you are making it available to one or more users, and the published application will follow the user(s) from workstation to workstation within an Active Directory domain. Users install a published application from the Add/Remove Programs icon in the Windows Control Panel or when they attempt to open a file with a file extension that is registered to that application (such as sheet1.xls, which would be associated with Microsoft Excel). You can publish an application only to users. When you assign a software application using a GPO, you are placing an icon for that application on the Start menu and associating its file extensions. You can assign applications to both computers and users. An assigned application actually gets installed the first time that a user opens the assigned program or attempts to open a file with a file extension that is registered to that application.

Windows Installer Packages are published or assigned to users through an Active Directory–based Group Policy. Perform the following steps to create a software installation Group Policy:

1. On an Active Directory domain controller, open Active Directory Users and Computers.

2. Select the domain to deploy the software to all users in the domain, or select a specific OU to deploy software to users just in that OU.

3. Right-click the domain or OU and choose Properties.

4. Select the Group Policy tab.

5. Click the New button to create a new Group Policy. Type a name for the Group Policy and press Enter.

6. Select the policy and then click Edit.

7. Under User Configuration, expand Software Settings. Next, right-click Software Installation and select New, Package.

8. Type the UNC path to the .MSI package on the network (for example, \\server1\ officeXP\proplus.msi, the MSI file for Microsoft Office XP Professional with Front Page).

9. Select either Published or Assigned from the Deploy Software dialog box and then click OK.

If you are using a transform, you must select Advanced Published or Assigned. You can't add an MST file to an existing deployment package using the GPO interface. (You can create a transform to install only specific applications from a software suite of applications or to customize the installation.)

10. Close the Group Policy Console and click the Close button for the OU Properties dialog box.

The software Group Policy will take effect when the users of the domain or the OU log on to the network. The users can then install the software. Software deployment through a GPO can be initiated for computer accounts only when the computer is rebooted and for user accounts when the user logs off and back on.

Publishing Applications

A software package is typically published to users when it is not mandatory that they have a particular application installed on their computer. This is a means to make the applications available for users if they decide they want to use them. After you have created a GPO to publish a software package, you can log on to your computer and use the Add or Remove Programs applet in the Windows XP Control Panel to find any applications that were published.

Select the Add New Programs button to see which applications have been published. Users can install a published application with user credentials. Windows Installer Service installs the published application with elevated privileges on behalf of users. This method provides a central location for users to install applications. This saves users from having to search for network-shared folders that contain applications they want to install.

Assigning Applications

Assigning an application is very similar to publishing one. When an application has been assigned, you can install it from Add or Remove Programs. Additionally, a shortcut for the application that has been assigned is placed on the Start, All Programs menu when users log on to their computer. The software does not get installed until users select the shortcut for the first time.

 Software that has been published or assigned is also installed if users double-click a file with the extension supported by the published or assigned application.

Repairing Applications

Windows Installer Service maintains configuration information on each application installed via the Windows Installer. The MSIEXEC.exe program can repair an application in the event that one or more of an application's files become damaged or deleted. MSIEXEC.exe offers several command-line switches. The default option, if no switches are specified on the command line, is /fpecms. For more details on using MSIEXEC.exe, go to the Windows XP Professional Help and Support Center (the Windows XP help system) and search on MSIEXEC.

The syntax for the repair options for MSIEXEC.exe is

```
MSIEXEC /f [p] [o] [e] [d] [c] [a] [u] [m] [s] [v]
➥filename.msi [ProductCode]
```

The commands in brackets are optional.

The syntax for advertising an MSI application is **MSIEXEC /j**, **MSIEXEC /ju** to advertise to the current user, or **MSIEXEC /jm** to advertise to all users of the computer. To apply a transform file (**MST**) to the installation, specify the **/t** switch on the command line. To write all installation errors to a log file, add the **/L*v logfile.txt** option to the command line.

Multiple-Language Support and Regional Options

Windows XP offers excellent support for multiple languages. It enables you to support people and companies that need to communicate in different languages by adding installed services for each input language that you need supported. Installed services include the input language and the keyboard layout for that input language. In addition, the Multilingual User Interface (MUI) Pack for Windows XP lets administrators or users specify the language for the user interface for any of the 33 supported languages. If your organization operates in a single language other than English, you can deploy one of 24 localized versions of Windows XP Professional. For example, if you are responsible for maintaining PC desktops in a company that operates only in French, you could obtain the French-localized version of Windows XP Professional. Your users would still have support to view, edit, and print in hundreds of languages, but the interface would be available only in French.

Windows XP Multilingual User Interface Pack

The MUI Pack is an add-on to the English version of Windows XP Professional and is available only via volume licensing programs to corporate users. The Windows XP MUI Pack eases the deployment and maintenance of multilingual computing environments by helping administrators to define a single corporate standard for desktops worldwide, enabling administrators to apply service packs or updates one time for all supported language environments, and allowing workstations to be shared by users who speak different languages. The MUI Pack also supports users logging on anywhere and getting the user interface in their own language.

Language Options

All versions of Windows XP Professional offer support for editing documents in multiple languages. Users or administrators can install Complex Script and Right-to-Left or East Asian language options as needed. All editions of Windows XP provide support for editing documents in several languages, and the world's languages have been categorized by Microsoft into three major Language Collections: Basic Collection, Complex Script Collection, and East Asian Collection. The Basic Collection includes support for languages spoken in Western and Central Europe and the United States, along with support for Baltic, Greek, Cyrillic, and Turkic languages. The Complex Script Collection is optionally installed depending on the localized language version of Windows XP and includes complex script support and right-to-left languages such as Thai, Hebrew, Arabic, Vietnamese, and Armenian. The East Asian Collection is always installed on the Asian versions of Windows XP Professional and can be optionally installed on all other versions. This collection includes Japanese, Korean, Simplified Chinese, as well as Traditional Chinese. The following are the three key areas of language configuration settings within the Regional and Language Options applet from the Windows XP Control Panel:

➤ Regional Options

➤ Languages

➤ Advanced

Regional Options: Locales

A *locale* is a collection of Windows XP Professional settings that reflects a specific country or region's language and cultural conventions. For example, the English (United Kingdom) and English (United States) locales reflect different countries or regions that may share a common language but use different dialects, currencies, and even date and time formats. Applications use the locale information to input the correct symbols and characters.

A locale contains information about standards and formats such as the following:

➤ Number

➤ Currency

➤ Time and date formats

➤ Localized calendar settings

➤ Character code page conversion tables

➤ Country abbreviation

The Regional Options tab on the Regional and Language Options dialog box gives you the capability to select a country from the Standards and Formats drop-down list box. When you select a country, the corresponding formats and standards for that locale are listed under Samples. To change the default settings for a locale, click the Customize button.

Configuring Regional Options

You configure all regional (locales) and language settings through the Regional and Language Options applet in the Control Panel folder (see Figure 4.14). Perform the following steps to select a regional setting for standards and formats:

1. Open the Regional and Language Options applet in the Control Panel.

2. Select the Regional Options tab.

3. Select your preferred locale from the Standards and Formats drop-down list.

4. Click OK.

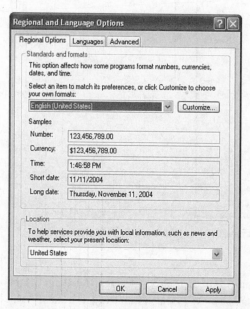

Figure 4.14 The Regional Options tab for the Regional and Language Options Control Panel applet.

No reboot is required. The change of locale takes effect immediately. In addition, applications that depend on these settings reflect the new locale immediately. As an alternative to selecting a specific locale, you can click the Customize button to individually adjust the regional settings for Numbers,

Currency, Time, and Date from the Customize Regional Options dialog box. To configure Windows XP for multiple locations, click the Location drop-down arrow at the bottom of the Regional Options tab and choose a different country than the one listed under Standards and Formats.

Configuring Text Services and Input Languages

You can add, remove, and configure support for input languages and associated keyboard layouts from the Languages tab on the Regional and Language Options dialog box. From this tab, you can add supplemental language support for East Asian languages and/or add support for complex script and right-to-left languages. Click the Details button to change the default input language, to add or remove Installed Services for input languages, or to set preferences for the Language Bar and Key Settings, as shown in Figure 4.15.

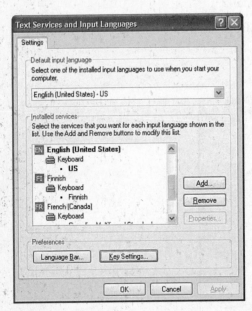

Figure 4.15 The Text Services and Input Languages dialog box for the Regional and Language Options Control Panel applet.

As soon as you add an additional input language (besides the default language), an icon appears on the taskbar next to the system tray; it indicates the input language that is currently being used. A quick way to select input languages (besides assigning hot keys) is to click the Language icon on the taskbar and then select the specific input language that you need, as shown in Figure 4.16. By clicking the Key Settings button on the Text Services and Input Languages dialog box, you can assign keystroke combinations for easy switching between different installed input languages.

Figure 4.16 Input language selections from clicking the Language icon on the taskbar.

Additional input locales are available for each new language that is installed. For example, if a user needs an input locale for Estonian, install the Baltic language setting.

Configuring Advanced Language Settings

Use the Advanced tab of the Regional and Language Options dialog box to specify the language to use for displaying menus and dialog boxes for non-Unicode applications. Use the Code Page Conversion Tables section to add or remove Code Page Conversion Tables on your Windows XP Professional computer. Click the Apply All Settings to the Current User Account and to the Default User Profile check box to allow all new user accounts on the computer to take advantage of all the Regional and Language Options dialog box settings that you have configured.

File Settings and Transfer Wizard

The new *File Settings and Transfer (FAST) Wizard* is a special GUI version of the User State Migration tool that has been available in the Windows 2000 Resource Kit. The FAST Wizard makes it easier to move user configuration settings, folders, and files from one computer to another. This wizard enables users to migrate Internet Explorer, Outlook Express, and Outlook settings; store dial-up connections, phone and modem options, accessibility settings, classic desktop screen saver settings, fonts, folder options, taskbar settings, mouse and keyboard settings, sound settings, regional options, Office settings, Network Drives and Printers folders, My Documents folder, My Pictures folder, Favorites folder, Cookies folder, common Office file types; and transfer user-specified files. The FAST Wizard supports three types of transfer techniques:

➤ Via direct cable connection using an RS-232 serial port or using a parallel (LPT) port

➤ Via floppy disk or other removable media such as Zip disks

➤ Via other media or connections, such as network drives or removable hard drives

The "old" computer that you want to transfer settings from must be running one of the following Microsoft operating systems:

➤ Windows 95

➤ Windows 98/Windows 98 Second Edition (SE)

➤ Windows Millennium Edition (ME)

➤ Windows NT 4

➤ Windows 2000

➤ Windows XP

Transferring Settings from One Computer to Another

The FAST Wizard offers several options for copying user and application settings to a new computer. The Direct Cable Connection and the Network Connection options are the fastest and easiest methods. To transfer settings and files from one computer to another using a network connection, follow these steps:

On the old computer:

1. Run the FASTWIZ.exe program from the \SUPPORT\TOOLS folder on the Windows XP Professional CD-ROM.

2. At the Welcome window, click Next to continue (see Figure 4.17).

3. Select a transfer method—To use a network connection, click either Home or Small Office Network or Other and specify a local or network folder in which to store the captured settings. Click Next.

4. If the wizard displays a message about certain applications that need to be installed on the new computer before you transfer settings, take note of them and click Next again.

5. Click Finish after the wizard notifies you that it has successfully copied all the files and settings that you specified.

On the new (Windows XP) computer:

1. Click Start, All Programs, Accessories, System Tools, File and Settings Transfer Wizard.

2. At the Welcome window, click Next to continue.

3. Click New Computer and click Next.

4. Click I Don't Need the Wizard Disk, I Have Already Collected My Files and Settings from My Old Computer, and click Next again.

5. Click Other (For Example, a Removable Drive or Network Drive) and specify the exact location of the FAST Wizard's transfer files (see Figure 4.18). Click Next. The transfer process will begin and you must wait for it to complete.

6. Click Finish to complete the wizard after it notifies you that your files and settings were transferred successfully.

7. Click Yes to log off. Log back on to have the new settings take effect.

Figure 4.17 FAST Wizard enables you to specify which files you want to transfer.

If the FAST Wizard fails at any time, you might want to check the Windows Firewall settings. There is an exception on the firewall that might be configured to not allow FAST to accept incoming network connections.

Figure 4.18 Choosing a method and location for copying settings to the new computer using the File Settings and Transfer Wizard.

Accessibility Options

Windows XP provides several options to make navigating and using the operating system easier. You can enhance the interface and keyboard settings for users who have limited vision, hearing, or manual dexterity.

Accessibility Options Applet

The *Accessibility Options applet* in the Control Panel contains several useful tabs: Keyboard, Sound, Display, General, and Mouse.

Keyboard Tab

Several options are available on the Keyboard tab to control repeat rate and key combinations:

➤ StickyKeys—Enables a user to press multiple keystrokes, such as Ctrl+Alt+Delete, by using one key at a time. To enable this feature, select the StickyKeys option in the Accessibility Options applet. You can also enable it by pressing the Shift key five times. At that point, a dialog box appears; it asks the user if this feature should be turned on. Click OK to enable and close the dialog box. In addition, a StickyKeys icon appears in the system tray. Double-clicking this icon opens the Accessibility Options applet.

➤ FilterKeys—Enables you to control the keyboard repeat rate, ignore repeated keystrokes, and control the rate at which a key repeats the keystroke if a user holds it down. You can apply granular settings to configure the repeat delay in number of seconds. If, for example, a user presses the L key and holds the key down, the letter L will repeat every x seconds (x represents the number of seconds for the repeat key delay). When you have enabled FilterKeys, an icon in the shape of a stopwatch appears in the system tray. You can also enable FilterKeys by holding down the right Shift key for 8 seconds.

 If a user has enabled FilterKeys but finds that the keystrokes repeat with no delay, either someone has selected the No Keyboard Repeat setting or the repeat time delay has been configured to its lowest setting.

➤ ToggleKeys—When enabled, this option causes a high-pitched sound to be played when the Num Lock, Caps Lock, or Scroll Lock key is pressed. This feature is enabled via the Accessibility Options applet or by holding down the Num Lock key for five seconds.

Sound Tab

On the Sound tab, you can enable the following two sound features to help notify users of warnings and other events:

➤ SoundSentry—When enabled, this option displays visual warnings when Windows XP generates audible alerts. This feature is helpful for users with a hearing impairment. A user can specify which part of the screen actually flashes when a sound is generated. The options are Flash Active Window, Flash Active Caption Bar, or Flash Desktop. To enable this feature, select the SoundSentry check box. No shortcut is available for this feature.

➤ ShowSounds—When applications use sounds to convey messages and information, this feature displays text captions that represent those sounds. Selecting the ShowSounds check box enables this feature. No shortcut is available for ShowSounds.

Display Tab

The Display tab enables you to specify high-contrast colors and fonts and to set cursor options:

➤ High Contrast—When enabled, this feature informs applications to change the color scheme to a High Contrast scheme to allow for easier reading. For example, you can enable a white-on-black scheme, a black-on-white scheme, or one of the many other high-contrast schemes, or you can choose from any of the installed appearance schemes on your Windows XP system. Doing so enables users to adjust colors and font sizes for Windows XP and all applications. To enable this feature, select the Use High Contrast check box or press the left Alt+left Shift+Print Screen keys as a shortcut. When you press these three keys at the same time, a dialog box appears that asks if the feature should be turned on.

➤ Cursor Options—You can adjust the Blink Rate slider bar to achieve a faster or slower blink rate for your Windows XP cursor. You can adjust the Width slider bar to set the cursor width to be narrower or wider.

Mouse Tab

The Mouse tab enables you to use the keyboard as a mouse using the following feature:

➤ MouseKeys—When enabled, this feature allows a user to use the numeric keypad to move the mouse pointer. The keypad can also perform single-click, double-click, and drag-mouse actions. In addition, you can assign settings that control the pointer speed. To enable this feature, select the MouseKeys check box or press left Alt+left Shift+Num Lock. A dialog box will appear asking whether the MouseKeys feature should be enabled. If you click the OK button, an icon will appear in the system tray to graphically indicate that the feature has been enabled.

General Tab

The General tab enables you to specify settings for all accessibility features:

➤ Automatic Reset—You can turn off StickyKeys, FilterKeys, ToggleKeys, SoundSentry, High Contrast, and MouseKeys after a specified idle period has passed. For example, you could assign a five-minute idle period. These six features would then all be turned off if the computer were idle for five or more minutes. To assign an idle period, click the Turn Off Accessibility Features After Idle For check box and select a timeout period from the drop-down list box.

➤ Notification—You can have the system alert you whenever an accessibility feature is turned on or off by having a warning message pop up and/or by having the system make a sound.

➤ SerialKey Devices—Enable this option for users who cannot use a standard keyboard and must install an alternative input device into a serial port.

➤ Administrative Options—You can choose Apply All Settings to Logon Desktop to allow the current user to use the Accessibility Options when logging on to the system. In addition, you can mark the check box Apply All Settings to Defaults for New Users to have the current settings applied to all new user accounts created by this Windows XP computer.

Accessibility Wizard

You can configure most of the accessibility options quite easily through the Accessibility Wizard. The wizard asks a series of questions to determine whether you need to configure keyboard, sound, display, and mouse accessibility features. For example, the wizard displays a sentence in varying font sizes. The user then selects a sentence with the font size that is easy to read. After the user has answered all the questions, the interface immediately changes to reflect larger fonts and any other options that were configured.

Additional Accessibility Features

Windows XP provides three additional accessibility tools that are not available in the Accessibility Options applet. These tools, which you can locate by navigating to Start, All Programs, Accessories, Accessibility, are the following:

➤ Narrator—This tool is for people who have low vision or who are completely vision-impaired. When enabled, the Narrator uses a synthesized voice to read what is displayed (such as menu options, text, dialog boxes, and alerts).

➤ Magnifier—This tool splits the screen into two portions, magnified and nonmagnified. The magnified portion of the screen magnifies the size of anything that the mouse pointer is hovering over. The nonmagnified area selects what needs to be magnified. You can increase or decrease the magnification level and the size of the magnification.

➤ On-Screen Keyboard—This tool displays a virtual keyboard on the Windows XP desktop. Users use the mouse pointer to press the virtual keys. They can also use a joystick with the onscreen keyboard to select keys.

Utility Manager

Utility Manager enables users to access these three accessibility tools from one central location. You can also use Utility Manager to check the status and start or stop the tools. An administrator can configure these tools to start when Windows XP starts. Users who have administrator privileges can configure one, two, or all three of these accessibility tools to start whenever Utility Manager launches. Users can also start these accessibility utilities before logging on to the computer by pressing the Windows key+U at the Welcome screen. Narrator, the built-in text-to-speech program, starts when Utility Manager opens so that users who have impaired vision can obtain immediate access to Utility Manager. Using Utility Manager, you can tell Windows to automatically start accessibility programs each time you log on to your computer, when you lock your computer desktop, or when Utility Manager starts. For example, you can specify that Magnifier launches automatically every time that you log on to your system.

Advanced Video Display Options

Windows XP Professional offers support for enhanced video-display features not found under previous operating systems, such as Windows 2000. One of the advanced video display options is ClearType, a font-smoothing technology for mobile computers and flat-screen monitors that use LCD technology. Another advanced display feature is called Dualview, which extends the Windows XP desktop over two computer displays using a mobile PC's built-in LCD screen plus an external monitor. Each of these advanced features enhances your computing experience when working with Windows XP.

ClearType Display Support

ClearType makes reading LCD screens easier by smoothing the display of fonts for mobile computer displays and flat-screen monitors. On ordinary (non-LCD) desktop monitors, ClearType may make the display appear blurry. ClearType is not compatible with the Magnifier utility. When you select either Standard or ClearType from the Use the Following Method to Smooth Edges of Screen Fonts drop-down list, the computer's video adapter and monitor must support at least 256 colors. High Color (24-bit) or Highest Color (32-bit) are recommended settings to use with ClearType. To enable ClearType technology:

1. Open the Display applet in the Control Panel.

2. Go to the Appearance tab and click the Effects button.

3. Mark the check box labeled Use the Following Method to Smooth Edges of Screen Fonts and select ClearType from the drop-down list box.

4. Click OK to close the Effects dialog box and then click OK to close the Display Properties window and enable ClearType.

Dualview Multiple Display Support

Dualview is related to the Multi-Monitor feature that was first introduced in Windows 98. The Multi-Monitor feature is also available under Windows XP, but Dualview extends the concept both to mobile computers that have only one video card installed and to desktop computers that have one video card installed with two video output ports. With Dualview, you cannot specify which monitor is the primary display. On mobile PCs, the primary display is always the built-in LCD screen. On desktop PCs, the primary display is always the monitor connected to the first video output port. To configure Dualview support, launch the Display applet in the Control Panel after you have connected and powered on the second (external) monitor. From the Display Properties window, click the Settings tab and then select the Extend My Windows Desktop onto the Monitor option.

 Not all display adapters are supported under Dualview. Be sure to check the Microsoft Hardware Compatibility List and Microsoft Knowledge Base article Q307397 for a list of supported adapters. Many video adapters come standard with multiple video outputs, which come with their own monitor control software.

Fax Features

Windows XP provides support for sending and receiving faxes via an internal or external modem or through a remote fax device connected over a network. The Windows XP Fax service is not installed by default when you first install Windows XP. To install the Fax service, open the Printers and Faxes folder from the Start menu and select Set Up Faxing from the Printer Tasks section, or select File, Set Up Faxing from the Printers and Faxes menu bar. As an alternative method, you can open the Add or Remove Programs applet from the Control Panel and select Add/Remove Windows Components. Mark the Fax Services check box, click Next, wait for the components to be installed, and then click Finish to complete the Windows Components Wizard.

After you have installed the Fax service, you need to configure the service using the Fax Console. The first time that you click Start, All Programs, Accessories, Communications, Fax, Fax Console after installing the Fax service, you'll be greeted by the Fax Configuration Wizard, which assists you in setting up your computer to send and receive faxes. Enter your Sender Information, specify which fax device to use, and configure fax send and receive options. By default, the Fax service is configured to allow users to only send faxes, not receive them. Mark the Enable Receive check box to turn on the fax-receiving feature. Enter your Transmitting Subscriber Identification (TSID) number and your Called Subscriber Identification (CSID) number through the Fax Configuration Wizard.

The wizard also asks you for routing options—whether to print a received fax on a certain print device and/or whether to store an additional copy of each fax within a specific folder. After you complete the wizard, the Fax Console window opens. You can access the Fax Console window by selecting Start, All Programs, Accessories, Communications, Fax, Fax Console, by right-clicking the Fax icon in the Printers and Faxes folder and selecting Open from the pop-up menu or simply by double-clicking the Fax icon in the Printers and Faxes folder.

To fax a document, follow these steps:

1. Click File, Send a Fax from the Fax Console, click File, Print from an application program, or click File, Send To, Fax Recipient.

2. If you select File, Print from an application, select the fax printer and then click OK to submit the fax. For any of the three options you choose, the Send Fax Wizard launches. The wizard enables you to enter the recipient's name and fax number, cover page information, and other configurations. Figure 4.19 shows the Send Fax Wizard.

The Fax Console: Managing Faxes, Settings, and Options

The Send Fax Wizard, seen in Figure 4.19, gathers some information, such as the sender's name and fax number. This information is gathered from settings contained in the properties of the Fax Console. To work with fax settings, right-click the Fax icon in the Printers and Faxes folder and select Properties. You can access the Printers and Faxes window from the Start menu or by clicking the Printers and Faxes icon in the Control Panel. The Fax Properties windows displays five tabs:

➤ General—Enables you to assign a location, comment, and configure specific fax features.

➤ Sharing—Fax sharing is not supported under Windows XP Professional.

➤ Devices—Enables you to specify fax device settings and send and receive options for each device.

➤ Tracking—Enables you to specify a fax device to monitor and to set send and receive notification options.

➤ Archives—Enables you to specify whether to archive incoming and/or outgoing faxes and where to store those archives.

Figure 4.19 The Send Fax Wizard.

To work with Fax Security permissions, right-click the Fax icon in the Printers and Faxes folder, press and hold down the Ctrl key, and then select Properties. The Fax Properties window will appear with an additional tab— Fax Security. By default, three groups have Fax Security permissions: Administrators, Everyone, and Interactive. Under default permissions, Interactive users can send documents as low-, normal-, or high-priority faxes. They can view fax jobs, manage fax jobs, view the Fax service configuration, and view incoming fax and outgoing fax archives. Administrators, by default, can additionally manage the Fax service configuration plus manage incoming and outgoing fax archives.

You use the Fax Console itself to troubleshoot and monitor fax transmissions. You can perform the following functions with the Fax Console:

➤ Send a fax

➤ Receive a fax

➤ Change sender information

➤ Manage personal cover pages

➤ Check fax printer status

➤ Run the Fax Configuration Wizard to reconfigure the Fax service

➤ Open the Fax Properties window

➤ Launch the Fax Monitor

The Fax Console window displays four folders for organizing faxes:

➤ Incoming

➤ Inbox

➤ Outbox

➤ Sent Items

If faxes aren't being sent or received, verify that a user has permission to use the fax device and make sure the fax device is configured to send and receive faxes. If those settings are correct and faxes are still not being sent or received, stop and restart the Fax service.

Scheduled Tasks

With the advent of Internet Explorer (IE) 5 (and later versions), Microsoft introduced the Scheduled Tasks folder, which replaced the older AT scheduler service. Under Windows XP, Microsoft has further refined this GUI utility that is designed to automatically run tasks at specified times. This utility is quite similar to the Windows 98 Task Scheduler.

You can open the Scheduled Tasks folder from the Control Panel by double-clicking the Scheduled Tasks icon or by clicking Start, All Programs, Accessories, System Tools, Scheduled Tasks. Unlike Windows 2000 Professional, the Scheduled Tasks folder is not shared by default. You still can, however, create a task on a Windows XP computer and then copy it to another Windows XP computer. This is helpful if a similar task needs to run on many computers. By copying the task from one computer to another, you don't have to re-create it multiple times.

Creating a Task

To create a new task, open the Scheduled Tasks folder and double-click the Add Scheduled Task icon to launch the Scheduled Task Wizard. This wizard steps users through the process of selecting a program, batch file, or script to run automatically at a scheduled time. The Scheduled Tasks service runs under the security context of the Windows XP local system account. However, for each scheduled task, you must specify a user account and password that determines the security context under which each scheduled task will execute. You still have the option of using the legacy AT command via the command line to set up scheduled events. Events scheduled using the AT command may be run under a different security context by selecting

Advanced, AT Service Account from the Scheduled Tasks folder's menu. You can then specify a particular user account whose security context will be used for all events that are scheduled using the AT command. Perform the following steps to create an automated task using the Scheduled Tasks folder:

1. Double-click the Add Scheduled Task icon and then click Next at the Scheduled Task Wizard window.

2. Select the application program that you want to schedule from the list, or click Browse to locate the appropriate program and click Next.

3. Choose how often the task should run and then click Next. The options are as follows:

   ➤ Daily

   ➤ Weekly

   ➤ Monthly

   ➤ One Time Only

   ➤ When My Computer Starts

   ➤ When I Log On

4. Depending on what you chose in step 3, users may have to set up what time of the day, what days of the week, or what months of the year the task should run. Choose the appropriate options and then click Next.

5. The next step requires you to enter a username and password. The username must have the right to run the selected application. Click Next.

6. The last dialog box of the wizard asks users whether to open the Advanced Properties dialog box after the task has been created. The Properties dialog box enables the user to edit the schedule, delete the task if it is not scheduled to run again, stop the task, start the task during idle periods, and not start the task if the computer is running on batteries. Also, you can assign security permissions to the task to control which users can modify the task options. Click Finish.

After you have closed the Scheduled Task Wizard and the Advanced Properties sheet, an icon that represents the task is created. Users can double-click a task to view and configure its advanced properties after they have created the task, as shown in Figure 4.20.

Figure 4.20 The Scheduled Tasks window displaying the advanced settings for a task.

Troubleshooting Tasks

The Scheduled Task Wizard makes it very easy to create tasks. However, sometimes tasks do fail to run. The most common reason for this is that the wrong username or password was entered for the task. If a task failed, verify that you entered the correct username and password on the task.

Another area where an incorrect account can cause problems is if a task has been created for old 16-bit applications. It may fail to run if the system account is used on the Task Service. If an error relating to the Task Service is generated, change the account used to run the service. Use the AT command to create a scheduled event and select Advanced, AT Service Account from the Scheduled Tasks folder's menu. You can then specify a particular user account whose security context will be used for all events that are scheduled using the AT command. If the task still won't run, stop and restart the Task Service. You can configure it to restart automatically if it fails. To do so, go to Start, Control Panel, Administrative Tools and open the Services Console. Right-click the Task Scheduler service and choose Properties. Click the Recovery tab and specify actions for service failures.

Exam Prep Questions

1. As a network administrator for your company, you log on to a Windows XP Professional workstation computer. You suspect that several users are logging on to this workstation, so you want to view all the user profiles that are stored locally. You look in the C:\Documents and Settings folder, but no user profiles exist. The C:\ drive is the only volume on the computer. What has happened to all the user profiles for this system?

   ○ A. The system is configured to use only roaming profiles.

   ○ B. The system is configured to use only mandatory roaming profiles.

   ○ C. Fast User Switching is turned on, so user profiles exist only on a domain controller.

   ○ D. The user profiles are located in `%systemroot%\Profiles`.

2. WRKSTN3 is a Windows XP Professional computer that is connected to a workgroup named SALESDEPT. All computers in the workgroup are configured with default settings. A user named Alexis makes sure that she shares her GROUPDOCS folder with the network and leaves the default settings for caching. A user named Brendan, working on WRKSTN7, connects to Alexis' GROUPDOCS share. He right-clicks one of the files in the shared folder to make it available offline; however, that option does not exist on the pop-up menu. How can Brendan solve this problem?

   ○ A. Make sure that his computer's DNS settings are correct.

   ○ B. Turn off Fast User Switching.

   ○ C. Run the Network Settings Wizard to enable Offline Files.

   ○ D. Make the computer a member of a Windows 2000 Server or a Windows .NET Server Active Directory domain.

3. Alison always works on several Excel files and Word documents at the same time. She's tired of having so many buttons cluttering her taskbar. What can Alison do to improve the organization of all the buttons representing all of her open application programs on the taskbar?

   ○ A. Enable Dualview display.

   ○ B. Enable the Taskbar Switching option.

   ○ C. Turn on the Group Similar Taskbar Buttons option in Control Panel, Display Properties.

   ○ D. Add the Quick Launch toolbar to the taskbar.

4. As a system administrator, you need to modify the Windows XP Professional boot settings so that the computer will generate a boot log file each time it restarts. You can't remember the exact boot option switch and you'd prefer not to edit the Boot.ini file directly. How can you accomplish this task?

   ○ A. Run the SYSEDIT utility.

   ○ B. Run the MSCONFIG utility.

   ○ C. Boot into Safe Mode and use the BOOTVRFY utility.

   ○ D. Use RegEdit to modify the Registry data for the value WindowsBoot under `HKEY_LOCAL_MACHINE\SOFTWARE\`
   `Microsoft\Windows NT\CurrentVersion\Winlogon`.

5. You want to use two legacy applications under Windows XP Professional. One application requires a Windows NT 3.51 environment. The other program requires a Windows NT 4 Service Pack 6a environment. Which application program can Windows XP provide legacy support for?

   - ○ A. The Windows NT 4 Service Pack 6a application.
   - ○ B. The Windows NT 3.51 application.
   - ○ C. Both applications can be properly supported.
   - ○ D. Neither application can be properly supported.

6. Jon is a network administrator who has created a ZAP file for a legacy 16-bit application. He wants to assign the application to the users in the Marketing OU within his company's Active Directory domain. How can Jon accomplish this using a software Group Policy?

   - ○ A. Create a Computer Configuration policy to assign the application using the ZAP file.
   - ○ B. Create a User Configuration policy to assign the application using the ZAP file.
   - ○ C. Create an MSI Windows Installer Package file for the legacy application using third-party repackaging software.
   - ○ D. Create an administrative template to add to the User Configuration settings for the Group Policy of the OU.

7. Zachary, a network administrator, wants to use the Windows Installer Program executable to advertise a new application to all users on a standalone Windows XP Professional workstation. The name of the program's installer package is App1.msi. He'd like to modify the installation with a transform file he's created by the name of App1.mst. He also wants to log any and all error messages to a file named Logfile.txt on the root of the C:\ drive. How can he accomplish this?

   - ○ A. Use the following command line syntax: `MSIEXEC.exe /jm c:\setup\app1.msi /t c:\setup\app1.mst /L*v c:\logfile.txt`.
   - ○ B. Run `setup.exe` to install the application and specify `/transform=c:\setup.app1.msi /log=c:\logfile.txt` as command-line arguments for the setup program.
   - ○ C. Create an MST Windows Installer Package Transform file for the legacy application using third-party repackaging software. Specify `MSIEXEC /t c:\setup\app1.mst` on the command line.
   - ○ D. Use the following command line syntax: `MSIEXEC.exe /fm c:\setup\app1.msi /t c:\setup\app1.mst /L*v c:\logfile.txt`.

8. Which computer configuration transfer techniques are supported by the File and Settings Transfer (FAST) Wizard? [Check all correct answers.]

   - ❑ A. Serial port connections (one RS-232 cable connected between two computers)
   - ❑ B. Parallel port connections (one LPT cable connected between two computers)
   - ❑ C. USB connections (one USB cable connected between two computers)
   - ❑ D. Zip or Jaz drive cartridges

❑ E. IEEE 1394 (FireWire) connections (one FireWire cable connected between two computers)

❑ F. Infrared connections

❑ G. Wireless 802.11 connections

Answers to Exam Prep Questions

1. Answer D is correct. The computer must have been upgraded from Windows NT Workstation 4. Upgraded systems continue to store user profiles in the same folder as the Windows NT 4 default location—%systemroot%\Profiles. All profiles get stored on the local computer, including roaming and mandatory roaming profiles, so answers A and B are incorrect. Fast User Switching has nothing to do with user profile locations.

2. Answer B is correct. The Offline Files feature, also known as Client-Side Caching, is disabled whenever Fast User Switching is turned on. DNS settings are used to ensure proper TCP/IP name resolution, so answer A is incorrect. Answer C is incorrect because the Network Settings Wizard does not configure Offline File support. A Windows XP Professional computer does not need to be a member of a domain for Offline Files to function; therefore, answer D is also incorrect.

3. Answer C is correct. By enabling the Group Similar Taskbar Buttons feature, all running application buttons will be grouped together on the taskbar. Answer A is incorrect because Dualview is related to the Multiple Monitor option that supports two displays from one video output port. Answer B is incorrect because no Taskbar Switching option exists. The Quick Launch toolbar adds icons to the taskbar for starting application programs, not for grouping program buttons that are already running. Therefore, answer D is incorrect.

4. Answer B is correct. The MSCONFIG utility allows you to set a variety of system startup options, including adding command-line switches to the Boot.ini file. The SYSEDIT tool does not allow you to modify any part of the Boot.ini file, so answer A is incorrect. The BOOTVRFY.exe command does not support editing the Boot.ini file, so answer C is incorrect. Values for the Boot.ini file are not stored in the Windows XP Registry, so answer D is also incorrect.

5. Answer D is correct. Windows NT 3.51 applications are not supported by Windows XP Compatibility Support. Although Windows NT 4 Service Pack 5 applications are supported, Windows NT 4 Service Pack 6a–specific programs are not explicitly supported. Other supported environments are Windows 95/98/ME/2000.

6. Answer C is correct. You can only publish, not assign, legacy applications using ZAP files. Answer A is incorrect because applications installed using ZAP files can only be published; therefore, you cannot use ZAP files for software Group Policies under Computer Configuration. Answer D is incorrect because you create software

Group Policies from the Software Settings folder of the Group Policy MMC snap-in, not by using additional Administrative Templates.

7. Answer A is correct. The syntax for MSIEXEC.exe is:

```
MSIEXEC [options] msi_filename.msi [/t transform_filename.mst]
➡ [/L*v driveletter:\logfile_name.txt]
```

The parameters in square brackets are optional. Answer B is incorrect because you need to run MSIEXEC to advertise applications using the command line option /ju to advertise to the current user or /jm to advertise to all users of the computer. Answer C is incorrect because you must specify both the Windows Installer Package (.msi) file as well as the Transform file, and no logging is specified. Answer D is incorrect because the /fm option means to perform a repair of an existing application by rewriting all computer-specific registry entries.

8. Answers A, B, D, F, and G are all correct. The FAST Wizard supports a direct cable connection using either serial ports or parallel ports and appropriate cables. Removable media are supported, which includes Zip and Jaz drives. Infrared connections are supported indirectly because you can copy the FAST Wizard's files via an infrared connection. Wireless networking support is also included, because any network connection will work. Answer C is incorrect because a direct USB connection between two computers is not supported. Answer E is incorrect because a direct FireWire connection between two computers is not supported.

Need to Know More?

Microsoft Corporation. *Microsoft Windows XP Professional Resource Kit*, 2nd ed. Redmond, WA: Microsoft Press, 2003. ISBN 0735619743 .This all-in-one reference is a compilation of technical documentation and valuable insider information that computer-support professionals and administrators can reference to install, customize, and support Windows XP.

Bott, Ed, and Carl Siechert. *Microsoft Windows XP Inside Out*, 2nd ed. Redmond, WA: Microsoft Learning, 2004. ISBN 073562044X. This book offers time-saving tips, troubleshooting techniques, and work-arounds. It focuses on techniques such as taking advantage of the rich integration of devices, applications, and web services in Windows XP.

Minasi, Mark. *Mastering Windows XP Professional*. Alameda, CA: Sybex, Inc., 2001. ISBN 0782129811. This book provides in-depth coverage of installing, configuring, and administering Windows XP Professional.

Search the Microsoft TechNet CD (or its online version through www.microsoft.com) using keywords such as "Offline Files", "MSCONFIG", "Fax", "Scheduled Tasks", and "Windows Installer Service".

Installing, Configuring, and Troubleshooting Hardware Devices and Drivers

Terms you'll need to understand:

- ✓ Universal Serial Bus (USB)
- ✓ Universal Plug and Play (UPnP)
- ✓ Advanced Power Management (APM)
- ✓ Advanced Configuration and Power Interface (ACPI)
- ✓ Add Hardware Wizard
- ✓ Device Manager
- ✓ Driver signing
- ✓ FireWire, or IEEE (Institute of Electrical and Electronics Engineers) 1394
- ✓ Driver Rollback
- ✓ Smart cards and smart card readers
- ✓ Multilink support
- ✓ DVD media
- ✓ Infrared Data Association (IrDA) devices
- ✓ Wireless networking
- ✓ Network adapter, or network interface card (NIC)
- ✓ Multiple monitor support
- ✓ Video adapter
- ✓ Power options
- ✓ Hardware profiles
- ✓ Multiprocessor support

Techniques you'll need to master:

- ✓ Installing, configuring, and troubleshooting hardware devices and drivers
- ✓ Updating drivers and system files
- ✓ Rolling back drivers to a previous version
- ✓ Managing and troubleshooting driver signing
- ✓ Managing and troubleshooting various types of input/output (I/O) devices
- ✓ Configuring and troubleshooting Multilink support for a dial-up connection
- ✓ Configuring and troubleshooting multiple monitor support, hardware profiles, and multiprocessor support

The term "computer hardware" includes any physical device that is connected to a computer which, in turn, is controlled by the computer's processors. It includes equipment connected to the computer at the time that it is manufactured as well as equipment that you add later. Modems, disk drives, CD drives, DVD drives, print devices, network cards, keyboards, display adapter cards, and USB cameras are all examples of devices. Each device attached to a system must also have a corresponding software driver, which allows the device to interface (communicate) with the computer's operating system. Supporting and troubleshooting hardware devices and their associated drivers is vital to maintaining a productive network. Administering, diagnosing, and resolving hardware-related issues are where productivity and this chapter begin.

Implementing, Managing, and Troubleshooting Hardware

Windows XP offers full support for Plug and Play (PnP) devices and partial support for non-Plug and Play devices. "Partial" support means only one thing: Some devices work, and others do not. Sometimes, testing a device may be the only sure way to determine whether it will work with Windows XP. It's a good idea to consult the Windows XP Hardware Compatibility List (HCL) before installing a new device. Unfortunately, the Windows XP HCL stopped being updated as of August 17, 2004, but it's still a good resource to review. You can also reference the Windows Catalog online (`http://www.microsoft.com/windows/catalog`), but it's not as comprehensive as the HCL.

For a device to work properly with Windows XP, software (a device driver) must be installed on the computer. Each hardware device has its own unique device driver(s), which the device manufacturer typically supplies. However, many device drivers are included with Windows XP and work even better with Windows XP than the manufacturer's own driver. Look for Microsoft to recommend using its own drivers for a given device rather than those of the manufacturer, because Microsoft understands the inner workings of the operating system better than anyone else.

Because Windows XP controls your computer's resources and configuration, you can install PnP hardware devices and many other devices without restarting your computer. Windows XP automatically identifies the new hardware and installs the drivers it needs. If you are using an older computer that does not support Advanced Power Management (APM) or the current standard, Advanced Configuration and Power Interface (ACPI), you must set up the device manually and restart your computer when installing new hardware devices. For now, you need ACPI-compliant hardware to make your Windows XP hardware setup experience smoother. We discuss APM and ACPI in greater detail later in this chapter.

Universal Plug and Play—Extending the PnP Standard

Starting with Windows 95, Microsoft has built hardware device PnP capabilities directly into the operating system, which makes installing and configuring peripherals on a personal computer a great deal easier. The Universal Plug and Play (UPnP) standard extends this simplicity to include the entire networked environment, enabling discovery and control of networked devices and services, such as network-attached printers, Internet gateways, and even consumer electronics equipment. UPnP is more than just a simple extension of the PnP peripheral model. It is designed to support zero-configuration, "invisible" networking, as well as automatic device discovery for a vast array of different types of devices developed by a wide range of manufacturers.

With UPnP, a device can dynamically join a network, obtain an IP address, communicate its capabilities, and discover the presence and capabilities of other devices—completely automatically. Devices can subsequently communicate with each other directly, further enabling transparent peer-to-peer networking (with no user intervention).

The scope of UPnP is large enough to encompass many exciting implementations, such as home automation, printing and imaging, audio and video entertainment, kitchen appliances, and automobile networks.

UPnP takes advantage of open, standard protocols such as TCP/IP, HTTP, and XML, enabling it to seamlessly fit into existing networks. Because UPnP is based on a distributed, open network architecture, it is not dependent on any specific operating system or programming language. UPnP does not require the use of specific APIs (application programming interfaces—calls to operating system functions) that applications must use. Operating system developers are free to create their own APIs that will meet their customers' needs. Devices on a UPnP network can be connected using any type of connection, including radio frequency (RF, wireless), phone lines, power lines, IrDA (Infrared), Ethernet (LAN), and IEEE 1394 (FireWire). In other words, any medium that can be used to connect network-enabled devices together can enable UPnP. An important issue to consider is whether the network connection being utilized supports the bandwidth required for the intended use.

Installing, Configuring, and Managing Hardware

You configure devices on Windows XP machines using the Add Hardware icon in the Control Panel or by clicking the Add Hardware Wizard button from the Hardware tab on the System Properties window. Keep in mind that, in most cases, to add, configure, and remove devices you need to be logged on to the local machine as a member of the Administrators group.

Installing PnP Devices

Connect the device to the appropriate port or slot on your computer according to the device manufacturer's instructions. You may need to start or restart your computer, but this happens much less often than it did with previous versions of Windows, such as Windows 9x, Windows NT 4.0, and even Windows 2000. If you are prompted to restart your computer, do so. Windows XP should detect the device and then immediately start the Found New Hardware Wizard.

Installing Non-PnP Devices

To install a device that is not Plug and Play compliant, follow these steps:

1. Click the Add Hardware icon in the Control Panel.

2. Click Next and then click Yes, I Have Already Connected the Hardware. Click Next again.

3. Scroll down the Installed Hardware list to the very bottom, select Add A New Hardware Device, and click Next.

4. Select one of the following options:

    ➤ Search for and Install the Hardware Automatically (Recommended)—Do this if you want Windows XP to try to detect the new non–Plug and Play device you want to install.

    ➤ Install the Hardware That I Manually Select from a List (Advanced)—Do this if you know the type and model of the device you are installing and you want to select it from a list of devices.

5. Click Next, and then follow the instructions on your screen.

6. You may be prompted to restart your computer, depending on the type of non–Plug and Play device you just installed.

The Hardware tab on the System Properties dialog box no longer displays the Add Hardware Wizard button under SP2 (see Figure 5.1). Fortunately, you can still access the Add Hardware Wizard from the Control Panel.

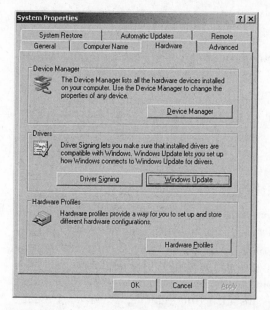

Figure 5.1 The Hardware tab on the System Properties dialog box under SP2.

Tips on Installing Devices

Using a PnP driver to install a non–PnP device may provide some PnP support. (But don't get your hopes up.) Although the system cannot recognize the hardware and load the appropriate drivers on its own, PnP can oversee the installation by allocating resources, interacting with Power Options in the Control Panel, and recording any issues in the Event Log.

If your computer is connected to a network, network policy (Group Policy) settings may prevent you from installing any devices on your computer. To add and set up a non–PnP device connected directly to your computer, you *must* be logged on as an administrator or a member of the Administrators group.

 If an administrator has already loaded the drivers for the device, you can install the device without having administrator privileges.

Troubleshooting Installed Hardware Devices

To troubleshoot an installed device, perform the following steps:

1. Click the Add Hardware icon in the Control Panel.

2. Click Next and then click Yes, I Have Already Connected the Hardware. Click Next again.

3. Select the installed hardware device that you are having trouble with and click Next.

4. Follow the subsequent instructions on your screen. To launch a troubleshooter from the Windows XP Help and Support Center, click Finish and go through the troubleshooter's steps to try to resolve the problem.

Device Driver Updates

Keeping drivers and system files updated ensures that your operating system performs at its peak level. Microsoft recommends using Microsoft digitally signed drivers whenever possible. The `Driver.cab` cabinet file on the Windows XP CD-ROM contains all the drivers that Windows XP ships with. This cabinet file is copied to the `%systemroot%\Driver Cache\i386` folder when Windows XP is installed (for example, `C:\windows\driver cache\i386`). Whenever a driver is updated, Windows XP looks in the `Driver.cab` file first. The location of `Driver.cab` is stored in a Registry key and can be changed via `HKLM\Software\Microsoft\Windows\CurrentVersion\Setup\DriverCachePath`.

Automatic Device Drivers Updates

Windows XP supports automatic updating of device drivers and other critical operating system files. In Windows XP Professional, you must be logged on as either the local administrator or as a member of the Administrators group to install updated components or to change Automatic Updates settings. If your computer is a member of a Windows Active Directory domain, Group Policy settings may further restrict your ability to modify these settings and install updated components.

To turn on, turn off, or modify Windows XP Automatic Updates notification settings, follow these steps:

1. Log on the computer as the administrator or as a member of the Administrators group.

2. Right-click the My Computer icon and select Properties.

3. Click the Automatic Updates tab.

4. Select from one of four available Notification Settings buttons, as shown in Figure 5.2:

> ➤ Automatic (recommended)—This is the *default* setting.

> ➤ Download Updates for Me, but Let Me Choose When to Install Them.

> ➤ Notify Me but Don't Automatically Download or Install Them.

> ➤ Turn Off Automatic Updates.

5. Click OK to accept the new settings.

 After the successful installation of certain updated components, Windows XP may prompt you to restart the computer. As a best practice, you should always restart the machine immediately as instructed. Failure to follow these instructions may result in an unstable computing environment and could cause data loss.

If you choose not to install one or more updates that have been downloaded to your PC, Windows XP deletes those update files from your computer. If you later decide that you want to install any of the updates that you have previously declined, click the link at the bottom of the Automatic Updates tab: Offer Updates Again That I've Previously Hidden. If any of the previously declined (hidden) updates still apply to your system, Windows XP will display them the next time the system notifies you of newly available updates.

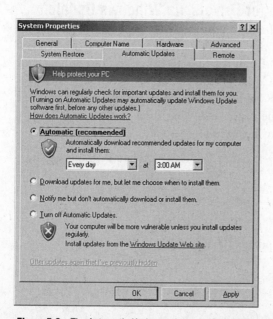

Figure 5.2 The Automatic Updates tab on the System Properties dialog box under SP2.

Manually Updating Drivers

To update individual drivers, perform the following steps:

1. Right-click My Computer and select Properties, or open the System applet from the Control Panel.

2. From the System Properties dialog box, click the Hardware tab and then click the Device Manager button.

3. Perform one of the following two steps:

   ➤ Right-click the device that you want to update, select Update Driver from the pop-up list, and follow the onscreen instructions.

   ➤ Right-click the device that you want to update and select Properties from the pop-up list. Click the Driver tab and then click the Update Driver button; follow the onscreen instructions.

 You can use the Driver Verifier utility to troubleshoot and isolate driver problems. It is *not* enabled by default. To use it, you must enable it by running the Driver Verifier Manager part of **Verifier.exe** by executing it from the GUI first, or by changing a Registry setting and then restarting the computer. When you run the Driver Verifier tool (**Verifier.exe**) from the command line, it offers several options for troubleshooting drivers. For example, if you run the command **verifier /all**, it verifies all the drivers installed on the system. See the Microsoft Knowledge Base article 244617 for more information.

 ## Automatically Searching for Drivers via Windows Update

Under SP2, you can specify whether Windows XP should automatically connect to Windows Update over the Internet to find a suitable driver when you install a new hardware device. From the System Properties dialog box, click the Hardware tab and then click the Windows Update button, as shown previously in Figure 5.1. At the Connect to Windows Update dialog box (see Figure 5.3), you can select one of the following three options to configure device driver search behavior using Windows Update:

➤ If My Device Needs a Driver, Go to Windows Update Without Asking Me

➤ Ask Me to Search Windows Update Every Time I Connect a New Device (default)

➤ Never Search Windows Update For Drivers

Figure 5.3 The Connect to Windows Update dialog box under SP2.

Updating Your System Files Manually from the Windows Update Website

Windows Update is a Microsoft database of items such as drivers, patches, help files, and Internet components that you can download to keep your Windows XP installation up to date. Using the Product Updates section of Windows Update, you can scan your computer for outdated system files, drivers, and help files, and automatically replace them with the most recent versions.

To update your system files using Windows Update, follow these steps:

1. Go to Windows Update at `http://windowsupdate.microsoft.com/`. (This website address may change at any time because Microsoft is prone to shuffling web page locations frequently.) You can also open Windows Update by clicking Start, All Programs, Windows Update.

2. Click Yes if you are prompted about whether to allow ActiveX or other components from Microsoft Corporation to be downloaded to your system.

3. Click Scan for Updates.

4. Follow the onscreen instructions to review and install all or some of the applicable updates to your system.

You may be required to be logged on as an administrator or a member of the Administrators group to complete the installation of certain Windows Update components or operations. If your computer is connected to a network, network (Group Policy) settings may prevent you from updating any system files or drivers.

The Driver Rollback Feature

Driver Rollback is a new feature of Windows XP. If you encounter problems with a hardware device after you have installed an updated driver for it, you can now easily revert back to the previously installed software driver for that device by using the Driver Rollback option. To restore a device driver back to its previously installed version, open Device Manager, right-click the device you are having trouble with, and select Properties. Click the Driver tab and then click the Roll Back Driver button, as shown in Figure 5.4. Unfortunately, the Driver Rollback feature does *not* work for printer drivers!

Figure 5.4 The Driver tab on a hardware device's Properties sheet provides the Roll Back Driver option.

Managing and Troubleshooting Device Conflicts

You configure devices using the Add Hardware Wizard in the Control Panel or from the Hardware tab on the System Properties window, which can also be accessed from the Control Panel. Each resource—for example, a memory address range, interrupt request (IRQ), input/output (I/O) port, Direct Memory Access (DMA) channel, and so on—that is assigned to your device must be unique or the device won't function properly. For PnP devices, Windows XP attempts to ensure automatically that these resources are configured properly. If a device has a resource conflict or is not working properly, you see next to the device name a yellow circle with an exclamation point inside it.

Device Manager uses three icons to indicate a device problem—a resource conflict, a disabled device, or a forced (manual) configuration setting. The three status icons for Device Manager are the following:

➤ Red X—This icon indicates that the device is disabled.

➤ Yellow !—This icon indicates that the device has some sort of problem and that it is not functioning or not functioning properly.

➤ Blue i—This icon indicates that the device has a forced (manually-set) resource configuration. You see this icon only when you display Device Manager in one of its two resource views: Resources by Type and Resources by Connection from the View menu.

Occasionally, two devices require the same resources, but keep in mind that this does not always result in a device conflict—especially if the devices are PnP compliant. If a conflict arises, you can manually change the resource settings to be sure that each setting is unique. Sometimes, two or more devices can share resources, such as interrupts on Peripheral Connection Interface (PCI) devices, depending on the drivers and the computer. For example, you may see Windows XP share IRQ 9 among multiple devices on many mobile computers.

When you install a non-PnP device, the resource settings for the device are not automatically configured. Depending on the type of device you are installing, you may have to manually configure these settings. The appropriate range of settings should be supplied in the user's manual that ships with your device.

In general, you should *not* change resource settings manually. When you manually modify resource settings, those manual settings become fixed and Windows XP has less flexibility for allocating resources to other devices. If too many resources retain static settings, Windows XP may not be able to install new PnP devices.

Managing and Troubleshooting Driver Signing

Microsoft is promoting driver signing for devices as a method to advance the quality of drivers and to reduce support costs for vendors and total cost of ownership (TCO) for customers. Windows XP uses a driver-signing process to make sure drivers have been certified to work correctly with the Windows Driver Model (WDM) in Windows XP. If you are having problems, it may be because you are using a driver not correctly written for Windows XP. To identify such drivers, use the Signature Verification tool. This utility, `Sigverif.exe`, helps you to quickly identify unsigned drivers if a device is not working or if you want to ensure that all drivers in use are properly signed.

Using the Signature Verification Tool

To use the Signature Verification tool, perform the following steps:

1. Click Start, Run, type `Sigverif.exe` into the Run box, and click OK.

2. In the Signature Verification tool, click the Advanced button.

3. Select the option Look for Other Files That Are Not Digitally Signed.

4. Mark the check box to include subfolders.

5. Click the Logging tab to make any changes for the log file and then click OK. Note the log file name: `Sigverif.txt`.

6. Click Start to run the utility.

Configuring Driver-Signing Options from the GUI

Windows XP offers a good degree of control over whether users can install signed or unsigned drivers, or both, for a chosen device. Signed drivers are software device drivers that have been tested by Microsoft for compatibility with Windows XP (or other versions of Windows). Microsoft embeds a digital signature into each device driver that successfully passes its compatibility test. Therefore, unsigned drivers are drivers that either have not been tested or that are actually not compatible with specific versions of Windows. To change the system's driver-signing options, right-click My Computer, select Properties, click the Hardware tab, and click the Driver Signing button. Select one of the following actions for Windows XP to take when you attempt to install an unsigned device driver (as shown in Figure 5.5):

➤ Ignore—Selecting this setting ignores whether a driver is signed, allowing the user to proceed with the driver installation.

➤ Warn—Selecting this setting issues a dialog box warning if an unsigned driver is encountered during a device installation. It gives the user the option of continuing with the installation or terminating the device's setup. This is the default setting under SP2, SP1, and the RTM version of Windows XP.

➤ Block—This option is the most restrictive of the three settings. To prevent the installation of any unsigned device drivers, this is the option you should select.

Figure 5.5   The Driver Signing Options dialog box under SP2.

Controlling the Use of Signed and Unsigned Drivers Using Group Policy

Instead of modifying the driver-signing options from the GUI, you can manipulate Windows XP driver-signing options using a Group Policy setting for the Local Computer Policy. This local policy setting is located in `Computer Configuration\Windows Settings\Security Settings\Local Policies\Security Options`. The policy is named Devices: Unsigned Driver Installation Behavior. To view or modify local policy settings, click Start, Run, type **gpedit.msc**, and click OK to launch the Local Group Policy Editor console. The three choices for the unsigned driver installation behavior policy (as shown in Figure 5.6) are the following:

➤ Silently Succeed—Selecting this setting ignores whether a driver is signed, allowing the user to proceed with the driver installation.

➤ Warn but Allow Installation—Selecting this setting issues a dialog box warning if an unsigned driver is encountered during a device installation. It gives the user the option of continuing with the installation or terminating the device's setup.

➤ Do Not Allow Installation—This option is the most restrictive of the three settings. To prevent the installation of any unsigned device drivers, this is the option you should select.

Figure 5.6 The local security settings for unsigned driver installation behavior.

Using Cameras and Scanning Devices

The Scanners and Cameras applet, part of the Control Panel, enables you to configure properties for scanners and digital cameras. If you have a PnP camera or scanner, Windows XP detects it and installs it automatically. You can use the Scanners and Cameras applet to install other scanners, digital still cameras, digital video cameras, and image-capturing devices.

After a device is installed, Scanners and Cameras can link it to a program on your computer. For example, when you push Scan on your scanner, you can have the scanned picture automatically open in the program you want.

Installing Scanners or Digital Cameras

To install a scanner or digital camera, perform the following steps:

1. Open Scanners and Cameras in the Control Panel.

2. Click Add an Imaging Device, and then follow the instructions on the screen.

Remember that you must be logged on as an administrator or a member of the Administrators group to complete this procedure. If your computer is connected to a network, network policy settings may prevent you from installing devices.

Testing Scanners or Digital Cameras

To test a scanner or digital camera, perform the following steps:

1. Open Scanners and Cameras in the Control Panel.

2. Right-click the scanner or camera you want to test, and then click Properties.

3. On the General tab, click Test Scanner or Camera.

An onscreen message tells you whether the camera or scanner completed the test successfully. You can also check the Event Log to see if the test was successful.

Using Modems for Dial-up Connections

At one time or another, if you've used a computer, you have probably used a modem to connect to your office or to an Internet service provider (ISP) using a dial-up connection. Although it seems that dial-up connections are rapidly become a relic, high-speed Internet connections such as DSL and cable have not completely replaced dial-up technology—at least not yet. This section details what you need to know about modem support and troubleshooting in Windows XP Professional.

Installing Modems

If Windows XP launches the Install New Modem dialog box for the Add Hardware Wizard as soon as your new modem is physically connected to your machine, you are in luck! You have nothing more to do than follow the prompts that the wizard provides (if any) to complete the setup of your new modem.

If the Add Hardware Wizard does not detect your modem or if you cannot find it listed, you are faced with installing an unsupported modem. Good luck on your mission. Windows XP cannot automatically detect certain internal modems. You must install the modem manually through the Add Hardware applet located in the Control Panel, or by following these instructions:

1. Open Phone and Modem Options in the Control Panel.

2. (Optional) If you are prompted for location information, enter dialing information for your location and click OK.

3. Click the Modems tab and then click the Add button.

4. Follow the instructions for the Add Hardware Wizard.

Leveraging Multilink Support

Multilinking, or multiple-device dialing, enables you to combine two or more modems or integrated services digital network (ISDN) adapters into one logical link with increased bandwidth. The Network and Dial-up Connections feature performs Point-to-Point Protocol (PPP) Multilink dialing over multiple ISDN, X.25, or modem lines. The feature combines multiple physical links into a logical bundle, and the resulting aggregate link increases your connection bandwidth. For example, you could use Multilink to combine the power of two 56Kbps modems to achieve a potential throughput of more than 100Kbps via a dial-up connection. Of course, the actual throughput depends on line noise, the distance from your location to the central telephone switching office, and other factors. Detailed information on Multilink support under Windows XP can be found in the Microsoft Knowledge Base article 307849.

Configuring Multilink

To configure Multilink, perform the following steps:

1. Open the Control Panel and double-click the Network Connections icon.

2. Right-click the connection on which you want to enable Multilink, and then select Properties.

3. On the General tab, mark the check box next to each device that you want to use with this connection, and click OK.

Multilink Tips

If you use multiple devices to dial a server that requires callback, only one of your Multilinked devices is called back, because only one phone number is stored in a user account. In this instance, only one device connects and all the other available devices fail to complete the connection, so your connection loses Multilink functionality. You can avoid this problem if the Multilinked phone book entry is for an ISDN line or for a modem with two channels that have the same phone number.

 To dial multiple devices, both your connection and your remote access server must have Multilink enabled.

Troubleshooting Modems

You can verify that your modem is working properly by clicking the Query Modem button found on the Diagnostics tab of the Properties dialog box for the modem (the Query Modem button is also accessible from the modem's Properties dialog box in Device Manager). Another option for troubleshooting a modem problem is to use the Troubleshoot button, which is also available from the modem's Properties dialog box, but you should use this only as a last resort because it invokes the Windows XP Help and Support Center and runs you through a basic troubleshooting checklist.

Configuring and Managing CD and DVD Media Devices

Windows XP supports a variety of optical media devices and formats, including CD read-only memory (CD-ROM), CD recordable (CD-R), CD rewritable (CD-RW), DVD read-only memory (DVD-ROM), DVD recordable (DVD-R and DVD+R), DVD rewritable (DVD-RW and DVD+RW), and DVD random access memory (DVD-RAM) drives and disc formats. Check with the most recent Hardware Compatibility List (HCL) or your hardware vendor to see if your CD or DVD device will work with Windows XP.

If the CD or DVD device is PnP compliant, you can rely on Windows XP to detect the device and install the appropriate drivers, as well as allocate system resources for the device. If you are using a CD or DVD drive that is not PnP compliant, use the Add Hardware applet in the Control Panel to install the drivers and assign resources for the device.

The Windows XP Compact Disc File System (CDFS) reads CDs that are formatted according to the ISO 9660 standard. Windows XP also supports the Joliet standard, which is an extension to the ISO 9660 standard. Joliet supports Unicode characters and supports a folder hierarchy extending deeper than eight levels of subfolders. Windows XP also offers integrated support for writing data directly onto CD-R and CD-RW media without requiring any third-party CD-burning software such as Roxio's Easy Media Creator. However, Windows XP, even under SP2, does not currently support writing data directly onto DVD recordable media without the use of a third-party tool.

DVD movies require either a hardware or software decoder to play movies on your Windows XP computer, even if you want to use the built-in Windows Media Player as the preferred playback device. The computer also requires a Windows XP–compatible sound card and video display card with their respective drivers to play multimedia DVD titles. Your decoder must be Windows XP compliant to play movies after you install Windows XP if you upgrade from a previous Windows version. You do not need a decoder for reading DVDs that contain only data.

Service Pack 2 installs an updated version of the Windows Media Player. The Windows Media Player 9 Series replaces the Windows Media Player 8 Series that shipped with the RTM version of Windows XP.

The Universal Disk Format (UDF)

UDF is based on the ISO 13346 standard, and Windows XP uses this standard for reading removable media such as DVDs, CD-ROMs, CD-Rs, CD-RWs, write once, read many (WORM) discs, and magneto-optical (MO) discs.

Windows XP supports UDF versions 1.02, 1.50, 2.0, and 2.01 through the Udfs.sys driver. You can format DVD-RAM discs with the FAT32 file system under Windows XP; however, you cannot natively format DVD-RAM discs using NTFS, nor can you write directly to UDF volumes (including DVD-RAM discs) without using a third-party utility.

Installing, Configuring, and Troubleshooting USB Devices

Windows XP offers built-in support for many Universal Serial Bus (USB) devices. Because all USB devices fully support Plug and Play, USB peripherals, by using standard USB cables and connectors, can be easily connected to (and disconnected from) Windows XP computers that have USB ports. In theory, USB devices can be safely connected and disconnected while the computer is running. Windows XP detects USB devices when they are plugged into the PC and attempts to install the proper device driver for each detected USB device. If Windows XP cannot locate an appropriate device driver, it will prompt you to insert a driver diskette or CD-ROM from the manufacturer of the device.

 All releases of Windows XP (RTM, SP1, and SP2) support both the USB 1.1 standard and the newer, faster USB 2.0 standard. Unfortunately, the hardware that Windows XP is running on may not support the newer USB 2.0 standard. You may need to install a USB 2.0 adapter card if the computer was manufactured with only USB 1.1 ports installed. Be mindful, however, that some motherboards and BIOSes still may not support the USB 2.0 specification.

Overview: USB Controllers, USB Hubs, and Daisy-Chaining USB Devices

To support USB, a computer needs either a USB host controller to be built in to the motherboard or a USB controller add-in adapter card to be installed. The USB host controller directs all USB traffic and also serves as a hub that USB devices connect to. Additional (external) USB hubs may be connected to enable multiple USB devices to be connected to the host controller, also known as the root hub. Hubs are either self-powered or bus powered. Some devices, such as mice and keyboards, can function fine when plugged into bus-powered USB hubs. Other devices, such as external hard drives, printers, and scanners, may require more power than bus-powered hubs can provide. Connect these kinds of USB devices to self-powered hubs. USB supports up to a maximum of 127 devices connected to one USB host controller (root hub) with no more than seven tiers (seven layers of USB hubs daisy-chained together). No more than five external hubs may be used in one physical chain of hubs. Each device can be no more than five meters away from the port of the hub that it is connected to.

 USB devices that install and function properly under Windows 98, Windows Me, or Windows 2000 are not guaranteed to work flawlessly under Windows XP. Be sure to check for upgraded drivers before you upgrade a computer to Windows XP. Verify that USB peripherals are on the Windows XP HCL or check with the USB device manufacturer regarding compatibility with Windows XP.

Viewing Power Allocations for USB Hubs

To view power allocations for USB hubs, perform the following steps:

1. Open Device Manager.

2. Expand the entry for Universal Serial Bus Controller.

3. Right-click USB Root Hub and then click Properties.

4. On the Power tab, view the power consumed by each device in the Attached Devices list.

 As mentioned previously, hubs for USB devices are either self-powered or bus powered. Self-powered hubs (hubs plugged into an electrical outlet) provide maximum power to the device, whereas bus-powered hubs (hubs plugged only into another USB port) provide minimum power. Devices that require a lot of power, such as cameras, should be plugged into self-powered hubs. Universal Serial Bus Controller appears only if you have a USB port on your computer. The Power tab appears only for USB hubs.

Troubleshooting USB Devices

Sometimes when you install a USB device on a computer, the computer might start functioning poorly or the system might even freeze entirely. The first step to take in such a scenario is to power off the computer, wait about 60 seconds, and then power it back on. If that doesn't help, try one or more of the following steps:

➤ Follow the manufacturer's installation instructions, which may require that you run a setup program before connecting the USB device to the computer.

➤ Connect the device to a different computer to verify that it is not defective.

➤ Plug the device directly into a USB hub on the back of the computer instead of plugging it into a USB hub.

➤ Look at the Windows XP Event Log for USB-related error messages.

➤ Check Device Manager to verify that all USB devices on the Universal Serial Bus Controller's tree are operating correctly.

➤ Check whether one or more USB devices are drawing more power (more than 500 milliamps) than the bus or hub can provide. Use a separate power adapter for high-power-consumption devices (if available) or use a self-powered USB hub for such devices.

➤ Try replacing the USB cables.

➤ Make sure that no more than five hubs are connected in one continuous chain.

 Ultra portable USB "thumb" drives (also known as keychain drives, jump drives, and flash drives) usually work seamlessly under Windows XP without the need to install a driver. Such is not the case under Windows 98—most of these small portable storage devices require that a driver be installed before they can be used.

Using Network Adapters

You can install network adapters using the Add Hardware applet in the Control Panel. You can make changes to the binding order of protocols and the network provider order by selecting the Advanced Settings option under the Advanced menu of the Network Connections window (accessed from the Network Connections icon in the Control Panel). Each network adapter has its own separate icon in the Network Connections folder. Right-click a network adapter icon to set its properties, install protocols, change addresses, or perform any other configuration changes for the connection.

Using Infrared Data Association (IrDA) Devices

Windows XP supports IrDA protocols that enable data transfer over infrared connections. This provides an infrastructure that allows other devices and programs to communicate with Windows XP through the IrDA interface. Windows XP installs with the Wireless Link tool, which transfers files to or from another computer that runs Windows XP, Windows 2000, or Windows 98.

Windows XP's PnP architecture automatically detects and installs the infrared component for computers with built-in IrDA hardware. For computers without built-in IrDA hardware, a user can attach a serial port IrDA transceiver to a serial COM port and use the Add Hardware Wizard to install the device under Windows XP.

After an infrared device is installed, the Wireless Link icon appears in the Control Panel. When another IrDA transceiver comes in range, the Wireless Link icon appears on the desktop and on the taskbar. You can then send a file over the infrared connection with any of the following actions:

➤ Specify a location and one or more files using the Wireless Link dialog box.

➤ Use drag-and-drop operations to move files onto the Wireless Link icon on the desktop.

➤ Right-click any selection of files on the desktop, in Windows Explorer, or in My Computer, and then click Send to Infrared Recipient.

➤ Print to a printer configured to use an infrared port.

In addition to sending or printing files, you can create a network connection that connects two computers using the infrared port. You can use this capability to map shared drives on a host computer and work with files and folders in Windows Explorer or My Computer. You can also use an infrared network connection to connect directly to another computer without modems, cables, or network hardware.

Enabling or Disabling Receiving Files via IrDA Connections

To enable or disable receiving files using an infrared link, perform the following steps:

1. Open the Wireless Link applet in the Control Panel.

2. On the Infrared tab, mark or clear the check box labeled Allow Others to Send Files to Your Computer Using Infrared Communications and click OK.

Wireless Networking Support

Windows XP Professional supports the IEEE 802.1x standard for wireless LANs, including the following popular wireless standards: 802.11a, 802.11b (also known as Wi-Fi), and 802.11g. Wireless networking support under Windows XP includes a roaming feature that enables the operating system to detect a move to a new wireless access point and forces reauthentication to verify appropriate network access at a new location. By default, wireless networking support under Windows XP uses the zero client configuration feature to automatically configure and use IEEE 802.1x authentication on the wireless network.

You can configure wireless networking settings by opening the Network Connections window from the Control Panel, right-clicking the wireless connection you want to modify, and selecting Properties. From the wireless connection's Properties dialog box, you can enable or disable the automatic wireless configuration, set up or disable IEEE 802.1x authentication, and specify a connection to a wireless network with or without a Wired Equivalent Privacy (WEP) Network Key. Windows XP wireless networking supports both the broadcasting and nonbroadcasting of service set identifiers (SSIDs), although nonbroadcasted SSIDs are a more secure option. Windows XP also supports network device filtering based on each network adapter's unique hexadecimal media access control (MAC) identification address, which is known as MAC filtering. By filtering out all unwanted network devices from connecting to a wireless access point, you add an extra layer of protection to the perimeter of your wireless network.

 SP2 offers several enhancements for wireless networking support under Windows XP. One of the biggest changes is the new Wireless Network Setup Wizard, which walks you through the steps necessary to configure a wireless network, including assigning an SSID and setting up either Wired Equivalent Privacy (WEP) encryption or Wi-Fi Protected Access (WPA) encryption. The Wireless Network Setup Wizard is available by double-clicking its icon in the Control Panel. The following new wireless networking features are also available under SP2:

➤ When connected to a wireless network, a new wireless network connection icon displays in the system tray.

➤ Wireless Provisioning Services (WPS)—This new feature provides wireless users with seamless connectivity to public Wi-Fi hotspots through the automatic configuration (provisioning) of the client and seamless roaming from one access point to another. WPS enables Wireless Internet Service Providers to use a standards-based platform to provide Wi-Fi hotspots with enhanced security that are easy to use and manage. WPS also offers organizations the capability to easily provide guest access to private wireless networks with enhanced security. WPS requires a network infrastructure based on Windows Server 2003 with Service Pack 1 installed in addition to Windows XP SP2 on the clients.

 Windows XP SP2 offers you two choices when configuring your wireless network adapter: connect to an *Ad-hoc* wireless network or to an *Infrastructure* wireless network. An Ad-hoc wireless network connects directly from one computer's wireless network adapter to another computer's wireless network adapter *without* going through a wireless access point (WAP) or wireless router. An Infrastructure-based wireless network requires either a wireless access point (WAP) or a wireless router that acts as a hub in which each computer's wireless signal must pass through to connect to other computers on the wireless network.

Installing, Configuring, and Supporting Video Display Adapters

When Windows XP is being installed, your system's BIOS selects the primary video display adapter based on PCI slot order. You can install and configure any additional video adapters you want to use with your system by using the Display applet or the Add Hardware applet in the Control Panel. Video problems often occur for one of the following four reasons:

➤ An incorrect video device driver has been installed.

➤ The display settings for the video adapter have been configured incorrectly.

➤ The monitor's refresh rate is set incorrectly.

➤ The graphics hardware acceleration setting has been set too high.

If you select an incorrect video driver or if you configure a video driver's settings incorrectly, your Windows XP system may become unuseable or even display the dreaded blue screen of death (BSOD). Fortunately, Windows XP offers several ways to restore the previous (functional) video display settings. When you restart the computer, press the F8 key as Windows XP is restarting, which enables you to select one of the following options from the Windows Advanced Options menu:

➤ Safe Mode—Enables you to manually update, remove, or even roll back the problem video driver.

➤ Enable VGA Mode—Enables you to boot the system using standard VGA 640×480 resolution with just 16 colors. You can then correct any incorrect video settings.

➤ Last Known Good Configuration (Your Most Recent Settings That Worked)—Enables you to revert the system's Registry and device driver configurations back to how they were the last time that a user started the computer and logged on successfully.

Configuring Multiple-Monitor Support

Windows XP continues to support multiple-monitor functionality that increases your work productivity by expanding the size of your desktop. Multiple displays still must use PCI or Accelerated Graphics Port (AGP) port devices to work properly with Windows XP. PCI or AGP video adapters that are built in to the motherboard are also supported under the multiple-monitor feature.

You can connect up to 10 individual monitors to create a desktop large enough to view several programs and windows onscreen at the same time.

You can easily work on more than one task at a time by moving items from one monitor to another or by stretching them across numerous monitors. Edit images or text on one monitor while viewing web activity on another. You can also open multiple pages of a single, long document and drag them across several monitors to easily view the layout of text and graphics. You can stretch a spreadsheet across two monitors so you can view several columns without scrolling.

One monitor serves as the primary display. This is the monitor on which you see the Logon dialog box when you start your computer. In addition, most programs display their windows on the primary monitor when you initially open them. You can set different resolutions and different color depths for each monitor. You can also connect multiple monitors to individual graphics adapters or to a single adapter that supports multiple outputs.

Arranging Multiple Monitors

To arrange multiple monitors, perform the following steps:

1. Open the Display applet in the Control Panel.

2. Click the monitor icons and drag them to positions that represent how you want to move items from one monitor to another, and then click OK or Apply to view the changes (see Figure 5.7). You can also click the Identify button to briefly flash the monitor number on each monitor's screen as assigned by Windows XP.

The icon positions determine how you move items from one monitor to another. For example, if you are using two monitors and you want to move items from one monitor to the other by dragging left and right, place the icons side by side. To move items between monitors by dragging up and down, place the icons one above the other. The icon positions do not have to correspond to the physical positions of the monitors. You can place the icons one above the other even though your monitors are side by side.

Changing the Primary Monitor

To change the primary monitor, perform the following steps:

1. Open the Display applet in the Control Panel.

2. On the Settings tab, click the monitor icon that represents the monitor you want to designate as the primary one.

Figure 5.7 The Display Properties dialog box enables you to configure multiple monitors when multiple video adapters are installed or when a single video adapter supports multiple video output signals.

3. Select the Use This Device as the Primary Monitor check box (see Figure 5.7). This check box is unavailable when you select the monitor icon that is currently set as your primary monitor.

The monitor that is designated as the primary monitor displays the Logon dialog box when you start your computer. Most programs display their window on the primary monitor when you first open them.

Moving Items Between Monitors or Viewing the Same Desktop on Multiple Monitors

To move items between monitors or to view the same desktop on multiple monitors, perform the following steps:

1. Open the Display applet in the Control Panel.

2. On the Settings tab, click the monitor icon that represents the monitor you want to use in addition to your primary monitor.

3. Select the Extend My Windows Desktop onto This Monitor check box (refer to Figure 6.7). Selecting this check box enables you to drag items across your screen onto alternative monitors. You can also resize a window to stretch it across more than one monitor.

Troubleshooting Multiple Displays

The default refresh frequency setting is typically 60Hz, although your monitors may support a higher setting. A higher refresh frequency might reduce flicker on your screens, but choosing a setting that is too high for your monitor may make your display unuseable, and may even damage your hardware.

If your refresh frequency is set to anything higher than 60Hz and your monitor display(s) goes black when you start Windows XP, restart the system in Safe Mode. Change your refresh frequency for all monitors to 60Hz. You may need to double-check this setting in your Unattended Installation script file, commonly called **Unattend.txt**, if Windows XP was installed on the computer using a customized unattended installation script file. You can find a sample **unattend.txt** file on the Windows XP Professional CD-ROM in the i386 folder.

Multiple-display support in Windows XP presents some challenges when you are dealing with some legacy applications and MS-DOS programs. If you start an MS-DOS application on your multiple-monitor Windows XP computer, and then both of your screens flicker and completely go dark, you can fix the problem without much difficulty. Multiple-display support allows you to adjust the display settings so that your application runs and is viewable on both monitors. First, you may need to restart your system. Then, select Safe Mode at the F8 startup menu. Finally, after you can see the contents of your desktop, you can configure the MS-DOS program to run in a window and change your Display settings from Default to Optimal.

Removable Storage Support

Windows XP Professional provides removable storage services for applications and network administrators that enhance the sharing and management of removable media hardware such as backup tape drives, optical discs, and automated (robotic) media pool libraries. Removable storage and media support in Windows XP precludes the need for third-party software developers to write custom application programs to support each type of removable media device. In addition, removable storage services allow organizations to leverage their investment in expensive removable storage equipment by having multiple removable storage applications share these devices.

Windows XP Removable storage implements a set of APIs that enable third-party software solutions to catalog all removable media, such as DVDs, tapes, and optical discs. Both offline (shelved) as well as online (housed in a library) media can be cataloged. Removable storage organizes media using media pools. These media pools control access to the removable media, categorize the media according to each type of use, and permit the media to be shared by applications. Removable storage tracks the application programs that share the removable media. Removable storage is logically structured into five basic components: media units, media libraries, media pools, work queue items, and operator requests. You manage removable storage from the MMC snap-in named, strangely enough, Removable Storage.

Managing Tape Devices

Windows XP provides comprehensive control of tape devices. You can back up or restore from tape devices, enable or disable specific tapes in your library, insert and eject media, and mount and dismount media. Tape devices are not the only media that the Windows Backup program supports. You can back up to network shares, to local hard drives, or to removable media such as USB external hard drives, FireWire external hard drives, or even Iomega Zip or Rev disks. Backing up to tape is still very popular, however, despite some of its drawbacks.

The Windows XP Backup utility does *not* support backing up data directly onto CD-R, CD-RW, DVD±R, or DVD±RW media. You can manually copy folders and files directly to CD-R, CD-RW, DVD±R, or DVD±RW discs using the native Windows XP CD burning capability for CD-R and CD-RW media or by using a third-party tool for writing to DVD media.

You can also copy backup files that were created by the Windows XP Backup utility to one or more CD-R, CD-RW, DVD±R, or DVD±RW discs using the native Windows XP CD burning capability for CD-R and CD-RW media or by using a third-party tool for writing to DVD media.

During a restore, the Windows XP Backup Utility program can *read* directly from optical media to perform the restore procedure; it just does not support *writing* backup data onto these types of optical media.

If the tape device is PnP compliant, you can rely on Windows XP to detect the device and install the appropriate drivers, as well as allocate system resources for the device. If you are using a tape device that is not PnP compliant, use the Add Hardware applet in the Control Panel to install the drivers and assign resources for the device. Use Device Manager to enable, disable, or edit settings for any tape device.

Upgrading a System from One to Two Processors

Windows XP Professional supports a maximum of two processors; Windows XP Home supports only one processor. When more than one processor (CPU) is present in the computer at the time the operating system is installed, Windows XP Professional uses symmetric multiprocessing (SMP). However, if Windows XP is installed with only one CPU present and you want to add a second processor later, you must use the Update Hardware Wizard to enable support for multiple processors.

To install support for multiple CPUs, perform the following steps:

1. Right-click My Computer and then select Properties.

2. Click the Hardware tab and then click the Device Manager button.

3. Expand the Processors node and note the type of support you currently have.

4. Right-click the icon for the currently installed processor and select Update Driver to launch the Update Hardware Wizard. Alternatively, you can right-click the icon for the currently installed processor, select Properties, and then click the Driver tab, as shown in Figure 5.8. Next, click the Update Driver button from this dialog box, and you will also launch the Update Hardware Wizard. Follow the onscreen instructions to load the proper Hardware Abstraction Layer (HAL) for the CPU that you have added.

Figure 5.8 The Processor Properties dialog box enables you to add support for a second processor by clicking the Update Driver button.

5. You must restart the computer for the change to take effect.

 Don't try this if your computer has only one processor! It may make your computer unbootable.

You can use the preceding steps only to upgrade from a single-processor HAL (Hardware Abstraction Layer) to a multiple-processor HAL. If you use this procedure to change from a standard HAL to an ACPI HAL (for example, after a BIOS upgrade) or vice versa, unexpected and undesired results may occur, including an inability to boot the computer. If you upgrade the BIOS from supporting APM to ACPI, you need to reinstall Windows XP so that the operating system will properly support that type of upgrade.

Mobile Computing

PC Card (formerly known as PCMCIA) adapters, USB devices, IEEE 1394 (FireWire) devices, and infrared devices are fully supported in Windows XP. You manage these through Device Manager. Support is provided in Windows XP Professional for both the APM and the ACPI power management standards, which are covered near the end of this chapter.

Hot (computer is fully powered) and cold (computer is in Suspend mode) docking and undocking are fully supported for computers with a Plug and Play BIOS. Hibernate (complete power down while maintaining the state of open programs and connected hardware) and Suspend (deep sleep with some power) modes are also supported for extending battery life.

When you install a PC Card, USB, FireWire, or infrared device, Windows XP automatically recognizes and configures it (if it meets Plug and Play specifications). If Windows does not have an entry in its Driver.cab file for the new hardware, you are prompted to supply the file path where the operating system can install a compatible driver.

Support for Offline Files enables mobile users to work with documents and other files even when they are disconnected from the network. Offline Files can be synchronized when users reconnect to the network. Folder Redirection enables administrators to redirect system folders, such as My Documents, to store users' files at an alternative location on a network server while making it appear to the users that the folder is local to their computer. This feature helps to ensure that users' data is stored in a central location that can be backed up. When used in conjunction with Offline Files, mobile users can take their data with them on the road and then synchronize their files when they return to the office.

Equipping mobile computers with Smart Cards and implementing the NTFS file system with the Encrypting File System decreases the likelihood of confidential data being compromised if the computer is stolen, lost, or placed into the wrong hands.

Managing Hardware Profiles

Hardware profiles store configuration settings in the Windows XP Registry for a collection of devices and services. Windows XP can store different hardware profiles so that a user's' needs can be met even when his computer may frequently require different devices and services to be enabled or disabled depending on different circumstances. A good example is a portable computer that is used in an office with a docking station. The computer is then undocked so the user can travel with the notebook PC. These two situations require different power management settings, possibly different network settings, and various other hardware configuration changes.

You can enable and disable devices in particular profiles through their Properties dialog box in Device Manager, as shown in Figure 5.9. You manage services using the Services snap-in for the MMC, as shown in Figure 5.10. You create and manage hardware profiles using the System applet in the Control Panel or by right-clicking My Computer and choosing Properties. Inside the System applet, go to the Hardware tab and click the Hardware Profiles button to open the Hardware Profiles dialog box, shown in Figure 5.11. At installation, Windows XP creates a single hardware profile called Profile 1 (Current), which you can rename. You are prompted to select a hardware profile at system startup only when two or more hardware profiles are stored on your machine. You can create and store as many hardware profiles on your machine as you like. You select the desired hardware profile at Windows XP startup to specify which device and service configuration settings you need for the current session.

To configure a hardware profile, copy the default profile and rename it appropriately. Restart the computer and select the profile you want to configure, if you are configuring hardware devices. In the Properties dialog box for any device, you can specify whether that device is enabled or disabled for the current profile. To configure services, you can specify which hardware profile a particular service is enabled or disabled for—the computer does not need to be restarted with a specific hardware profile when you configure services.

If Windows XP detects that your computer is a portable (laptop or notebook), it tries to determine whether your system is docked or undocked; it then selects the appropriate hardware profile for the current conditions. Do not confuse *hardware profiles* with *user profiles*—the two are not related!

Figure 5.9 The properties sheet for a device allows you to enable or disable it for the current hardware profile using the Device Usage drop-down list box.

Figure 5.10 The Log On tab of the properties sheet for a service allows you to enable or disable it for each hardware profile stored on the computer.

Hardware Profiles   [?][X]

    You can set up hardware profiles for different hardware
    configurations. At startup, you can choose the profile you
    want to use.

Available hardware profiles:

ZIP Drive (Current)
No ZIP Drive   [↑]

                                                     [↓]

[Properties]   [Copy]   [Rename]   [Delete]

Hardware profiles selection
When Windows starts:

○ Wait until I select a hardware profile

◉ Select the first profile listed if I don't select a profile in
  [30 ▲▼] seconds

                            [OK]   [Cancel]

Figure 5.11 The Hardware Profiles dialog box enables you to copy, rename, configure, and delete hardware profiles.

Hardware profiles deal with devices and services settings for the entire computer; user profiles deal with user configuration settings for individual users.

Power Management Support

Windows XP offers a variety of options for managing and conserving power consumption for both mobile and desktop computers. Monitoring battery power levels and maximizing the efficient use of electricity is critical for mobile users on the go. The Advanced Power Management (APM) specification was popular around the time when Windows 2000 was first released. However, APM was quickly replaced by the newer and improved standard, Advanced Configuration and Power Interface (ACPI). Virtually all new mobile computers sold today support ACPI; only older mobile computers support the APM standard and many of those are no longer in use. For optimal power management under Windows XP, make sure that the computer supports ACPI.

APM

Windows XP supports the APM version 1.2 specification. APM helps to greatly reduce your computer's power consumption, which is particularly helpful for mobile users. You use the Power Options applet in the Control Panel to configure power management settings on your computer. If your computer does not have an APM-compliant BIOS, Windows XP cannot install APM. This means no APM support for your machine, and no APM tab in the Power Options applet in the Control Panel. Keep in mind, though, that your machine can still function as an ACPI computer if your BIOS is ACPI compliant. The ACPI-based BIOS will take over your system configuration and power management from the Plug and Play BIOS.

ACPI

ACPI is an open-industry specification that defines a flexible and extensible hardware interface for your system board. Windows XP is a fully ACPI-compliant operating system. Software developers and designers use the ACPI specification to integrate power management features throughout a computer system, including hardware, the operating system, and application software. This integration enables Windows XP to determine which applications are active and to handle all the power management resources for computer subsystems and peripherals.

ACPI enables the operating system to control power management on a wide range of mobile, desktop, and server computers and peripherals. ACPI is the foundation for the OnNow industry initiative, which allows manufacturers to deliver computers that will start at the touch of a key on a keyboard.

ACPI design is essential when you want to take full advantage of power-management and UPnP features in Windows XP. If you are not sure if your computer is ACPI compliant, check your manufacturer's documentation. To change power settings that take advantage of ACPI, use the Power Options applet in the Control Panel.

If you upgrade a computer's BIOS so that the computer will support the ACPI standard, you must *reinstall* Windows XP if you want the system to take advantage of ACPI features.

Power Options Overview

By using Power Options in the Control Panel, you can reduce the power consumption of several computer hardware components, or you can have it impact your entire system. You do this by choosing a power scheme, which is a collection of settings that manages your computer's power usage. You can create your own power schemes or use the ones provided with Windows XP.

You can also adjust the individual settings in a power scheme. For example, depending on your hardware, you can do the following:

➤ Turn off your monitor and hard disks automatically to save power.

➤ Put your computer in Standby mode, which puts your entire system in a low-power state, if you plan to be away from your computer for a while. While in Standby mode, your entire computer switches to a low-power state, where devices such as the monitor and hard disks turn off and your computer uses less power. When you want to use the computer again, it comes out of Standby quickly, and your desktop is restored exactly as you left it. Standby is useful for conserving battery power in portable computers.

 Standby mode does *not* save your desktop state to disk, so if a power failure occurs while the computer is in Standby mode, you can lose unsaved information. If an interruption in power occurs, information in memory is lost. If this concerns you, using Hibernate mode or completely powering off may be better choices to consider.

➤ Put your computer in Hibernate mode. When you restart your computer, your desktop is restored exactly as you left it. It takes longer to bring your computer out of Hibernate mode than out of Standby. Put your computer in Hibernate mode when you will be away from the computer for an extended period of time.

 The Hibernate feature saves everything in memory to disk, turns off your monitor and hard disk, and then powers off the computer.

Managing Battery Power on a Mobile Computer

Using the Power Options applet in the Control Panel, you can reduce consumption of battery power on your portable computer and still keep the computer available for immediate use. You can view multiple batteries separately, or as a whole, and set alarms to warn you of low-battery conditions.

Managing Power When Installing a Plug and Play Device

The Windows XP Plug and Play feature works with the Power Options applet in the Control Panel to make sure that your system runs efficiently while you are installing or removing hardware devices. The Power Options applet controls the power supply to the devices attached to your computer, supplying power to those components that you are using and conserving power for those components that you are not currently using. Windows XP automatically manages the power for devices; however, some devices may have options you can set in Device Manager.

To take full advantage of Plug and Play, you need to use Windows XP on an ACPI-compliant computer that is running in ACPI mode, and the hardware devices must be PnP and/or ACPI compliant. In an ACPI-compliant computer, the operating system, not the hardware, configures and monitors the computer's devices. Windows XP Professional supports ACPI wake events for ACPI-compliant devices. These events include wake-on-ring for modems, wake-on-LAN for network cards, and wake-on-critical-battery.

Managing Card Services

Card services play an important role in Windows XP Professional. Support for card services includes PC Cards as peripheral devices and Smart Card technology for logon authentication. The operating system supports both the PC Card standard as well as the CardBus (PC Card 32) standard. The many benefits of these devices include their compact size, low power requirements, and support for the Plug and Play standard. The CardBus specification is a combination of the PC Card 16 standard and the Peripheral Component Interconnect (PCI) standard. This combination provides 32-bit performance and the PCI bus in a compact, portable size. You can find several types of PC Cards that are usually used in mobile computers: network adapter cards, hard drive cards, modem cards, wireless network cards, and so on.

Working with Smart Cards

Support for Smart Card technology is fully integrated into Windows XP. Smart Cards play an important role in Windows XP's Public Key Infrastructure (PKI) security architecture for logon authentication and other security-related services. Smart Cards are credit-card–sized devices that have integrated circuits built in to them. These electronic cards securely store both public and private encryption keys and also perform cryptographic functions such as digital-signature and key-exchange operations.

Microsoft supports only PnP-compliant Smart Card reader devices. Smart Card readers connect to standard PC interfaces such as serial (RS-232) ports, PS/2 ports, USB ports, and PC Card slots. To install a Smart Card reader, use the Add Hardware applet in the Control Panel. Smart Card configurations typically use the Extensible Authentication Protocol-Transport Level Security (EAP-TLS) authentication protocol. When you use a Smart Card to log on to a Windows XP Professional computer, at least one Cryptographic Service Provider (CSP) service must be installed and running on the system. CSPs enable other application programs to have access to the cryptographic services of a Smart Card, such as digital signature, key generation, and key exchange.

Before a user can log on to a system with a Smart Card, the user must be enrolled for a Smart Card certificate by an administrator who has the proper security privileges to enroll other users. This enrollment process creates a certificate and a public encryption key for the user. The user also needs to create or to be assigned a personal identification number (PIN) code, which must be used in conjunction with the Smart Card when logging on to a Smart Card–enabled computer.

Exam Prep Questions

1. Brendan has just installed a brand new updated version of the software driver for his Zip drive removable media device. After the driver installs successfully, he is prompted to restart his Windows XP computer. Unfortunately, whenever he attempts to copy files to a Zip disk now, he receives an error message and the files do not get copied to the disk. He doesn't have the original Zip disk driver diskette, but he wants to replace the new driver with the previous version. What is the fastest and easiest way that he can accomplish this?

   ○ A. Restart the computer, press the F8 key during startup, and select the Last Known Good Configuration option.

   ○ B. Restart the computer, press the F8 key during startup, and select the Safe Mode option. Uninstall the printer and then reinstall it and let Windows locate the correct driver.

   ○ C. Open Device Manager, right-click the Zip device, select Properties, click the Driver tab, and click the Roll Back Driver button.

   ○ D. Click Start, All Programs, Windows Update, and download a driver from the Windows Update website.

2. Brandy is a network administrator who wants to control the type of device drivers that can be installed in the Windows XP Professional workstations in her office. Which Group Policy Object (GPO) can she use along with which setting so that unsigned device drivers cannot be installed?

   ○ A. Brandy can go to User Configuration, Windows Settings, Security Settings, Local Policies, Security Options, and set the Devices: Unsigned Driver Installation Behavior policy to Silently Succeed.

   ○ B. Brandy can go to Computer Configuration, Administrative Templates, System, and set the Devices: Unsigned Driver Installation Behavior policy to Silently Succeed.

   ○ C. Brandy can go to User Configuration, Administrative Templates, System, and set the Devices: Unsigned Driver Installation Behavior policy to Do Not Allow Installation.

   ○ D. Brandy can go to Computer Configuration, Windows Settings, Security Settings, Local Policies, Security Options, and set the Devices: Unsigned Driver Installation Behavior policy to Do Not Allow Installation.

3. Alexis has several USB devices plugged into different USB hubs that are all connected to a USB port on her Windows XP computer. She buys a new USB mouse and plugs it into one of the daisy-chained USB hubs using a USB cable that is 12 feet in length. The computer does not detect the new mouse. Even when she tries to install it using the Add Hardware Wizard, the system cannot find the new USB device. What is the most likely cause of this problem?

    ○ A. The mouse is not compatible with Plug and Play or Universal Plug and Play.

    ○ B. The USB hub that the mouse is plugged into is connected as the sixth hub in a row of hubs.

    ○ C. The 12-foot USB cable used for the mouse is longer than the supported USB cable length.

    ○ D. The USB mouse requires a self-powered hub instead of a bus-powered hub.

4. Which of the following five methods can you employ to fix a severe video driver problem where the display is no longer visible? (Check all correct answers.)

    ❑ A. Restart the computer in Safe Mode and then update or change the driver.

    ❑ B. Don't restart the computer and use the Driver Rollback feature.

    ❑ C. Restart the computer in VGA Mode.

    ❑ D. Restart the computer under the Last Known Good Configuration option.

    ❑ E. Restart the computer and select a different hardware profile.

5. How many monitors will Windows XP support if you install one PCI video adapter, one AGP video adapter, and one ISA video adapter, and the computer already has an integrated AGP video adapter on the motherboard?

    ○ A. The computer will support three monitors.

    ○ B. The computer will support four monitors.

    ○ C. The computer will support two monitors.

    ○ D. The computer will support one monitor.

6. What is the most efficient way that you can update Windows XP Professional to support a second processor if only a single processor was present when you first installed the operating system?

    ○ A. Use the Uptomp.exe utility from the Windows XP Professional Resource Kit.

    ○ B. Reinstall Windows XP Professional on the system.

    ○ C. Launch the Hardware Update Wizard by right-clicking the existing processor in Device Manager and selecting Update Driver.

    ○ D. Copy the `Halmps.dll` file from the Windows XP Professional Setup CD-ROM to the `%systemroot%\system32` folder and then restart the computer.

7. How can you update Windows XP to support ACPI after you have upgraded the computer's BIOS from supporting APM to supporting ACPI?

    ○ A. Go to the Power Options applet in the Control Panel, click the Advanced tab, click the Enable ACPI option button, and then restart the computer for the change to take effect.

    ○ B. Reinstall Windows XP Professional on the system.

    ○ C. Launch the Hardware Update Wizard by right-clicking the existing processor in Device Manager and selecting Update Driver.

    ○ D. Copy the `Halacpi.dll` file from the Windows XP Professional Setup CD-ROM to the `%systemroot%\system32` folder and then restart the computer.

8. Which of the following statements about support for DVD and CD media *are not true* under Windows XP Professional? (Check all correct answers.)

   ❏ A. You can write to CD-R and CD-RW media under Windows XP without using any third-party applications.

   ❏ B. You can write to DVD-R and DVD-RW media under Windows XP without using any third-party applications.

   ❏ C. You can play back DVD movies without third-party decoder software or hardware by using the new Windows Media Player that ships with Windows XP.

   ❏ D. You cannot read DVD data discs without using a third-party application.

9. Which of the following types of encryption for wireless networking does Windows XP SP2 offer? Choose two.

   ❏ A. Wired Equivalency Privacy

   ❏ B. Wi-Fi Protected Mode

   ❏ C. SSID-based encryption

   ❏ D. WPS filtering

   ❏ E. MAC filtering

10. Which of the following options must you select from when you click the Windows Update button on the Hardware tab of the System Properties dialog box under Windows XP SP2? Choose three.

    ❏ A. If My Device Needs a Driver, Go to Windows Update Without Asking Me

    ❏ B. Turn Off Automatic Updates

    ❏ C. Notify Me but Don't Automatically Download or Install Them

    ❏ D. Download Updates for Me, but Let Me Choose When to Install Them

    ❏ E. Ask Me to Search Windows Update Every Time I Connect a New Device

    ❏ F. Never search Windows Update for drivers.

Answers to Exam Prep Questions

1. Answer C is correct. The Driver Rollback feature is the quickest and easiest way to return a device driver to its previous version. Answer A is incorrect because the Last Known Good Configuration option can't help you after you have successfully logged on to the computer after a configuration change. Answer B is incorrect because Safe Mode is no better for installing drivers than booting normally, and this action would not return the driver to its previous version. Answer D is incorrect because the Windows Update website would also not return the driver to its previous state.

2. Answer D is correct. The policy setting for Devices: Unsigned Driver Installation Behavior is a global, computer-related GPO, and the setting Do Not Allow Installation blocks unsigned drivers from being installed on the system. Answer A is incorrect because the policy setting for Devices: Unsigned Driver Installation Behavior is a global, computer-related GPO; it is not user-specific, and the setting Silently Succeed allows both signed and unsigned drivers to be installed. Answer B is

incorrect because the setting Silently Succeed allows both signed and unsigned drivers to be installed. Answer C is incorrect because the GPO is not located in the User Configuration container and the policy is not under Administrative Templates.

3. Answer B is correct. No more than five external hubs can be used in one physical chain of hubs. Answer A is incorrect because all USB devices are PnP–compatible. Answer C is incorrect because the maximum supported cable length between a USB device and a USB hub or port is 5 meters (12 feet is less than 5 meters). Answer D is incorrect because high power consumption devices such as hard drives, cameras, and scanners often require self-powered hubs. Generally, devices such as keyboards and mice do not.

4. Answers A, C, and D are correct. You can restart the computer in Safe Mode to fix the driver problem, you can restart the computer and select VGA Mode and then fix the problem, or you can simply restart the computer under the Last Known Good Configuration option and the video settings will revert back to how they were previously. Answer B is incorrect because you can't use the Driver Rollback feature if you can't see the display. Answer E is incorrect because the computer may have only one hardware profile present, and any other hardware profiles may not necessarily apply to the video display settings.

5. Answer A is correct. Windows XP supports the multiple-monitor feature using only PCI or AGP video display adapters. It's okay if one adapter is built in to the motherboard. Answer B is incorrect because the multiple-monitor feature is not supported for ISA video adapters. Answer C is incorrect because the multiple-monitor feature is supported on both PCI and AGP adapters. Built-in adapters are also acceptable.

6. Answer C is correct. Windows XP Professional supports a maximum of two processors. To upgrade the operating system to support a second installed processor, you use the Hardware Update Wizard. Answer A is incorrect because the Uptomp.exe utility was used for Windows NT 4, but is not used for Windows XP. Answer B is incorrect because although performing a reinstallation should update the system to support multiple processors, it would take much more time than to simply run the Hardware Update Wizard. Answer D is incorrect because copying DLL files from the Windows XP CD-ROM is not supported for upgrading support for two processors.

7. Answer B is correct. The only way that you can enable ACPI support after you have upgraded your system's BIOS to support ACPI is to reinstall Windows XP. Answer A is incorrect because there is no option button for Enable ACPI under the Power Options applet in the Control Panel. Answer C is incorrect because the Hardware Update Wizard does not support enabling ACPI on systems that were not installed with ACPI support. Answer D is incorrect because copying DLL files from the Windows XP CD-ROM is not supported for upgrading the operating system to support ACPI.

8. Answers B, C, and D are correct. You cannot write to DVD-R or DVD-RW media without a third-party utility. You cannot play back DVD movies without third-party decoder hardware or software. You can read DVD data discs natively under Windows XP without requiring a third-party utility. Answer A is incorrect because Windows XP does support writing to both CD-Rs and CD-RWs natively.

9. Answers A and B are correct. Answer C is incorrect because SSIDs are used only for wireless networks to identify themselves, not for signal encryption. Answer D is incorrect because WPS provides wireless provisioning services and does not offer any type of encryption. Answer E is incorrect because MAC filtering permits only specified network adapters to connect based on each adapter's unique hexadecimal address; no encryption is involved with MAC filtering.

10. Answers A, E, and F are correct. Answer B is incorrect because the options for configuring Automatic Updates are listed on the Automatic Updates tab of the System Properties dialog box. Answer C is incorrect because the option Notify Me but Don't Automatically Download or Install Them is also one of the options for Automatic Updates, but not for searching for device drivers under Windows Update. Answer D is incorrect because the option Download Updates for Me, but Let Me Choose When to Install Them is another option for Automatic Updates, but not for Windows Update.

Need to Know More?

 Bott, Ed, and Carl Siechert. *Microsoft Windows XP Inside Out*, 2nd ed. Redmond, WA: Microsoft Learning, 2004. ISBN 073562044X. This book offers timesaving tips, troubleshooting techniques, and workarounds. It focuses on techniques such as taking advantage of the rich integration of devices, applications, and web services in Windows XP.

 Microsoft Corporation. *Microsoft Windows XP Professional Resource Kit*, 2nd ed. Redmond, WA: Microsoft Press, 2003. ISBN 0735619743. This all-in-one reference is a compilation of technical documentation and valuable insider information that computer-support professionals and administrators can reference to install, customize, and support Windows XP.

Minasi, Mark. *Mastering Windows XP Professional*. Alameda, CA: Sybex, Inc., 2001. ISBN 0782129811. This book provides in-depth coverage of installing, configuring, and administering Windows XP Professional.

Search the Microsoft TechNet CD (or its online version through www.microsoft.com) using keywords such as "ACPI", "Driver Signing", "Universal Plug and Play", "Hardware Profiles", "Wireless Networking", "Automatic Updates", "FireWire or IEEE 1394", "USB", "Multiple Monitors", "SP2", and "Service Pack 2".

Implementing, Managing, and Troubleshooting Disk Storage

Terms you'll need to understand:

- ✓ Basic versus dynamic disks
- ✓ Partitions, volumes, and logical drives
- ✓ Simple, spanned, and striped volumes
- ✓ Diskperf.exe utility
- ✓ Diskpart.exe utility
- ✓ File allocation table (FAT or FAT16) file system
- ✓ 32-bit file allocation table (FAT32) file system
- ✓ NTFS file system
- ✓ Convert.exe utility
- ✓ Mounted drives and mount points
- ✓ Disk quotas
- ✓ NTFS file compression
- ✓ NTFS data encryption
- ✓ Universal Serial Bus (USB) storage devices

Techniques you'll need to master:

- ✓ Using the Disk Management Console
- ✓ Monitoring and troubleshooting disks using the Performance Console
- ✓ Using the Disk Cleanup Wizard and Disk Defragmenter
- ✓ Selecting a file system for Windows XP Professional
- ✓ Using Convert.exe to convert a FAT drive letter to NTFS
- ✓ Using Diskpart.exe to manage disk drives, partitions, and volumes from the command line
- ✓ Creating mounted volumes
- ✓ Managing NTFS compressed files and folders
- ✓ Managing NTFS encrypted files and folders

If you are familiar with managing hard disks, disk partitions, and disk volumes under Windows 2000, you should feel quite at home working with disk storage administration in Windows XP. Hard disk management under Windows XP Professional is strikingly similar to the Disk Management Console under both the Server and Professional editions of Windows 2000. For administrators who are more accustomed to working with Windows NT 4, Windows XP Professional introduces some different concepts, such as basic and dynamic disk storage. Even so, the Disk Management MMC (Microsoft Management Console) snap-in has a resemblance to the old Disk Administrator utility used under Windows NT 4.

Disk Storage Management

This chapter discusses how to manage and troubleshoot hard disks and their associated logical drives, basic partitions, and dynamic volumes in Windows XP Professional. It looks at the available options under Windows XP for creating partitions and volumes on a hard disk, creating and formatting drive letters, and working on other disk administration chores. In addition, this chapter uncovers the features of the different disk storage types that were first introduced under Windows 2000. Windows XP Professional supports two disk configuration types—basic storage and dynamic storage. This chapter compares and contrasts the differences between basic and dynamic disks and explains how to manage both types of disks and their associated partitions and volumes.

The *system* partition or volume contains hardware-specific files and the required system files from which Windows XP starts the boot process. These files include **ntldr**, **ntdetect.com**, and **boot.ini**, among others, and they are usually stored on the root of the C: drive.

The *boot* partition or volume contains the Windows XP operating system files, and they are usually stored in the C:*windows* folder, which is the default installation location.

Basic Disks

A Windows XP basic disk is similar to the standard disk configuration used under previous versions of Windows, such as Windows 9x and Windows NT 4. A basic disk is a physical disk with primary and/or extended partitions. As long as you use the file allocation table (FAT) file system (discussed in detail later in this chapter), Windows XP Professional and Home editions, Windows 2000, Windows NT, Windows 9x/Me, and MS-DOS operating systems can access basic disks. You can create up to three primary partitions and one extended partition on a basic disk, or just four primary partitions.

You can create a single extended partition with logical drives on a basic disk; however, in general, you cannot extend a partition on a basic disk (the section "Partitions and Logical Drives on Basic Disks" later in this chapter discusses how you can extend a basic partition under certain circumstances). Extending a disk partition enables you to add a second disk partition for more storage capacity while the operating system makes the additional partition appear to be part of the original disk partition. You gain more disk storage while maintaining the same drive letter. In all cases, you can only extend a partition formatted as NTFS.

Basic disks store their configuration information in the master boot record (MBR), which is stored on the first sector of the hard drive. The configuration of a basic disk consists of the partition information on the disk. Basic fault-tolerant sets inherited from Windows NT Server 4 are based on these simple partitions, but they extend the configuration with some extra partition relationship information, which is stored on the first track of each disk within each set.

Basic disks may contain spanned partitions (volume sets), mirrored partitions (mirror sets), striped partitions (stripe sets), and Redundant Array of Independent (or Inexpensive) Disks (RAID) level 5 partitions (stripe sets with parity) that were created using Windows NT 4 or earlier. These kinds of partitions are covered later in this chapter.

 Mirrored and RAID-5 volumes are fault-tolerant volumes that are available only under the Windows 2000 Server or the Windows Server 2003 family of network operating systems. These types of volumes cannot be created on basic or dynamic disks using Windows XP Professional. Fault-tolerant volumes are designed to withstand a single disk failure within a set of disks and to continue functioning until the failed disk is replaced. A mirror set duplicates data to a second physical disk; a RAID-5 set writes data across several disks (between 3 and 32 physical disks) and stores parity information across all the drives to be able to retrieve data in the event of a single failed disk.

Dynamic Disks

A Windows XP dynamic disk is a physical disk that does not use partitions or logical drives. Instead, a single volume is created that includes the entire disk, which can then be divided into separate volumes. Also, dynamic disks do not have the same constraints of basic disks. For example, a dynamic disk can be resized on-the-fly without requiring a reboot. Dynamic disks are associated with disk groups, which are disks managed as a collection, which helps to organize dynamic disks. All dynamic disks in a computer are members of the same disk group. Each disk in a disk group stores replicas of the same configuration data. This configuration data is stored in a 1MB region at the end of each dynamic disk.

Dynamic disks can contain any of the types of volumes discussed later in this chapter. You can extend a volume on a dynamic disk. Dynamic disks can contain an unlimited number of volumes, so you are not restricted to four volumes per disk, as you are with basic disks. Regardless of the type of file system employed, only computers running Windows XP, Windows 2000, or Windows Server 2003 can directly access dynamic volumes on hard drives that are physically connected to the computer. However, computers that are not running Windows XP, Windows 2000, or Windows Server 2003 can access the dynamic volumes remotely when they are connected to shared folders over the network.

Dynamic disks are not available under Windows XP Home edition or for mobile computers.

Comparing Basic Disks to Dynamic Disks

When you install Windows XP, the system automatically configures the existing hard disks as basic disks. Windows XP does not support dynamic disks on mobile PCs (laptops or notebooks), and, if you're using an older desktop machine that is not Advanced Configuration and Power Interface (ACPI)-compliant, the Upgrade to Dynamic Disk option (discussed later in this chapter) is not available. Dynamic disks have some additional limitations. You can install Windows XP on a dynamic volume that you converted from a basic disk, but you can't extend either the system or the boot partition. The process of upgrading volumes is covered later in this chapter. Any third-party troubleshooting tools that cannot read the dynamic Disk Management database work only on basic disks.

Dynamic disks are supported only on desktop or server systems using Small Computer System Interface (SCSI), Fibre Channel, Serial Storage Architecture (SSA), Integrated Drive Electronics (IDE), Enhanced Integrated Drive Electronics (EIDE), Ultra Direct Memory Access (DMA), Advanced Technology Attachment (ATA) interfaces, or Serial Advanced Technology Attachment (SATA) interfaces. Portable computers, removable disks, and disks connected via Universal Serial Bus (USB) or FireWire (IEEE 1394) interfaces are not supported for dynamic storage. Dynamic disks are also not supported on hard drives with a sector size that is not equal to 512 bytes. You can use the **fsutil fsinfo ntfsinfo** command or the **chkdsk** command to determine a disk's sector size. Cluster disks—groups of several disks that serve to function as a single disk—are not supported either.

Basic and dynamic disks are Windows XP's way of looking at hard disk configuration. If you're migrating to Windows XP from Windows NT 4, the dynamic disk concept might seem odd in the beginning; but after you understand the differences, working with dynamic disks is not complicated. You can format both basic disk partitions and dynamic disk volumes with the FAT16, FAT32, or NTFS file systems. FAT and NTFS are discussed later in this chapter. However, you can format a dynamic volume as NTFS only from the Disk Management Console. You must use the Windows XP Explorer or the `for-mat.exe` command-line tool to format a dynamic volume as FAT or FAT32. Table 6.1 compares the terms used with basic and dynamic disks.

Table 6.1	A Cross-Reference of Terms Used with Basic and Dynamic Disks
Basic Disks	**Dynamic Disks**
Active partition	Active volume
Extended partition	Volume and unallocated space
Logical drive	Simple volume
Mirror set	Mirrored volume (servers only)
Primary partition	Simple volume
Stripe set	Striped volume
Stripe set with parity	RAID-5 volume (servers only)
System and boot partitions	System and boot volumes
Volume set	Spanned volume

Upgrading Disks

When you perform a new installation of Windows XP Professional or when you perform an upgrade installation from Windows 98, Windows ME, or Windows NT Workstation 4, the computer system defaults to basic disk storage. Only if you upgrade from Windows 2000 Professional (or if you import a "foreign disk" from Windows 2000 Server or Windows Server 2003) could one or more of the disk drives be configured as dynamic. Dynamic disks are proprietary to Windows 2000, Windows Server 2003, and Windows XP Professional, and they provide support for advanced disk configurations such as disk striping and disk spanning. On Windows 2000 Server and Windows Server 2003, dynamic disks provide support for fault-tolerant configurations such as disk mirroring and disk striping with parity (also known as Redundant Array of Inexpensive Disks--RAID level 5).

Upgrading Basic Disks to Dynamic Disks

You use Windows XP's Disk Management Console (an MMC snap-in) to upgrade a basic disk to a dynamic disk. To access Disk Management, click Start, (All) Programs, Administrative Tools, Computer Management. Or right-click the My Computer icon from the Start menu and select Manage. You'll find Disk Management by expanding the Storage folder. You must be a member of the local Administrators group to make any changes to the computer's disk management configuration.

For the upgrade to succeed, any disks to be upgraded must contain at least 1MB of unallocated space. Disk Management automatically reserves this space when creating partitions or volumes on a disk, but disks with partitions or volumes created by other operating systems may not have this space available. (This space can exist even if it is not visible in Disk Management.) Before you upgrade disks, close any programs that are running on those disks. Windows XP requires this minimal amount of disk space to store the dynamic database, which is maintained by the operating system that created it. This is why it is generally not a good idea to dual-boot between Windows XP and Windows 2000 (or Windows Server 2003) if you are using dynamic disks.

To change or convert a basic disk to a dynamic disk from the Disk Management Console, perform the following steps:

1. Open the Disk Management tool.

2. Right-click the basic disk you want to change to a dynamic disk and then click Convert to Dynamic Disk.

When you convert a basic disk to dynamic, any system partition or boot partition is converted to a dynamic volume after the computer is restarted. All other basic partitions get converted to dynamic volumes immediately. If a basic partition on the disk that you are converting is in use, Windows XP performs a "force dismount" on the disk, which means that any programs using the basic partition are automatically disconnected from accessing the disk. If the partition cannot be force dismounted (for example, if there is an active paging file on the partition), the disk conversion does not complete until you restart the computer.

The good news is that you do not need to select a special command such as Commit Changes Now before restarting your computer or closing the Disk Management tool.

To change or convert a basic disk to a dynamic disk from the Windows XP command line, perform these steps:

1. Open a command prompt window, type **diskpart**, and press Enter.

2. Type **commands** or **help** to view a list of available commands.

3. Type **select disk 0** to select the first hard disk (**select disk 1** to select the second hard disk, and so on) and press Enter.

4. Type **convert dynamic** and press Enter.

5. Type **exit** to quit the diskpart.exe tool and then restart the computer to have the new configuration take effect (see Figure 6.1).

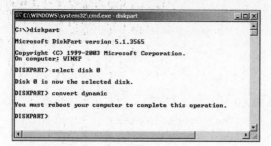

Figure 6.1 Using the diskpart.exe command-line utility to convert a basic disk to a dynamic disk.

In addition to **diskpart.exe**, Windows XP administrators can take advantage of another command-line tool for managing FAT, FAT32, and NTFS file systems—**Fsutil.exe**. With **Fsutil.exe**, Windows XP administrative users can perform tasks such as managing disk quotas, using reparse (mount) points, and several other advanced disk-related tasks. Type **Fsutil /?** at a command prompt to view a list of supported commands.

When you upgrade a basic disk to a dynamic disk, any existing partitions on the basic disk become simple volumes on the dynamic disk. Any existing mirrored volumes, striped volumes, RAID-5 volumes, or spanned volumes become dynamic mirrored volumes, dynamic striped volumes, dynamic RAID-5 volumes, or dynamic spanned volumes, respectively.

You cannot dual-boot to another operating system if you upgrade a basic disk to a dynamic disk, which typically isn't an issue for servers. However, it's something to consider for Windows XP Professional machines. After you upgrade a basic disk to a dynamic disk, you cannot easily change the dynamic volumes back to basic partitions. To revert a dynamic disk back to a basic disk, you first must delete all dynamic volumes on the disk and then use the Convert to Basic Disk command.

Upgrading to a dynamic disk is a *one-way* process. Yes, you can convert a dynamic disk with volumes back to a basic disk, but you'll lose all of your data on that disk. Obviously, this is a major downside! In the event that you do find yourself needing to convert a dynamic disk back to basic, first back up your data on the dynamic disk, delete all dynamic volumes on the disk, convert the disk to basic, and then restore your data.

Because the upgrade from basic to dynamic is per physical disk, all partitions or volumes on a physical disk must be either basic or dynamic. Again, you do not need to restart your computer when you upgrade from a basic to a dynamic disk from the Disk Management Console. You must restart your computer only if you use the diskpart.exe command-line tool or if you upgrade your startup disk.

When you convert a basic disk to a dynamic disk, at least 1MB of free space must be available for the dynamic disk database. Under normal circumstances, this should not be a problem.

Converting Dynamic Disks to Basic Disks

You must remove all volumes from the dynamic disk before you can change it back to a basic disk. After you change a dynamic disk back to a basic disk, you can create only partitions and logical drives on that disk. After being upgraded, a dynamic disk cannot contain partitions or logical drives, nor can any operating systems other than Windows XP, Windows 2000, or Windows Server 2003 access it.

To convert a dynamic disk to a basic disk, perform the following steps:

1. Open Disk Management.

2. Right-click the dynamic disk you want to change back to a basic disk and then click Convert to Basic Disk.

Moving Disks to Another Computer

To move disks to another computer, perform the following steps:

1. Before you disconnect the disks, look in Disk Management and make sure the status of the volumes on the disks is healthy. If the status is not healthy, repair the volumes before you move the disks.

2. Turn the computer off, remove the physical disks, and then install the physical disks on the other computer. Restart the computer that contains the disks you moved.

3. Open Disk Management.

4. Click Action and then click Rescan Disks.

5. Right-click any disk marked Foreign, click Import Foreign Disks, and then follow the instructions on your screen.

Guidelines for Relocating Disks

Every time you remove disks from or import disks to a computer, you must click Action, Rescan Disks from the Disk Management Console menu and then verify that the disk information is correct. Aside from following the preceding steps 1 through 5, you can choose which disks from the group you want to add by choosing the Select Disk option when you right-click a Foreign disk. You do not have to import all the new disks at the same time.

Disk Management describes the condition of the volumes on the disks before you import them. Review this information carefully. If any problems exist, you will know what will happen to each volume on these disks after you have imported them. After you import a dynamic disk from another computer, you can see and use any existing volumes on that disk. Be sure to move together all disks that are part of a volume set or a stripe set. If you move only some of the disks that are members of a volume set or stripe set, you render the set unusable. You may even damage the set and lose the data stored on the set if you do not move all the disks that make up the set. You can also use the diskpart.exe command-line tool to import disks.

Reactivating a Missing or Offline Disk

A dynamic disk may become missing when it is corrupted, powered down, or disconnected. Only dynamic disks can be reactivated—not basic disks. Sorry!

To reactivate a missing or offline disk, perform the following steps:

1. Open Disk Management.

2. Right-click the disk marked Missing or Offline, and then click Reactivate Disk.

3. The disk should be marked Online after the disk is reactivated.

Basic Partitions

Basic partitions include disk partitions and logical drives, as well as disk partitions created using Windows NT 4 or earlier operating systems. Before Windows 2000, basic disks contained all volume types: partitions, volume sets, stripe sets, mirror sets, and stripe sets with parity (also known as RAID level 5 sets). For Windows 2000, Windows Server 2003, and Windows XP, these volumes have been renamed to spanned volumes, striped volumes, mirrored volumes, and RAID-5 volumes. Under Windows XP, you can create basic partitions on basic disks only. In addition, fault-tolerant volumes (mirrored volumes and RAID-5 volumes) can be created on dynamic disks only under the Windows 2000 Server or Windows Server 2003 server-based operating systems. See the upcoming section titled "Dynamic Volumes" to find out how to migrate data from stripe sets or volume sets that are stored on a basic disk under Windows NT 4 Workstation or Windows 2000 Professional.

Because Windows XP Professional is a desktop (client-side) network operating system, it does not support any type of fault-tolerant volumes, even on dynamic disks. Only Microsoft server operating systems support fault-tolerant features such as mirrored volumes and RAID-5 volumes (stripe sets with parity). Windows 2000 Server and Windows Server 2003 offer software-based fault-tolerant volumes; these fault-tolerant volumes must be created on dynamic disks. However, hardware-based fault-tolerant volumes are operating-system independent—hardware-based RAID volumes do not need to be converted to dynamic disks.

Partitions and Logical Drives on Basic Disks

You can create primary partitions, extended partitions, and logical drives only on basic disks. You should create basic partitions instead of dynamic volumes if your computer dual-boots or multiboots to a down-level Microsoft operating system, such as Windows 98, which does not support dynamic disks. You must be an administrator or a member of the Administrators group to create, modify, or delete basic partitions.

Partitions and logical drives can reside only on basic disks. You can create up to four primary partitions on a basic disk or up to three primary partitions and one extended partition. You can use the free space in an extended partition to create multiple logical drives.

You can extend a basic partition, but you must use the **diskpart.exe** command-line tool. The basic partition that you want to extend must be formatted as NTFS, it must be adjacent to contiguous unallocated space on the same physical disk, and it can be extended only onto unallocated space that resides on the same physical disk. You cannot extend the system or boot partitions using either the Disk Management Console or the **diskpart.exe** utility.

You should create basic partitions, such as partitions or logical drives, on basic disks if you want computers running earlier versions of Microsoft operating systems to be able to access those volumes.

Creating or Deleting a Partition or Logical Drive

To create or delete a partition or logical drive, you can use the diskpart.exe command-line tool or use the GUI and perform the following steps:

1. Open the Disk Management Console.

2. Right-click an unallocated region of a basic disk and then click New Partition. Alternatively, you can right-click an area of free space in an extended partition and then click New Logical Drive. To remove the partition, select Delete Partition from the right-click menu.

3. Using the Create Partition Wizard, click Next. Click Primary Partition, Extended Partition, or Logical Drive and follow the instructions presented by the wizard.

If you choose to delete a partition, all data on the deleted partition or logical drive is lost. You cannot recover deleted partitions or logical drives (well, you can't recover deleted partitions or logical drives using standard Microsoft tools, anyway). You cannot delete the system partition, boot partition, or any partition that contains an active paging file. The operating system uses one or more paging files on disk as virtual memory that can be swapped into and out of real system memory as the system's load and volume of data dictate.

 Windows XP requires that all logical drives or other volumes in an extended partition be deleted before you can delete the extended partition.

Dynamic Volumes

What used to be called sets (such as mirror sets and stripe sets) under previous versions of Windows are now referred to as *volumes* (such as mirrored volumes and striped volumes) in Windows 2000 and Windows XP. Dynamic volumes are the only type of volume you can create on dynamic disks. With dynamic disks, you are no longer limited to four volumes per disk (as you are with basic disks). You can install Windows XP Professional onto a dynamic volume; however, these volumes must contain the partition table (which means that these volumes must have been *converted* from basic to dynamic under Windows XP, Windows 2000, or Windows Server 2003). In other words, you cannot install Windows XP onto a dynamic disk that was created directly from unallocated space—the dynamic disk must have been converted from a basic disk.

Only computers running Windows XP Professional, the Windows 2000 family of operating systems, or the Windows Server 2003 family of products can access dynamic volumes stored on locally attached disks. The five types of dynamic volumes are *simple, spanned, mirrored, striped,* and *RAID-5*.

 Windows XP Professional supports only simple, spanned, and striped dynamic volumes.

You must be an administrator or a member of the Administrators group to create, modify, or delete dynamic volumes.

Simple Volumes

A simple volume is made up of disk space on a single physical disk. It can consist of a single area on a disk or multiple areas on the same disk that are linked together.

To create a simple volume, perform the following steps:

1. Open Disk Management.

2. Right-click the unallocated space on the dynamic disk where you want to create the simple volume and then click New Volume.

3. Using the New Volume Wizard, click Next, click Simple, and then follow the instructions on your screen.

Following are guidelines for simple volumes:

➤ You can create simple volumes on dynamic disks only.

➤ Simple volumes are not fault tolerant.

➤ Simple volumes cannot contain partitions or logical drives.

➤ Neither MS-DOS nor Windows operating systems other than Windows XP, Windows 2000, and Windows Server 2003 can access simple volumes.

Spanned Volumes

A spanned volume is made up of disk space from more than one physical disk. You can add more space to a spanned volume by extending it at any time.

To create a spanned volume, perform the following steps:

1. Open Disk Management.

2. Right-click the unallocated space on one of the dynamic disks where you want to create the spanned volume and then click New Volume.

3. Using the New Volume Wizard, click Next, click Spanned, and then follow the instructions on your screen.

The following are guidelines for spanned volumes:

➤ You can create spanned volumes on dynamic disks only.

➤ You need at least two dynamic disks to create a spanned volume.

➤ You can extend a spanned volume onto a maximum of 32 dynamic disks.

➤ Spanned volumes cannot be mirrored or striped.

➤ Spanned volumes are not fault tolerant.

Extending a Simple or Spanned Volume

To extend a simple or spanned volume, perform the following steps:

1. Open Disk Management.

2. Right-click the simple or spanned volume you want to extend, click Extend Volume, and then follow the instructions on your screen.

The following are guidelines for extending a simple or a spanned volume:

➤ You can extend a volume only if it contains no file system or if it is formatted using NTFS. You cannot extend volumes formatted using FAT or FAT32.

➤ You can extend a simple volume within its original disk or onto additional disks, provided that the volume was converted to a dynamic volume under Windows XP (not Windows 2000). *If you extend a simple volume across two or more disks, it becomes a spanned volume.*

➤ After a volume is extended onto multiple disks (spanned), you cannot mirror or stripe it.

➤ After a spanned volume is extended, no portion of it can be deleted without the entire spanned volume being deleted.

➤ You can extend a simple or extended volume only if the volume was created as a dynamic volume. You cannot extend a simple or extended volume that was upgraded from basic to dynamic under Windows 2000.

➤ You can extend simple and spanned volumes on dynamic disks onto a maximum of 32 dynamic disks.

➤ Spanned volumes write data to subsequent disks only as each disk volume fills up. Therefore, a spanned volume writes data to physical disk 0 until it fills up, then it writes to physical disk 1 until its available space is full, and then it writes to physical disk 2, and so on. If just one disk fails in the spanned volume, only the data contained on that failed disk is lost for that spanned volume.

 For dynamic disks—You cannot extend a system volume or boot volume. You also cannot extend striped, mirrored, and RAID-5 volumes.

Striped Volumes

A striped volume stores data in stripes on two or more physical disks. Data in a striped volume is allocated alternately and evenly (in stripes) to the disks within the striped volume. Striped volumes can substantially improve the speed of access to your data on disk.

To create a striped volume, perform the following steps:

1. Open Disk Management.

2. Right-click unallocated space on one of the dynamic disks where you want to create the striped volume and then click New Volume.

3. Using the New Volume Wizard, click Next, click Striped, and then follow the instructions on your screen.

The following are guidelines for striped volumes:

➤ You need at least two physical, dynamic disks to create a striped volume.

➤ You can create a striped volume onto a maximum of 32 disks.

➤ Striped volumes are not fault tolerant and cannot be extended or mirrored.

Mirrored Volumes and RAID-5 Volumes

You can create mirrored volumes and RAID-5 volumes only on dynamic disks running on Windows 2000 Server or Windows Server 2003 computers.

 Mirrored and RAID-5 volumes are available only on computers that are running Windows 2000 Server or Windows Server 2003. Windows XP Professional computers can use basic and dynamic disks, but they cannot *host* (locally store) software-based fault-tolerant disk configurations such as mirrored volumes and stripe sets with parity (RAID-5) volumes. You can, however, use a computer running Windows XP Professional to create mirrored and RAID-5 volumes on a *remote* computer running Windows 2000 Server or Windows Server 2003. The Disk Management MMC snap-in can administer both local and remote computers.

Limitations of Dynamic Disks and Dynamic Volumes

You can use dynamic disks and dynamic volumes in specific circumstances; you need to understand when you can and cannot use them.

When You Are Installing Windows XP

If you create a dynamic volume from unallocated space on a dynamic disk, you cannot install Windows XP on that volume. This installation limitation occurs because Windows XP Setup recognizes only dynamic volumes that contain partition tables. Partition tables appear in basic partitions and in dynamic volumes when dynamic volumes have been upgraded from basic to dynamic. If you create a new dynamic volume on a dynamic disk, that new dynamic volume does not contain a partition table.

When You Are Extending a Volume

If you upgrade a basic partition to dynamic (by upgrading the basic disk to a dynamic disk), you can install Windows XP on that volume, *but you cannot extend the volume*. The limitation on extending volumes occurs because the boot volume, which contains the Windows XP systems files, cannot be part of a spanned volume. If you extend a simple volume that contains a partition table (that is, a volume that was upgraded from basic to dynamic), Windows XP Setup recognizes the spanned volume but cannot install to it, because the boot volume cannot be part of a spanned volume.

You can extend volumes that you created only after you convert the disk to a dynamic disk. You can extend volumes and make changes to the disk configuration in most cases without rebooting your computer. If you want to take advantage of these features in Windows XP, you must change or upgrade a disk from basic to dynamic status, as covered earlier in this chapter. Use dynamic disks if your computer runs only Windows XP and you want to create more than four volumes per disk or if you want to extend, stripe, or span volumes onto one or more dynamic disks.

When You Are Upgrading from Windows NT 4 with Volume Sets on a Basic Disk

If you need to upgrade a computer running Windows NT 4 that has hard drives configured as volume sets or stripe sets, you must first back up all the data stored on each volume set or stripe set, because Windows XP Professional does not support volume sets or stripe sets on basic disks. Striped and spanned volumes are supported only by dynamic disks under Windows XP Professional.

To migrate data on volume sets or stripe sets from Windows NT 4 to Windows XP Professional, perform the following steps:

1. Under Windows NT 4, back up the data.

2. Delete the volume(s).

3. Upgrade the operating system to Windows XP Professional.

4. Convert the appropriate hard disks from basic to dynamic disks.

5. Create the appropriate volume(s).

6. Restore the backed up data.

When You Are Upgrading from Windows 2000 Professional with Volume Sets on a Basic Disk

If you need to upgrade a computer running Windows 2000 Professional that has hard drives configured as volume sets or stripe sets, you must still back up all the data stored on each volume set or stripe set, because Windows XP Professional does not support volume sets or stripe sets on a basic disk. Under Windows 2000 Professional, volume sets and stripe sets are supported on basic disks for backward compatibility, although you cannot create such sets on basic disks. Under Windows XP Professional, volume sets and stripe sets are strictly not supported. Windows XP Professional Setup will not allow an installation to complete if stripe sets or volume sets exist on basic disks.

To migrate data on volume sets or stripe sets stored on basic disks from Windows 2000 Professional to Windows XP Professional, perform the following steps:

1. Under Windows 2000, back up the data.

2. Under Windows 2000, use the Disk Management Console to convert the basic disks to dynamic disks.

3. Upgrade the operating system to Windows XP Professional.

Troubleshooting Disks and Volumes

If a disk or volume fails, naturally you want to repair it as soon as possible to avoid losing data. The Disk Management snap-in makes it easy to locate problems quickly. In the Status column of the list view, you can view the status of a disk or volume. The status also appears in the graphical view of each disk or volume.

Diagnosing Problems

To diagnose disk and/or volume problems, perform the following steps:

1. Open Add Hardware in the Control Panel. Click Next. Windows XP tries to detect new Plug and Play devices.

2. Click Yes, I Have Already Connected the Hardware, and then click Next.

3. Choose the device you want to diagnose and fix, and then click Next.

4. The wizard will inform you of the device's current status. Click Finish to invoke the Hardware Troubleshooter as part of the Help and Support Center, or click Cancel to exit the Add Hardware Wizard.

Another way to troubleshoot hardware problems is with Device Manager. Right-click the My Computer icon and select Properties. Click the Hardware tab and then click the Device Manager button. Expand the hardware category that you need to troubleshoot and right-click the device that you want to inquire about. Select Properties from the context menu to display the Properties dialog box for that device, as shown in Figure 6.2. All the pertinent information about the device is available from this window, including its device status as determined by the operating system.

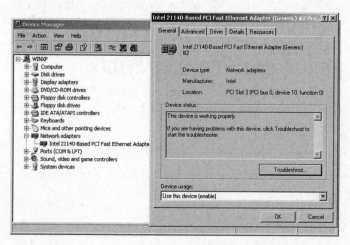

Figure 6.2   Using Device Manager to troubleshoot hardware issues.

Monitoring Disk Performance

The Windows XP performance monitoring tool is composed of two parts: System Monitor and Performance Logs and Alerts. The MMC snap-in is named Performance. With System Monitor, you can collect and view real-time data about disk performance and activity in graph, histogram, or report form. Performance Logs and Alerts enables you to configure logs to record performance data and to set system alerts to notify you when a specified counter's value is above or below a defined threshold.

To open Performance, perform the following steps:

1. Click Start, Control Panel.

2. In the Control Panel, double-click Administrative Tools, and then double-click Performance. You will use System Monitor within Performance to monitor disk activity.

The Diskperf.exe command-line tool was used to control the types of physical and logical disk counters that you could enable for monitoring system performance under earlier versions of Windows. Under Windows XP, disk performance counters are permanently enabled and the LogicalDisk object counters have been removed. Instead of using the LogicalDisk object counters for measuring disk performance, Windows XP maps physical drives to logical drives by applying the same instance name. For example, if a computer contains a dynamic volume that is composed of two physical hard disks, the logical drives might appear as Disk 0 C: and Disk 1 C:, which denotes that drive C spans physical disks 0 and 1. For a PC that has three logical volumes on one physical disk, the instance would appear as Disk 0 C: D: E:.

Detecting and Repairing Disk Errors

In previous Windows operating systems, ScanDisk detected and fixed disk errors. In Windows XP, you can use the Error-Checking tool to check for file system errors and bad sectors on your hard disk.

To run the Error-Checking tool, perform the following steps:

1. Open My Computer and right-click the local disk you want to check.

2. Select Properties.

3. Click the Tools tab.

4. Under Error-Checking, click Check Now.

5. Under Check Disk Options, select the Scan for and Attempt Recovery of Bad Sectors check box and click Start.

All files must be closed for the Error-Checking process to run. Your volume is not available to run any other tasks while this process is running. If the volume is currently in use, a message asks if you want to reschedule the disk checking for the next time you restart your system. Then, the next time you restart your system, disk-checking runs. If your volume is formatted as NTFS, Windows XP automatically logs all file transactions, replaces bad clusters automatically, and stores copies of key information for all files on the NTFS volume.

You should also be aware of two valuable command-line utilities for troubleshooting and repairing disk problems—chkdsk and chkntfs. The chkdsk tool looks for errors on the disk drive that you specify and it can also attempt to repair the errors that it finds. The chkntfs utility displays and can modify which disk drives are marked as "to be checked" at the time of the next reboot. Obviously, chkntfs works only on drive letters, partitions, and volumes formatted as NTFS.

The Disk Defragmenter Tool

Disk Defragmenter rearranges files, programs, and unused space on your computer's hard disk(s), allowing programs to run faster and files to open more quickly. Putting the pieces of files and programs in a more contiguous arrangement on disk reduces the time the operating system needs to access requested items.

To run Disk Defragmenter, perform the following steps:

1. Click Start, (All) Programs, Accessories, System Tools, and then click Disk Defragmenter. Alternatively, you can right-click a drive letter in My Computer, select Properties, click the Tools tab, and click Defragment Now.

2. Select which disk(s) you would like to defragment and any additional options you would like to set.

3. Click the Defragment button to start the defragmentation process.

> Windows XP Professional ships with a command-line version of the disk defragmenter—**defrag.exe**. You can run this program within a batch file or inside of a Windows script, which in turn can be scheduled to run automatically using the Scheduled Tasks folder.

Understanding Why Files Are Not Moved to the Beginning of NTFS Partitions and Volumes

On NTFS-formatted drives, Windows XP reserves a portion of the free space for a system file called the master file table (MFT). The MFT is where Windows stores all the information it needs to retrieve files from the partition or volume. Windows stores part of the MFT at the beginning of the partition or volume. Windows reserves the MFT for exclusive use, so Disk Defragmenter cannot and does not move files to the beginning of partitions and volumes.

Using the Disk Cleanup Wizard

Disk Cleanup helps free up space on your hard drive by searching your drive(s) and then showing you a list of temporary files, Internet cache files, and potentially unnecessary program files that you can safely delete. You can instruct Disk Cleanup to delete none, some, or all of those files.

To use the Disk Cleanup Wizard, perform the following steps:

1. Click Start, (All) Programs, Accessories, System Tools.

2. Click the Disk Cleanup icon and follow the onscreen instructions.

File Systems Supported in Windows XP

The Compact Disc File System (CDFS) has full support for CD-based media in Windows XP. Although Windows XP does not support the High Performance File System (HPFS) as used under IBM's OS/2 operating system, it fully supports the FAT, FAT32, and NTFS file systems.

FAT and FAT32

Windows XP has full FAT (also known as FAT16) and FAT32 file system support with the following conditions and parameters:

➤ Preexisting FAT32 partitions up to 2TB are supported in Windows XP.

➤ By design, Windows XP allows you to create new FAT32 partitions or volumes only with a data storage capacity not exceeding 32GB. You cannot create FAT32 partitions or volumes larger than 32GB under Windows XP; however, Windows XP will read from and write to FAT32 partitions or volumes larger than 32GB that were created by a different operating system or by a third-party tool.

➤ FAT partitions and volumes are limited to a maximum size of 4GB and can support a maximum file size of 2GB.

➤ FAT32 partitions and volumes can support a maximum file size of 4GB. If you attempt to copy a file larger than 4GB to a FAT32 partition or volume, Windows XP gives you an error message stating that there is not enough disk space, even if there is more than enough disk space available.

➤ You can install Windows XP onto a FAT, FAT32, or NTFS partition. Keep in mind that you have no local security permissions for files or folders under Windows XP unless you place the operating system on an NTFS partition or volume.

➤ If you initially install Windows XP onto a FAT or FAT32 partition and then later use the Convert.exe utility to convert the partition to NTFS, default security settings are not applied to the %systemroot% folder or its subfolders. The %systemroot% environment variable maps to the Windows XP system folder, which, by default, is installed as the \Windows folder located on the root of the designated boot drive. Under Windows 2000 and previous versions of Windows NT, the %systemroot% folder was named the \Winnt folder by default.

The Windows XP NTFS File System

Windows XP Professional inherits the Windows 2000 NTFS version 5 file system. NTFS is Windows XP's native file system. This version of NTFS includes capabilities such as support for very granular file and folder permissions, support for disk quotas, the Encrypting File System (EFS), and a number of other useful features. The disk quotas feature is covered later in this chapter.

When you install Windows XP, existing legacy NTFS volumes and partitions are automatically upgraded to NTFS 5. No options are presented to you to choose NTFS version 5 during the installation. Any existing volumes or partitions are converted to NTFS 5 whether you want them to be or not.

When you install Windows XP to an NTFS partition or volume, part of the Setup process is to apply default security settings to the system files and folders located on the boot partition (essentially the \Windows and \Program Files folders).

All local NTFS partitions and volumes, including removable media, are upgraded to the new version 5 of NTFS. This occurs after you restart your computer the first time after the graphical portion of Setup. Any NTFS volumes that are removed or powered off during the installation or upgrade process are upgraded automatically when those drives are mounted. If, during the installation, the system detects a version of Windows NT earlier than Windows NT 4 with Service Pack 4 (SP4), you will see a warning message indicating that an earlier version of Windows NT was found and that Windows NT will not be accessible if you continue. Windows NT Workstation 4 can be upgraded to Windows XP Professional without applying service packs. However, if you want to create a new installation of Windows XP and dual-boot with Windows NT 4, you will see the warning.

If you want to configure your computer to dual-boot Windows NT 4 and Windows XP, you need to upgrade your version of Windows NT 4 to SP4 or later. An updated NTFS.SYS driver that enables NT 4 to read from and write to NTFS 5 volumes created with Windows 2000 or Windows XP is included in NT 4 SP4 and later SPs. If you expect to dual-boot Windows 98 (or Windows Me) with Windows XP, remember that Windows 98/Me can read from and write to FAT and FAT32 file systems only; they *cannot* access NTFS drives without a third-party utility.

Converting from One File System to Another

Windows XP supports converting from one file system to another, with some special caveats and limitations that you need to be well aware of.

Converting a FAT or FAT32 Partition to an NTFS Partition

Suppose that you want to convert drive D: to NTFS, from either FAT or FAT32. No problem! *However, before you perform the conversion, be sure to create a restore point using the System Restore feature, in case you change your mind about the conversion prior to restarting the computer.* From the command line (click Start, Run, type `cmd.exe`, and click OK), type `c:` and press Enter, and then type the command `convert d: /fs:ntfs` and press Enter.

If the FAT or FAT32 partition is the boot partition, the conversion takes place when the machine next reboots, because many of the operating system files are locked in memory. This command is a one-way ticket only and is not reversible. However, if you convert the boot volume, you do have one option before the computer restarts. The boot volume should not be confused with what Microsoft calls the system volume (the first logical operating system partition, usually denoted as the C: drive). Figure 6.3 shows an example of the Disk Management Console where both the system and boot volumes are identified in parentheses for the C: drive and the F: drive, respectively. Of course, the system volume and the boot volume often are one and the same.

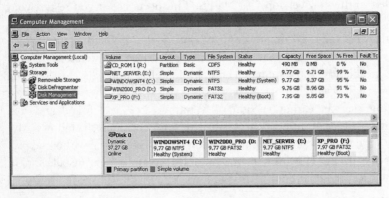

Figure 6.3 The Disk Management Console shows which drive letter is the system volume and which is the boot volume.

If you decide to undo the conversion to NTFS for the boot volume (the volume that contains the \Windows folder, also known as the %systemroot% folder), before you restart the computer, you may use the restore point that you made prior to performing the conversion, or you may edit the Windows XP Registry to remove the NTFS file system conversion flag that gets placed there by the Convert.exe utility. Warning: Editing the Windows XP Registry is a risky procedure that can render a computer unstable or unbootable. Be sure to have a good, recent, reliable backup before editing the Registry. You can use the Regedit.exe tool to modify the following Registry entry:

```
HKEY_LOCAL_MACHINE\CurrentControlSet\Control\Session Manager
```

Change the `BootExecute` value data from `autoconv` `\DosDevices\` `x:` `/FS:NTFS` to `autocheck autochk*`, where x: denotes the drive letter flagged to be converted.

After the conversion, NTFS file permissions are set to Full Control for the Everyone group. However, if the `%systemroot%` folder resides on a newly converted NTFS volume, the permissions for the `\Windows` folder and `\Program Files` folder and associated files should be properly secured using NTFS permissions.

You cannot convert an NTFS partition or volume to a FAT partition or volume (at least not with standard Microsoft tools). A conversion such as this is not possible with the **Convert.exe** command-line utility. Your only course of action, if you want to keep the data, is to back up all the data on the drive. Then use the Disk Management tool to reformat the disk to the flavor of FAT you prefer and restore your backed up data to your newly formatted disk.

Reapplying Default NTFS Permissions

You may need or want to reapply the default NTFS permissions to the system boot partition if you changed them or never applied them to begin with (because you converted the boot partition to NTFS after installation). To reapply the default NTFS permissions, use the `Secedit.exe` utility from the command prompt, which comes with Windows XP. The computer must still be bootable under Windows XP for this approach to work.

Assigning, Changing, or Removing Drive Letters

To assign, change, or remove a drive letter, perform the following steps:

1. Open Disk Management.

2. Right-click a partition, a logical drive, or a volume, and then click Change Drive Letter and Paths.

3. Do one of the following:

   ➤ To assign a drive letter—Click Add, select the drive letter you want to use, and then click OK.

   ➤ To change a drive letter—Click Change, select the drive letter you want to use, and then click OK.

   ➤ To remove a drive letter—Click Remove, either click Yes to confirm the removal or click No to cancel the removal, and then click OK.

An old "gotcha" still applies. Be careful when assigning drive letters, because many MS-DOS and Windows applications refer to a specific drive letter, especially during installation. For example, the PATH environment variable shows specific drive letters in conjunction with program names.

You can use up to 24 drive letters, from C: through Z:. Drive letters A: and B: are reserved for floppy disk drives. However, if you do not have a floppy disk drive B:, you can use the letter B: for a network drive. *You cannot change the drive letter of the system partition or volume or the boot partition or volume.*

An error message may appear when you attempt to assign a letter to a volume, CD or DVD drive, or other removable media device, possibly because a program in the system is using it. If this happens, close the program that is accessing the volume or drive and then click the Change Drive Letter and Paths option again.

Windows XP allows you to statically assign drive letters on volumes, partitions, and CD and DVD drives. This means that you can permanently assign a drive letter to a specific partition, volume, CD, or DVD drive. When you add a new hard disk to an existing computer system, it does not affect statically assigned drive letters. You can also mount a local drive through an empty folder on an NTFS volume by using a drive path instead of a drive letter. This feature is known as using mounted drives.

Mounted Drives

Mounted drives, also known as mount points or mounted volumes, are useful for increasing a drive's size without disturbing it. For example, you could create a mount point to drive E: as `C:\CompanyData`, thereby appearing to increase the size available on the C: partition, which would specifically allow you to store more data in `C:\CompanyData` than you could otherwise. Drive paths are available only on empty folders on NTFS drive letters. The NTFS partition or volume can be basic or dynamic.

Creating a Mounted Drive

To create a mounted drive, perform the following steps:

1. Open Disk Management.

2. Right-click the partition or volume you want to mount and then click Change Drive Letter and Paths.

3. Do one of the following:

➤ To mount a volume—Select Add. Click Mount in the Following Empty NTFS Folder and type the path to an empty folder on an NTFS volume, or click Browse to locate it.

➤ To unmount a volume—Select the drive letter path and then click Remove. Confirm your selection by clicking Yes to remove the mount point, or click No to retain it.

When you mount a local CD-ROM drive, DVD drive, or a disk partition or volume within an empty folder on an NTFS drive letter, Windows XP assigns a *drive path*, rather than a drive letter, to that local CD-ROM drive, DVD drive, or disk partition or volume. This feature lets you access the specified CD-ROM drive, DVD drive, or disk partition or volume without using a drive letter; you can simply access it as a subfolder on the host drive.

To modify a drive path, remove it and then create a new drive path using the new location. You cannot modify the drive path directly. If you are administering a local computer, you can browse NTFS folders on that computer. If you are administering a remote computer, browsing is disabled and you must type the path to an existing NTFS folder.

Support for FAT32 on DVD-RAM Disks

Under Windows XP Professional, DVD-RAM disks can be used as CD-ROM devices, as DVD-ROM devices, or as recordable and rewritable media. Windows XP employs the FAT32 file system for both read and write operations on DVD-RAM disks. The Universal Disk Format (UDF) file system is utilized for read-only operations. Windows XP support for DVD-RAM disks includes multiple session recording and logical block addressing. See the Windows XP Hardware Compatibility List (HCL) on the Microsoft website (https://winqual.microsoft.com/download/hcl/WinXPHCLx86.txt) for a current listing of supported DVD-RAM drives.

Disk Quotas

Windows XP disk quotas track and control disk usage on a per-user, per-volume basis. You can apply disk quotas only to Windows XP NTFS volumes. Quotas are tracked for each partition or volume, even if the partitions or volumes reside on the same physical disk. The per-user feature of quotas enables you to track each user's disk space usage regardless of which folder the user stores files in.

Disk quotas do not use compression to measure disk space usage, so users cannot obtain or use more space simply by compressing their own data. To enable disk quotas, open the Properties dialog box for a disk, select the Quota tab, and configure the options as shown in Figure 6.4.

Figure 6.4   The Quota tab of the Properties dialog box for an NTFS drive letter enables you to configure Windows XP disk quota options.

When a user no longer stores data on a volume, you need to delete disk quota entries. The catch to this is that you can delete the user's quota entries only after you have removed from the volume all files that the user owns, or after another user has taken ownership of the files. By default, only members of the Administrators group can view and change quota entries and settings. In addition, all members of the Administrators group inherit unlimited disk quotas by default. To work with disk quota entries, click the Quota Entries button on the Quota tab of an NTFS drive letter's properties sheet. The Quota Entries window is shown in Figure 6.5.

Status	Name	Logon Name	Amount Used	Quota Limit	Warning Level	Percent Used
Above Limit		WINXP\Dan	1.02 GB	50 MB	45 MB	2106
OK		BUILTIN\Administrators	1.33 GB	No Limit	No Limit	N/A
OK		NT AUTHORITY\NETWORK S...	288 KB	50 MB	45 MB	0
OK		NT AUTHORITY\LOCAL SERV...	330 KB	50 MB	45 MB	0
OK		NT AUTHORITY\SYSTEM	166 KB	50 MB	45 MB	0

5 total item(s), 1 selected.

Figure 6.5   The Quota Entries window enables you to set and remove disk quota limits and warning levels for individual users.

Data Compression

Windows XP Professional supports two types of data compression: NTFS compression and Compressed (Zipped) Folders. Files and folders compressed using the Compressed (Zipped) Folders feature remain compressed under all three supported file systems—NTFS, FAT, and FAT32. Compressing any system folders, such as the \Windows folder or the \Program Files folder, is not recommended. Compressed (Zipped) Folders are identified by a zipper icon that is part of the folder's icon.

To create a Compressed (Zipped) Folder, right-click a folder, point to Send To, and click Compressed (Zipped) Folder. This action creates a Zip file that Windows XP recognizes as a Compressed (Zipped) Folder that contains the folder you selected to be compressed along with all of that folder's contents. You can also use any popular third-party utility, such as WinZip or PKZip, to read, write, add, or remove files to any Compressed (Zipped) Folder. Unless you install a third-party zip utility, Windows XP "sees" standard zip *files* as Compressed (Zipped) *Folders*.

The NTFS file system under Windows XP enables you to compress individual files and folders so that they occupy less space on the NTFS drive letter. Any Windows- or MS-DOS-based program can read and write to NTFS compressed files without having to decompress them first. The compressed files decompress when opened and recompress when closed. The Windows XP NTFS file system handles this entire process transparently to the user. You can use the Windows Explorer to have compressed files and folders displayed in a different color from uncompressed items.

Setting the compression state (compressed or uncompressed) on a file or folder is as simple as setting a file or folder attribute. Right-click the file or folder that you'd like to compress or uncompress and select Properties. On the General tab, click the Advanced button. Check or clear the Compress Contents to Save Disk Space check box. Click OK twice to exit both dialog boxes.

Instead of compressing individual files or even individual folders, you can choose to compress an entire NTFS drive letter. To compress an entire NTFS partition or volume, right-click an NTFS drive letter in My Computer or in the Windows Explorer, select Properties, and mark the check box labeled Compress Drive to Save Disk Space, as shown in Figure 6.6. Click OK to close the drive volume's Properties dialog box.

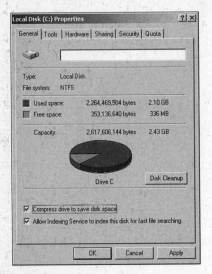

Figure 6.6   The Properties dialog box for an NTFS drive letter, where you can mark the check box labeled Compress Drive to Save Disk Space.

Moving and Copying Compressed Files and Folders

A simple method exists for remembering whether the original compression attribute of an object is retained or inherited when you are moving and/or copying files and folders. Compressed (Zipped) Folders retain their compression no matter where they are copied to. For NTFS-compressed files and folders: When you move a compressed or uncompressed file or folder from one location to another within the same NTFS volume, the original compression attribute is retained. That is all you need to remember about NTFS compression, because in all other scenarios, the compression attribute is inherited from the new, or target, location.

NTFS Compression Guidelines

NTFS allocates disk space based on the *uncompressed* size of a file. If you try to copy a compressed file to an NTFS volume with enough space for the compressed file, but not enough space for the uncompressed file, you get an error message telling you there is inadequate disk space available to copy the file to the target. So, you really need to plan ahead.

If you attempt to copy or move an NTFS-compressed file to a floppy disk, be prepared for an Insufficient Disk Space error. If the uncompressed size of the file is larger than the capacity of the floppy, you cannot copy or move the file. Create a Compressed (Zipped) Folder for this purpose or use a third-party compression tool, such as WinZip, to be able to successfully copy the file(s) to a floppy disk.

Make it a standard practice to use NTFS compression only on static data and not on data that frequently changes; applying or removing the compression attribute does require system overhead. NTFS encryption and compression are mutually exclusive. You can encrypt or compress a file or folder, but not both. Windows XP does not support NTFS compression for volumes with cluster sizes larger than 4KB because of the performance degradation it would cause.

Data Encryption

The NTFS file system for Windows XP Professional also supports data encryption. Just as with NTFS data compression, data encryption is set as an advanced attribute for a file or a folder. With NTFS data encryption, Microsoft has given you a secure method for keeping confidential documents private.

Keeping Data Private with the Encrypting File System (EFS)

Microsoft designed EFS for Windows XP to ensure the confidentiality of sensitive data. EFS employs public key/private key–based cryptography. EFS works only with the NTFS 5 file system under Windows XP, Windows 2000, and Windows Server 2003. It is transparent to users: You can either compress or encrypt files and folders, but you can't do both. Files that are encrypted using EFS remain encrypted even if you move or rename them, as long as they remain on a NTFS disk. Encrypted files that are backed up or copied also retain their encryption attributes as long as they reside on NTFS-formatted drive letters. EFS leaves no file remnants behind when it modifies an encrypted file, nor does it leave any traces of decrypted data from encrypted files in temporary files or in the Windows XP paging file. You can encrypt and decrypt files and folders from the graphical user interface (GUI) by using the Windows Explorer, or from the command line by using the Cipher.exe tool.

Encrypting Folders and Files

The best practice for using encryption is to first encrypt a folder and then move files into the encrypted folder. Folders do not actually become encrypted; folders get marked with the encryption attribute. The files contained within an encrypted folder are the objects that actually become encrypted. You can also individually encrypt files without placing them within a folder that is marked for encryption. To encrypt and decrypt files physically located on a Windows 2000 server or on a Windows Server 2003 computer over the network, that server must be *trusted for delegation*. By definition, domain controllers are already trusted for delegation. Member servers require this Trust for Delegation setting. To encrypt a file or folder from the Windows Explorer, follow these steps:

1. Right-click the file or folder and select Properties.

2. From the General tab, click the Advanced button.

3. Click the Encrypt Contents to Secure Data check box in the Advanced Attributes dialog box.

4. Click OK.

5. Click OK in the Properties dialog box. The folder then becomes encrypted, and any files and folders that are placed within it are encrypted. If subfolders or files exist within the folder, the Confirm Attribute Changes dialog box appears, as shown in Figure 6.7.

Figure 6.7 The Confirm Attribute Changes dialog box.

6. Click either Apply Changes to This Folder Only or Apply Changes to This Folder, Subfolders and Files to specify the object(s) that you want encryption to affect.

7. Click OK; the encryption attribute is applied to the appropriate objects.

If you want to unencrypt a file or folder, perform the same steps as outlined previously and clear the Encrypt Contents to Secure Data check box on the Advanced Attributes dialog box.

Issues to Remember About Using EFS

Only files and folders located on NTFS partitions or volumes may be encrypted. If you encrypt a file or folder that is already compressed using NTFS compression, that file or folder will become uncompressed. You cannot (and should not) encrypt any files that are marked with the System attribute, nor can you encrypt files that are stored within the %systemroot% folder structure, which, by default, is the \Windows folder. Windows XP offers you the option of displaying both compressed and encrypted folders and files in different colors. This feature enables you to readily identify objects that have one of these advanced attributes. You configure this feature as a part of the View tab of the Folder Options dialog box available from the Control Panel, as shown in Figure 6.8.

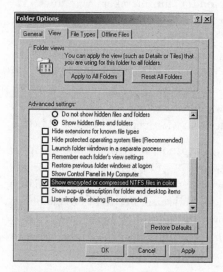

Figure 6.8 The Show Encrypted or Compressed NTFS Files in Color option on the View tab of the Folder Options dialog box.

Accessing Encrypted Files and Data Recovery Agents (DRAs)

Encryption is just an extended (or advanced) attribute of a file or folder. If you set NTFS permissions to deny the Write Attributes permission on a file or folder, the users to whom you have assigned this Deny permission cannot use encryption. To work with NTFS permissions on a Windows XP computer that is not a member of an Active Directory domain, you must clear the Use Simple File Sharing (Recommended) check box from the Folder Options dialog box. After a file has the encryption attribute, only the user who encrypted it or the DRA can access it. DRAs are users who are designated as recovery agents for encrypted files. Only these users have the capability to decrypt *any* encrypted file, no matter who has encrypted it. Other users who attempt to access an encrypted file receive an Access Is Denied message. The default DRAs are as follows:

➤ Users who are members of the local Administrators group for Windows XP Professional nondomain member computers

➤ Users who are members of the local Administrators group for Windows 2000 Server and Windows Server 2003 nondomain member servers

➤ Users who are members of the Domain Administrators group for Windows 2000 Server or Windows Server 2003 domain controllers, Windows domain member servers, and Windows XP Professional domain member computers

DRAs can log on to a system and decrypt files and folders so that they are again accessible to other users. Nondomain member Windows XP Professional computers issue a default self-signed certificate that designates the default Administrator user as the DRA. If you remove any and all DRAs from a standalone Windows XP computer or from a Windows Active Directory domain, no Data Recovery policy is in place and, therefore, EFS will prohibit users from encrypting files and folders. You can manage the EFS recovery policy for the local Windows XP computer via the local Group Policy snap-in (gpedit.msc) for the Microsoft Management Console (MMC).

Click Start, Run, type **gpedit.msc**, and expand the Group Policy snap-in node for Computer Configuration\Windows Settings\Security Settings\ Public Key Policies. Select the Encrypting File System subnode. Right-click the Encrypting File System subnode and select Properties to enable or disable EFS on the computer, as shown in Figure 6.9. By default, EFS is turned on for all users. To turn off EFS, you must clear the Allow Users to Encrypt Files Using Encrypting File System (EFS) check box.

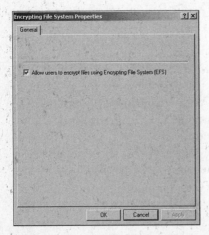

Figure 6.9 The local computer policy properties sheet for enabling or disabling the Encrypting File System.

Moving and Copying Encrypted Files

Encrypted files that are moved or copied to another NTFS folder remain encrypted. Encrypted files that are moved or copied to a FAT or FAT32 drive volume become decrypted because EFS is supported only on NTFS 5 volumes. Files also become decrypted if they are moved or copied to a floppy disk or CD-R. EFS-protected files can be easily deleted by any user unless proper NTFS security permissions are applied to EFS-protected files, which is true for all files whether encrypted or not. Unless users have been granted shared access to an encrypted file or folder, the following rules apply:

➤ Users who did not originally encrypt a file or folder receive an Access Is Denied message if they try to copy an encrypted file or folder.

➤ If users other than the one who encrypted the file attempt to move it to a different NTFS volume or to a FAT or FAT32 drive volume, they receive an Access Is Denied error message.

➤ If users other than the one who encrypted the file attempt to move the encrypted file to a different folder located on the *same* NTFS volume, the file is moved.

Whereas EFS is designed to safeguard files that are stored on local NTFS partitions and volumes, EFS actually *decrypts* files when they are transmitted over the network. Whenever a user who encrypted a file with EFS copies it across the network or sends it via e-mail, the file is automatically decrypted before it is sent so that it will be readable on the computer that receives it.

For unsecured or poorly secured wireless networks, users who send EFS-encrypted files wirelessly run a great risk of compromising their data because of the absence of adequate data encryption. EFS does not work over a local area network (LAN) unless the server and the workstations operate within the same Active Directory forest and the server has been "trusted for delegation." By default, only domain controllers within an Active Directory network are trusted for delegation.

Sharing Access to Encrypted Files with Other Users

You can now share confidential access to encrypted files under Windows XP Professional. This shared access applies only on a file-by-file basis; it does not apply to folders. To grant other users access to an encrypted file, each user must have already encrypted at least one file or folder previously so that either the local Windows XP system or the Active Directory domain has issued the user an EFS-compatible certificate. To add or remove users for shared access to encrypted files, you must be the original user who encrypted the file or you must be one of the users already listed as having shared access to the file. Perform the following steps to share access to an encrypted file with one or more other users:

1. Right-click a file that you have already encrypted under EFS and select Properties.

2. Click the Advanced button from the General tab.

3. Click the Details button to display the Encryption Details dialog box for the encrypted file.

4. Click the Add button to display the Select User dialog box, as shown in Figure 6.10. The Find User button is available only when the computer is a member of an Active Directory domain.

Figure 6.10 The Select User dialog box enables you to pick other users with whom to share access to an encrypted file.

5. Click the user with whom you want to share access to this file and then click OK. Repeat this step for each user with whom you want to share access to this file.

6. Click OK to close the Encryption Details dialog box. This dialog box should display all the users who can transparently access the encrypted file, similar to Figure 6.11.

7. Click OK to close the Advanced Attributes dialog box, and then click OK again to close the encrypted file's properties dialog box.

Figure 6.11 The Encryption Details dialog box enables you to view, add, and remove users who have shared access to the encrypted file.

Data Protection from Removable USB Storage Media

Keychain drives, jump drives, pen drives—however you care to refer to them—these small and portable USB 2.0 storage devices are everywhere these days. Until Windows XP SP2, an IT manager had a difficult decision: disable the mass storage device driver for storage devices that connect via USB or allow the default settings and hope that no authorized user steals any company data. No middle ground exists in this debate because disabling the storage driver over USB connections turns off support for *all* USB storage devices.

Making USB Storage Drives Read-only

Because SP2 is focused on enhancing and improving computer security, Microsoft created a new storage device policy named WriteProtect to prevent users from moving or copying data onto USB-connected drives. Even under SP2, this new Registry setting does not exist by default; you must manually create the appropriate Registry entries if you want to take advantage of this new security feature. This new WriteProtect policy is a per-computer setting, not a per-user setting. A warning mentioned earlier in the chapter, and throughout this book—editing the Windows XP Registry is a risky procedure that can render a computer unstable or unbootable. Be sure to have a good, recent, reliable backup before editing the Registry. To turn on the USB storage WriteProtect feature, perform the following steps using the Windows XP Registry Editor:

1. Click, Start, Run, type regedit, and click OK.

2. Navigate to the HKEY_LOCAL_MACHINE\SYSTEM\ CurrentControlSet\Control key.

3. Right-click the Control subkey as described in step 2 and select New, Key.

4. Type the name for the new subkey—**StorageDevicePolicies**.

5. Right-click the new subkey that you just created StorageDevicePolicies, and click New, DWORD value.

6. Type the name of the new value, **WriteProtect**, and then click somewhere other than on this new value name to save the name you entered.

7. Double-click the new WriteProtect value name so that you can enter the *decimal* value data of **1** to enable this new setting (see Figure 6.12). The value data of **0** *turns off* the WriteProtect setting for USB storage devices.

8. Exit the Windows XP Registry Editor.

Figure 6.12 Creating the WriteProtect setting for USB storage devices under SP2 using the Windows XP Registry Editor.

Exam Prep Questions

1. Brendan wants to convert one of the hard drives connected to his Windows XP Professional desktop computer from a basic disk to a dynamic disk. In the Disk Management Console, he right-clicks the physical disk designated as Disk 1, but the option to Convert to Dynamic Disk is unavailable. Why would the option to convert the drive to a dynamic disk be disabled?

   ○ A. There are already drive volumes with data stored on that physical disk.

   ○ B. The drive is an external drive connected via USB or IEEE 1394 bus connections.

   ○ C. The drive is an external Fibre Channel device.

   ○ D. The drive has a sector size greater than 512 bytes.

2. Alexis wants to convert physical hard disk number 2 on her Windows XP Professional desktop computer from a basic disk to a dynamic disk using only the command line. Is a command-line tool available to accomplish this task? If so, what is the name of this utility and does it differ from the Disk Management Console?

   ○ A. The command-line tool is called Diskperf.exe. Only administrative users may use it.

   ○ B. No command-line tool equivalent to the Disk Management MMC exists.

   ○ C. The command-line tool is called Diskpart.exe. You must restart the computer for the conversion process to take effect.

   ○ D. The command-line tool is called Convert.exe. You do not need to restart the computer for the conversion to take place unless you are converting the boot disk.

3. What are the three types of dynamic volumes that are supported by dynamic disks under Windows XP Professional? (Check all correct answers.)

   ❑ A. Spanned volumes

   ❑ B. Extended volumes

   ❑ C. RAID-5 volumes

   ❑ D. Simple volumes

   ❑ E. Volume sets

   ❑ F. Striped volumes

   ❑ G. Mirrored volumes

4. Sue has a Windows XP Professional computer that has two physical hard drives installed—both disks have been converted to dynamic disks. The first disk (disk 0) has a capacity of 20GB with 11GB of unallocated free space, a drive C: (system and boot) volume of 2GB, and a drive D: volume of 7GB. The second disk (disk 1) has a capacity of 30GB with 20GB of unallocated free space. Sue needs to extend drive D: (a simple volume) on her computer so that the volume will have an

increased amount of total disk space--from 7GB to 14GB. How can she accomplish this without deleting any existing data? (Check all correct answers.)

- ❏ A. Repartition and reformat drive C:.
- ❏ B. Extend drive D: to an area of free space on disk 1.
- ❏ C. Extend drive D: to an area of free space on disk 0.
- ❏ D. Convert disk 1 to basic and extend the volume.

5. To make accessing different hard drive volumes and removable drives easier on a local Windows XP computer, you want your users to be able to access each drive volume through different folder names located on the same drive letter. How can you accomplish this?

- ○ A. Use the Subst.exe command-line utility to specify each folder as a unique drive letter.
- ○ B. Use the Disk Management Console to create mount points for each hard drive volume letter through empty folders on the same FAT or FAT32 volume.
- ○ C. Use diskpart.exe to create mount points for each hard drive volume letter through empty folders on the same NTFS volume.
- ○ D. Use diskperf.exe to create mount points for each hard drive volume letter through empty folders on the same NTFS volume.

6. What is the easiest way to convert an NTFS drive volume configured as drive D: to the FAT32 file system without losing any existing data? Assume that the volume is not the system or boot volume.

- ○ A. Use the command `convert d: /fs:fat32`.
- ○ B. Use the command `convert d: /fs:-ntfs`.
- ○ C. Use the Disk Management Console to revert the volume back to FAT or FAT32.
- ○ D. Back up all the data stored on the NTFS drive volume, use diskpart.exe or the Disk Management Console to delete the volume, create a new volume, format the volume as FAT32, and then restore the backed up data.

7. How can you set disk quotas on NTFS drive volumes for the Power Users group and for the Administrators group?

- ○ A. Right-click the drive letter in My Computer, select Properties, click the Quota tab, and mark the check boxes for Enable Quota Management and Deny Disk Space to Users Exceeding Quota Limit. Click Apply and click the Quota Entries button. Configure quota entries for the Power Users group and for the Administrators group.
- ○ B. Right-click the drive letter in My Computer, select Properties, click the Quota tab, and mark the check boxes for Enable Quota Management and Deny Disk Space to Users Exceeding Quota Limit. Click Apply and click the Quota Entries button. Configure quota entries for the Power Users group.
- ○ C. Right-click the drive letter in My Computer, select Properties, click the Quota tab, and mark the check boxes for Enable Quota

Management and Deny Disk Space to Users Exceeding Quota Limit. Click Apply and click the Quota Entries button. Configure quota entries for each member of the Power Users group.

❍ D. Create a new local group named Super Users and make all the members of the Power Users group and the Administrators group members of this new group. Right-click the drive letter in My Computer, select Properties, click the Quota tab, and mark the check boxes for Enable Quota Management and Deny Disk Space to Users Exceeding Quota Limit. Click Apply and click the Quota Entries button. Configure quota entries for the Super Users group.

8. Brandy wants to move an NTFS-compressed file from NTFS drive D: to an uncompressed folder on NTFS drive F:. What will happen to the file when she performs this operation?

❍ A. The compressed file will become uncompressed when it is moved to drive F:.

❍ B. The compressed file will remain compressed when it is moved to drive F:.

❍ C. Windows XP will prompt the user as to whether the file should remain compressed or should be uncompressed after it is moved.

❍ D. Brandy will receive an error message when she attempts to move the file to an uncompressed folder.

9. Terry encrypts an NTFS folder named SECRET DOCS on the hard drive of a Windows XP Professional computer. Terry is the only user with access to all the encrypted files in the SECRET DOCS folder (except for the DRA). Terry shares the computer with her associate, Kim. Kim is not the DRA. Later, Kim logs on to the same computer and attempts to copy one of the files stored inside of the SECRET DOCS folder, named Salaries.xls, to a floppy disk in drive A. After that, Kim tries to move the same file to an unencrypted folder on the same NTFS drive volume named PUBLIC DOCS. What are the results of Kim's file operations?

❍ A. Kim will receive an error message for trying to copy the encrypted file to a floppy disk, but he will be able to move the encrypted file to the PUBLIC DOCS unencrypted NTFS folder, where the file will remain encrypted.

❍ B. Kim will receive an error message for trying to copy the encrypted file to a floppy disk and he will also receive an error message for attempting to move the encrypted file to the PUBLIC DOCS unencrypted NTFS folder.

❍ C. Kim will receive an error message for trying to copy the encrypted file to a floppy disk, but he will successfully move the encrypted file to the PUBLIC DOCS unencrypted NTFS folder, where it will lose its encryption attribute.

❍ D. Kim will successfully copy the encrypted file to a floppy disk, where it will remain encrypted, and he will successfully move the encrypted file to the PUBLIC DOCS unencrypted NTFS folder.

Answers to Exam Prep Questions

1. Answer B is correct. Hard disks connected via USB or FireWire (IEEE 1394) buses are not supported for dynamic disks. Answer A is incorrect because you are allowed to convert disks with existing drive volumes and data to dynamic disks; you cannot convert back to a basic disk without deleting all existing volumes (and therefore the data on those volumes), however. Answer C is incorrect because dynamic disks do support Fibre Channel drives. Answer D is incorrect because only disks that have a sector size of less than 512 bytes are not supported by dynamic disks.

2. Answer C is correct. Diskpart.exe is the command-line equivalent to Disk Management. You must restart the computer for the conversion to take effect. Answer A is incorrect because diskperf.exe enables and disables hard disk performance counters on earlier versions of Windows; it does nothing for converting basic disks to dynamic disks. Answer B is incorrect because a command-line utility functionally equivalent to Disk Management exists—diskpart.exe. Answer D is incorrect because the Convert.exe command-line tool is used to convert a FAT or FAT32 volume to NTFS.

3. Answers A, D, and F are correct. Spanned volumes enable you to store data sequentially over two or more physical disks, but Windows XP displays the disks as one logical drive volume. Simple volumes are the most fundamental dynamic volumes, with each simple volume residing on only one physical disk. Striped volumes are also supported under Windows XP, enabling you to store data in stripes across two or more physical disks, but Windows XP displays the disks as one logical drive volume. Answer B is incorrect because there is no such volume as an extended volume on a dynamic disk. Answer C is incorrect because Windows XP Professional does not support the fault-tolerant RAID-5 volume configuration. Answer E is incorrect because volume sets were supported for basic disks under Windows NT; these are known as spanned volumes under Windows XP. Answer G is incorrect because Windows XP Professional does not support the fault-tolerant mirrored volume configuration.

4. Answers B and C are correct. A simple volume on a dynamic disk may be extended onto unallocated free space of additional dynamic disks up to a maximum of 32 dynamic disks. This automatically turns the volume into a spanned volume. A simple volume on a dynamic disk may also be extended onto an area of unallocated free space on the same dynamic disk. Answer A is incorrect because repartitioning and reformatting a disk deletes any data stored on the disk. Answer D is incorrect because converting a disk from dynamic to basic deletes any data stored on the disk.

5. Answer C is correct. You may use either diskpart.exe or the Disk Management MMC snap-in to create mount points for a drive letter through empty NTFS folders. Answer A is incorrect because the Subst.exe command associates a specific drive letter path with a different drive letter root folder. Answer B is incorrect because you can create mount points only on empty NTFS folders. Answer D is incorrect because diskperf.exe enables and disables hard disk performance counters on earlier versions of Windows.

6. Answer D is correct. Windows XP does not offer a conversion tool for converting an existing NTFS volume to FAT, FAT32, or any other file system. You must back up all the data on the volume, create a new volume, format it, and restore the data. Answer A is incorrect because the Convert.exe command does not support the conversion to the FAT or FAT32 file system. Answer B is incorrect because the Convert.exe command-line tool supports only a conversion to NTFS—adding a minus sign (-) to the NTFS parameter is not supported. Answer C is incorrect because the Disk Management Console only supports reformatting an existing NTFS drive volume to convert it to the FAT or FAT32 file system.

7. Answer C is correct. Windows XP Professional supports disk quotas on NTFS drive volumes only for individual users, not for groups. Therefore, you would have to create a quota entry for each member of the Power Users group—you cannot assign a quota limit to a group. All members of the Administrators group inherit a no-limit disk quota by default, so you cannot set quotas on members of this group. Answer A is incorrect for the reasons just cited. Answer B is incorrect because you cannot set quotas on groups. Answer D is incorrect for the same reason.

8. Answer A is correct. When you move a compressed file from one NTFS volume to a different NTFS volume, the file inherits the compression attribute from the target location. Answer B is incorrect because an NTFS compressed folder or file retains its compression attribute only when it is moved to another folder on the same NTFS volume. Answer C is incorrect because Windows XP never prompts the user as to whether a folder or file should remain compressed or uncompressed. Answer D is incorrect because Windows XP does not generate error messages for moving compressed files to an uncompressed folder.

9. Answer A is correct. Only the user who originally encrypted the file (or any users given shared access to the encrypted file) may copy the file to a non-NTFS drive volume or to any type of removable media. In addition, only the user who originally encrypted the file (or any users given shared access to the encrypted file) may copy the file or move it to a folder located on a different NTFS volume. A user without shared access to an encrypted file is permitted to move the file only to another

folder located on the same NTFS volume, where the file remains encrypted. Answer B is incorrect because, although Kim will receive an error message when he attempts to copy the file to a floppy disk, he will not receive an error message when he attempts to move the encrypted file to an unencrypted NTFS folder located on the same NTFS volume. Answer C is incorrect because, although Kim will receive an error message when he attempts to copy the file to a floppy disk, he will be allowed to move the encrypted file to an unencrypted NTFS folder located on the same NTFS volume, but the file will not lose its encryption attribute. Answer D is incorrect because Kim will receive an error message when he attempts to copy the encrypted file to a floppy disk.

Need to Know More?

Bott, Ed, and Carl Siechert. *Microsoft Windows XP Inside Out*, 2nd ed. Redmond, WA: Microsoft Learning, 2004. ISBN 073562044X. This book offers time-saving tips, troubleshooting techniques, and workarounds. It focuses on techniques such as taking advantage of the rich integration of devices, applications, and web services in Windows XP.

Microsoft Corporation. *Microsoft Windows XP Professional Resource Kit*, 2nd ed. Redmond, WA: Microsoft Press, 2003. ISBN 0735619743. This all-in-one reference is a compilation of technical documentation and valuable insider information that computer-support professionals and administrators can reference to install, customize, and support Windows XP.

Minasi, Mark. *Mastering Windows XP Professional*. Alameda, CA: Sybex, Inc., 2001. ISBN 0782129811. This book provides in-depth coverage of installing, configuring, and administering Windows XP Professional.

Search the Microsoft TechNet CD (or its online version through www.microsoft.com) using keywords such as "fsutil", "diskpart.exe", "disk quotas", "Encrypting File System (EFS)", "dynamic disks", "basic disks", "disk management", "data compression", "USB storage writeprotect", "SP2", and "Service Pack 2".

7

Implementing, Managing, and Troubleshooting Network Protocols and Services

Terms you'll need to understand:

✓ Transmission Control Protocol/Internet Protocol (TCP/IP)
✓ Dynamic Host Configuration Protocol (DHCP)
✓ Domain Name System (DNS)
✓ Windows Internet Naming Service (WINS)
✓ Automatic Private IP Addressing (APIPA)
✓ File Transfer Protocol (FTP)
✓ Simple Mail Transfer Protocol (SMTP)
✓ Address Resolution Protocol (ARP)

✓ ipconfig
✓ ping
✓ route
✓ tracert
✓ TCP/IP profiles
✓ Remote Desktop
✓ Remote Assistance
✓ Nbtstat
✓ Loopback address
✓ Variable length subnet mask

Techniques you'll need to master:

✓ Configuring and troubleshooting TCP/IP
✓ Configuring protocols to interoperate with Unix and Novell
✓ Configuring a network bridge
✓ Using Windows Messenger

✓ Configuring and troubleshooting Remote Desktop
✓ Configuring and troubleshooting Remote Assistance

The idea of a protocol in the networking world is rather simple. When one computer needs to communicate with another computer, they must speak the same language and be on the same connection. The protocol is the language that the computers speak, and the network itself (typically an Ethernet network) is the connection over which the protocols travel. Many different protocols exist to choose from, including NetBEUI, IPX/SPX, and TCP/IP. Microsoft supports all three of these protocols and more. Windows XP Professional must be configured with TCP/IP if it is going to be communicating on a network that runs Microsoft's Active Directory. The configuration of the TCP/IP protocol can be confusing, and troubleshooting communication problems related to TCP/IP can be more difficult. However, after an overview of the technology, configurations, and tools, the confusing aspects of protocols and network services will become crystal clear.

Configuring and Troubleshooting TCP/IP

TCP/IP encompasses a vast array of utilities and network services. This suite of services has evolved to become the industry standard for both the Internet and for local area networks (LANs) using personal computer network operating systems like Novell NetWare 5, Unix, and Windows XP.

TCP/IP is the default protocol when you install Windows XP Professional. It provides a means for connecting dissimilar computer systems. TCP/IP scales well and is typically the best choice for any size of organization. TCP/IP and its name resolution partner, Domain Name System (DNS), are both required components for implementing Active Directory in the Windows 2000/2003 Server family of products.

Deciphering the TCP/IP Protocol Suite for Windows XP

TCP/IP is more than a standardized specification for data transport over a network wire. It is a sophisticated toolbox of data transport services, name resolution services, and troubleshooting utilities. Microsoft's implementation of TCP/IP for Windows XP includes the following network services and components:

➤ Dynamic Host Configuration Protocol (DHCP)—This service is based on an industry-standard specification for automatically assigning (or leasing) IP addresses to computers connected to the network. The addresses are assigned from a predefined pool (or scope) of IP addresses that an administrator must configure. DHCP makes the chore of assigning and maintaining TCP/IP addresses on hundreds or thousands of computers much easier than having to maintain an exhaustive list of IP addresses and computer names by hand. However, administrators should manually assign static IP addresses for domain controllers, file and print server computers, and printers. You can install the DHCP service only in the Windows 2000/2003 Server product line, but DHCP can assign addresses to both servers and workstations. Any operating system that can make DHCP-enabled requests for IP addresses can use a DHCP server that is running Windows 2000. DHCP-enabled operating systems include Windows 3.x, 9x, ME, NT, 2000, 2003 and XP.

➤ DNS server—Computers understand and work well with numbers, but humans remember names much more easily than numbers. TCP/IP requires that each network device be assigned a numeric IP address. DNS, in conjunction with DNS servers, maps numeric IP addresses to computer (host) names and vice versa. DNS employs a hierarchical system of domains and subdomains that helps to make this name resolution service very scalable. DNS servers mitigate the need for a manually maintained HOSTS file to be stored on each computer. Windows 2000/2003 DNS servers offer added functionality such as Active Directory Integrated Zones, Incremental Zone Transfers, and Secure Dynamic Updates. DNS is a requirement for implementing Active Directory.

➤ Windows Internet Naming Service (WINS)—This service is Microsoft's implementation of a name resolution mechanism to match IP addresses to NetBIOS computer names and vice versa. WINS servers can greatly reduce NetBIOS traffic on networks by decreasing the amount of broadcast traffic that occurs when computers attempt to resolve unknown NetBIOS computer names to IP addresses. For an Active Directory–based network in Windows 2000/2003 native mode with no applications that require NetBIOS, nor any legacy Windows clients, WINS becomes unnecessary.

➤ Automatic Private IP Addressing (APIPA)—Microsoft first introduced this feature in Windows 98. For computers that are configured to obtain an IP address automatically, APIPA kicks in if no DHCP server is available on the network to lease out an IP address. APIPA automatically queries the other computers on the network to ensure it does not duplicate an IP address, and then assigns a unique IP address to the local computer using the IP address scheme of 169.254.x.y with the subnet mask of 255.255.0.0. The Internet Assigned Numbers Authority (IANA) has reserved the IP address range of 169.254.0.0 through

169.254.255.255 for APIPA. This ensures that any IP address that APIPA generates does not conflict with any public, routable addresses. This feature is turned on by default in Windows XP Professional.

➤ Serial Line Internet Protocol (SLIP)—This specification is an older Unix standard for serial communications. Windows XP supports SLIP for backward-compatibility purposes. You can use SLIP only for outbound connections on Windows XP Professional.

➤ Point-to-Point Protocol (PPP)—PPP has effectively replaced SLIP. PPP is a remote access/dial-up protocol that supports industry-standard network protocols such as TCP/IP, NWLink, NetBEUI, and AppleTalk. PPP is optimized for low-bandwidth connections, so it is the preferred remote access protocol for dial-up/modem connections.

➤ Point-to-Point Tunneling Protocol (PPTP)—The only Virtual Private Network (VPN) protocol that shipped with Windows NT 4, PPTP encapsulates TCP/IP, Internet Protocol Exchange (IPX), or NetBEUI data packets and encrypts the data being transmitted as it is tunneled through the Internet. PPTP clients can connect to any Microsoft-compatible PPTP servers via the Internet with proper security credentials. This service, shipped with Windows XP Professional, allows users to connect to the Internet using local (non–long-distance) connections and offers them a way to connect to PPTP computers in remote locations without incurring toll charges or requiring dedicated data lines.

➤ Layer 2 Tunneling Protocol (L2TP)—An alternative to PPTP, L2TP was new to Windows 2000 and offers similar functionality to PPTP. However, L2TP is an industry-standard VPN protocol and is shipped with Windows XP Professional. L2TP also encapsulates TCP/IP, IPX, or NetBEUI data packets and encrypts the data being transmitted as it is tunneled through the Internet. You can also use L2TP in conjunction with Microsoft IP Security (IPSec) for enhanced security. L2TP is covered in more detail later in this chapter.

➤ IPSec—This is a relatively new Internet security protocol, also referred to as *Secure IP*. It provides computer-level authentication in addition to data encryption for VPN connections that use the L2TP protocol. IPSec negotiates between the client computer and the remote tunnel server before an L2TP connection is established, which secures both authentication passwords and data. L2TP uses standard PPP-based authentication protocols, such as Extensible Authentication Protocol (EAP), Microsoft Challenge Handshake Authentication Protocol (MSCHAP), CHAP, Shiva Password Authentication Protocol (SPAP), and Password Authentication Protocol (PAP) with IPSec.

➤ World Wide Web (WWW) publishing service—This is a major component of Internet Information Services (IIS), which ships with Windows XP Professional. Although not installed by default in Windows XP Professional, IIS and the WWW publishing service provide web page hosting for HTML-based and Active Server Pages (ASP)-based documents.

➤ File Transfer Protocol (FTP) service—This is another major component of IIS. FTP is an industry-standard protocol for transferring files between computers over TCP/IP-based networks, such as the Internet.

➤ Simple Mail Transfer Protocol (SMTP)—The Microsoft SMTP service implements the industry-standard SMTP to transport and deliver email messages. The SMTP service for Windows XP is also a component of IIS.

Understanding TCP/IP Computer Addresses

TCP/IP assigns a unique set of numbers to each computer that is connected to a TCP/IP-based network or internetwork. This set of numbers consists of four separate numbers, each delimited by a period or a dot (.). For example, an IP address of 192.168.1.20 illustrates this concept, known as dotted-decimal notation. Each device on a TCP/IP-based network must be assigned a unique IP address so that it can send and receive data with the other devices on the network. A network device can be a computer, a printer, a router, a firewall, and so on.

We write IP addresses in a dotted-decimal format for ease and convenience. However, TCP/IP addresses are actually 32-bit binary numbers! By converting these binary numbers into decimal, most of us can work with these addresses much more easily than if we had to work with them in their native binary format. The real binary address of 192.168.1.20, previously mentioned, translates into 11000000.10101000.00000001.00010100.

 If you're not sure how to convert decimal numbers into binary or vice versa, just use the Windows Calculator by selecting Start, Run, typing **calc**, and clicking OK. Select View, Scientific and you can easily perform these conversions.

Certain IP addresses are reserved for specific functions:

➤ The address 255.255.255.255 (11111111.11111111.11111111.11111111 in binary) is reserved for *network broadcasts*.

➤ The IP address 127.0.0.1 (1111111.00000000.00000000.00000001 in binary) is reserved as a *loopback address* for testing proper configuration of the IP address(es) for the local host computer.

➤ The address schemes 192.168.x.y, 172.16.0.0 to 172.31.255.255, and 10.0.x.y have been *reserved as nonroutable* by the bodies that govern the Internet.

Therefore, IP addresses such as 192.168.1.20 and 10.0.0.7 are restricted to use only for the internal addressing of LANs. By definition, you cannot route these addressing schemes onto the Internet. Routers (devices that route network data packets) do not forward any data packets that originate with a non-routable addressing scheme.

Understanding Classful IP Addressing

A look at Classful IP addressing takes us back to the beginning of TCP/IP itself. Classful addressing was adopted as RFC 791 and was the first major addressing scheme. Three address classes were used for typical network communication. These three ranges include A, B, and C class ranges. The difference between each class was the number of bits that made up the class prefix. For example, an IP address of 10.1.1.1 would be in the Class A range because the first octet, 10, starts with a prefix that is within the Class A range. Table 7.1 shows the different classes and the corresponding prefix ranges.

 You can quickly determine the class ranges by starting off with an octet of all zeros and turning on bits from the left-most part of the octet range. For a Class A range, the starting number would be an octet of all zeros up to an octet with the first bit turned on, 10000000. This would be a range of 0 to 127. The actual value of the octet with the first bit turned on is 128, which is the start of the next range. Then the end of the next range would be up to the second bit turned on, 11000000. So, the Class B would be a range of 128 to 191. If you follow this pattern for the remaining ranges, you will never be at a loss as to which range an IP address falls into.

When you see a reference to a Classful IP address scheme, it is referring to an address scheme that does not break up these classes. It is no surprise that because of the influx of the Internet, these address ranges are already purchased. If you want to get a range of IP addresses, you will need to contact an Internet service provider (ISP).

Understanding Variable-Length Subnet Masks

When you contact that ISP, you might be surprised that you can't obtain your own Class B range. What you might get instead is a portion of a Class B range.

When a Classful IP address range is broken down into smaller pieces, you need to use a *variable-length subnet mask* (VLSM), as shown in Figure 7.1. The standard subnet masks that come with the Classful IP ranges are as follows:

➤ Class A—255.0.0.0

➤ Class B—255.255.0.0

➤ Class C—255.255.255.0

Table 7.1   Classful IP Address Prefix Ranges and Their Associated Address Classes

Prefix Range	Address Class
0–127	A
128–191	B
192–223	C
224–239	D
240–255	E

When you want to use only a portion of the address class range, you need to alter the standard subnet mask. A typical example of using VLSM is when you need to break up a Class C range into smaller ranges. A typical Class C range contains 254 IP addresses for hosts. Many smaller companies don't need this many addresses, so they will use a Class C address range that uses a VLSM to break up the range. This is done to create smaller pools of IP addresses. If you had a company that needed only 50 IP addresses, you could use a subnet mask of 255.255.255.192 with a Class C range of IP addresses. This subnet mask would break up the original Class C range and create four IP address ranges containing 62 IP addresses each.

Understanding Classless Interdomain Routing

The technology that we just looked at, VLSM, takes a Classful IP address range and makes more IP networks with fewer IP addresses. This is great for smaller companies or companies that want to break up the network into segments to reduce broadcasts. However, what if you are a larger company and you require additional IP addresses for one network segment? For this solution, you will need to combine IP address ranges. This is called Classless Interdomain Routing (CIDR). With CIDR, multiple subnets are seen as a single logical network of IP addresses. CIDR does have limitations, such as routing protocols and hardware devices. However, if your network can support CIDR, it just might be the solution that you are looking for.

When you are determining whether two IP address ranges can be combined with CIDR, you need to first determine if they share the higher-order bits. The following examples help explain how this works:

Example 1	Bits
10.1.2.0/24	00001010.00000001.00000010.00000000
10.1.3.0/24	00001010.00000001.00000011.00000000

Example 2	Bits
10.3.2.0/24	00001010.00000011.00000010.00000000
10.1.3.0/24	00001010.00000001.00000011.00000000

The first example can use CIDR because the first 23 bits are the same and therefore can be combined into a single network by the use of a classless network. This would be accomplished by using a new subnet mask of 255.255.254.0, which would result in a new subnet that would have a total of 510 host addresses. The second example will not work with a shortened CIDR subnet because only the first 14 bits are the same.

> **NOTE**
> To get more information on CIDR, refer to **http://www.petri.co.il/what's_cidr.htm** on the Internet or review the Microsoft Windows Server 2003 Resource Kit, "Internet Protocol (IP) Addresses: Getting Started" section.

Configuring TCP/IP

TCP/IP is installed by default when you install Windows XP Professional. However, you can override this default setting if your network does not require it or if you will not be on a network with Active Directory. In addition, the protocol's default configuration is to *obtain an IP address automatically*. This means that the computer automatically requests a unique TCP/IP address for your network from a DHCP server. If no DHCP server is available, the operating system invokes APIPA to query the other computers that are currently powered on and connected to the network so that it can assign itself a unique IP address.

To work with TCP/IP, you need to become familiar with the following terms:

➤ Subnet mask—This is essentially an IP address filter that gets applied to each unique IP address. The subnet mask determines which part of the IP address for a computer specifies the network segment where the computer is located, versus which part of the IP address specifies the unique host address for that individual computer. As an example, an IP address of 192.168.1.20 with a subnet mask of 255.255.255.0 is determined to have the network ID of 192.168.1. The host address for the computer, therefore, is 20. This is analogous to the street name of a postal address versus the actual house number of the address. The street may have many houses, but only one house has a house number of 20.

➤ Default gateway—This IP address specifies the router for the local network segment (or subnet). If this address is absent, the computer cannot communicate with other computers that are located outside of the local network segment. Default gateway information is often obtained through DHCP if the computer is configured to obtain an IP address automatically.

➤ Preferred and alternate DNS servers—Having more than one DNS server on a network helps provide load balancing and fault tolerance for client computers that need to perform hostname-to-IP address lookups as well as IP address-to-hostname lookups. DNS is also used to find domain-based services such as domain controllers, DFS roots, and Global Catalog servers. Name resolution is a critical issue in TCP/IP. DNS server information is often obtained through DHCP if the computer is configured to obtain an IP address automatically.

➤ WINS server addresses—WINS provides name resolution between NetBIOS computer names and IP addresses. WINS server addresses are often obtained through DHCP if the computer is configured to obtain an IP address automatically.

To manually set up a Windows XP Professional computer with a static IP address for the TCP/IP network protocol, click Start, Control Panel, Network Connections, and then select the Local Area Connection that you want to configure. Right-click the Local Area Connection icon and then click Properties. To configure the necessary settings so that TCP/IP can communicate with other computers and devices over the network, follow these steps:

1. Click Internet Protocol (TCP/IP) and then click Properties.

2. Click Use the Following IP Address.

3. Type the IP Address, Subnet Mask, and Default Gateway.

4. Type the proper IP address for a Preferred DNS Server and an Alternate DNS Server (if any).

5. Click the Advanced button to add additional IP addresses and default gateways. You can also add, edit, or remove DNS server address information, and you can change other DNS settings. You can specify IP addresses for any WINS servers on the network, enable NetBIOS name resolution using an LMHOSTS file, and enable or disable NetBIOS over TCP/IP. You can also set up IPSec and TCP/IP filtering as optional settings from the Advanced TCP/IP Settings properties sheet.

6. Click OK to close the Advanced TCP/IP Settings Properties dialog box.

7. Click OK to close the Internet Protocol (TCP/IP) Properties dialog box.

8. Click OK to close the Local Area Connection Properties dialog box.

Troubleshooting TCP/IP

Windows XP Professional comes with several software tools and utilities to help you isolate and resolve TCP/IP-related issues. You must run these utilities from the command line. Connectivity tools include the following:

➤ Finger—Displays information about a user for a particular computer. The target computer must be running the Finger service.

➤ FTP—Transfers files to and from FTP servers over a TCP/IP connection.

➤ LPR—Sends one or more files to be printed via a line printer daemon (LPD) printer.

➤ RCP—Copies files between a Windows XP Professional computer (or a computer running Windows Server 2003) and a computer system running the remote shell daemon (RSHD). Windows 2000 Professional and Windows XP clients cannot run the RSHD daemon, but Unix systems can.

➤ REXEC—Executes commands on remote computer systems that are running the REXEC service. Windows 2000, Windows XP, and Windows Server 2003 systems all have the capability to run the REXEC service.

➤ RSH—Executes commands on remote computer systems that are running the RSH service. Windows 2000, Windows XP, and Window Server 2003 systems do not run the RSH service.

 A utility included with the Windows 2000 Server Resource Kit enables the RSH service to run on a Windows 2000 system. The utility is called **RSHSVC.EXE**. The Windows Server 2003 Resource Kit does not include this utility.

➤ Telnet—Establishes a terminal emulation session for working on remote systems, including environments such as Unix, Mainframe, and mini-computers.

➤ Trivial File Transfer Protocol (TFTP)—Copies files to and from remote computers that are running the TFTP service.

Diagnostic tools include the following:

➤ Address Resolution Protocol (ARP)—Lists and edits the IP-to-Ethernet (or Token Ring) physical translation tables that ARP uses.

➤ HOSTNAME—Lists the name of the local host (computer).

➤ IPCONFIG—Shows all current TCP/IP configuration settings for the local computer, such as its IP address, subnet mask, and any WINS servers and DNS servers assigned to the computer.

Special optional parameters for the **IPCONFIG** command deal with the DNS portion of the IP session. These include the **/registerdns**, **/displaydns**, and **/flushdns** switches. These switches register the client with DNS, show the current DNS cache, and flush out the DNS cache, respectively. You can use the **IPCONFIG** command to release and renew an automatically assigned IP address from a DHCP server with the **/release** and the **/renew** switches.

➤ LPQ—Shows the current status of the print queue on a computer that is running the LPD service.

➤ NBTSTAT—Delineates network protocol statistics and lists the current connections that are using NetBIOS over TCP/IP.

Don't forget about the **–R** and **–RR** switches that can help refresh the cache, send release packets to WINS, and then refresh the client connection.

➤ NETSTAT—Delineates network protocol statistics and lists the current TCP/IP connections.

➤ PING—Used to test TCP/IP-related connectivity to remote computers. This command also verifies the proper TCP/IP configuration of the local host computer by attempting to ping the loopback address for the local host (computer). For example: `ping 127.0.0.1`

➤ ROUTE—Edits the local computer's routing tables.

➤ TRACERT—Displays the route (path) that data packets follow as they travel from the local computer to a remote destination computer.

Troubleshooting TCP/IP Configuration and Connectivity

Whenever you initially set up TCP/IP, you should always test and verify that the protocol is working properly. Following are the steps you can take to check the computer's TCP/IP configuration and test its connectivity:

1. Open a command prompt window (`ipconfig` and `ping` are command-line-only utilities).

2. Run `ipconfig` to display the computer's current IP configuration. Use `ipconfig /all` to display more detailed information, as shown in Figure 7.1.

3. Use the `ping` command to ping a computer's loopback address, which is 127.0.0.1, by default (for example, `ping 127.0.0.1`). This tests whether TCP/IP is correctly installed and properly bound to the network adapter card(s). Figure 7.2 shows the response from pinging the loopback IP address.

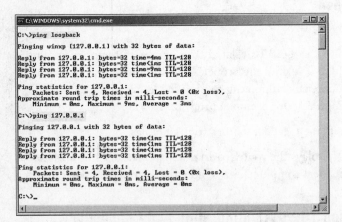

Figure 7.1 Running the **ipconfig** command with the **/all** option.

Figure 7.2 Running the *ping* command using the computer's loopback IP address.

4. Ping the IP address of the local computer to verify the uniqueness of the IP address on the network.

5. Ping the IP address of the default gateway for the local subnet to check that the default gateway is up and running. This step also demonstrates whether the computer can successfully communicate over the local network segment.

6. Ping the IP address of a computer that is located on a different network segment. This step indicates whether the computer can send and receive network data packets through a router.

Using APIPA

If a computer is set up to obtain an IP address automatically from a DHCP server, but no DHCP servers are available, APIPA temporarily assigns an IP address to the local computer while it searches the network to make sure that no other network devices have been assigned the same IP address. By running `ipconfig`, you can view the current TCP/IP information for the local computer. An address such as 169.254.x.y generally indicates that APIPA is currently in effect.

Windows XP clients do not indicate that they are unable to obtain an IP address from a DHCP server. By default, instead of a notification, a Windows XP computer obtains an APIPA address without any warning or message. It is essential that the help desk and IT staff be made aware that this is the default behavior and that they can be sure to add it to their list of items for troubleshooting TCP/IP communication issues.

Working with TCP/IP Profiles

You now know that when a DHCP-enabled client can't find a DHCP server, it will be allocated an IP address within the allocated APIPA range. A nice feature that Windows XP offers is the alternate TCP/IP configuration option, sometimes referred to as a TCP/IP profile. This feature is excellent for mobile users who need to connect to multiple networks. A good example might be an executive who receives a DHCP-allocated IP address at work, but needs a static IP address for the home office network.

The alternate IP address assignment process takes place as follows:

1. The DHCP-enabled client attempts to locate a DHCP server.

2. The client will attempt to contact a DHCP server for approximately 60 seconds and then will try to configure its own IP address.

3. The computer will use the information configured on the Alternate Configuration tab to determine whether to use APIPA or the alternate configuration information. Figure 7.3 illustrates the options available for the Alternate Configuration tab.

Figure 7.3 The Alternate Configuration tab for specifying a TCP/IP address for the local computer when a DHCP server cannot be contacted.

The Alternate Configuration tab is available only if the initial TCP/IP configuration is set to Obtain an IP Address Automatically.

Connecting to Novell NetWare Networks and Unix-Based Computer Systems

Microsoft has always made an effort to allow its client operating systems the connectivity needed to communicate with other network operating systems. Windows XP does not stray from these efforts. Microsoft's OSs have always had the capability to connect with Novell networks, and Microsoft continues to add capabilities to connect to other companies' network OSs as they become more common in the business marketplace.

Novell NetWare Connectivity

When connecting to a Novell network, the version of NetWare and connectivity requirements will determine the Windows XP configuration. We are all familiar with the protocol that is used to communicate with most of the Novell networks in existence: IPX/SPX. Microsoft has renamed its version of this protocol to incorporate NetBIOS, which it calls NWLink. If you are running Novell NetWare 3.x or 4.x, you will need to install NWLink on some, if not all, of your Microsoft clients for communication. If you are running Novell NetWare 5.x, you can run TCP/IP natively, allowing for a limited number of protocols to be installed on the Microsoft clients.

Beyond the protocol, you also need to consider the client redirector. Since the NT days, the Microsoft client redirector for a Novell network has been Client Service for NetWare (CSNW). This client allows Microsoft clients access to file and print sharing with NetWare servers. When this client is installed, the client also installs the NWLink protocol to function properly.

Another service designed to help the communication gap with NetWare is Gateway Service for NetWare (GSNW). This service is available only on Microsoft servers; it functions as a proxy between the Microsoft network and the NetWare network. If this service is implemented, the clients running Windows XP need only TCP/IP installed. The server running the service will need both TCP/IP and NWLink installed to communicate with both the Microsoft network and the NetWare network.

CSNW and GSNW do not function with TCP/IP, even with NetWare 5.x servers. These services are designed to function only with the IPX/SPX protocol suite.

Another important aspect of communicating with a NetWare network is the frame type that is associated with the IPX/SPX protocol. Remember that the earlier versions of Netware use the higher-numbered frame type! To ensure that communication is upheld, be sure to check with the following list of frame types when configuring your Windows XP Professional clients:

➤ Netware 3.12 and later—Use frame type 802.2

➤ Netware 2.x through 3.11—Use frame type 802.3

An option is available to set the frame type to autodetect, but it will detect only one type at a time. The order in which the frame types are detected is 802.2, 802.3, ETHERNET_II, and 802.5. The frame type 802.5 is used with Token Ring and is not usually used.

Unless you are running some form of metadirectory or software to synchronize the account information between Microsoft and NetWare, you will need to change your password for the NetWare environment separately from the Microsoft environment. One option is to use the SETPASS.EXE command from the Windows XP Professional client. The other option is to change the NetWare password from the Change Password option available when you press Ctrl+Alt+Delete. This enables Windows XP Professional users to change their password on a NetWare 4.x and higher server that is running Novell Directory Services (NDS).

Unix Connectivity

Microsoft has made a valiant effort to incorporate better connectivity with Unix servers and has produced many new services and applications that allow better communication. However, the tools still have not made their way into the base operating system. The following standard tools are available with Windows XP:

➤ Print Services for Unix—This service enables Line Printer Remote (LPR) ports to be installed on your Windows XP client. An LPR port can send a document to a print spooler service on another computer or Unix printer. The Line Printer Daemon (LPD) service is also installed with Print Services for Unix. This allows the receipt of a print job.

➤ Services for Unix (SFU)—This service can be installed on a Windows system to allow the Windows system to communicate with Unix file and print servers. The different services that are installed include Telnet client, Telnet server, Unix shell and utilities, and Client for NFS. SFU is not a free product, but can be purchased online or from a Microsoft vendor.

Network Bridging

The Windows XP network bridge option is similar to a typical network bridge. It connects different network segments into a single network, appearing to exist as a single network subnet. This can have some benefits for small office and home office (SOHO) networks. The technology allows different network media to be bridged as well, which might include Ethernet, FireWire, and wireless Ethernet.

To get the network bridge established, you highlight both of the network adapters that will be part of the bridge. After highlighting the adapters, right-click one of them and select the Bridge Connections menu option. After the bridge is established between the two network cards, the bridge functions as a single, logical network card. The two original network cards will not be configurable, because they are now part of the bridge. The bridge will obtain an IP address and will function as a single network card between the two networks.

 You can confirm that the bridge is working properly by running the **ipconfig** command. The results of the command should indicate that the network bridge is the only connection and that it now has the IP address and TCP/IP configurations needed to communicate with both networks.

It is possible to add more than two network cards to a network bridge. Actually, it is possible to add as many network cards as your computer will support. After the network card is added to the network bridge, it is located under the Network Bridge section in the Network Connections properties interface, as shown in Figure 7.4.

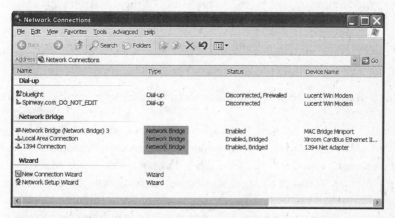

Figure 7.4   The Network Connections window shows which connections are a part of the network bridge.

Windows Messenger

It is no surprise that Microsoft put a messenger service inside Windows XP. The popularity of Microsoft Instant Messenger is nothing new to computer users. The tool that Microsoft placed into the Windows XP default configuration replaces MSN Messenger. However, MSN Messenger is the tool that you will continue to use on your pre–Windows XP clients. If you are a NetMeeting user, you will also be able to switch over to Windows Messenger for your collaboration and communication needs.

If you have not used MSN Messenger before, you will most likely become very familiar with the application as soon as you get your XP client running. Windows Messenger allows you to communicate with other users on the Internet and share files, as well. The following is a list of functions that you can perform with Windows Messenger:

➤ Chat with employees, clients, or friends who are also online.

➤ Use the contact list and notification capabilities to determine whether other employees, clients, or friends are online. This reduces the time spent attempting to contact someone who is not available.

➤ Communicate with employees, clients, or friends using audio and video conferencing.

➤ Make voice calls using the built-in capabilities of the messenger application.

➤ Communicate to cell phones and pagers by sending text messages.

➤ Transfer files and documents quickly and easily.

➤ Share a whiteboard or program online to collaborate with employees, clients, or friends.

To get Windows Messenger up and running, you need to establish a .NET Passport account. You can either establish a Passport with a free MSN (or Hotmail) account or link it to an existing email account that you own. The Passport information can be saved with your user account, either as a domain or local account. After you have the information stored with your user account, you will have pass-through authentication with a single username and password.

One way to ask for Remote Assistance is directly through Windows Messenger menu options.

This new Windows Messenger is compatible with the older MSN Messenger for the capabilities of MSN Messenger. However, if you are attempting to communicate with a NetMeeting user, you will find that it is not compatible.

If you still need to have NetMeeting on your XP Pro clients to communicate with others who are running NetMeeting, you can access NetMeeting from the XP Pro CD-ROM.

Remote Desktop

Remote Desktop comes with Windows XP and is a big improvement on the Terminal Services client software that you previously had to download manually and install on Windows 2000 and earlier desktop operating systems. Like the Terminal Services client, the Remote Desktop Connection software for Windows XP allows you to connect to a terminal server computer. Microsoft wanted to allow you to access a session that is running on your computer while you are sitting at another computer. This is a great solution for those employees who want to connect to their computer at work while working from home. You will have access to applications, files, and other network resources from the comfort of your home. You will even be able to see the existing applications that were left open on your desktop. Remote Desktop Connections use the Remote Desktop Protocol (RDP) over TCP/IP for all Remote Desktop Connection sessions.

Configuring Remote Desktop

To get Remote Desktop up and running, you will need to configure the computer that will be connected to, called the *work computer* in this discussion. The computer that will be connecting to the work computer is called the *home computer*. We will look at the requirements for the home computer in just a little bit.

For the work computer, you must be running Windows XP Professional. You must enable the work computer to allow Remote Desktop. To access this option, right-click the My Computer icon and select Properties. Next, click the Remote tab. After you get to the interface for this path, you can enable Remote Desktop, as shown in Figure 7.5.

Only computers running Windows XP Professional can act as a host (allow another computer to connect to it via RDP) for a Remote Desktop session. However, both Windows XP Professional and Home editions can *connect to* another Windows XP Professional computer running Remote Desktop (or to a Windows server running terminal services).

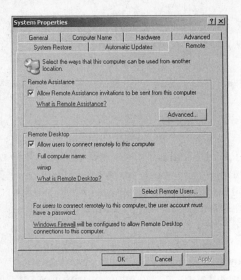

Figure 7.5 Remote Desktop options on the Remote tab of the System Properties dialog box.

After you get Remote Desktop enabled, you need to configure which users will have the capability to connect. This is accomplished by adding the correct users to the Remote Desktop Users group, which is the group that users must belong to in order to gain access to the work computer from the home computer. You can add users to this group by clicking the Select Remote Users button shown in Figure 7.5 or by using the Local Users and Groups option in the Computer Management snap-in.

All users who are members of the local Administrators group automatically have Remote Desktop Connection access *without* being placed into the local Remote Desktop Users group.

Connecting with Remote Desktop

When users want to connect to a computer that has Remote Desktop Connections enabled, they will only need to run a simple application installed by default on all Windows XP computers. To access the application, go to Start, (All) Programs, Accessories, Communications, Remote Desktop Connection. You will be prompted to input the computer name (or IP address) of the work (remote) computer. After clicking the Connect button, you will be prompted for a username and password for the Remote Desktop connection.

Microsoft put in a security feature for the work computer. The feature locks the desktop and puts up a screen so no one can see what you are working on remotely. *As long as you are connected to the computer through Remote Desktop, no one will be able to connect to the computer locally.* For you to gain access to your computer after you get back to work, you press Ctrl+Alt+Delete to be prompted for your username and password, enabling you to unlock the system.

If you have accidentally left the connection established from your home computer to your work computer, the connection at home will automatically be logged off when you unlock the work computer.

Remote Desktop Web Connection

Another feature of Remote Desktop is the capability to allow users to connect through a web browser. This is a feature that was first introduced with Terminal Services and is ported over to Remote Desktop. To get the Remote Desktop web service installed, you need to follow these steps:

1. Open Add or Remove Programs in Control Panel.

2. Select Add/Remove Windows Components.

3. Select Internet Information Services (IIS) and click the Details button for this option.

4. After selecting World Wide Web Service in the IIS Details window, click the Details button for this option.

5. Select the Remote Desktop Web Connection option and click OK for each of the dialog boxes that you have opened. Click Next when you get to the Windows Components Wizard window.

This selection will install the Remote Desktop capabilities, which are really a portion of IIS. If you go into the IIS management tool, you will see a virtual directory named `tsweb` that supports the Remote Desktop functionality.

The connecting computer needs to have Microsoft Internet Explorer (IE) version 4.0 or later. To make the connection, open the browser and type in the following URL: `http://<computername>/tsweb`. This will prompt the user for the computer to connect to and for the proper username and password for authentication. Figure 7.6 shows the web page for connecting through the Remote Desktop Web Connection.

Whether you are connecting through the Remote Desktop Web Connection page or through the standard Remote Desktop Connection client, you must enter a valid username and password to connect. *A blank password is not acceptable* for connecting to another computer via a Remote Desktop Connection.

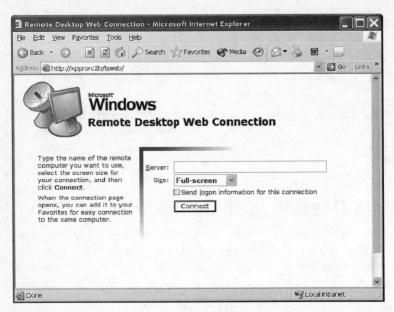

Figure 7.6 The Remote Desktop Web Connection page for connecting to another computer via RDP.

Understanding Remote Assistance

The underlying technologies of Remote Desktop and Remote Assistance are the same, but the application is much different. As you just saw with Remote Desktop, the goal is to allow users access to their work computer from their home computer. With Remote Assistance, the goal is to have another user, typically a helpdesk technician or a system administrator, remotely help end users with issues that they are experiencing on their Windows XP Professional computer.

Remote Assistance is similar to third-party remote control software that you may have used, such as PCAnywhere, Funk Proxy, or VNC. However, this software is built into the OS and allows for better control and security. With this technology, end users are able to invite someone to help them troubleshoot or walk through an issue that they are having on their desktop. The end user simply fills out a small questionnaire, called an *invitation*, and sends it to the desired support personnel. Before end users can create and successfully send invitations, they need to enable Remote Assistance on their computer. This is accomplished by right-clicking the My Computer icon and selecting Properties. Next, click the Remote tab and mark the check box labeled Allow Remote Assistance Invitations to Be Sent from This Computer, as shown in Figure 7.7.

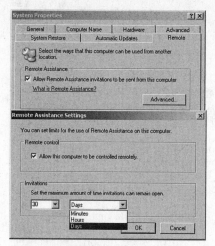

Figure 7.7 Turning on Remote Assistance and specifying option settings on the Remote tab of the System Properties dialog box.

The dialog boxes shown in Figure 7.7 also allow for advanced options to be configured for the Remote Assistance sessions. Click the Advanced button to work with the Remote Assistance Settings dialog box. The first advanced option is the capability to allow the computer to be controlled remotely. If this option is selected, it indicates that the support person not only is able to see the desktop, but also can take control of it using a mouse and keyboard. The second option controls the amount of time for which an invitation is valid. It is not wise to leave an invitation open for too long, because of security concerns.

To create an invitation, the user selects the Invite a Friend to Connect to Your Computer with Remote Assistance link from the Help and Support Center off the Start menu. The invitation has many steps that need to be well understood. The first step is to determine how you will contact your support person, also called an *assistant* or *expert*, as they are referred to in the Remote Assistance dialog boxes. You have three options for sending an invitation:

➤ Windows Messenger—This requires that you have an existing MSN Messenger account or have configured a .NET Passport.

➤ Email—This requires that you have Microsoft Outlook or Outlook Express configured.

 To use the email invitation method, both you and the assistant must have Windows Messenger or a MAPI-compliant email program such as Microsoft Outlook or Outlook Express.

➤ File—This is the advanced option, but it gives you the most freedom in getting the invitation out to the assistant.

During the creation of the invitation, you first are prompted to give the name that will appear on the invitation and the duration for which the invitation will be valid. Next, you are asked to give the invitation a password. This is a critical step for the overall security of the process. It is highly recommended that you configure the password so that you make the password difficult for a stranger to guess. Here are some tips to ensure the password is complex, which makes it difficult for others to easily discover:

➤ The password should contain multiple characters, at least six or seven.

➤ The password should contain more than one type of character, such as a combination of alpha and numeric characters.

➤ The password should not contain the computer name or username.

➤ The password should not be a common word, especially one that can be referenced from a dictionary.

 Because the password is not sent with the invitation, it must be communicated to the assistant so that the assistant can use the invitation to connect using Remote Assistance. You can send the password via email; however, relaying the password to the assistant through a simple phone call is a much more secure way to send it.

After the invitation is filled out, it needs to be saved. The name of the invitation ticket can be anything, but it helps if it is descriptive for the event. The invitation file extension is .msrcincident by default, and it should not be changed. The file is actually an XML-formatted file that gives the pertinent information for the invitation and for connecting to the remote computer.

After you have sent the invitation or created the invitation file, you can access the log of invitations through the Windows XP Help and Support Center. Just click Start, Help and Support, and then click the Invite a Friend to Connect to Your Computer with Remote Assistance link. Select the View Invitation Status link to view all the invitations you have created and sent on the local computer.

When the assistant (expert) receives the invitation, she will click to accept the invitation and connect to your computer. After she connects, she will be able to view your desktop and chat with you in real-time, as shown in Figure 7.8. Both the assistant and the computer being controlled must be running Windows XP Professional. If the computer being controlled has been configured to allow remote control, the assistant will be able to use her mouse and keyboard to control the remote desktop. The remote control option requires permission—it is not turned on by default. Another feature that is possible after the connection is made is audio help. If both parties have full-duplex sound cards or sound through the USB port, speakers, and a microphone, they can communicate verbally to help resolve any issues *without any long distance phone charges!*

Figure 7.8 Getting help from an expert using Remote Assistance.

To stop Remote Assistance, you click the Stop option on the chat window. Another option is to press the Esc key, which will also close the current session. If you want to disconnect the current session, but keep the Remote Assistance window open, you can select the Disconnect option in the chat window.

Some final comments about Remote Assistance concern security. Not all firewalls will allow Remote Desktop or Remote Assistance traffic to pass through. To allow this Remote Desktop and/or Remote Assistance data traffic to freely flow to and from your Windows XP client computers, you need to start by opening ports TCP 3389 and UDP 3389 on the firewall. All of the sessions are encrypted, so the security of the information being transferred back and forth should be fairly high. As far as creating a new invitation, you can do this at the command line if you feel so inclined. The HELPCTR.EXE tool can create almost any view of the Help and Support Center, including starting a Remote Assistance session.

Always keep in mind that even though both ends of Remote Desktop and Remote Assistance sessions are encrypted, that does not deter hackers from attempting to break into Windows XP Professional computers that are hosting or standing by to host those sessions. Strongly encrypted virtual private network (VPN) tunnels provide a much more secure communications channel with which to use both the Remote Desktop and Remote Assistance features. Unfortunately, there may be many scenarios in which using a VPN tunnel is not practical for your environment. In those cases, *keep port 3389 open only for the duration of each remote session and disable the Remote Desktop and Remote Assistance services except when expressly needed.*

Exam Prep Questions

1. You are the administrator of a small company that has 20 nodes on the network. The network is currently split into two distinct network segments. You are looking for an inexpensive solution to allow the computers on one network segment to communicate with the users on the other network segment. What will you implement to allow this communication?

   ○ A. Set up a DHCP relay agent.
   ○ B. Configure ICS on one of the client computers.
   ○ C. Configure a TCP/IP profile for each node.
   ○ D. Set up a network bridge.

2. You have just been promoted to the sales manager for the Braincore.net corporation. As part of your job responsibilities, you are required to access a database to monitor the sales trends. You discover that the database is not updated until well after you get home in the evenings, but your report is due early in the morning. You do not want to make the drive into work to generate the report from the database information. What do you do instead?

   ○ A. Configure your system at work to allow Remote Assistance.
   ○ B. Configure your system at work to receive dial-up access.
   ○ C. Configure your system at work to allow Remote Desktop access.
   ○ D. Configure your system at work to allow a Virtual Private Network connection.

3. You are the network administrator for a growing web-development company. You have needed to purchase multiple Class C address ranges to keep up with the growth of the company and the number of computers. You need to combine two of the Class C licenses that you have to increase the number of clients on a single network segment. How will you accomplish this?

   ○ A. Use DHCP instead of statically configuring your IP addresses.
   ○ B. Use Classless Interdomain Routing to combine the two IP address ranges into one.
   ○ C. Use Classful IP address ranges to combine the two IP address ranges into one.
   ○ D. Use variable-length subnet masking to combine the two IP address ranges into one.

4. You have just acquired an application that runs on a NetWare 3.11 server. Numerous Windows XP clients need to gain access to this application, to the files that are generated from the application that are placed on the NetWare server, as well as the other domain-based Microsoft resources on the network. These clients cannot have static IP addresses, because of the limited number of IP addresses that are available. What protocols or services will these Windows XP clients need to run? (Check all correct answers.)

- ❑ A. TCP/IP that is dynamically configured
- ❑ B. IPX/SPX that uses frame type 802.2
- ❑ C. TCP/IP that is manually configured
- ❑ D. GSNW
- ❑ E. IPX/SPX that uses frame type 802.3
- ❑ F. CSNW

5. You are attempting to connect to your Windows XP Professional computer at work named XPPROWORK. This computer has an IP address of 24.15.199.1. You are attempting to connect from your Windows 98 computer at home, named HOME. This computer has been assigned an IP address of 20.1.20.1 from your ISP. You do not have the correct client installed on your Windows 98 computer, but have installed the Remote Desktop Web Connection on the work computer. How will you connect to the work computer from the Windows 98 computer?

- ○ A. You cannot connect to a Windows XP Professional computer from a Windows 98 computer using Remote Desktop.
- ○ B. Connect using Internet Explorer and a URL of `http://HOME/tsweb`.
- ○ C. Connect using Internet Explorer and a URL of `http://XPPROWORK/tsweb`.
- ○ D. Connect using Internet Explorer and a URL of `http://20.1.20.1/tsweb`.

6. You are having trouble getting an application to work properly on your Windows XP Professional computer. You know of another person in the IT department who can help you with the issue, but that person is working at home today. What Windows XP component will allow him to help you with your issue?

- ○ A. Remote Desktop Web Access
- ○ B. Remote Desktop
- ○ C. Remote Assistance
- ○ D. Application Compatibility

7. You have been given the task of documenting the IP network and the Classful subnets that make up your network. To make the correct classification for the subnets, you need to have the correct ranges for each different class of IP address. You also need to specify which IP address ranges are functional on the internal network, but not routable on the Internet. Which is the correct set of IP address ranges for the A, B, and C classes, and which is the set of IP addresses that are within these ranges, but are not routable on the Internet? (Check all correct answers.)

- ❑ A. 0 to 128 for Class A, 129 to 192 for Class B, and 193 to 224 for Class C
- ❑ B. 0 to 126 for Class A, 128 to 191 for Class B, and 192 to 223 for Class C
- ❑ C. Nonroutable ranges of 10.x.y.z and 192.168.x.y
- ❑ D. Nonroutable ranges of 127.x.y.z and 192.168.x.y

8. You are trying to find the last Remote Assistance file that you created, but are unable to track down the location where you stored the file. When you saved the file, you did not use the default location, to increase the security of the invitation. Now you need to try to search for the file. What file extension will you look for?

- ○ A. .msrcincident
- ○ B. .assistant
- ○ C. .help
- ○ D. .info

9. You are a desktop administrator for Que Certification. The network consists of a single Active Directory domain. All users have computers running Windows XP Professional with SP2, and their computers utilize DHCP for their TCP/IP configurations. A new employee reports that he cannot access network resources. No other employees report problems. When you run the `ipconfig.exe` command on the problem computer, you receive the following information, as shown in Figure 7.9.

You must ensure that the new employee can connect to the network. What should you do?

- ○ A. Run the `Netstat -e` command on the new user's computer.
- ○ B. Run the `IPconfig/renew` command on the new user's computer.
- ○ C. Run the `Nbtstat -RR` command on the new user's computer.
- ○ D. Add the IP address of the DHCP server to the HOSTS file.
- ○ E. Disable Automatic Private IP addressing (APIPA) on the new user's computer.

10. You are the desktop administrator for Bunyip Computers. Your network consists of a single Active Directory domain including Windows Server 2003 computers and Windows XP Professional SP2 client computers. Except for the domain controllers (DCs), all computers network using DHCP for their TCP/IP configuration. During the business day, you

perform emergency maintenance on a file server (non-DC) named
Server1. After restarting, Server1 appears fully operational. However,
users receive the error message, Network path not found when they try to
access files on Server1. No problems can be found with Server1. You
need to ensure that all users can access Server1. What command should
you instruct users to run?

O A. nbtstat -R

O B. nbtstat -RR

O C. ipconfig /flushdns

O D. ipconfig /registerdns

Answers to Exam Prep Questions

1. Answer D is correct. A network bridge connects different network segments into a single network, allowing them to appear as a single network subnet. Answer A is incorrect because the DHCP relay agent is
   only for DHCP clients, not for allowing normal network traffic communication. Answer B is incorrect because it does not allow a network
   of computers access to the Internet through a single computer. Answer
   C is incorrect because a TCP/IP profile is designed to allow a single
   computer multiple IP configuration options at boot time.

2. Answer C is correct. Remote Desktop allows someone to access a session that is running on one computer while sitting at another computer. This is an excellent solution for someone who works at home and
   needs to gain access to their computer at work. Answer A is incorrect
   because Remote Assistance allows for another person to access your
   computer to help you with an issue. Answers B and D are incorrect;
   the Remote Desktop option is preferred because of security and access
   permissions. If you were to configure your computer at work to accept
   dial-up or VPN access, there would need to be a local account for
   authentication, which is frowned upon in most enterprises.

3. Answer B is correct. Classless Interdomain Routing (CIDR) is the
   technology that allows two or more IP address ranges to appear as if
   they are on the same network segment. Answer A is incorrect because
   CIDR will still be needed, even if DHCP is used. Answer C is incorrect because a Classful IP address range will not solve the problem of
   combining the two Class C licenses. Answer D is incorrect because
   VLSM would make more network segments, not less.

4. Answers A, E, and F are correct. To have the client automatically
   receive an IP address, it must be configured to dynamically receive an
   IP address. Another term for this is to be *DHCP-enabled*. Because the
   version of NetWare that is being used is 3.x, the frame type must be
   802.3. The use of IPX/SPX is also a requirement because the NetWare
   server cannot communicate with the XP Pro client without it. The

Windows XP client must also have CSNW installed to allow communication to the file and print services running on the NetWare server.
Answer B is incorrect because the 802.2 frame type would not be correct for the NetWare 3.11 server that is being used. Answer C is incorrect because the question clearly states that static or manual IP
addresses are not allowed. Answer D is incorrect because the GSNW
service is for servers, not for Professional computers.

5. Answer C is correct. As long as the Windows 98 client has IE4 or later,
it can connect to the Windows XP computer using the virtual directory
that was configured on that system for Remote Desktop. The virtual
directory is named tsweb by default and can be referenced with either
the computer name or the IP address. Answer A is incorrect because it
is possible to connect to a Windows XP Professional computer from a
Windows 98 computer using Remote Desktop. Answer B is incorrect
because HOME is the name of the Windows 98 computer, not the
Windows XP computer. Answer D is incorrect because this is the IP
address of the Windows 98 computer, not the Windows XP computer.

6. Answer C is correct. Remote Assistance will allow someone to gain
access to your computer and assist you with a problem or issue. This
tool allows remote control, chat, and voice communications. Answers A
and B are incorrect because they are related to Remote Desktop, not
Assistance. With Remote Desktop, someone can take control of your
computer, but can't assist you with the problem. Answer D is incorrect
because Application Compatibility will attempt to run applications in
another OS environment, not help someone connect to your computer.

7. Answers B and C are correct. The Classful ranges for IP addresses go
up to the binary range of the number, but don't include the next value.
For example, the Class A range includes 0 to 126, but does not include
128, which is the beginning of the next range of addresses. The nonroutable ranges include the 10.x.y.z range from Class A and 192.168.x.y
from the Class C range. There is another range that is not routable,
which is 172.16.0.0 to 172.31.255.255 from the Class B range. Answer
A is incorrect because the IP address ranges are too large, not leaving
room between the Class ranges. Answer D is incorrect because
127.x.y.z is not a functional address range; it is used for local computer
configurations.

8. Answer A is correct. When an invitation for Remote Assistance is saved
to a file, the default file extension is .msrcincident. Another extension is
valid, but you will manually have to connect the file to the correct
application when accessing it. Answers B, C, and D are incorrect
because these are not the correct extensions for the Remote Assistance
files.

9. Answer B is correct. You can tell from the information presented by running the `ipconfig` command that the computer has been assigned an Automatic Private IP addressing (APIPA) address because it was not able to connect to a DHCP server. After you make sure that the computer is connected to the corporate network and that at least one DHCP server is up and running, you need to renew the IP address by typing **`ipconfig /renew`** at a command prompt. Answer A is incorrect because the `netstat -e` command displays only network interface statistics. Answer C is incorrect because the `nbtstat -RR` command refreshes only the NetBIOS names that are currently registered on the computer. Answer D is incorrect because adding the IP address of the DHCP server to the local computer's HOSTS file is not necessary for the DHCP server to assign IP addresses automatically. Answer E is incorrect because disabling APIPA does not help a computer obtain an IP address automatically from a DHCP server.

10. Answer C is correct. Because the question states that Server1 is operationally sound, but has been rebooted, it must have obtained a different IP address via DHCP. Only the DCs have static IP addresses on this network. Because the other computers have not been restarted, the DNS cache on these PCs still contains the old IP address of Server1, which is now incorrect. By running the `ipconfig /flushdns` command at a command prompt, the old DNS information is cleared from memory and the new IP address for Server1 can be discovered from the DNS server(s) on the network. Answer A is incorrect because the `nbtstat -R` command only purges and preloads the NetBIOS over TCP/IP (NBT) Remote Cache Name Table. Answer B is incorrect because the `nbtstat -RR` command refreshes only the NetBIOS names that are currently registered on the computer. Answer D is incorrect because the `ipconfig /registerdns` command refreshes all the local DHCP leases on the computer and reregisters the DNS names, but it does not clear the current DNS cache from memory.

Need to Know More?

Bott, Ed, and Carl Siechert. *Microsoft Windows XP Inside Out*, 2nd ed. Redmond, WA: Microsoft Learning, 2004. ISBN 073562044X. This book offers time-saving tips, troubleshooting techniques, and workarounds. It focuses on techniques such as taking advantage of the rich integration of devices, applications, and web services in Windows XP.

Microsoft Corporation. *Microsoft Windows XP Professional Resource Kit*, 2nd ed. Redmond, WA: Microsoft Press, 2003. ISBN 0735619743. This all-in-one reference is a compilation of technical documentation and valuable insider information that computer-support professionals and administrators can reference to install, customize, and support Windows XP.

Minasi, Mark. *Mastering Windows XP Professional*. Alameda, CA: Sybex, Inc., 2001. ISBN 0782129811. This book provides in-depth coverage of installing, configuring, and administering Windows XP Professional.

Search the Microsoft TechNet CD (or its online version through www.microsoft.com) using keywords such as "TCP/IP", "APIPA", "DNS", "Network Bridge", "Remote Assistance", "Remote Desktop", "DHCP", "SP2", and "Service Pack 2".

System Monitoring, Performance Optimization, and Recovery Features

Terms you'll need to understand:

✓ Windows XP Backup
✓ Normal Backup
✓ Differential Backup
✓ Incremental Backup
✓ System State
✓ Volume Shadow Copy Service (VSS)
✓ Advanced startup options
✓ Safe Mode
✓ Last Known Good Configuration

✓ Recovery Console
✓ System Restore
✓ Automated System Recovery (ASR)
✓ Performance Counters
✓ Performance Objects
✓ Sample (or Update) interval
✓ Baselining
✓ Paging file

Techniques you'll need to master:

✓ Backing up and restoring data
✓ Starting a Windows XP system in the appropriate Safe Mode
✓ Using the Last Known Good Configuration
✓ Installing and using the Recovery Console
✓ Using and configuring System Restore
✓ Using the Automated System Recovery (ASR) tool

✓ Creating restore points
✓ Using System Monitor
✓ Creating a log with Performance Logs and Alerts
✓ Setting performance alerts
✓ Monitoring performance with Task Manager

After a Windows XP system has been successfully installed, configured, and secured, one of the major goals of a system administrator is to ensure stable, reliable, and optimal performance. Windows XP Professional offers more system troubleshooting and recovery features than any previous Microsoft operating system. This chapter explores the skills required to properly prepare for and recover from computer system failures. This chapter also examines how to maintain systems to run under peak conditions by providing a foundation for performance monitoring and system optimizing.

Backing Up and Restoring Data

Under Windows XP, Windows Backup helps you plan for and recover from data loss by enabling you to back up and restore files, folders, and System State data (which includes the Registry) manually, or on a schedule. The new-and-improved backup tool supports all kinds of storage devices and media, including tape drives, logical drives, and removable disks. Recordable CDs and DVDs are minimally supported as *restore-only* media; the Windows Backup program (NTBackup.exe) does *not* support backup operations to CD-R, CD-RW, DVD-R, DVD-RW, DVD+R, or DVD+RW media.

The term "media" refers to any fixed or removable objects, such as hard disks, floppy disks, tape cartridges, compact discs (CDs), and Digital Versatile Discs (DVDs), that store computer data. The Windows Backup tool also has wizards to help administrators new to Windows XP to implement backup and recovery processes.

Using Windows Backup

To run the Windows Backup utility, perform one of the following actions:

➤ Click Start, Run, type **ntbackup**, and click OK.

➤ Select Start, (All) Programs, Accessories, System Tools and click Backup.

➤ Use the NTBackup.exe tool from the command line. Run ntbackup /? from a command prompt window to view its command-line options.

By default, Windows Backup runs the Backup or Restore Wizard, which steps you through the choices and configurations related to backing up and restoring data. To change this default behavior, clear the Always Start in Wizard Mode check box. You can bypass the wizard by clicking the Advanced Mode link on the Welcome to The Backup or Restore Wizard window.

Required Permissions for Backing Up Files

To successfully back up or restore data on a Windows XP system, users must have appropriate security permissions. Users who are members of either the local Administrators group or the local Backup Operators group may back up any and all files on a local Windows XP computer. Users who are members of either the Administrators group or the Backup Operators group for a Windows domain may back up any and all files on any Windows XP Professional computer that is a member of that domain. If a user is not a member of one of these groups, he or she must be an owner of all the files and folders to be backed up. If a user is neither an owner of the files and folders nor a member of Backup Operators or Administrators, the user must be granted at least one of the following permissions on those files and folders: Read, Read and Execute, Modify, or Full Control. Only members of Administrators are permitted to back up System State data, which contains very important internal configuration information for Windows XP systems, including the Registry. Moreover, System State data can be backed up only on a local computer. You cannot back up the System State remotely over the network to another Windows XP computer.

Backup Types

Several types of backup jobs enable you to create a backup procedure that maximizes efficiency, minimizes media used, and minimizes performance impact. Each file has an archive attribute, also called a *backup marker*. When a file is changed, the archive attribute or marker is set, indicating that the file has been modified since the last backup. This marker is the focus of the different backup types because some types look for the marker; others do not. Some types clear the marker; others do not. Table 8.1 clarifies the different backup types.

NOTE

The Windows XP Backup program skips backing up and restoring certain files by default. These include temporary files such as **Pagefile.sys**, **Hiberfil.sys**, **Win386.swp**, **386spart.par**, **Backup.log**, and **Restore.log**. Files that are open or locked during the backup procedure are also skipped unless they reside on local NTFS volumes and enough disk space is available on a local NTFS drive volume for a volume shadow copy to be created. Volume shadow copies are covered later in this chapter.

NTFS File System Offers the Change Journal Attribute

The Change Journal is a new and faster method for keeping track of changes under the NTFS 5 file system used in Windows XP and Windows 2000. The Change Journal keeps track of changes similar to the archive attribute, but it goes beyond the archive attribute in that it can also keep track of changes to permissions and changes to a document's name. These are features that the archive attribute doesn't offer.

Table 8.1	Windows XP Backup Types		
Backup Type	Looks for Marker	Clears Marker	Backup Set Created
Normal	No	Yes	Backup of all selected files and folders. The most complete backup and the most straightforward to recover, but also the lengthiest to create.
Copy	No	No	Copies all selected files and folders.
Differential	Yes	No	Backup of selected files that have changed since the last normal backup. If you create a normal backup, and one week later create a differential backup, and then another week later create another differential backup, you could restore all data using the normal backup and the second differential backup, which contains all files that have changed since the normal backup. You could, in this example, discard the first differential backup.
Incremental	Yes	Yes	Backup of all data that has changed since the most recent (normal or incremental) backup. If you create a normal backup, and one week later create an incremental backup, and then another week later create a second incremental backup, you would need all three backups to recover data.
Daily	Yes	No	Backup of all files and folders that have changed during the day.

Backup Strategies

Backup strategies generally combine different backup types. Some backup types require more time to create the backup. A normal backup takes the most time to create because it backs up all selected files; however, it creates a "baseline," or complete backup. The second backup could be incremental or differential—the result would be the same. The third and subsequent backups are where the difference starts to be significant. If the second and third backups are differential, the third backup includes all files changed since the normal backup. If the second and third backups are incremental, the third backup includes only files changed since the second (incremental) backup.

So why wouldn't you just do a normal backup and then do incremental backups until the end of time? Because incremental backups take longer than a differential backup to recover. Imagine recovering a machine that had a normal backup one year ago and an incremental backup every week since. To recover that system after a catastrophe, you would have to restore the normal backup and then restore 51 incremental backups. If you had used differential backups, you would have to restore only the normal backup first and then the most recent differential backup.

Therefore, you should balance the "cost" of backup time against the cost of recovery time. Also, factor in the media required to support your backup plan. You must save incremental backups until the next normal backup. You need to keep only the most recent differential backup, along with the most recent normal backup.

Configuring File and Folder Backup Jobs

When you create a backup job using the Backup Wizard or the Backup tab of the Windows Backup utility, you can specify the following:

➤ Drives, files, or folders to back up. Place a check mark next to the drive, file, or folder that you want to back up. The selected items are backed up according to the backup type. Items whose check boxes are cleared are not backed up. A grayed-out but marked check box indicates a container (disk or folder) in which only some, but not all, of its contents are selected.

➤ A backup destination. You can back up to a file or to any other storage device configured on your system. However, you cannot back up directly to CD-R or CD-RW media.

➤ A path and filename for the backup file, or a tape to use.

➤ Backup options such as backup type and log file type.

➤ A description of the job, to help you identify the job.

➤ Whether the backup medium already contains existing backup jobs.

➤ Advanced backup options, including compression and data verification.

The Windows XP Backup utility *does not support* backing up directly to CD-R, CD-RW, DVD-R, or DVD+R media. You can back up to a local or network drive and then copy the backup file onto CD-R, CD-RW, DVD-R, or DVD+R media. Fortunately, you can *restore* directly from one or more CD-R, CD-RW, DVD-R, or DVD+R discs with the Windows XP Backup program.

Backing Up the System State

The Backup tool can back up what is called *System State data*, which includes critical files that you can use to rebuild the system. You can reinstall a failed system with the Windows XP CD-ROM. Then you can restore the System State data, bringing the system back to its original condition as of the date of the System State backup.

Be familiar with backing up the System State. You should understand that the backup program can provide you with a backup of the system's Registry as a whole, but *it cannot back up individual components* of System State data.

System State data includes the following:

➤ The Registry.

➤ Files stored under Windows File Protection.

➤ The component services class registration database—Component Object Model + (COM+) objects.

➤ All system files and boot files.

➤ Certificate Services database—Applies only to Windows 2000 Server and Windows Server 2003 domain controllers (DCs) and member servers running Certificate Services, not Windows XP.

➤ Active Directory—Applies only to DCs, not Windows XP.

➤ Sysvol folder—Applies only to DCs, not Windows XP.

Configuring the System State Backup

To configure the System State backup using the Backup Wizard, perform the following steps:

1. In the Backup Wizard, on the What Do You Want to Back Up? page, select Let Me Choose What to Back Up and then click Next.

2. On the Items to Back Up page, expand My Computer and mark the check box for System State, click Next, and follow the remaining instructions from the wizard.

To configure the System State backup using Advanced Mode, perform the following steps:

1. Click the Backup tab.

2. Expand My Computer and mark the check box for System State, click Next, and follow the remaining onscreen instructions.

Scheduling Backup Jobs

You can use the Backup utility in conjunction with Task Scheduler to schedule backups to occur at regular intervals or during periods of relative inactivity on the network.

Scheduling a Backup with the Backup Wizard

To schedule a backup when using the Backup Wizard, perform the following steps:

1. In the Backup Wizard, on the Completing the Backup or Restore Wizard page, click the Advanced button.

2. Select the backup type, if you need to change it, and click Next.

3. Select any options that you want, such as Verify Data After Backup, and click Next again.

4. Select either Append This Backup to the Existing Backups or Replace the Existing Backups and then click Next.

5. On the When to Back Up page, click Later, type in a Job Name, and click the Set Schedule button.

6. Specify the schedule for the backup job as shown in Figure 8.1 and click OK.

Figure 8.1 The Schedule Job dialog box for the Windows Backup program.

7. Click Next to display the Set Account Information dialog box. Type in the user account under which this scheduled backup job will run, type in the password for the user account, and then confirm the password. Click OK.

8. Click Finish to complete the wizard.

Configuring a Job Using the Scheduled Jobs Tab

To configure a job using the Scheduled Jobs tab, perform the following steps:

1. In the Windows Backup utility, click Advanced mode, and click the Scheduled Jobs tab.

2. Double-click the day you want to start scheduled backups, or click the Add Job button at the bottom of the Scheduled Jobs window.

3. Complete the information for the Backup Wizard.

Volume Shadow Copy Technology

Microsoft introduces Volume Shadow Copy Technology, also known as the Volume Shadow Copy Service (VSS), to enable backups to be created from data files and application files *even when they are currently locked in memory and in use*! Whenever a backup procedure begins, an instant shadow copy snapshot is taken of the original drive letter(s) being backed up. VSS is enabled by default.

 Volume shadow copies are created only for *NTFS-formatted* drive letters running under Windows XP Professional. Enough available free disk space must exist on *any* available local NTFS drive letter for the shadow copy to be made. If none of the local NTFS drive letters contain enough free disk space to hold the shadow copy, no shadow copy is created.

By creating an exact duplicate copy of the original files to be backed up, the Backup program can back up all the files from the shadow copy snapshot instead of backing up the files directly from the original volume. After the shadow copy snapshot is made, *it does not change*, even if data on the original volume changes during the backup operation. After the backup operation is completed, the shadow copy snapshot is deleted. VSS enables applications and services to be backed up even when they are still running. Open files appear closed on the shadow copy snapshot for backup purposes and the data within those open files is frozen as of the moment in time that the shadow copy is created. Open files on the original volume remain open and their data may continue to change.

Restoring Files and Folders

You can restore files and folders by using the Backup utility, through the Restore Wizard, or by manually restoring them (without using the wizard). When you restore files and folders, you must specify which ones to restore, the restore location (original location, alternative location, or a single folder), and options (such as to replace existing files with backup files).

If you backed up data from an NTFS volume, you must restore data to an NTFS 5 disk volume to preserve security permissions, Encrypting File System

(EFS) settings (encryption), disk quota settings, mounted drive configuration settings, and remote storage information. Restoring files backed up from a Windows XP NTFS volume onto a FAT or FAT32 volume will result in *all* NTFS settings being lost. If you attempt to restore Windows XP NTFS-stored files onto an NTFS volume running under Windows NT 4, you will lose all EFS settings, disk quota settings, advanced NTFS 5 permissions, and Remote Storage configuration information.

Troubleshooting and Repairing Windows XP Professional Systems

Windows XP Professional offers several advanced startup options for troubleshooting and repairing the operating system. In addition to supporting various options when you restart the computer, Windows XP also offers more effective ways to recover from reconfiguration errors or from intentional or accidental system damage than any other previous Microsoft operating system. With Windows XP, disaster recovery no longer needs to be an overly arduous process.

Safe Mode and Other Advanced Startup Options

Safe Mode enables you to start your system with a minimal set of device drivers and services. For example, if newly installed device drivers or software are preventing your computer from starting, you may be able to start your computer in Safe Mode and then remove the software or device drivers from your system. Safe Mode does not work in all situations, especially if your system files are corrupted or missing, or if your hard disk is damaged or has failed. All Safe Modes start using standard VGA and create a boot log, which is useful when you are determining the exact cause of system startup problems. As a precautionary measure, when you boot into Safe Mode, Windows XP does not update the Last Known Good Configuration information. So, you always have the option of booting the computer using the Last Known Good Configuration even after you have restarted the computer under Safe Mode and perhaps changed some settings. You can go back to the original settings under the Last Known Good Configuration and discard any changes you may have made under Safe Mode.

In Safe Mode, Windows XP uses default settings, including the VGA monitor, Microsoft mouse driver, no network connections, and the minimum device drivers required to start Windows. Support for audio devices, as well as for most USB and FireWire (IEEE 1394) devices, is disabled by Safe Mode. Users' applications that normally run at startup do not run at startup under Safe Mode. If your computer does not start successfully using Safe Mode, you may need to use the Recovery Console feature or the Automated System Recovery (ASR) feature, covered later in this chapter, to repair your system.

Windows XP also provides several startup modes to help you troubleshoot and repair Windows XP systems, as well as recover from various types of disaster. Understanding each mode enables you to make informed decisions about the best startup method to use in a particular crisis situation. To select an advanced startup option, press the F8 key during the Windows XP startup process. The startup options definitely provide extra troubleshooting capabilities for your Windows XP machines. The following sections describe the Windows Advanced Options menu items that are available when you press the F8 key during startup for Windows XP Professional.

Safe Mode

As previously mentioned, this option loads only a minimal set of drivers and system services so that Windows XP can run in a very basic state. User startup programs do not load automatically.

Safe Mode with Networking

This option starts Windows XP using only Safe Mode drivers, services, and drivers required to enable network connections. Logon scripts run, security settings get applied, and Group Policy settings get applied. If you are confident that network issues are not the cause of your problem, it can be useful to boot to this mode, which enables you to connect to a remote system, access installation files, install service packs, or back up data.

Safe Mode with Command Prompt

This option uses the Safe Mode configuration, but displays the command prompt instead of the Windows graphical user interface (GUI) after you log on successfully. This is useful if you believe that a process spawned by the Explorer shell may be causing your problem.

Enable Boot Logging

This option starts Windows XP and creates a log file that details all drivers and services that the operating system loads (or fails to load). The log file is called Ntbtlog.txt and is located in the %systemroot% folder (by default, this is the \Windows folder). Safe Mode, Safe Mode with Networking, and Safe Mode with Command Prompt also create a boot log file. This option creates the log file without booting into Safe Mode. The boot log is useful when you are determining the exact cause of system startup problems.

Enable VGA Mode

This option employs the extremely stable and well-debugged standard VGA driver for Windows XP. This mode is useful when you have installed a new video card, if you have configured incorrect settings for the video display, or if you have installed a corrupted or poorly written video device driver. Video is a common troubleshooting issue in the Windows environment. This stable video driver is used when booting into each of the Safe Modes.

Last Known Good Configuration

Windows XP starts using the Registry configuration (ControlSet) that was saved at the last successful logon to Windows XP. Last Known Good Configuration helps you recover from incorrect configuration of hardware device drivers and services. However, it does not solve problems caused by corrupted or missing drivers or files. Any changes made to the ControlSet key of the Registry since the last successful startup and logon are lost when you select the option to start up with the Last Known Good Configuration. You should try this option before resorting to the Automated System Recovery feature, discussed later in this chapter.

Directory Services Restore Mode

This option applies only to Windows 2000 Server and Windows Server 2003 domain controllers and is used to restore Active Directory and the sysvol folder. This option is not applicable to Windows XP, even though it is one of the menu choices.

Debugging Mode

In this mode, Windows XP can send debugging information through a serial cable to another computer for troubleshooting the operating system kernel and system analysis.

Start Windows Normally

This option starts Windows XP normally without selecting any advanced startup option.

Reboot

This option restarts Windows XP Professional.

Return to the OS Choices Menu

This option takes you back to the operating system selection menu, if your computer has more than one operating system installed.

System Recovery Settings

To specify Windows XP's behavior if the system stops unexpectedly, follow these steps:

1. Right-click the My Computer icon (not a shortcut) and then select Properties.

2. On the Advanced tab, click the Settings button under the Startup and Recovery section. From the System Failure section and from the Write Debugging Information section, select the actions that Windows XP should perform if a stop error occurs, which shuts down the operating system and usually results in the infamous BSOD (Blue Screen Of Death).

Available Recovery Actions

The following are the available recovery actions that only members of the Administrators group may configure from the Startup and Recovery dialog box, as shown in Figure 8.2:

Figure 8.2 Setting System Startup, System Failure, and Write Debugging Information options.

➤ Write an Event to the System Log

➤ Send an Administrative Alert

➤ Automatically Restart

➤ Small Dump Directory—Specify the small memory dump location and folder name

➤ Dump File—Specify the dump file location and filename

The Write Debugging Information drop-down list enables you to select from four options: None, Small Memory Dump (64 KB), Kernel Memory Dump, and Complete Memory Dump. The Complete Memory Dump option requires a paging file on the boot volume at least as large as the computer's installed physical RAM, plus 1MB. If you select the Kernel Memory Dump option, Windows XP writes only kernel information to the listed file instead of the entire contents of system memory. The Small Memory Dump option requires at least a 2MB paging file on the boot volume.

If you contact Microsoft Product Support Services about a stop error, the support engineer may ask for the system memory dump file generated by the Write Debugging Information options. Except for small memory dumps, Windows always writes to the same filename for each dump file generated. To save successive dump files, change the filename after each stop error, or change the location path or filename setting in the Dump File text box. For small memory dumps, a new filename is created each time the system stops unexpectedly.

Setting Up Recovery Actions to Occur When a Service Fails

To set up recovery actions to take place when a service fails, perform the following steps:

1. Open the Services MMC snap-in.

2. Right-click the service for which you want to set recovery actions and then click Properties.

3. On the Recovery tab, select the actions you want the system to take for the First Failure, Second Failure, and Subsequent Failures, as shown in Figure 8.3.

If you select the Run a Program option, do not specify programs or scripts that require user input. If you select Restart the Computer, you can specify how long to wait before restarting the computer by clicking the Restart Computer Options button. You can also create a message to send to remote users before the computer restarts.

Figure 8.3 The Recovery tab of a service's Properties dialog box enables you to select actions that the system will take if the service fails.

The Recovery Console

The Recovery Console is a startup option that provides you with a command-line interface that enables you to repair system problems using a limited set of command-line commands. Using the Recovery Console, you can start and stop services, read and write data on a local drive (including drives formatted as NTFS), format drives, repair a corrupted master boot record, and perform many other administrative tasks. This feature gives you maximum control over the repair process; only advanced users and administrators should use it.

The Recovery Console is particularly useful if you need to repair your system by copying a file from a floppy or a CD-ROM to your hard drive. It can also help you when you need to reconfigure a service that is preventing your computer from starting properly. You should try this option if the Last Known Good Configuration option is unsuccessful and if you cannot start the system in Safe Mode.

Running the Recovery Console on a System That Will Not Start

To run the Recovery Console on a system that will not start, perform the following steps:

1. Be sure that your computer is configured to boot from the CD-ROM drive by selecting the proper options in the BIOS settings. Insert the Windows XP Professional Setup CD-ROM into your CD-ROM or DVD-ROM drive.

2. Restart your computer.

3. Follow the directions on the screen; you may need to press a key to boot from the CD. It may take several minutes to load the files. Choose the option to repair your Windows XP installation (press R) to start the Recovery Console. If you have other installations of Windows XP or Windows 2000 on your computer, the Recovery Console will prompt you to select which installation you want to work with.

4. Type the Administrator password and press the Enter key when prompted.

Before you encounter a system failure, open a command prompt window in Windows XP, and from the i386 folder on the Windows XP CD-ROM or from a shared network installation folder, enter the command **winnt32.exe /cmdcons**. Doing so installs the Recovery Console on the local hard drive (this requires 7MB of disk space) and configures it as a valid startup option. Then if you want to start the system using the Recovery Console, you do not need the Windows XP CD-ROM. Simply boot the machine and press the F8 key to display the startup options. *When you upgrade a Windows XP computer to SP2, you must reinstall the Recovery Console using a Windows XP Setup CD-ROM that contains the slip-streamed SP2 version of the setup files.*

Launching the Recovery Console

The Recovery Console is quite powerful, so only advanced users who have a thorough understanding of personal computers and Windows XP should use it. Also, you should install the Recovery Console on each Windows XP machine so that it is always an available startup option.

If you install the Recovery Console as a startup option on a FAT or FAT32 volume and then convert that drive to NTFS, the *Recovery Console will no longer function.* You must reinstall the Recovery Console if you convert the system's boot drive to NTFS.

After you start the Recovery Console, you must choose which installation of Windows XP or Windows 2000 that you want to log on to (if you have a dual-boot or multiboot system), and you must log on with a local administrator account and password. You are allowed three attempts to enter the correct password. If you enter three incorrect passwords, the system automatically restarts the computer. The design of the Recovery Console grants the administrator access to the root of the hard drives, the \Cmdcons directory if it exists, and the \Windows directory and all directories below it. You have read-only access to CD-ROM drives, to floppy drives, and to other removable media. These limitations are in place for security concerns, and access to other devices or systems is functionally beyond the scope and purpose of the Recovery Console. The main purpose of the Recovery Console is to allow you to repair the existing installation and to successfully boot Windows XP.

Recovery Console Commands

The easiest way to work in the Recovery Console—as in any unfamiliar environment—is to type help at the command prompt and then press the Enter key. The commands available in the Recovery Console are listed in Table 8.2.

 You can use Group Policy in conjunction with a **Set** command to enable write access for removable media while using the Recovery Console. Run **GPEdit.msc** from the Start, Run box to launch the Group Policy snap-in and then expand **Computer Configuration\Windows Settings\Security Settings\Local Policies**. Click Security Options. Double-click the policy named Recovery Console: Allow Floppy Copy and Access to All Drives and All Folders and click the Enabled button. Click OK to save the new setting and exit from the Group Policy snap-in. The next time that you boot into the Recovery Console, type the following command: **Set AllowRemovableMedia = TRUE**. Be sure to insert a space before and after the equal sign. When you enable this environment variable setting after turning on the Group Policy setting, you have access to all local hard drives and folders, in addition to being able to copy files *to* floppy disks and other removable media.

Table 8.2	Recovery Console Commands
Command	**Description**
attrib	Changes file attributes
batch	Runs a list of commands stored in a text file
bootcfg	Scans the hard drives to modify or rebuild the Boot.ini file so that the system will boot properly
chdir (cd)	Displays the name of the current folder or changes the current folder
chkdsk	Checks a disk and displays a status report
cls	Clears the screen
copy	Copies a single file to another location
delete (del)	Deletes one or more files
dir	Displays a list of files and subfolders in a folder
disable	Disables a system service or a device driver
diskpart	Adds and deletes hard drive partitions
enable	Starts or enables a system service or a device driver
exit	Exits the Recovery Console and restarts your computer
expand	Expands compressed files such as Windows XP setup files and CAB files
fixboot	Writes a new partition boot sector onto the system partition

(continued)

Table 8.2	Recovery Console Commands *(continued)*
Command	**Description**
fixmbr	Repairs the master boot record of the partition boot sector
format	Formats a disk
help	Displays a list of the commands that you use in the Recovery Console
listsvc	Displays all available services and drivers installed on the system along with their startup status
logon	Logs on to a Windows 2000, Windows Server 2003, or Windows XP installation
map	Displays the drive letter mappings
mkdir (md)	Creates a folder
more	Displays a text file
net	Maps a network share to a drive letter
rename (ren)	Renames a single file
rmdir (rd)	Deletes a folder
set	Specifies environment variables for the Recovery Console session
systemroot	Sets the current folder to the **%systemroot%** folder for the system that you are currently logged on to
type	Displays contents of a text file

System Restore

The System Restore feature enables you to restore a Windows XP Professional system back to a prior operational state and configuration. This feature can be quite helpful if you ever want to go back to a previous configuration because the system is encountering a problem with a new setting or a new driver—or even if the system is having compatibility problems with a new application program that you installed. If a newly installed program is causing a problem or not working properly, you should uninstall the program *before* you attempt to use System Restore to restore Windows XP to a previous point in time. You must be a member of the Administrators group to work with System Restore.

System Restore monitors several critical operating system files and application program files that are listed in a file named FileList.xml located in the %systemroot%\system32\restore folder. The main function of System Restore is the capability to get a Windows XP computer up and running properly again; its job is not to act as a backup and restore agent for user data files. Several data folders and files are not tracked by the System Restore feature, such as: the paging file; data files stored in My Documents; Favorites;

temporary folders; BMP, JPG, and EPS image files; and any data files not listed in `FileList.xml`, including filenames ending in .doc, .xls, .mdb, and .pst.

Restore Points

System Restore automatically creates restore points based on several types of events. You can also manually create your own restore points. The initial restore point is created when you start your Windows XP system for the very first time, either after performing an upgrade installation or a brand new installation. After that, Windows XP automatically creates its own restore points every 24 hours, or every 24 hours that the computer remains powered on. If the machine is powered off for more than 24 hours, a restore point is created the next time that the computer is turned on. Restore points are automatically created whenever you update the system, perform a recovery from the Windows XP Backup utility, install a new application that supports System Restore, restore the system from a restore point, or install an unsigned device driver.

To change the amount of disk storage allocated to System Restore, right-click the My Computer icon (not a shortcut), click Properties, and click the System Restore tab. System Restore is enabled by default. To turn off this feature, click the Turn Off System Restore on All Drives check box. To increase or decrease the amount of disk space used for restore points, select a drive letter from the Available Drives list and click the Settings button. Drag the slider bar (as shown in Figure 8.4) to the right to increase the amount of disk space used for restore points, or drag it to the left to decrease the amount of disk space used.

Figure 8.4 The Settings dialog box for configuring disk space usage for restore points under System Restore.

The System Restore Wizard

Use the System Restore Wizard to manually create restore points and to restore the system to an earlier configuration by selecting a previously created restore point. You find the System Restore Wizard by clicking Start, All Programs,

Accessories, System Tools, System Restore. To manually create a restore point, launch the System Restore Wizard and click the Create a Restore Point button. Click Next. Type in a restore point description and click Create.

To restore the system to a previous state, launch the System Restore Wizard and click the Restore My Computer to an Earlier Time button. Click Next and then click a boldfaced date on the calendar (boldfaced dates indicate restore points). More than one restore point may exist for a given date—select the restore point that you want, and then click Next. Click Next again to confirm the restore point selected after you close all open applications. Your Windows XP system will shut down and then restart using the configuration settings specified by the restore point that you chose.

Automated System Recovery

The new Automated System Recovery (ASR) feature replaces the Emergency Repair Disk (ERD) used with Windows 2000 and Windows NT. ASR is an advanced feature of the Windows XP Professional Backup program (`NTBackup.exe`). The aim of ASR is to get a Windows XP Professional system back up and running when other recovery tools such as Safe Mode, the Recovery Console, or the Last Known Good Configuration won't work because of issues such as physical problems with a hard drive, for example. ASR is not for backing up or restoring data! ASR actually formats the system drive letter (the drive letter denoted by the `%systemdrive%` environment variable, usually the C: drive). Any data files that exist on this drive letter will be lost if an ASR restore is performed.

 You should always attempt to restore the system using the System Restore feature *before* you decide to use ASR. ASR should be reserved as a *last resort*.

Creating an ASR Backup

You use the Windows XP Backup program to create ASR backups. One floppy disk is required in addition to using backup media to store the operating system files, settings, and the System State data. To create an ASR backup, perform the following steps:

1. Launch the Windows XP Backup program and use Advanced mode.

2. Click the Automated System Recovery Wizard button and click Next at the welcome screen.

3. Select a backup media type and name and click Next.

4. Click Finish to complete the wizard and begin the backup process, and then follow the instructions on the screen.

Performing an ASR Restore

The ASR restore process requires three critical components: the bootable Windows XP Professional CD-ROM, your most recent ASR backup floppy disk, and your system's most recent ASR backup media set (usually stored on tape or other removable media). To perform an ASR restore, follow these steps:

1. Insert the Windows XP Professional CD-ROM and restart the computer.

2. Press a key when prompted to Press a Key to Boot from CD as the computer starts.

3. When prompted to invoke Automated System Recovery, press the F2 key as the Windows Setup program loads.

4. Insert your ASR floppy disk when prompted by Windows Setup.

5. Insert your ASR backup media when prompted by Windows Setup.

6. Specify a location for the %systemroot% folder (for example, C:\Windows).

7. Follow the instructions on the screen to complete the process.

You should specify the same folder name for the **%systemroot%** target folder as on the backup media. You cannot perform an ASR restore from an ASR backup residing on a network share. The ASR backup must be stored on a locally attached device such as a tape drive, a Zip or Jaz drive, a CD drive, a DVD drive, other removable media, or other hard disks.

Performance Optimizing and Troubleshooting

Although Windows XP Professional performs extremely well as a general workstation platform, with the right tools, techniques, and knowledge, you can further optimize the operating system for particular roles and you can more easily troubleshoot performance challenges. This section looks at System Monitor, Performance Logs and Alerts, Task Manager, and other tools that you can use to improve Windows XP's performance.

System Monitor

The System Monitor feature is part of the Performance MMC snap-in (accessed by selecting Start, (All) Programs, Administrative Tools, Performance) and is available for inclusion in custom MMC consoles. This tool enables you to visually inspect the activity of system components, such as the memory, processor, disk subsystem, network cards, paging file, and applications. The plethora of performance metrics, or *counters*, available for monitoring can make the task a daunting one, indeed. We will examine the most useful counters after a tour of the Performance Console's major components.

Configuring System Monitor

System Monitor, like all MMC snap-ins, is best controlled by right-clicking. If you right-click the main portion of the Details pane, you can select Add Counters, which opens the Add Counters dialog box shown in Figure 8.5. Counters are the basic elements that track specific aspects of system performance. The thousands of available counters are organized hierarchically as follows:

> ➤ Computer—You can monitor performance of the local system (default) or of a remote system.

> ➤ Performance Object—Any system component, such as processor, memory, disk, network protocol, or service.

> ➤ Counter—You use these objects as performance metrics related to the specific performance object on the specific computer selected. Literally thousands of counters may be available for monitoring, so take advantage of the Explain button in the Add Counters dialog box. Clicking Explain produces a description of the selected counter.

Figure 8.5 The Add Counters dialog box from the Performance Console enables you to monitor various aspects of a system's performance.

➤ Instance—When an object occurs more than once on a computer, you see instances. For example, a multiprocessor machine has instances for each processor when you select the processor object. When you select the logical disk object, you see instances for each drive volume on a system. Often, instances are numbered, with the first instance being 0, the second instance 1, and so on. Usually, an additional instance provides the total for all the instances. For example, a dual processor system has a "_Total", which reflects the combination of processors 0 and 1.

After you select a computer, object, counter, and instance (if necessary), click Add to add the counter to your System Monitor view. By right-clicking the view (the right pane of the Performance Console) and choosing Properties, you can alter all properties of the System Monitor view, including the display color of counters, the scale and sample rate, and the format of the monitor's display—which can be in a graph (default), a histogram (bar chart), or a report (numeric display) format.

Performance Logs and Alerts

The Performance Logs and Alerts snap-in, also part of the Performance Console, enables you to collect and save performance data, as well as proactively configure a system to send notifications based on various performance thresholds.

Configuring Alerts

Alerts enable you to generate actions based on a counter reaching a particular threshold. For example, you might want to be notified when a disk's capacity reaches 90%, because you might want to increase the disk's capacity before it fills up. By specifying a counter (such as %Free Space for a logical disk) and a threshold (under 10%), you can cause an event to be logged, a program to be run, a log to be started, or a network message to be sent.

To configure alerts, select the Alerts node in the Performance Logs and Alerts snap-in. Then right-click in the Details pane and choose New Alert Settings. Enter a name for your alert settings—the name is for your use only. Then in the Properties dialog box, add the counter(s) appropriate for the alert you are configuring. For each counter, you must specify a threshold (over or under a particular amount). You select either Under or Over from the Alert When the Value Is drop-down list, and then specify the threshold amount in the Limit text box on the General tab. You can then configure, on the Action tab, what will happen when those alerts are generated. The General and Action tabs are shown in Figure 8.6. On the Schedule tab, you can specify when the selected counters should be scanned. If you specify no schedule, scanning will begin as soon as you click OK. The alert settings you have specified will appear in the Alerts node of the Performance Logs and Alerts snap-in. Right-click an alert setting to change its configuration, to delete it, or to stop or start scanning.

Figure 8.6 The General tab of an alert's properties dialog box enables you to set counters and thresholds, and the Action tab enables you to specify what actions should be taken when the alert conditions are met.

Configuring Logs

Logs collect and store performance counters' data. You can view logs by using System Monitor, retrieve them in a spreadsheet such as Excel, or import them into a database. The following are the two types of logs:

➤ Counter logs—Record data captured over a span of time; useful for detecting trends, setting baselines of performance, and spotting performance bottlenecks. Baselines are discussed later in this chapter.

➤ Trace logs—Collect performance data when an event such as a process creation, disk input/output (I/O), or page fault occurs. Trace logs are useful for troubleshooting and debugging.

To create a counter log, select the Counter Logs node of the Performance Logs and Alerts snap-in and then right-click the Details (right) pane and choose New Log Settings. Give the log a name that will help you identify it in the future, and then click OK. On the General tab of the new log's Properties dialog box, add one or more counters to be recorded and then specify the sample rate—the interval at which counter data will be collected. Obviously, a shorter sample rate provides more data but also fills up the log more quickly.

You can also configure and manage counter logs and trace logs directly from the command line by using the new **Logman.exe** tool. Type **Logman.exe /?** at a command prompt to view this command's syntax, parameters, and options.

Logs are stored, by default, in the \Perflogs folder off the root of the same drive letter where the %systemroot% folder is located. The default format is binary (.blg extension). You can stop and start logs as desired and view them in System Monitor. To view a log using the System Monitor, click System Monitor, right-click the right (view) pane of the Performance Console, and choose Properties. Then, on the Source tab, click Log Files and click Add to browse for the log filename. To analyze a log with Microsoft Excel, Microsoft Access, or other database and reporting tools, save the log as a comma- or tab-delimited file (.csv or .tsv extension, respectively).

Managing Performance

Monitoring, troubleshooting, and optimizing performance are some of the most important tasks you will perform as an administrator of Windows XP Professional systems. Managing performance involves several steps:

1. Create a baseline.

2. Proactively monitor.

3. Evaluate performance.

4. Identify potential bottlenecks.

5. Take corrective action.

6. Monitor the effectiveness and stability of the change.

7. Return to step 2.

Creating a Baseline

One of the most important, and most often overlooked, steps of managing performance is creating a baseline. A *baseline* is a range of acceptable performance of a system component under normal working conditions. Baselining, or establishing a baseline, requires that you capture key counters while a system performs with normal loads and all services running. Then you can compare future performance against the baseline to identify potential bottlenecks, troubleshoot sudden changes in performance, and justify system improvements.

A baseline should cover a relatively large timeframe so that it captures a range of data reflecting acceptable performance. The sample interval for the log should be somewhat large as well so that the baseline log does not become enormous. You should generate baselines regularly, perhaps even once a month, so that you can identify performance trends and evaluate bottlenecks pertaining to system and network performance. If you follow these guidelines, you will produce a baseline that gives an accurate overview of system performance.

The most useful objects to understand and monitor are the following:

➤ Cache—Physical memory used to store recently accessed disk data.

➤ Memory—RAM used to store code and data.

➤ Paging file—The file used to extend physical RAM and create virtual memory.

➤ Physical disk—The disk drive or redundant array of independent disks (RAID) device. A physical disk may contain multiple logical disks.

➤ Logical disk—The disk volume, including simple, logical, spanned, striped, mirrored, or RAID-5 volumes. A logical disk may span multiple physical disks.

➤ Process—Executable programming code that represents a running application.

➤ Processor—The Central Processing Unit (CPU).

➤ Server—The server service, which offers data and print services, even on a Windows XP Professional system.

➤ System—Counters that apply to all system hardware and software.

➤ Thread—Executable programming code that the processor is processing.

Baselines should include these critical objects as well as the other counters discussed in this chapter.

Managing Memory Performance

The counters in the Memory object represent the memory available via the system's physical RAM and via the system's virtual memory (paging file). The most important counters in the memory object are the Pages/sec counters and the Available Bytes counter:

➤ Memory:Pages/sec, threshold over 20 pages/sec—This counter and all related counters (including Page Reads/sec, Page Writes/sec, Page Faults/sec, Page Inputs/sec, and Page Outputs/sec) reflect the transfer of data and code from physical RAM to the virtual paging file and

paging-related events. When any one of these counters is high, it indicates a potential memory shortage because when a system does not have
enough RAM to satisfy its needs, inactive data and code are moved from
physical RAM to the virtual paging file to make room for active data and
code.

➤ Memory:Available Bytes, threshold under 4MB—Available Bytes reflects
the amount of physical RAM available after the working sets of applications and the cache have been served. Windows XP Professional trims
working sets and page memory to the disk to maintain at least 4MB of
available RAM. If this counter is consistently lower than 4MB, it generally indicates a memory shortage.

Memory is often the first performance bottleneck in the real world. The counters
related to processor and hard-drive utilization might be well beyond their thresholds simply because inadequate memory is causing paging, which impacts those
two components. So always check the memory counters to make sure that they are
not the "root cause" of the performance bottleneck.

To correct a memory shortage, your first reaction might be to add more
RAM, which is certainly one solution. However, it is often equally valid to
optimize memory usage by stopping unnecessary services, drivers, and background applications, or by moving services or applications to systems with
excess capacity.

Managing the Paging File

Just as every Windows 2000 and Windows Server 2003 computer requires a
paging file to avoid dismally slow performance, each Windows XP system
needs a paging file as well. When physical RAM is not sufficient to support
active processes, the Virtual Memory Manager (VMM) moves less active data
or code from physical RAM to virtual memory stored in the paging file.
When a process later attempts to address data or code currently in the paging file, the VMM transfers that memory space back into physical RAM. The
paging file thus provides for efficient utilization of a system's physical RAM
and allows a system to support more activity than its physical RAM alone
would allow. Transfer of pages, 4KB blocks of memory, to and from the paging file is normal on any system, but excessive paging, or *thrashing*, indicates
a memory shortage. In addition, the paging file itself can impede performance if it is not properly optimized.

You configure the paging file using the System applet in Control Panel. Click
the Advanced tab, click the Performance Options button, and then, in the
Virtual Memory section, click Change. The paging file, called `Pagefile.sys`, is

created on the %systemroot% volume by default. Microsoft recommends that the Initial paging file size should be 1.5 times the amount of physical RAM installed in the computer and that the Maximum paging file size should be 3 times the initial paging file size. For example, on a Windows XP computer with 512MB of physical RAM installed, the *Initial* paging file size should be 768MB and the Maximum paging file size should be 2304MB (768MB × 3 = 2304MB).

You can configure the paging file to be placed on other volumes or to be split across multiple volumes, in which case there will be a Pagefile.sys file on each selected drive letter. The total size of the paging file is considered to be the sum total of all the paging files that the system uses. You can configure the paging file's Initial Size (the space created initially by the VMM and reserved for paging activity) and its Maximum Size (a setting that can permit the VMM to expand the paging file to a size greater than the Initial Size).

You can optimize paging by performing the following:

➤ Remove the paging file from the system and boot partitions. The system partition is technically the partition that is used to start the system—it contains the NTLDR file and the boot sector. To make things confusing, the boot partition contains the operating system and is indicated by the variable %systemroot%. Luckily, most computers are configured with Windows XP on the C: drive (the first partition or volume), making the boot partition, the system partition, and %systemroot% all equal to C:. To remove the paging file from a partition, set its Initial Size and Maximum Size to zero (0) and click the Set button.

➤ Configure the paging file to reside on multiple physical disks. The paging subsystem then spreads written pages evenly across all available Pagefile.sys files.

➤ Configure the paging file to reside on fast, less active drives. If you have drives of various speeds, put the paging file on the fastest one. If you have drives that are less active, put the paging file on those so that the paging system doesn't have to compete as often with other read or write operations.

➤ Before moving the paging file, defragment the volumes on which you will put the paging file. This practice helps to prevent a fragmented paging file.

An optimal paging file configuration is to set up one paging file that is stored on the boot partition or volume while you also create a second paging file on a drive letter that resides on a different physical disk that is rarely accessed by application programs, assuming that a different physical disk is available.

For improved performance, you should put the paging file on a drive letter that resides on a different physical disk than the system and boot partitions or volumes. In this configuration, Windows XP can accommodate multiple input/output (I/O) requests with greater speed. When the paging file is stored on the boot partition or volume, the operating system must perform disk reads and writes for both the system folder and the paging file. When the paging file is stored on a separate partition or volume on a completely different physical disk, one physical disk handles I/O for the system folder and the other physical disk takes care of I/O for the paging file.

Keep in mind, however, if you remove the paging file from the boot partition or volume, Windows XP cannot create a dump file (Memory.dmp) in which to write debugging information in the event that a kernel mode Stop Error message occurs (also known as the "Blue Screen Of Death," or BSOD). The absence of a memory dump file could be problematic if you had to troubleshoot such a Stop error message.

If possible, you should create a second paging file that is stored on its own drive letter, without any data or operating system files. By design, Windows XP uses its own internal algorithm to determine which paging file to use based on the amount of disk I/O occurring. Windows XP will utilize the paging file that resides on the partition or volume with the lighter amount of disk access as compared to more heavily accessed partitions or volumes, such as the boot partition or volume.

When you put a paging file on its own drive letter, the paging file does not become fragmented, which is another performance advantage. When a paging file resides on a drive letter that contains other data, it may become fragmented because of having to increase its size to provide the extra virtual memory space needed. Without question, an unfragmented paging file offers faster virtual memory access.

Managing Disk Performance

The PhysicalDisk and LogicalDisk performance objects collect metrics related to individual disk drives and logical disk volumes, respectively. PhysicalDisk counters focus on a storage device, so you should use them to analyze hardware performance. Use LogicalDisk counters, which focus on a specific drive letter, to analyze disk read and write performance.

For Windows XP and Windows Server 2003 systems, you no longer need to enable LogicalDisk counters with the **Diskperf.exe** command so that you can monitor their performance with the System Monitor snap-in—LogicalDisk counters are automatically enabled on demand. **Diskperf.exe** is needed only for remote administration on computers running Windows NT 4.0 and Windows 2000.

The following disk counters will help you to monitor and manage disk performance:

➤ PhysicalDisk/LogicalDisk: %DiskTime, threshold close to 100%—This reports the amount of time that a disk is busy servicing read or write requests.

➤ PhysicalDisk/LogicalDisk: Disk Queue Length, threshold 2—The Average and Current disk queue length counters reflect the read/write requests that are pending and being serviced. If the queue is long, processes are being delayed.

When disk performance is a bottleneck, you can add capacity; replace disks with faster hardware; move applications, services, or data to underused disks; or implement spanned, striped, or RAID-5 volumes.

Managing Network Performance

Although Windows Server 2003 and Windows 2000 Server can support Network Monitor for relatively sophisticated network traffic analysis, Windows XP Professional has limited network performance tools. Counters are available for the number of bytes and packets received and sent over a particular network interface. However, you cannot analyze the contents or properties of packets using only Windows XP Professional tools from the GUI.

To conduct detailed network analysis for a Windows XP Professional system, perform the following steps:

1. Install the Network Monitor driver.

2. From the Network Connections folder, right-click a connection, choose Properties and then click Install.

3. Select the Protocol component and click the Add button. Select Network Monitor Driver and click OK.

4. Click Close to exit from the connection's Properties dialog box.

The Network Monitor Driver can collect packets that the Windows XP system's network interfaces send or receive. You can then analyze those packets using a version of Network Monitor that ships with Systems Management Server (SMS), Windows 2000 Server, or Windows Server 2003. You can also use a new tool that ships with Windows XP Professional, the Netcap.exe command-line utility, to analyze your system's network packets.

Managing Processor Performance

A system's processor is one of the more difficult components to optimize, because every other component impacts it. Low memory leads to paging, which increases processor usage; fragmented disk drives increase processor usage; hardware interrupts keep the processor busy; and, of course, applications and services place many demands on the processor. Therefore, to optimize a processor, you need to look at Processor counters, as well as counters for other objects. Some of the most useful Processor counters are the following:

➤ Processor:%ProcessorTime, threshold near 100%—A processor being fully utilized (100%) is not necessarily a sign of a performance bottleneck—in fact, you might hope that you would be using this expensive system component at its full capacity. Therefore, although `%ProcessorTime` is a flag that indicates a potential bottleneck, it is not in itself enough to prescribe a solution. Check Memory:Pages/sec to examine paging and determine whether low memory is causing excessive paging.

➤ Processor:Interrupts/sec, threshold varies—A malfunctioning hardware device may send excessive interrupts to the processor. Compare this counter to a baseline; a significant increase in this counter without a corresponding increase in system activity may indicate a bad device. Network cards are particularly notorious for generating bogus interrupts.

➤ System:Processor Queue Length, threshold 2—A queue length that is regularly above 2 indicates that threads are backing up as they wait for processor attention.

➤ Process:%ProcessorTime (Instance: each service or application)—This counter enumerates the activity of individual applications and services, allowing you to identify processes that are placing demands on the processor.

If Processor Queue Length is low and %ProcessorTime is averaging above 85% for extended periods of time, these settings indicate that a single threaded application or service is keeping the processor busy. A faster processor may improve performance of such a system. However, if Processor Queue Length is high, a second processor would be a better solution, or you might consider moving processes to underutilized systems.

Task Manager

Task Manager enables you to view applications and processes and a number of other common performance counters. To open Task Manager, right-click the taskbar and choose Task Manager, or press Ctrl+Shift+Esc on the keyboard. The Applications tab enumerates active applications. The Processes tab can display a number of process-related counters. With the Processes tab displayed, click View, Select Columns from the menu bar to specify which counters you want to view. The Performance tab displays useful performance metrics such as CPU usage and paging file usage; these statistics start running whenever Task Manager is opened. The Networking tab is new to Windows XP—it displays the network utilization percentage for the system.

Managing Application Performance

Windows XP preemptively multitasks active processes, ensuring that all threads gain access to the processor. Processes do run at different priorities, however. Priority levels of 0 to 31 are assigned to a process, and higher-level processes are executed before lower-level processes. As a user, you can specify process priority using Task Manager. Right-clicking a process on the Processes tab enables you to set a process's priority. Processes are assigned a priority of Normal by default. Choosing Above Normal or High will increase the priority of a process and thereby increase the frequency with which its threads are serviced. Choosing Below Normal or Low will diminish the servicing of a process.

Do not use the Real-time priority. This priority should be reserved for real-time data gathering applications and operating system functions. Setting an application to Real-time priority can cause system instability, which can be difficult to reverse without restarting the computer.

Process priority can also be controlled when an application is launched, using the start command with the /low, /belownormal, /normal, /abovenormal, /high, and /realtime option parameters.

On dual-processor Windows XP Professional computers, you can also assign one or more specific processes to a specific processor of your choosing. When you right-click a process in Task Manager from the Processes tab, the Set Affinity option is available in addition to the Set Priority option. The Set Affinity option is not displayed at all on single CPU systems.

Monitoring Event Logs

The new Eventtriggers.exe command-line tool displays and configures actions to be taken based on events (system messages, warnings, and failures) that occur, which are tracked by the Windows XP Event Viewer. The Eventtriggers.exe utility works on both local and remote computers and monitors the Application log, the System log, the Security log, the DNS Server log, and the Directory log. *You must be a member of the Administrators group to use* Eventriggers.exe. To view a current list of event triggers, type **eventtriggers** (without any parameters) at a command prompt. For more details on this tool, search on the keyword "eventtriggers" in the Windows XP Professional Help and Support Center, or type **eventtriggers /?** at a command prompt.

Proactively Managing Security Threats

Windows XP Service Pack 2 introduces the Data Execution Prevention (DEP) feature. To improve Windows XP's memory buffer overflow defenses, Microsoft redesigned the way that the operating system monitors and protects different areas of memory where application programs execute their code. These areas of memory include the *stack*, the *paged pool*, and the *session pool*. In fact, Microsoft actually recompiled the programming code for the entire operating system to implement the DEP feature. DEP is optimized to run on computers with 64-bit processors installed, such as the AMD Opteron, the AMD Athlon, the Intel D series of processors, and the Intel Itanium 2 processor. Sixty-four-bit processors support the *NX* flag, which marks specified memory pages as nonexecutable. Unfortunately, 32-bit CPUs do not have built-in NX support. So, on 32-bit systems, SP2 acts as a software "watchdog," doing its best to prevent programming code from executing "out of the stack" and performing some mischief.

By default, DEP monitors only essential Windows XP programs and services. Fortunately, you can force DEP to monitor all programs and services. You can also specify individual exceptions for programs that may not run properly with DEP turned on. To configure DEP settings, follow these steps:

1. Right-click My Computer and select Properties to display the System Properties dialog box.

2. Select the Advanced tab.

3. Click the Settings button located in the Performance section.

4. For the Performance Options dialog box, select the Data Execution Prevention tab.

5. To change the default settings, click the Turn on DEP for All Programs and Services Except Those I Select option button (see Figure 8.7).

6. If you want to exclude specific programs or services from being monitored by DEP, click the Add button and specify them.

7. Click OK to save the DEP settings.

8. Click OK for the message box that appears, notifying you that you must restart the computer for the new settings to take effect.

9. Click OK to exit from the System Properties dialog box and restart the computer.

Figure 8.7 Turning on DEP for all programs and services under Windows XP Service Pack 2.

Exam Prep Questions

1. If your Windows XP system gets a stop error (blue screen) after you have installed an updated video driver, what is the best and most efficient course of action to take to get your system back up and running so that you can fix the problem?

   ○ A. Restart the system using the Last Known Good Configuration advanced startup option.

   ○ B. Restart the system using the Recovery Console.

   ○ C. Perform a restore operation using the Automated System Recovery feature.

   ○ D. Restart the system using the Enable VGA Mode advanced startup option.

2. Jan's Windows XP Professional computer does not have a tape drive installed on it. Fortunately, the important data that she needs to back up requires only about 575MB of storage space. Jan remembers that Windows XP supports writing directly to CD-R and CD-RW media, so she runs the Windows XP Backup program to create a backup of her data onto a CD-R disc. How can Jan get her data backed up onto a CD-R?

   ○ A. Specify a CD-R as the target media for the Windows Backup program.

   ○ B. Specify a CD-RW as the target media for the Windows Backup program.

   ○ C. Use the Windows XP Backup program to back up the data to a different hard drive or to a network drive, and then copy the backup file onto CD-R or CD-RW media.

   ○ D. Specify a DVD-R as the target media for the Windows Backup program.

3. Bob has a Windows XP Professional computer that has applications processing data 24 hours a day, 7 days a week. He upgraded the computer to Windows XP from Windows 98 and he has left the file systems intact. He knows he needs to have frequent, regular backups, but he's concerned about not being able to back up several important data files that are always open and critical application files that are always locked. What can Bob do to back up his important data and application files?

   ○ A. Turn off 50% of the important applications and close their data files during nonpeak intervals and perform a backup of those files; turn off the other 50% at different nonpeak intervals and perform a second backup of those files.

   ○ B. Rely on Windows XP's Volume Shadow Copy Technology to enable the Windows XP Backup program to back up those open data files and locked application files.

   ○ C. Let the Windows XP Backup program skip the open and locked files for now; those files may be closed and unlocked during the next scheduled backup.

   ○ D. Use the Inuse.exe utility from the Windows 2000 Professional Resource Kit to unlock any locked files and then perform a backup.

4. How can you boot your Windows XP system into the Recovery Console after you have just installed Windows XP Professional on the computer? (Check all correct answers.)

❑ A. Restart the system, press the F8 key as Windows XP starts up, and select Recovery Console from the default list of advanced startup options.

❑ B. Restart the system by booting from the Windows XP Professional CD-ROM and select the repair option when prompted.

❑ C. Click Start, Run, and run the command winnt32.exe /cmdcons from the i386 folder on the Windows XP Professional CD-ROM. Restart the system, press the F8 key as Windows XP starts up, and select Recovery Console from the list of advanced startup options.

❑ D. Restart the system, press the F8 key as Windows XP starts up, and select Safe Mode Using Recovery Console from the default list of advanced startup options.

5. After making several configuration settings changes, Edie wants to restore her Windows XP Professional system to the configuration that it had yesterday, before she made any changes. Unfortunately, she forgot to set any restore points. Her computer has been left powered on in her office for the last week. Can she restore her system to its previous state, and if so, using which technology?

○ A. Yes, she can use the System Restore Wizard to restore her system.

○ B. No, she can't restore her system to its previous state from yesterday, but she can restore it to its original state when it was first installed using the System Restore Wizard.

○ C. Yes, she can easily restore her system to its previous state using the Last Known Good Configuration.

○ D. Yes, she can restore her system's configuration using the Windows XP Professional CD-ROM, an ASR floppy disk, and the ASR tape backup that she created from the night before.

6. Which of the following system tools is best suited to help you create a historical baseline of overall system performance for a Windows XP Professional computer?

○ A. Performance Logs and Alerts

○ B. System Monitor

○ C. Task Manager

○ D. Network Monitor Driver and the Netcap.exe utility

7. Which of the following actions represents a best practice approach to configuring virtual memory on a Windows XP Professional computer that has three physical hard disks (assigned as drives C, D, and E), the %systemroot% folder located on the C: drive, and 256MB of memory installed?

○ A. Place the paging file on the C: drive with an initial size of 192MB and a maximum size of 256MB.

○ B. Place a paging file on the D: drive with an initial size of 192MB and a maximum size of 192MB, and place a second paging file on the E: drive, also with an initial size of 192MB and a maximum size of 192MB.

○ C. Place a paging file on the E: drive with an initial size of 128MB and a maximum size of 256MB.

○ D. Place a paging file on the E: drive with an initial size of 192MB and a maximum size of 192MB, and place a second paging file on the C: drive, also with an initial size of 192MB and a maximum size of 192MB.

8. Which of the following Windows XP system components can you configure or monitor from the Task Manager window for a dual-processor computer? (Check all correct answers.)

❑ A. Network utilization and current condition

❑ B. Processor usage and page file usage

❑ C. Processor affinity for specific processes

❑ D. Processor priority for specific processes

❑ E. Available system memory

❑ F. List of processes running from all users

Answers to Exam Prep Questions

1. Answer D is correct. Restarting the system under VGA mode would be the fastest and most efficient way to get back into the system, and either roll back or uninstall the poorly behaving video driver. Answer A is incorrect because the Last Known Good Configuration would also erase any other configuration changes that you might have made just prior to updating the video driver. Answer B is incorrect because you do not need to boot into the Recovery Console just to change the video driver. Answer C is incorrect because an Automated System Recovery restore formats the system drive and reinstalls Windows XP, which would be time-consuming and completely unnecessary in this case.

2. Answer C is correct. The Windows XP Backup program does not support backing up directly to CD-R or CD-RW media, but you can copy a previously created backup file to a CD-R or CD-RW disc. Answer A is incorrect because the Windows XP Backup program does not support backing up directly to CD-Rs. Answer B is incorrect because the Windows XP Backup program does not support backing up directly to CD-RWs. Answer D is incorrect because the Windows XP Backup program does not support backing up directly to DVD-Rs, nor can you natively write to DVD-RAM media.

3. Answer A is correct. Volume Shadow Copy Technology (VSCT) is not available for data or application files stored on FAT or FAT32 drive volumes; Bob must create a backup window interval during which the Backup program can back up his important files. Answer B is incorrect

because VSCT is not available for data or application files stored on
FAT or FAT32 drive volumes. Answer C is incorrect because open and
locked files do not get backed up, and you should not leave good backups to chance. Answer D is incorrect because the `Inuse.exe` tool is
meant for replacing locked operating system files, not for helping to
back up locked or open files.

4. Answers B and C are correct. You can boot into the Windows XP
Recovery Console by booting from the Windows XP Professional CD-
ROM and selecting the repair option, or by first installing the
Recovery Console onto your system using the `winnt32.exe /cmdcons`
command. Then you can restart the system and select Recovery
Console as an advanced startup option. Answer A is incorrect because
the Recovery Console is not a default startup option; you must manu-
ally install it first. Answer D is incorrect because there is no Safe Mode
Using Recovery Console advanced startup option.

5. Answer A is correct. By default, System Restore automatically creates a
restore point every 24 hours or every 24 hours that the computer is
powered on. She can use the System Restore Wizard to restore her
system from the restore point that was created approximately 24 hours
earlier. Answer B is incorrect because she can restore her system to its
previous state from approximately 24 hours earlier. Answer C is incorrect because the Last Known Good Configuration holds the
CurrentControlSet information after you successfully log on to the
system. It cannot revert to a previous configuration after successfully
logging on to the system. Answer D is incorrect because when you perform an ASR restore, it reformats the system drive and returns all settings to their installation defaults.

6. Answer A is correct. The Performance Logs and Alerts snap-in captures performance activity for all of the objects and their associated
counters that you add to a performance counter log. By tracking such
activity over time for key components, such as memory, processor, network interfaces, physical and logical disks, you can create a baseline
against which to compare future activity. Answer B is incorrect because
the System Monitor snap-in displays only current activity or past activity—it does not store such data. Answer C is incorrect because the Task
Manager displays only current activity for applications, processes, performance, and networking—it does not store such data. Answer D is
incorrect because the Network Monitor Driver and the `Netcap.exe`
utility capture and analyze network data packets; they do not store any
other performance-related data.

7. Answer B is correct. The optimal paging file configuration is to split it
evenly over multiple physical disks without placing it on the system or
boot volumes. The recommended paging file size is 1.5 times the
installed memory. For a system with 256MB RAM installed, that would

be 384MB split over two drives (192MB each). Answer A is incorrect because it is not a best practice to place the paging file on the system or boot volumes. Answer C is incorrect because it is not optimal to make the initial size lower than the maximum size; this will cause the paging file to be expanded, which takes system resources. Answer D is incorrect because it is not a best practice to place the paging file on the system or boot volumes, even if you place other paging files on different volumes.

8. Answers A, B, C, D, E, and F are all correct. Network utilization percentage is displayed on the Networking tab, processor and page file usage is displayed on the Performance tab, and processor affinity settings and processor priority settings for specific processes are managed on the Processes tab. Available system memory is shown on the Performance tab, and you can expand the list of processes to include all users on the machine by marking the Show Processes from All Users check box at the bottom of the Processes tab.

Need to Know More?

 Bott, Ed, and Carl Siechert. *Microsoft Windows XP Inside Out*, 2nd ed. Redmond, WA: Microsoft Learning, 2004. ISBN 073562044X. This book offers time-saving tips, troubleshooting techniques, and workarounds. It focuses on techniques such as taking advantage of the rich integration of devices, applications, and web services in Windows XP.

 Microsoft Corporation. *Microsoft Windows XP Professional Resource Kit* 2nd ed. Redmond, WA: Microsoft Press, 2003. ISBN 0735619743. This all-in-one reference is a compilation of technical documentation and valuable insider information that computer-support professionals and administrators can reference to install, customize, and support Windows XP.

 Minasi, Mark. *Mastering Windows XP Professional*. Alameda, CA: Sybex, Inc., 2001. ISBN 0-78212-981-1. This book provides in-depth coverage of installing, configuring, and administering Windows XP Professional.

 Search the Microsoft TechNet CD (or its online version through www.microsoft.com) using keywords such as "Windows Backup", "System Restore", "Automated System Recovery (ASR)", "Safe Mode", "System Monitor", "Performance", "Volume Shadow Copy", "Last Known Good Configuration", "paging file", "SP2", and "Service Pack 2".

Windows XP SP2 Problem Solver.
http://www.michna.com/kb/WxSP2.htm

Installing, Administering, and Troubleshooting Remote Access Services

Terms you'll need to understand:

✓ Authentication protocol
✓ Internet Protocol Security (IPSec)
✓ Point-to-Point Tunneling Protocol (PPTP)
✓ Layer 2 Tunneling Protocol (L2TP)
✓ Extensible Authentication Protocol (EAP)
✓ Smart Card
✓ Encryption
✓ Dial-up connection
✓ Virtual Private Network (VPN)
✓ Windows Firewall (WF)
✓ Windows Security Center
✓ Internet Connection Sharing (ICS)
✓ **netsh** command
✓ COM and DCOM
✓ Microsoft Distributed Transaction Coordinator

Techniques you'll need to master:

✓ Configuring the proper authentication for a remote access client
✓ Determining when it is best to use PPTP or L2TP for your VPN connections
✓ Establishing the requirements and configurations to use a Smart Card
✓ Knowing what the default encryption levels are for your remote access connections
✓ Configuring WF to secure your computer on the Internet
✓ Knowing when to configure ICS to allow multiple computers on your network access to the Internet
✓ Working with the Windows Security Center
✓ Managing network security settings with group policy
✓ Managing network security settings with the **netsh** command
✓ Configuring RPC, COM, DCOM, and DTC security settings

Dial-up connectivity still maintains an important role for connecting remote computers. In Microsoft terms, *dial-up connections* generally refer to client computers dialing out to server computers. Remote Access Services (RAS) generally refer to server computers that accept inbound remote connections from dial-up clients. Dial-up connections usually involve regular phones using analog modems and/or dial-up integrated services digital network (ISDN) lines. Security is always a big concern whenever you work with remote access solutions. Network authentication, data encryption, Windows Firewall configuration, and best practices for other important remote access security settings are the major themes for this chapter.

Authentication Protocols

Windows XP Professional provides advanced support for remote access authentication protocols over older versions of Windows operating systems. These new authentication protocols offer enhanced security and dynamic bandwidth allocation for remote access. These authentication protocols authenticate the logon credentials for all users who attempt to connect to a Windows-based network. Windows XP Professional supports all the authentication protocols that Windows 2000 offered, including PAP, CHAP, MSCHAP (v1 and v2), EAP, SPAP, PPTP, and L2TP. Figure 9.1 shows the new interface for configuring an XP Professional's authentication protocols.

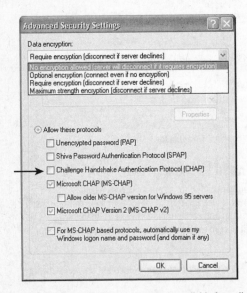

Figure 9.1 Authentication protocols available for a dial-up or VPN connection.

The Security tab has two configuration options: Typical and Advanced. Choosing the Typical option enables you to make a fast configuration setting. If you want to see what the Typical settings are and perhaps make changes to them, select the Advanced option and then click the Settings button, which gives all the detailed settings that are configured for the current settings.

The default authentication protocols for a dial-up connection are PAP, SPAP, MS-CHAP, and MS-CHAPv2. The default protocols for a VPN connection are MS-CHAP and MS-CHAPv2.

Extensible Authentication Protocol (EAP)

Extensible Authentication Protocol (EAP) is an extension of PPP for dial-up networking (DUN), L2TP, and PPTP clients. EAP supports a negotiated authentication model where the actual authentication mechanism is determined between the dial-up connection client and the remote access server. EAP provides support for a few authentication protocols, including the following:

➤ Message Digest 5 Challenge Handshake Authentication Protocol (MD5-CHAP)—Encrypts usernames and passwords using its own MD5 algorithm.

➤ Transport Level Security (TLS)—Works with Smart Cards and other types of security certificates. A Smart Card stores a user's security certificate and private key electronically on the card. Smart Card technology requires physical cards and card readers.

By using EAP application programming interfaces (APIs), software developers can design and implement new authentication methods for Smart Cards, generic token cards, and even biometric devices such as fingerprint identification scanners. In this way, EAP can support authentication technologies that will be developed in the future. To add EAP authentication methods, go to the Security tab of the remote access server's Properties dialog box.

IP Security (IPSec)

IP Security (IPSec) is a suite of security-related protocols and cryptographic functions for establishing and maintaining private and secure IP connections. IPSec is easy to implement and offers superb security for potential network traffic sniffing. IPSec-enabled clients establish a Security Association (SA) with the server that serves as a private key for encrypting data. IPSec uses simple on/off configurations, or you can configure policies for configuring its security services. IPSec policies support different gradations of security levels for different types of network traffic. Administrators can set IPSec policies at the Local, Organizational Unit, Domain, or Site levels. You configure IPSec policies with the IP Security Policy Management snap-in of the Microsoft Management Console (MMC).

Layer 2 Tunneling Protocol (L2TP)

You can compare the Layer 2 Tunneling Protocol (L2TP) to the Point-to-Point Tunneling Protocol (PPTP) in that it provides an encrypted "tunnel" for data to pass through an untrusted (public) network such as the Internet. Both L2TP and PPTP use PPP to establish initial communication. Some of the major differences between L2TP and PPTP include the following:

➤ L2TP exploits IPSec for encryption services; PPTP uses the encryption functions of PPP.

➤ L2TP offers support for tunnel authentication; PPTP does not support tunnel authentication. If you implement IPSec tunneling in conjunction with L2TP or PPTP, L2TP tunnel authentication isn't needed, because this will be handled by the IPSec tunnel.

Remote Authentication Dial-in User Service (RADIUS)

Remote Authentication Dial-in User Service (RADIUS) offers accounting services and centralized authentication functions for distributed dial-up connections. Windows XP Professional can take on the role of a RADIUS server or a RADIUS client, or it can assume the roles of both. A RADIUS client is often used as a remote access server for an Internet service provider (ISP). The RADIUS client forwards authentication requests to a RADIUS server. You configure RADIUS client settings from the Security tab of the remote access server's Properties dialog box.

RADIUS servers validate requests from RADIUS clients. For authentication, Windows 2000 provides Internet Authentication Services (IAS) as an optional Windows component that you can add during installation or through the Add/Remove Programs icon in the Control Panel. RADIUS servers maintain RADIUS accounting data from RADIUS clients in associated log files.

Bandwidth Allocation Protocol (BAP)

Bandwidth Allocation Protocol (BAP) works in conjunction with the Bandwidth Allocation Control Protocol (BACP) as an enhancement to the Multilink feature found in Windows NT 4. Multilink enables you to bind together two or more modems or ISDN lines, enabling you to achieve higher throughput (more bandwidth) than you would if you used the lines individually. BAP and BACP work together to dynamically add or drop lines for multilinked devices on an on-demand basis. Both protocols serve as PPP control protocols. These protocols provide a means for optimizing bandwidth while holding down connection costs by responding to network bandwidth needs on demand. For organizations that incur line-usage charges based on bandwidth use (such as ISDN lines), BAP and BACP can significantly cut costs.

Administrators can turn on the Multilink feature as well as BAP and BACP from the PPP tab of each remote access server's Properties dialog box. You configure BAP settings using remote access policies. By implementing a remote access policy using BAP, you can specify that an extra line should be dropped if the connection for that line falls below a specified percentage. If two users need to have different BAP settings, multiple remote access policies can be configured in which each of them uses a different percentage. The easiest way to configure the different remote access policies is to associate the settings to a Windows group, which will easily apply the policy settings to the correct type of user.

Encryption

Encryption is the technology of locking down data or network traffic with digital keys. These keys are available only to those who are transferring the information. Multiple levels of encryption exist, and with each increase in a level of encryption, a hit to performance occurs. It simply takes longer to create and decode higher encryption.

By default, dial-up connections have the encryption level set to optional, and VPN connections have the encryption level set to required. In these instances, a dial-up session does not have to use encryption, whereas VPN sessions do. Of course, the main reason for this is the lack of security that VPNs endure, because they are traveling across the Internet. You can alter this default behavior, but in the case of the VPN, it is always best to keep the security at this level or higher.

The following are the four encryption levels that you can set on any remote network connection, as shown in Figure 9.2:

➤ No Encryption Allowed—This does not allow the dial-up or VPN client to connect with any form of encryption. Not allowing any encryption will be rare, but in the case of a very slow connection, this can be useful.

➤ Optional Encryption—This will use encryption if the remote access server is suggesting that it be used or requiring that encryption be used.

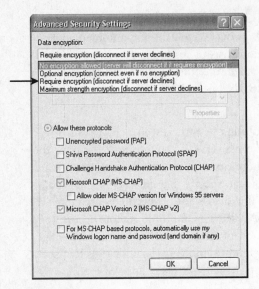

Figure 9.2 Security configurations for a dial-up or VPN connection.

➤ Require Encryption—This will require that the remote access client use encryption with the remote access server. The encryption level used will be the standard level for either the MPPE or IPSec.

➤ Maximum Strength Encryption—This will require that both the remote access client and server negotiate the communication with strong encryption.

Two different levels of encryption can be required for a remote access connection. Table 9.1 gives you the information about how the levels are seen in the interface and what each means.

Table 9.1 Encryption Levels			
Interface Text	**Encryption Level**	**MPPE**	**IPSec**
Require Encryption	Standard	40-bit	56-bit (DES)
Maximum Strength Encryption	Strong	128-bit	168-bit (3DES)

Connecting to Remote Access Servers

You create new connections to remote access servers from the Network Connections window. You can make new connections as well as modify or delete existing network connections from this window. To create a new network connection, you start the New Connection Wizard from the Network Connections window. During this wizard, you can create connections for your LAN, dial-up, VPN, or direct connection. Figure 9.3 shows the wizard in action, including some of the available options.

Figure 9.3   New Connection Wizard options for connecting to a workplace.

As soon as you complete the New Connection Wizard for a remote access connection, a Connect dialog box appears. It prompts you for a User Name and a Password. Click the Connect button to initiate the connection. Click the Properties button to modify the remote connection's properties.

You can modify the properties of any network connection listed in the Network Connections window by right-clicking the connection's icon and selecting Properties. From the connection's Properties dialog box, you can configure connection devices (modems and so on), list alternate phone numbers, and configure dialing options and redialing options. You can specify security options, configure dial-up server settings, and modify network connection components. You can also set up Internet Connection Sharing (ICS) from the Sharing tab, if this connection will be used to connect other users on the network to the Internet. ICS is covered in more detail later in this chapter.

The Networking tab of a dial-up connection's Properties dialog box enables you to configure several essential components for successful connections (see Figure 9.4). Be sure to specify the proper dial-up server type to which you will be connecting (either PPP or SLIP). You can change PPP settings by clicking the Settings button (as shown in Figure 9.5). Be sure that your connection has at least one dial-up network protocol in common with the remote access server to which it will be attempting to connect. You can install and uninstall networking components, such as protocols, from the Networking tab. You can also enable or disable any listed component by marking or clearing its check box.

Figure 9.4 The Networking tab of a dial-up connection's Properties dialog box.

Figure 9.5 The PPP Settings dialog box.

Setting Up and Configuring VPN Connections

Setting up and configuring VPN connections is similar to establishing dial-up connections. VPN connections enable you to connect to remote computers anywhere in the world by tunneling through the Internet using a VPN protocol such as PPTP or L2TP. VPN protocols encapsulate TCP/IP, NetBEUI, or NWLink data packets for transport over TCP/IP via the Internet. PPTP and L2TP use encryption to secure all the data that they encapsulate as it travels to the destination VPN server.

Start the Make the New Connections Wizard in the Network Connections folder to set up a new VPN connection. When you double-click the Virtual Private Connection icon to access a VPN server, you are prompted to connect to the Internet using the dial-up connection you specified. After you have established a connection to the Internet, Windows XP Professional attempts to connect to the remote VPN server.

The IPSec Network Address Translation traversal (NAT-T) behavior has changed in Windows XP SP2. The reason for this change is due to a rare, but possible, security vulnerability that was exposed when connecting to a VPN L2TP/IPsec VPN server that was behind a NAT.

The change is rather dramatic, in that Windows XP no longer supports an IPSec NAT-T security association to a VPN server that is located behind a device that uses NAT.

It is possible to alter this behavior to allow such a connection, but because of the security vulnerability and rare situation in which this would occur, it is suggested that you don't change this setting.

Configuring Windows Firewall

Windows Firewall (WF) has changed slightly since the original version of XP. The changes came along with Windows XP SP2. The first change you will notice is that the name has changed. The original name, Internet Connection Firewall (ICF), has now become Windows Firewall. The overall behavior of WF has not changed, but the finer details certainly have. You can work with Windows Firewall settings by either double-clicking the Windows Firewall icon in Control Panel or by selecting the Advanced tab on the properties sheet for a network connection and clicking the Settings button.

Under SP2, the Windows Firewall is enabled by default. From the General tab of the Windows Firewall dialog box, you have the option of turning the firewall on or off, as shown in Figure 9.6. You also have the option of not allowing any exceptions when the firewall is turned on by marking the Don't Allow Exceptions check box.

The key aspects of WF that have not changed include the following:

➤ WF is a stateful firewall, in that it monitors all aspects of the traffic that crosses the interface, including the source and destination addresses.

➤ WF tracks traffic that originates from the computer and from the computers connecting to it from the Internet.

➤ WF still works with ICS to allow internal computers to connect to the Internet through the computer running WF and ICS.

➤ WF will work hand-in-hand with the ICS translation table to verify and route all incoming traffic to the appropriate internal computer.

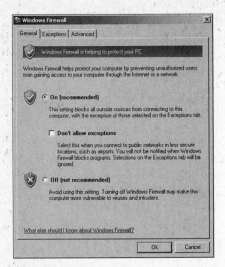

Figure 9.6 Configuring Windows Firewall settings.

➤ All traffic originating from the Internet will be dropped by default where WF is enabled. This can be altered by configuring the services that Internet users can communicate with on the Services tab of the interface where WF is enabled, as shown in Figure 9.7.

Figure 9.7 Services tab for an WF interface connection.

➤ Allowed WF services can be configured by providing the name or IP address of the computer on the network that is running the selected service. If the service is new to the standard WF list, you will need to add the port and transport type along with the IP address of the computer, as shown in Figure 9.8.

Figure 9.8 Custom service window for use with WF.

There are some other changes to how Windows XP works with WF after SP2 is installed. Again, the overall functions are the same, but some major differences should be noted. The following list highlights the differences you should know:

➤ There is a boot-time policy that allows the computer to perform basic networking tasks while it boots, but protects the network traffic during this time. The basic networking tasks that are still allowed include DNS, DHCP, and basic communication with the domain controllers.

➤ As soon as SP2 is installed, WF is enabled and ready for action. This can cause some negative results, depending on the applications that are running on the computer. Because of some changes in the network stack, memory, and firewall filters, some applications might not function anymore.

Many MMC snap-ins will no longer function after SP2 is installed. This is because port 445 is blocked. After you enable port 445, all of the "broken" MMC snap-ins will begin to work again.

Remote control applications might also be at risk of failing to function after SP2 is installed. Again, this is caused by ports not being available; in addition, file sharing might be disabled. To get your remote control applications to function, you need to find out which ports need to be opened up and potentially allow file sharing to allow them to work again.

➤ A new command-line tool can be used to control every aspect of WF and its configurations. The command-line tool that you will use is `netsh firewall`, and plenty of switches are available. The tool is built in to the system, so you can just go to a command prompt and type **`netsh firewall /?`** to get a full listing of the switches. The `netsh firewall show config` command, as shown in Figure 9.9, displays the current WF configuration. Some of the more important tasks that you perform using the `netsh` tool include the following:

➤ Modifying the firewall configurations

➤ Showing the configuration script

➤ Resetting the firewall configurations back to the default values

➤ Displaying the current firewall configurations

Figure 9.9 Displaying the current Windows Firewall settings using the *netsh* command-line tool.

 The **netsh** command can also be used to generate scripts that can automatically configure a group of Windows Firewall settings for both the traditional Internet Protocol version 4 (IPv4) standard as well as for the newer Internet Protocol version 6 (IPv6) standard.

➤ You can now control WF through a myriad of Group Policy Object (GPO) settings. These GPO settings were not available in any other operating system, including Windows Server 2003 (although they will be available with Windows Server 2003 SP1). These GPO settings will behave like all other GPO settings; however, they will target computers running only Windows XP SP2. Figure 9.10 shows the list of GPOs that configure WF.

 These GPO settings for WF are located only on Windows XP Professional computers that have SP2 installed. If you want to configure these new SP2 GPO settings from a Windows 2000 or Server 2003 computer, you will need to import the appropriate ADM templates to the computer from which you are administering the GPOs.

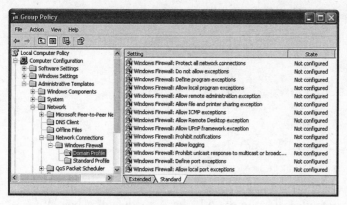

Figure 9.10 GPO settings for Windows Firewall.

➤ There is a manual method for controlling the configuration of WF. The manual method consists of modifying the netfw.inf file, which resides in the C:\windows\inf folder of the client computer. The benefit of using this manual method is that you can quickly update computers by replacing this file with an updated file. After updating this file, you will need to run the netsh firewall reset command on each computer where the new file is placed.

➤ WF allows for "scoping" of services. This feature allows you to control which networks will be affected by the firewall rules. For example, you might want the File and Printer Sharing service to function within the LAN, but want to deny Internet users from connecting with the File and Printer Sharing ports (TCP 139 and 445, UDP 137 and 138). This option is available when you edit the list of programs and services on the Exceptions tab for the WF properties by following these steps:

1. Open the Connection Properties sheet for the connection that has WF enabled.

2. On the Advanced tab, click the Settings button under the Windows Firewall section.

3. Select the Exceptions tab.

4. Highlight the service or application that you want to scope, and then click the Edit button.

5. Highlight the port that you want to scope, and then click the Change Scope button.

6. Select the scope of the port by clicking the appropriate option button, as shown in Figure 9.11.

Figure 9.11 The scope of a port for a service can be changed.

➤ WF can be controlled down to the NIC level. By default, when WF is enabled it is enabled for every NIC on the computer. However, if one NIC or interface needs to be more open or does not require WF to be enabled, it can be controlled. You can see this setting under the Advanced tab in the WF properties sheet, as shown in Figure 9.12.

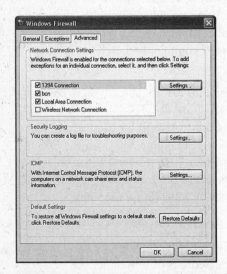

Figure 9.12 WF can be enabled and disabled per NIC.

➤ WF can control specific ports and services at the individual NIC level. Similar to having the capability to enabled or disable WF per NIC, this option allows the configuration of services that will be available to Internet users, depending on which interface they communicate through. This option is available by clicking the Settings button for the individual NICs, shown in Figure 9.12. A new configuration window opens, which allows the configuration of services for the NIC, as shown in Figure 9.13.

Figure 9.13   Each NIC can have a different configuration of services available through WF.

➤ WF can control the configurations of the firewall depending on whether the computer is joined to a domain. If the computer is joined to a domain, two profiles can be associated with the computer. One profile controls the computer when it is connected to the corporate network (the network with Active Directory). The other profile controls the computer when it leaves the corporate network. This is designed to allow a more strict firewall configuration when the computer is not connected to the corporate network, which most likely has a corporate firewall in place.

 WF handles this dynamic firewall configuration by using GPOs. In the GPO section under Windows Firewall, there are configurations for both Standard and Domain profiles. These will be applied to the computer based on whether the computer is connected to a network with domain controllers or one without domain controllers. If the computer is not joined to a domain, it will have only a single profile.

WF is tied into the Windows Security Center and can be accessed from this interface. The Windows Security Center is designed to help centralize the control of WF, Automatic Updates, Antivirus, and Internet Explorer security.

The Windows Security Center

One of the most visible new security features for computers that are not members of an Active Directory domain is the Windows Security Center, as shown in Figure 9.14. You can access the Security Center from Control Panel. Under SP2, both the Automatic Updates feature and the new Windows Firewall component are turned on by default. In addition to SP2 checking the operating system for installed and running antivirus software, the Windows Security Center provides you with a central interface for managing the Windows Firewall, Automatic Updates, Virus Protection monitoring, and Internet Explorer (IE) options.

By default, the Windows Security Center does not display automatically for computers that are members of an Active Directory domain. For nondomain member computers, the Windows XP prompts you to view the Security Center interface the first time that you log on after you have successfully installed SP2.

Figure 9.14 The Windows Security Center displaying the computer's current security settings.

On some computers, the Security Center may report that no antivirus software is currently installed, as Figure 7.9 indicates. This may occur because no antivirus product is installed or it may be because Windows is not able to accurately detect the antivirus program that is currently installed and enabled. If the PC already has an antivirus tool loaded that Windows does not detect, you can click the Recommendations button in Virus Protection section to stop Windows from sending you unnecessary alerts about the computer's virus protection status (see Figure 9.15). On the Recommendation dialog box, mark the I Have an Antivirus Program That I'll Monitor Myself check box and click OK to turn off Windows virus protection notifications.

Figure 9.15 Turning off Windows virus protection monitoring from the Security Center's Recommendation dialog box.

Configuring Windows Firewall Exceptions

By default, *File and Printer Sharing*, *Remote Desktop*, and *UPnP Framework* programs and services are listed but disabled on the Exceptions tab of the Windows Firewall dialog box, as shown in Figure 9.16. You can allow a specific application program to connect through the Windows Firewall as an exception by clicking the Add Program button and selecting the particular program. You can open a specific network port on the Windows Firewall by clicking the Add Port button and specifying the port's name, port number, and whether it's a TCP (connection-oriented) or UDP (connectionless) port.

Figure 9.16 Configuring Windows Firewall Exception settings.

You can also enable or disable individual port numbers that are associated with specific programs or services. For example, you can select the File and Printer Sharing service name and click the Edit button to open or block selective ports, as shown in Figure 9.17. In addition, you have the option of specifying a particular network segment (subnet) or a list of computers for which a particular network program or service is allowed to pass through the firewall and not be blocked (see Figure 9.18). Specifying a set of computers for which a port or service is to be *unblocked* is referred to as *changing scope* in Windows Firewall parlance. To change the scope, click the Change Scope button from one of the following dialog boxes: Edit a Service, Add a Program, or Add a Port.

Figure 9.17   Configuring individual port numbers associated with a Windows service or program.

 The Windows Firewall blocks only incoming network traffic, not outgoing network traffic. If your network environment requires a more feature-rich software firewall, you should consider one of the many third-party Internet security utilities on the market, such as Norton Internet Security from Symantec Corporation, Zone Alarm from Zone Labs, or Black Ice Defender from Internet Security Systems. As an optional (or additional) security measure, you may also choose to implement Internet Protocol Security (IPSec) to block outgoing network traffic.

Figure 9.18   Changing the scope for a port, program, or service.

WF Logging

When there is traffic that is dropped by the WF service, no message appears to the user of the system. The reason for this is obvious: If there is an abundance of dropped packets, there could be an overwhelming number of messages hindering the user. In many instances, the information about dropped packets will be important, whether for troubleshooting or for tracking down security issues. For these cases where it is important to get information about the traffic that is being dropped, a log file is available that can store information about the dropped packets, successful connections, or both.

The overall logging has not changed for WF, but the access of the logging options has. To access logging with SP2 installed, go to the Advanced tab of **SP2** the WF window. Then click the Settings button for the Security Logging section. This opens up a Log Settings window similar to the way it was with Internet Connection Firewall, as shown in Figure 9.19.

Figure 9.19   Log file configuration for the WF service.

Remember that HTTP traffic will be logged as port 80 and FTP traffic will be logged as ports 20 and 21.

WF log is stored in a file named **pfirewall.log**. The log can be controlled to log dropped packets and/or successful connections. You can also change the location of the log, which is by default located under **C:\Windows**.

Configuring and Troubleshooting ICS

Windows XP Professional enables you to have one IP address from an ISP and share that connection (through the Windows XP Professional computer) with other computers on the network. This feature is known as Internet Connection Sharing (ICS). ICS translates (or maps) a set of nonroutable IP addresses (by default, from the 192.168.x.y network range) to an external (public) IP address that exists on the Internet. Computers on the LAN can then access external resources on the Internet, such as websites and FTP sites, but the LAN computers are somewhat sheltered from outside intrusions because the LAN computers are using nonroutable IP addresses.

Configuring ICS

To set up ICS, perform the following steps:

1. Click Start, Control Panel, Network Connections.

2. Right-click a connection icon for an Internet connection and select Properties.

3. Click the Advanced tab.

4. Click the Allow Other Network Users to Connect Through This Computer's Internet Connection check box. After you have marked this check box, the other settings for ICS become available.

5. Select the Establish a Dial-Up Connection Whenever a Computer on My Network Attempts to Access the Internet check box if you want this Internet connection to automatically dial and establish a connection to the Internet when another computer on the LAN attempts to access Internet resources through this computer.

6. Click the Settings button. On the Services tab, you can mark the check boxes for each Internet-related service you want to enable for this shared connection. You can also add services that are not currently listed by clicking the Add button.

7. Click OK to close the Internet Connection Sharing Settings dialog box.

After you have set up ICS, you should verify that the computer's IP address is now set to 192.168.0.1 with a subnet mask of 255.255.255.0. Test the local Internet connection to verify that the computer can connect to the Internet successfully. For each Windows XP Professional computer on the LAN that wants to take advantage of the shared Internet connection, perform the following steps:

1. Click Start, Control Panel, Network Connections.

2. Right-click the LAN connection and select Properties.

3. Click Internet Protocol and then click Properties.

4. Configure TCP/IP to obtain an IP address automatically. This is the preferred method to use with ICS (as opposed to obtaining the address manually, covered shortly). When you enable ICS, the Windows XP Professional DHCP Allocator uses the default IP addressing range of 192.168.0.2 through 192.168.0.254, and the DNS Proxy service becomes enabled so that clients on the network can connect to the shared Internet resource.

As an alternative, you can manually set up workstations to work with ICS; however, this is not the recommended method according to Microsoft. To do this, perform these steps:

1. Click Start, Control Panel, Network Connections.

2. Right-click the LAN connection and select Properties.

3. Click Internet Protocol and click Properties.

4. Click Use the Following IP Address and type a unique IP address in the range from 192.168.0.2 through 192.168.0.254.

5. Type `255.255.255.0` for the Subnet Mask.

6. Type `192.168.0.1` for the Default Gateway (the IP address for the Windows XP Professional computer that is hosting the shared Internet connection).

7. Type the Preferred DNS Server according to your ISP's documentation (if your ISP does not provide this information automatically).

8. Type the Alternate DNS Server according to your ISP's documentation (if your ISP does not provide this information automatically).

9. Click OK in the Internet Protocol (TCP/IP) Properties dialog box.

10. Click OK in the LAN connection Properties dialog box.

Troubleshooting ICS

Following are some tips for troubleshooting ICS:

➤ If you encounter problems with computers on the network not being able to connect to websites through the shared Internet connection, verify the DNS server IP addresses with your ISP.

➤ To verify that the new IP settings have taken effect, type **ipconfig** at a command prompt; sometimes you need to restart the computer for all the settings to become active.

➤ Check the subnet mask; it must read 255.255.255.0 or else the computer that is attempting to connect to the ICS computer cannot connect.

➤ Make sure that each IP address that you assign to the other computers on the network falls within the range of 192.168.0.2 through 192.168.0.254, with no duplicate addresses on any computer.

> If you have network devices that need to have static IP addresses while using ICS, you will need to modify the Registry. The update will modify the STOP value, which needs to be set to the maximum IP address within the 192.168.0.0/24 network that will be given out to clients. For example, if you set the STOP value to 192.168.0.220, the DHCP service within the ICS service will only give out IP addresses between 192.168.0.1 and 192.168.0.220. You would set your network devices to an IP address above 192.168.0.221.

➤ If computers on the network can connect to the Internet only after you manually initiate the Internet connection from the ICS host computer, make sure that Establish a Dial-Up Connection Whenever a Computer on My Network Attempts to Access the Internet is checked on the Advanced tab of the Internet connection's Properties dialog box.

Managing Enhanced Network Security Under SP2

Windows XP Service Pack 2 introduces several security-related enhancements to the operating system. Microsoft essentially reengineered SP2 so that Windows XP would become a more fortified computing environment able to fend off many common attacks from high-tech germs such as viruses, trojans, worms, and spyware. The SP2 security improvements include limitations on TCP/IP Raw Sockets, restricting the number of outbound TCP/IP connections, and changes to the default behaviors of Remote Procedure Calls (RPCs), the Distributed Transaction Coordinator (DTC) service, the Component Object Model (COM), and the Distributed Component Object Model (DCOM).

Understanding Restrictions to TCP/IP Raw Sockets

Some application programs use a feature of TCP/IP called *Raw Sockets* that enable those programs to create TCP/IP data packets that are subject to less security and integrity scrutiny by the TCP/IP protocol stack than ordinary packets. Malicious programs (viruses) could potentially use raw sockets as an intrusion technique or for mounting a denial of service (DoS) attack. Therefore, SP2 limits the capability to send data over raw sockets while still allowing data to be received via raw sockets. SP2 restricts sending network traffic over raw sockets in the following two ways:

➤ Sending Transmission Control Protocol (TCP) data packets over raw sockets is prohibited.

➤ Sending User Datagram Protocol (UDP) packets that contain invalid source addresses over raw sockets is prohibited. Unless the IP source address for an *outbound* UDP datagram (packet) exists on one of the local computer's network interfaces, the packet gets dropped.

Understanding TCP/IP Outbound Connection Limits

Microsoft has modified the TCP/IP stack under SP2 to restrict the number of simultaneous incomplete outbound TCP connection attempts. This change is designed to slow down the rate at which malware (viruses, worms, and the like) can spread to infect other computers on the network. A common technique of computer viruses and worms is to send out multiple simultaneous connection attempts to random IP addresses in the hope of reaching more machines to infect. Because most of the randomly sent connection attempts fail, such a sudden burst of failed connections can often indicate that a malicious program has infected the local computer.

These new TCP/IP outbound connection limits attempt to mitigate malware proliferation. The exact number of outbound connections allowed is not documented by Microsoft, although some people believe the number to be around 10. If outbound connections exceed the limit, subsequent connections are placed into a queue and the queued connections eventually get sent at an undisclosed rate. When the outbound connection limit is reached, System Event ID 4226 is recorded in the local computer's event log.

The TCP/IP outbound connection limit under SP2 is not configurable or changeable; it also cannot be disabled.

Managing Changes to RPCs, DTC, COM, and DCOM

SP2 adds options to and changes the default behaviors of several important internal communications services such as Remote Procedure Calls (RPCs), the Distributed Transaction Coordinator (DTC), Microsoft's Component Object Model (COM), and Microsoft's Distributed Component Object Model (DCOM). All these changes are designed to provide better security for local and remote Windows XP computers. Communications are locked down much better between the application programs and the operating system and between remote machines communicating over the network.

Under SP2, both the Alerter service and the Messenger service are turned off by default. Their startup values are set to *disabled,* as you can verify in the services snap-in. Prior to SP2, the Messenger service defaulted to Automatic startup and the Alerter service defaulted to Manual startup.

Restricting the RPC Interface

SP2 turns off anonymous access to RPCs for unauthenticated clients. Application programs that are written to expect and receive RPCs from remote anonymous RPC clients may fail to run properly. SP2 introduces the RestrictRemoteClients Registry key to limit or allow remote anonymous RPC calls. Even if this Registry key does not exist, the default value of DWORD=1 (restrict access to all RPC interfaces) still applies. You can work with the RestrictRemoteClients Registry key using the Group Policy editor. Navigate to Computer Configuration\Administrative Templates\System\Remote Procedure Call. The policy setting is named Restrictions for Unauthenticated RPC Clients, as shown in Figure 9.20. When you enable this policy setting, you must select one of three options:

➤ Authenticated—This is the default setting under SP2 (DWORD=1) and it restricts access to all unauthenticated RPC interfaces. All anonymous calls are rejected by the RPC service. RPCs within application programs that have registered certain security callbacks and provide the RPC_IF_ALLOW_CALLBACKS_WITH_NO_AUTH flag are exempt from this setting.

➤ Authenticated Without Exceptions—This setting rejects all remote anonymous RPC requests with no exceptions (DWORD=2).

➤ None—This setting completely bypasses the RPC interface restrictions (DWORD=0). This is the default setting for pre-SP2 systems.

Figure 9.20 Configuring the Restrictions for Unauthenticated RPC Clients policy setting using the Group Policy editor.

SP2 also restricts RPC support for calls over the network to operating system services, such as remote computer management, remote Windows Management Instrumentation (WMI) configuration, and calls from within scripts that are designed to manage remote clients and servers. These types of remote services rely on the RPC Endpoint Mapper, which by default under SP2, requires client authentication. Windows Firewall permits RPCs to pass through only when the RPC originates from one of the following security contexts:

➤ Local System

➤ Network Service

➤ Local Service

Managing Restricted DTC Network Transactions

Under SP2, the Distributed Transaction Coordinator (DTC) component blocks network transactions by default. Users who need to connect to network services running on Microsoft Commerce Server and/or Microsoft SQL Server require that changes are made to their client computers' configurations. Perform the following steps to enable network access for the Microsoft Distributed Transaction Coordinator (MSDTC):

1. In Control Panel, double-click the Administrative Tools icon and then double-click Component Services.

2. Expand the Component Services node in the left pane.

3. If a Windows Security Alert message box appears, click Unblock.

4. Under the Component Services node, expand the Computers folder and then expand the My Computer container.

5. Right-click the My Computer container and select Properties.

6. Click the MSDTC tab.

7. Click the Security Configuration button to open the Security Configuration dialog box.

8. Mark the Network DTC Access check box.

9. *Only if you are connecting to a Windows 2000 Server computer from Windows XP SP2*, select the No Authentication Required option button.

10. Click OK to save your settings and exit from the Security Configuration dialog box for the MSDTC. The MSDTC service on the local Windows XP SP2 computer will then be stopped and restarted (see Figure 9.21).

11. Click Yes to continue.

12. Click OK to save your settings and exit from the My Computer Properties dialog box.

13. Exit from the Component Services MMC snap-in.

Figure 9.21 Configuring the security configuration settings to allow (unblock) network access for the MSDTC.

Administering Restricted COM and DCOM Settings

SP2 changes the default security settings for the types of users that are permitted to launch, activate, and access (call) local RPC services (COM) versus network RPC services (DCOM). These new, tighter restrictions permit local (COM) services to be launched, activated, and accessed from unauthenticated users by assigning such permissions to the Everyone group. However, the tighter restrictions prohibit, by default, network remote procedure calls (DCOM) from unauthenticated users. This is accomplished by assigning Allow Permissions for Remote Launch and Remote Activation only to the local Administrators group by default, as shown in Figure 9.22.

 Microsoft does not recommend changing the default COM and DCOM permissions. You can view (and edit) these permissions from the COM Security tab on the My Computer Properties dialog box found in the Component Services MMC snap-in (**%windir%\System32\Com\Comexp.msc**).

Figure 9.22 The Launch Permission properties sheet showing that unauthenticated users (Everyone group) do not have Remote Launch or Remote Activation permissions for DCOM-based programs or services under SP2.

Exam Prep Questions

1. Bob is a consultant for an IT outsourcing company. He has a number of clients that have network infrastructures that enable him to access their internal networks via a Virtual Private Network (VPN). One of his new clients, ACME Corp., needs Bob to check the status of its Exchange Server. Bob configures a VPN connection for ACME on his Windows XP Professional workstation to use a Smart Card. Bob tries to check Automatically Use My Windows Logon Name and Password, but the option is grayed out. What should Bob do to enable this option?

   ○ A. Change the Security option setting from Use Smart Card to Require Secured Password.

   ○ B. Change the Security option setting from Typical to Advanced.

   ○ C. Change the Security option setting from Require Secured Password to Allow Unsecured Password.

   ○ D. Disable his Smart Card.

2. Your manager informs you that you need to set up dial-up networking for all the clients in your network. She is concerned about ensuring that the clients use the appropriate authentication protocols as the remote users dial in to the network. You want to calm her fears. Which authentication protocols does Windows XP Professional install, by default, when dial-up networking is installed on the computer? (Check all correct answers.)

   ❑ A. PAP

   ❑ B. SPAP

   ❑ C. MS-CHAP

   ❑ D. MS-CHAPv2

   ❑ E. CHAP

3. You are the network administrator of an international tar factory. You have 200 Windows 2000 servers and 4,500 Windows XP Professional workstations. Of the Windows XP Professional workstations, 250 are for the remote sales force. This remote sales force will access the corporate LAN via Virtual Private Networking and connect to a Windows 2000 Advanced Server running RRAS. You instruct the remote users on how to configure their workstations to use the corporate network via VPN. A few days later, one of the remote users calls you, explaining that he cannot access the Internet when he is connected to the corporate LAN. How should you resolve the issue?

○ A. Clear the check box Use Default Gateway on Remote Network on the General tab of the TCP/IP dialog box.

○ B. Ensure that the check box Use Default Gateway on Remote Network on the General tab of the TCP/IP dialog box is checked.

○ C. Ensure that the check box Allow Other Network Users to Connect Through This Computer's Internet Connection on the Internet Connection Sharing section on the Advanced Dial-Up properties sheet is checked.

○ D. Clear the check box Require Data Encryption (Disconnect if None) on the Security tab of the VPN Properties dialog box.

4. You have several clients that have installed Windows XP Professional on their corporate workstations. One of your clients calls, requesting that you connect to his machine using Remote Desktop. You have a direct Internet connection and Windows Firewall (WF) enabled. You attempt to connect to your client's network via VPN. You have problems connecting to the client's machine. What is the first thing you should do?

○ A. Disable Windows Firewall on the VPN connection.

○ B. Ensure that Windows Firewall on the VPN connection is enabled.

○ C. Check the Dial Another Connection First box on the General tab of the VPN Properties dialog box.

○ D. Disable your direct Internet connection and dial in to your client's network.

5. You have 250 Windows XP Professional computers in various OUs in your domain. You have 100 remote Windows XP Professional computers that use VPN connections to connect to the corporate LAN. You want the connections to be encrypted, so you use L2TP with IPSec on the VPN connection. What type of authentication is being used by default during the negotiation of security settings?

○ A. Preshared key authentication

○ B. Certificate-based authentication

○ C. Pass-through authentication

○ D. Internet Authentication Service

6. John is the network administrator for SofaKing, Inc., which has 15 print devices distributed throughout the enterprise. SofaKing uses Internet Connection Sharing in its company to provide Internet access to its users. The users' computers receive an address from the server that is sharing the Internet connection. The print devices must have static TCP/IP addresses. You want to ensure that the Dynamic Host Control Protocol (DHCP) service does not assign a conflicting IP address. How should you accomplish this?

○ A. Edit the Registry and change the STOP value to 192.168.0.200.

○ B. Edit the Registry value, STOP, to 192.168.0.1.

○ C. Exclude the print devices' IP address from the DHCP scope.

○ D. Exclude the servers' IP address from the DHCP scope.

7. You are the administrator for a national bank and your current protocol requires that you use Smart Cards for both local and remote user logons. You want the remote users to be able to use the Internet while connected to the corporate LAN. You do the following:

   ➤ Enable a Smart Card logon process for the domain.

   ➤ Enable the Extensible Authentication Protocol (EAP) and configure the Smart Card or other certificate (TLS) EAP type on the remote access router computer.

   ➤ Enable Smart Card authentication on the VPN connection on the remote access client computer.

   What else must you do to ensure the successful connection of your VPN clients? (Check all correct answers.)

   ❑ A. Install a computer certificate on the remote access router.

   ❑ B. Configure remote access on the remote access router.

   ❑ C. Ensure that the check box Use Default Gateway on Remote Network on the General tab of the TCP/IP Properties sheet is checked.

   ❑ D. Ensure that Internet Connection Firewall on the VPN connection is enabled.

8. You want to host a family website from your home on your Windows XP Professional workstation. You want to enable your family to access the website and add content via FTP. You create the site, register its name, and enable Windows Firewall. Later, you receive reports that your family can access the web page without problems, but no one can upload their files. What can you do to resolve the issue?

   ○ A. Ensure that the FTP box on the Services tab of the Advanced Settings page of the WF VPN Properties dialog box is checked.

   ○ B. Ensure that the FTP box on the Services tab of the Advanced Settings page of the WF VPN Properties dialog box is cleared.

   ○ C. Ensure that the HTTP box on the Services tab of the Advanced Settings page of the WF VPN Properties dialog box is checked.

   ○ D. Ensure that the HTTP box on the Services tab of the Advanced Settings page of the WF VPN Properties dialog box is cleared.

9. You are the network administrator for XYZ Roofing Company. All the workstations in the company have been upgraded to Windows XP Professional Service Pack 2. You notice that one of the workstations in the sales department is repeatedly getting Event ID 4226 in its System Event Log. What does this event indicate?

○ A. Too many inbound connections are overwhelming the Windows Firewall.

○ B. TCP/IP Raw Sockets are timing out because of the new security restrictions in SP2.

○ C. The Microsoft Distributed Transaction Coordinator (MSDTC) is blocking unauthenticated network RPC requests.

○ D. TCP/IP reports too many outbound connection requests—an outbound connection queue has been created.

○ E. Authentication is required for network DTC access because the Windows XP SP2 computer is attempting to connect to a Microsoft SQL Server database stored on a computer running Windows 2000 Server.

10. You are the network administrator for your department. You want to enable the logging feature for the Windows Firewall under SP2 on four of the department's workstations. What is the default name and location of the Windows Firewall security log?

○ A. `Wfirewall.txt` located in `%windir%`

○ B. `Pfirewall.log` located in `%windir%`

○ C. `Wfirewall.txt` located in `%windir%\System32`

○ D. `Wfirewall.log` located in `%windir%\Pfirewall`

○ E. `Pfirewall.log` located in `%windir%\Wfirewall`

○ F. `Winfwlog.txt` located in `%windir%`

Answers to Exam Prep Questions

1. Answer A is correct. The option Automatically Use My Windows Logon Name and Password is available only when the Security option setting Require Secured Password is selected. When using a Smart Card for authorization, the logon name and password entry will be secured and there is no need to have the system require a secured password. Answer B is incorrect because selecting Advanced on the Security option setting will gray out the option, not make it available. Answer C is incorrect because the Allow Unsecured Password option is available only with dial-up clients. Answer D is incorrect because you cannot disable the Smart Card and allow Bob to log on.

2. All the answers are correct. An authentication protocol is a set of standards for exchanging logon name and password information between the two network devices. Microsoft Windows XP supports the most common authentication protocols and includes their own version of CHAP. For a dial-up connection, all these protocols are selected and are supported for the remote access client.

3. Answer A is correct. The check box applies when you are connected to a local network and a dial-up network simultaneously. When checked, data that cannot be sent on the local network is forwarded to the dial-up network. Answer B is incorrect because the browser is using the remote server as its gateway (which is incorrect) and will not be able to connect to the Internet. Answer C is incorrect because the issue is about connecting to remote computers, not computers connecting to the user's computer. You would check the box if you wanted others to access the Internet through your computer. Answer D is incorrect because it wouldn't affect whether the user could access the Internet.

4. Answer A is correct. Because it will interfere with the operation of file sharing and other VPN functions, you should not enable WF on VPN connections. Answer B is incorrect because, by default, the option is already enabled. Answer C is incorrect because you would have the same problems with WF. Although it seems that answer D would work, nothing in the scenario suggests that it is possible to dial in to the network.

5. Answer B is correct. When you make an L2TP with IPSec connection, an IPSec policy is automatically created to specify that the Internet Key Exchange (IKE) will use certificate-based authentication during the negotiation of security settings for L2TP. This means that both the L2TP client and L2TP server must have a computer certificate (also known as a machine certificate) installed before a successful L2TP-over-IPSec connection can be established. Answer A is incorrect because Microsoft does not recommend frequent use of preshared key authentication, because the authentication key is stored, unprotected, in the IPSec policy. Preshared key methodology is provided only for interoperability purposes and to adhere to the IPSec standards set forth by the Internet Engineering Task Force (IETF). Answer C is incorrect because pass-through authentication is for access to resources, not the negotiation of security settings. Answer D is incorrect because IAS performs centralized authentication, authorization, auditing, and accounting of connections for dial-up and VPN remote access and demand-dial connections; it does not negotiate security settings.

6. Answer A is correct. To ensure that the Dynamic Host Control Protocol (DHCP) service does not assign a conflicting IP address, you must edit the Registry and change the STOP value to 192.168.0.200. You would then assign to the printers static IP addresses from the range above 192.168.0.200, including 192.168.0.201 through 254. Answer B is incorrect because the value expressed in the answer would not allow enough addresses for the clients on the network. Answer C is incorrect because the DHCP scope is hard-coded and cannot be modified. Answer D is incorrect because the server IP addresses would not be in the DHCP scope.

7. Answers A and B are correct. You must install a computer certificate on the remote access router because you are using Smart Cards. You must also configure remote access on the remote access router that remote clients can connect to. Answer C is incorrect because it would cause the remote clients to not be able to connect to the Internet. Answer D is incorrect because it would cause the remote clients to have connectivity problems if ICF is installed.

8. Answer A is correct. Any service that you want to provide for remote clients must be enabled on the Services tab of the Advanced Settings page on the WF VPN Properties dialog box. Answer B is incorrect because the FTP service option must be selected, not cleared. Answer C is incorrect because the scenario clearly indicates that users are able to connect to the website, so the option had to have been checked. Answer D is incorrect because that would cause the users to not be able to connect to the website, which is not what you want.

9. Answer D is correct. When TCP/IP outbound connections exceed the hard-coded (and unchangeable) threshold under SP2, an outbound connection queue is created and the outbound connections are resolved at an undocumented rate of speed. Answer A is incorrect because Event ID 4226 is not associated with an excessive number of inbound TCP/IP connections. Answer B is incorrect because Event ID 4226 is not associated with TCP/IP Raw Socket connections. Answer C is incorrect because Event ID 4226 is not associated with the behavior of the MSDTC. Answer E is also incorrect because Event ID 4226 is not associated with the behavior of the MSDTC.

10. Answer B is correct. The default filename for the Windows Firewall log file is Pfirewall.log and its default location is the %windir% folder, which is usually the c:\Windows folder. Answer A is incorrect because the default log filename is not Wfirewall.txt. Answer C is incorrect because the default log filename is not Wfirewall.txt. Answer D is incorrect because the default log filename is not Wfirewall.log. Answer E is incorrect because even though the default log filename is Pfirewall.log, it is not located in the %windir%\Wfirewall folder by default. Answer F is incorrect because the default log filename is not Winfwlog.txt.

Need to Know More?

 Microsoft Corporation. *Microsoft Windows XP Professional Resource Kit*, 2nd ed. Redmond, WA: Microsoft Press, 2003. ISBN 0735619743. This all-in-one reference is a compilation of technical documentation and valuable insider information that computer-support professionals and administrators can reference to install, customize, and support Windows XP.

 Microsoft Corporation. *Microsoft Windows 2000 Professional Resource Kit*. Redmond, WA: Microsoft Press, 2000. ISBN: 1576108082. This book reviews the core aspects of TCP/IP and the related protocol tools.

 Search the Microsoft TechNet CD (or its online version through www.microsoft.com) and the Windows 2000 Professional Resource Kit CD using the keywords "RAS", "L2TP", "PPTP", "VPN", "WF", and "ICS", "Windows Firewall", "netsh command", "Windows Security Center", "COM", "DCOM", "Distributed Transaction Coordinator", "Raw Sockets", "SP2", and "Service Pack 2".

Practice Exam I

1. You have a multiprocessor Windows XP Professional workstation. You are running a SQL Server database application on your server and a customized SQL client application on your workstation. You also run a custom Internet client application on your machine. You notice that performance sometimes is sluggish. You open Task Manager and see that one processor is being used much more than the other. What should you do to increase performance?

   O A. Set the processor affinity for the applications in Task Manager.

   O B. Add more RAM.

   O C. Increase the size of your pagefile.

   O D. Add another processor.

2. You have a file that is encrypted. You want to use EFS file sharing to add one of your team members, Bob, to the file. How should you accomplish this?

   O A. You cannot. EFS does not support file sharing between multiple users on a single file.

   O B. You must place the users in a group first, and then you will have the opportunity to add Bob.

   O C. You first must encrypt the folder where the file is, and then you will be able to add Bob.

   O D. File sharing is enabled through a new button in the UI.

3. Anne recently installed Windows XP onto a relatively small drive C: and is concerned about unnecessary use of storage space on drive C:. Anne knows that the default document folder, My Documents, is on drive C:, and she uses her computer extensively to create and edit digital photos, vector-based graphic art, and desktop publishing (DTP) files. Knowing that these types of documents can quickly consume a lot of disk storage space, she moves the data files to a different drive volume that has lots of available disk space. In addition, she creates a volume mount point, called Art, on drive C: under the My Documents folder; it references the new folder where she has moved all the files. What should Anne do for this to be successful?

   ○ A. Anne should ensure that the host drive is formatted with NTFS.

   ○ B. Anne should ensure that the mounted drive is formatted with NTFS.

   ○ C. Anne should ensure that the mounted drive is on a dynamic disk.

   ○ D. All of the above.

   ○ E. None of the above.

4. Bob is a member of the Sales group, a member of the Engineering group, and a member of the Marketing group. A server in the domain, SRV1, has a shared folder named STUFF with Allow Read NTFS permissions for the Sales group. Also on SRV1 is a shared folder named TECH with Allow Modify NTFS permissions for the Marketing group. The Engineering group needs access to both folders. Bob tries to create a file in the TECH folder but is denied access. What should you do to remedy the situation without giving Bob excessive permissions?

   ○ A. Make Bob a member of the Engineering group.

   ○ B. Make Bob a member of the Administrators group.

   ○ C. Remove Bob from the Marketing group.

   ○ D. Change the Deny Write permission for the Engineering group to Allow Modify on the TECH folder.

5. You have 250 Windows XP Professional computers in various OUs in your domain. You have 100 remote Windows XP Professional computers that use VPN connections to connect to the corporate LAN. You are concerned about the security of the files in certain folders, so you set up a hidden share called SECRET$. In the folder is a file named Hrdays.txt. You want to monitor this file to prevent unauthorized changes with the least amount of administrative effort. What should you do?

   ○ A. Enable auditing and select Account Management.

   ○ B. Enable auditing and select Directory Service Access.

   ○ C. Enable auditing and select Object Access.

   ○ D. Use Network Monitor.

6. John is the network administrator for ACME High, Inc., an international rope company. It has 1,500 print devices distributed throughout the enterprise. ACME High uses Internet Connection Sharing (ICS) in its company to provide Internet access to its users. John is having problems doing this with his Windows XP Professional workstation computers and enlists the help of Microsoft. The Microsoft technical support engineer tells John to enable the built-in support account. John does so and tries to use Remote Desktop. The Microsoft technical support engineer is still unable to connect to John's computer. What should John do next? (Check all correct answers.)

- ❏ A. Edit the local policy setting in User Rights to enable Deny Access from Network.
- ❏ B. Edit the local policy setting in User Rights to enable Deny Log On Locally.
- ❏ C. Edit the local policy setting in User Rights to disable Deny Access from Network.
- ❏ D. Edit the local policy setting in User Rights to disable Deny Log On Locally.

7. You are the administrator for a small office network of 15 workstations that participate in a workgroup. All the users are using Windows XP Professional computers. You share a printer and a volume on a Windows XP Professional computer for office documents. Intermittently, people are not able to print. How should you resolve the issue?

- ○ A. Install the printer on a Windows 2000 Server.
- ○ B. Install a printer pool.
- ○ C. Change the network protocol to NetBEUI.
- ○ D. Install Active Directory.

8. You are the administrator of a medium-sized network. On a Windows XP Professional workstation that one of your users is assigned to, you need to modify the Boot.ini file and restart the computer, starting only the essential services needed to boot. How would you accomplish this with the least amount of administrative effort?

- ○ A. Use SYSEDIT.
- ○ B. Use MSCONFIG.
- ○ C. Modify Boot.ini manually.
- ○ D. Use DXDIAG.

9. You work for an international carpet company and are responsible for the network in the Latin American region. You need to create documents using both English and Spanish. How would you accomplish this with the least amount of administrative effort?

   ○ A. Install the Microsoft Select version of Windows XP Professional on all the client computers.

   ○ B. Install the Spanish version of Windows Office XP on all the client computers.

   ○ C. Click the Language icon in the system tray notification area and select Spanish.

   ○ D. Purchase Spanish-language keyboards for the client computers in the Latin American region.

10. You are the administrator for a company that hires many employees who have accessibility issues. Many of the employees have problems holding down two keys at once. Which accessibility option should you enable?

    ○ A. High Contrast

    ○ B. FilterKeys

    ○ C. MouseKeys

    ○ D. StickyKeys

11. You are the administrator of a medium-sized network. You use offline files on your laptop to help optimize your efficiency. You attempt to modify a document, but the document does not appear in your Offline Files folder. How should you resolve the issue with the least amount of administrative effort? (Check all correct answers.)

    ❏ A. Select Manual Caching of Documents.

    ❏ B. Select Automatic Caching of Documents.

    ❏ C. Select Automatic Caching of Programs and Documents.

    ❏ D. Copy all the files to your laptop and copy them back to the server.

    ❏ E. Open the file the next time you are connected to the server.

12. You are the manager of a help desk team at a soft drink company. Your users use Windows 98 computers and participate in a Windows NT 4 Server domain. The company has decided to purchase new computers and adopt Windows XP Professional for the desktop users. Most of your users will require all their settings from their old computers to be migrated to their new computers. What should you do to accomplish this task with the least amount of administrative effort?

    ○ A. Use the File and Settings Transfer Wizard.

    ○ B. Use the Active Directory Migration Tool.

    ○ C. Use the Windows Backup and Restore Wizard.

    ○ D. Use the Automated System Restore (ASR) utility with the Windows Backup program.

    ○ E. Copy all the files from the old computer to the server and then copy them back to the new computer.

13. You are installing a new device on your computer. You make a backup of the System State. After installing the device and rebooting, everything works as it should. Six months later, you notice that the manufacturer has updated the driver for the device. You download the new driver and select Install from This Location. After you reboot and log on, the device no longer works. What should you do to get the device to work again with the least amount of administrative effort?

○ A. Boot into Safe Mode, remove the driver, boot normally, and reinstall the previous driver.

○ B. Use the Driver Rollback feature.

○ C. Use the Last Known Good Configuration feature.

○ D. Use System Restore.

14. You install security patches on your Windows XP Professional computer to prevent malicious users from attacking your system. After installing the patches and rebooting, you receive a series of checksum error messages. What tool should you use to help resolve this issue?

○ A. Hfnetchk.exe

○ B. Sigverif.exe

○ C. Eventtriggers.exe

○ D. Boot into Safe Mode

15. You've just installed Windows XP Professional by accepting all the default settings. You want to be able to send and receive faxes from the fax modem installed on your Windows XP Professional computer. What do you need to do to set up this feature?

○ A. Double-click the Fax icon in the Printers and Faxes window and use the Fax Console to configure the Fax service.

○ B. Install a third-party fax program such as WinFax Pro.

○ C. First, open the Services Console, right-click the Fax service, and select Start. Next, double-click the Fax icon in the Printers and Faxes window and use the Fax Console to configure the Fax service.

○ D. Click Start, Control Panel, Add or Remove Programs. Click Add/Remove Windows Components, select the Fax Services entry, click Next, and follow the onscreen instructions to complete the installation. Use the Fax Console to configure the Fax service.

16. You are currently in an area where the power is not reliable. There are long periods of time when there is no electricity. You need your laptop computer to power down in a fashion that protects it from a serious power failure. You need to ensure that if you do power down, your computer is returned to its previous state as quickly as possible without losing any information. Which power option should you choose?

○ A. Standby

○ B. Hibernate

○ C. Shut Down

○ D. Restart

17. You are the administrator for a law firm that has 30 users who use laptops with Windows XP Professional installed. One of the partners, Bob, uses a docking station to access network resources while at work. He calls you and reports that every time he boots up from home, he gets error messages concerning his network interface card (NIC). He does not receive those errors when he boots his computer at work. What should you do to resolve Bob's issue?

○ A. Use Hardware Profiles and create one profile that includes the drivers for the NIC and one profile that disables the drivers for the NIC.

○ B. Use Hardware Profiles and disable the NIC for Profile 1.

○ C. Have Bob boot into Safe Mode while at home.

○ D. Have Bob boot normally while at work and boot into Safe Mode with Networking while at home.

18. You've just performed a default installation of Internet Information Services (IIS) 5.1 on your Windows XP computer. You go to set up an FTP site for some users at your company by clicking Start, All Programs, Administrative Tools, Internet Information Services. In the Internet Information Services Console, you see the Default Web Site and the Default SMTP Virtual Server containers; however, no container is present for the Default FTP Site. What do you need to do to enable the FTP Server feature for Windows XP Professional?

○ A. Install Windows 2000 Server, because the FTP Server feature is not available under Windows XP Professional.

○ B. Click Start, Run, type in `Services.msc`, click OK, and right-click the FTP Server service to start it and to set it to Automatic startup.

○ C. Click Start, Control Panel, Add or Remove Programs. Click Add/Remove Windows Components, select the Internet Information Services (IIS) entry, and click Details. Mark the check box for File Transfer Protocol (FTP) Service, click OK, click Next, and follow the onscreen instructions to complete the installation.

○ D. Purchase and install the Plus! Pack for Windows XP or download and install the Windows XP Professional Resource Kit tools.

19. You have a desktop with Windows XP Professional installed on it that contains three hard disks, and you want to ensure that you will be able to continue working if any one of the drives ceases to function properly. What should you do to accomplish this? (Check all correct answers.)

❏ A. Convert from basic to dynamic disks.

❏ B. Implement disk spanning.

❏ C. Implement disk striping with parity.

❏ D. Implement disk mirroring.

❏ E. Format the disk and install Windows 2000 Server.

20. You upgrade a Windows 98 computer with a single drive and single partition to Windows XP Professional, and you want to use the Encrypting File System (EFS). When you attempt to encrypt a folder, the option is not available. What should you do to accomplish this with the least amount of administrative effort?

    ○ A. Format the drive with the NTFS file system.

    ○ B. Convert the drive to the NTFS file system.

    ○ C. Install Windows 2000 Server.

    ○ D. Run the CIPHER command from the command prompt.

21. You are the administrator for a banking company. Your network environment is currently supported by a Windows Active Directory domain with 300 Windows XP Professional workstations. Currently, the users save all their documents and files in their personal folders on a file server named FSRVR1. You notice that drive space is becoming an issue on FSRVR1, and you decide to implement disk quotas. You give a certain user, User5, a quota of 20MB. Later, you look at his personal folder and see he is currently occupying 55MB of disk space. You check to see that disk quotas have been set up properly and enabled. You also verify that there is a quota entry for User5 and that the quota setting denies user access if the quota is exceeded. You verify that all the information is correct. What should you check next?

    ○ A. Check to see if User5 is a member of the Domain Administrators group.

    ○ B. Check to see if User5 is a member of the Server Operators group.

    ○ C. Check to see if the drive where the user's folders are located is formatted with NTFS.

    ○ D. Check to see if User5 is a member of the domain.

22. You want to back up *only* your system files and create a floppy disk to recover your system in case of a failure, but when you start the Backup or Restore Wizard, you do not have this option. What should you do to accomplish this with the least amount of administrative effort?

    ○ A. In the wizard, select All Information on This Computer.

    ○ B. In the wizard, select Let Me Choose.

    ○ C. Select Advanced Mode and select Automatic System Recovery.

    ○ D. In the wizard, select Everyone's Documents and Settings.

23. You are the manager of application development for a custom software company. The developers' program builds (versions) are tested daily. The files of the old versions are backed up and stored to tape. One build caused a stop error screen. You need to restore the old build using the old files. Using the Windows Backup or Restore Wizard, which restore option should you choose?

    ○ A. Do Not Replace the File on My Computer

    ○ B. Replace the File on Disk Only if the File on Disk Is Older

    ○ C. Always Replace the File on My Computer

    ○ D. None of the above

24. You install an application on your Windows XP Professional server that installs a new service. After installing the application and rebooting, you log on normally and begin working. Suddenly, your system becomes unstable and you receive a stop error. You investigate the nature of the error and discover that it is caused by a driver and a service that the application uses. You need to remove the driver and the service that is causing the stop error. What should you do to successfully remove the driver and service so that you can return the computer to its previous state with the least amount of administrative effort?

- ○ A. Use the System Restore feature.
- ○ B. Boot into the Recovery Console and remove the driver and the service.
- ○ C. Boot into Safe Mode and remove the driver and the service.
- ○ D. Boot into the Last Known Good Configuration.

25. You are running two 16-bit applications, App16A.exe and App16B.exe. Your Windows XP Professional computer is also running two 32-bit applications, App32A.exe and App32B.exe. Each 16-bit application runs in its own memory space. You notice severe performance degradation on the system and you want to determine which application is causing the problem. Which tool is best suited to measure and monitor the operational efficiency of your system?

- ○ A. Task Manager
- ○ B. The Performance Logs and Alerts snap-in from the Performance Console
- ○ C. The System Monitor snap-in from the Performance Console
- ○ D. The Windows XP Event Log with auditing enabled for Process Tracking

26. You are the network administrator for a state bank. Security is of the highest priority, so you want to ensure that unauthorized access is kept to a minimum. You implement System and Group Policy to ensure a standard environment for your users, who work with various client operating systems. Your remote users use Windows XP Professional on their laptops. These users do not always log on to the Windows 2000 domain you have set up. These remote users' computers contain highly confidential information, and you want to prevent them from copying to floppy. How should you accomplish this task?

- ○ A. Make a copy of the default hardware profile on all the laptops, and then change the hardware profile on all the laptops to disable the floppy drive. Then delete the default hardware profile.
- ○ B. Create a group called Remote Users and then put it in an OU called Remote. Create a Group Policy that disables the floppy drives for users in the Remote OU.
- ○ C. Create a group called Remote Users and then create a System Policy that disables the floppy drive for everyone in the group.
- ○ D. Encrypt the remote users' hard drives.

27. You are the network administrator for ACME Metals, Inc. and have 20 Windows 2000 Servers, 300 Windows 2000 Professional workstations, 50 Windows XP Professional workstations, and 150 Windows 98 computers. You have a single Windows 2000 Active Directory domain and implement roaming profiles. You have a drive on a server called FSRVR1; you designate it as X and create a folder for your users called USERS. You share the folder as USERS. You want to use GPOs to manage the roaming profiles. You create a policy and specify the target location as `X:\folders`. You receive an error message. What should you do?

   O A. Specify the target location as `\\FSRVR1\users`.
   O B. Share the USERS folder with the name of PROFILE.
   O C. Move the USERS folder to the SYSVOL drive and share it as `%systemroot%\USERS`.
   O D. Do nothing. Select OK and proceed.

28. You are the system administrator and enterprise administrator for an engineering company. Your network is comprised of four Windows 2000 Active Directory domains. One of your assistants, Bob, is a domain administrator. Bob tries to log on to a remote Windows XP Professional computer, which is a member of the domain, using Remote Desktop but is unsuccessful. What should you do to ensure that Bob can log on using Remote Desktop without giving Bob unnecessary rights?

   O A. Remove and add Bob to the Domain Admins group.
   O B. Explicitly grant Bob's user account the capability to connect remotely.
   O C. Make Bob a member of the Enterprise Administrators group.
   O D. Give Bob the right to log on locally to the server.

29. You are a sales representative for a garage door company. You use Windows 95 on your laptop and use a dial-up connection to access your network via Remote Desktop to your Windows XP desktop computer at your office. You frequently get disconnected from your RDP session with your Windows XP computer. You sometimes are not able to reestablish a connection. What should you do?

   O A. Disable APM on the laptop.
   O B. Upgrade your operating system on the laptop to Windows XP.
   O C. Disable PPP.
   O D. Change the network interface card.

30. You have been recently hired as the lead help desk associate. The enterprise network has a Windows 2000 Active Directory domain, which has all new Windows XP Professional clients. You want to reduce the overall support costs, so you will use Remote Assistance to resolve many of the problem tickets that you will face in your company. What Remote Assistance options will your users have to use when they need to request assistance? (Check all correct answers.)

   - ❑ A. Email
   - ❑ B. MSN Messenger
   - ❑ C. Sending a file
   - ❑ D. Internet Explorer

31. As the lead help desk associate, you receive many trouble tickets in a day. As you are going through the tickets and open an invitation for help, you receive a message that the invitation has expired. The request came from an officer of the company and you need to help this person. How should you resolve this as quickly as possible?

   - ○ A. Change the expiration time and connect to the remote computer.
   - ○ B. Send a message to the officer to resend the invitation.
   - ○ C. Connect to the remote computer via Remote Desktop, bypassing the security.
   - ○ D. Change your system time and open the invitation again.

32. You are the network administrator for a corporate network whose environment does not have an Internet connection. Your company's growth is demanding that you develop a way to assist them with user issues in an efficient manner. You would like to use Remote Assistance in conjunction with Windows Messenger to accomplish this task. What other service must be in place before your solution will function properly?

   - ○ A. Exchange
   - ○ B. DNS
   - ○ C. Microsoft .NET Passport
   - ○ D. Remote Desktop

33. You are the network administrator for a corporate network of three divisions: Marketing, Sales, and Engineering. You have a Windows 2000 domain with three child domains named after the divisions. Each division has a different configuration for its computers, and you create a template from which to create answer files, as well as multiple answer files for each division. You need to deploy 300 Windows XP Professional computers using Remote Installation Services (RIS) while ensuring that each answer file cannot be altered. What should you do to accomplish the task with the least amount of administrative effort?

   ○ A. Set NTFS permissions on the template to Everyone READ.

   ○ B. Set NTFS permissions on each SIF answer file to Everyone READ.

   ○ C. Set NTFS permissions on the \RemoteInstall directory to Everyone READ.

   ○ D. Set NTFS permissions on the %systemroot% directory to Everyone READ.

34. You are the system administrator of a network that has a root Windows 2000 Active Directory domain with two child domains. You have several OUs with each domain. To help with the administration of the domains, you want to give Bob, one of your assistants, the capability to add computers, users, and groups to OUs. Bob later reports that he is unable to add computers to the OUs. What should you do to resolve this issue with the least amount of administrative effort and without giving Bob unnecessary rights?

   ○ A. Give Bob the Create All Child Objects permission in the Delegation of Control Wizard.

   ○ B. Make Bob a member of the Enterprise Administrators group.

   ○ C. Give Bob the Full Control permission in the Delegation of Control Wizard.

   ○ D. Make Bob a member of the Domain Administrators group.

35. You are the IT manager for an automobile manufacturer that is opening a new branch in Phoenix. You want to use RIPrep and create an answer file. After running RIPrep, you want to create the answer file, as well as put the answer file in the correct location to ensure a successful unattended installation. What should you do?

   ○ A. Place the file in the Sysvol directory.

   ○ B. Place the answer file in the \RemoteInstall directory.

   ○ C. Place the answer file in the %systemroot%\system32 directory.

   ○ D. Do nothing.

36. Your company has opened a new branch in New York. You need to purchase 300 more computers. You use three vendors, purchasing 100 computers from each. You image one system, run RIPrep, and then attempt to apply this image to the rest of the systems. When you do this, 200 machines get a stop error. What should you do to accomplish the task of imaging all 300 machines with the least amount of administrative effort?

   - ○ A. Copy the `Hal.dll` file from the source machine and place it in the `\i386` directory.
   - ○ B. Run RIPrep on one machine per vendor and use the corresponding image on the target computers.
   - ○ C. Run an unattended installation with a UDF file for all 300 computers.
   - ○ D. Run an unattended installation with a UDF file for each vendor.

37. You have 200 client computers that need Windows XP Professional and 20 applications. After installation of Windows XP Professional and the applications, you run RIPrep on the Windows XP Professional computer that contains two partitions, C and D. The applications reside on the D partition. When you attempt to run RIPrep and restore the image to the target computer, none of the applications are installed and you receive several error messages. How should you resolve this issue in the least amount of time?

   - ○ A. On the source machine, reinstall the applications on the C partition and then rerun RIPrep.
   - ○ B. Run RIPrep on each partition individually.
   - ○ C. On the target machines, create a D partition and install the applications.
   - ○ D. Run an unattended installation with a UDF file.

38. You work at an OEM called SBU Industries. For all computers that you sell, you use a SYSPREP image that has Windows XP Professional. This image is used on all computers and then shipped out. Customers are complaining about strange entries in the system log. What should you do to resolve the issue?

   - ○ A. Run Sysprep –reseal.
   - ○ B. Run Sysprep –factory.
   - ○ C. Run Sysprep –pnp.
   - ○ D. Run Sysprep –quiet.

39. You are the lead IT associate in your company. You and your team have finally upgraded your network to a purely Windows 2000 environment. All file, DNS, DHCP, and WINS servers are running Windows 2000 Server. All applications and services have been upgraded to use only DNS name resolution. You have decommissioned all WINS servers. What should you do next to optimize the network?

   - ○ A. Decommission your DNS servers.
   - ○ B. Disable NetBIOS over TCP on your servers.
   - ○ C. Decommission your DHCP servers.
   - ○ D. Disable TCP/IP on your servers.

40. You are the IT manager of an international plastics company. You have a team of 20 personnel, 5 of which are spread out over Latin America. Your assistant in Mexico, Tom, has a file server called Srv1 whose IP address is 206.109.180.10. Srv1 is relocated to Houston and a new IP address is assigned, which is 206.109.50.18. You manually change this information in DNS. Later, Tom reports that he cannot connect to Srv1. You check DNS and everything appears to be in order. What should you do next?

　○　A. Run IPCONFIG /renew and then IPCONFIG /release.

　○　B. Restart the DNS server.

　○　C. Run IPCONFIG /flushdns.

　○　D. Restart the DHCP server.

41. You recently bought a retail copy of Windows XP Professional for your own personal home use. You enjoy using it and are learning new features. As you surf the Web, you notice that you have to authenticate and reauthenticate at several sites. What can you do so that you might not have to authenticate and reauthenticate at different websites?

　○　A. Enable cookies in your browser.

　○　B. Sign up for .NET Passport services.

　○　C. Disable cookies in your browser.

　○　D. Set the security level for the Internet zone to Low.

42. You want to host a family website from your home on your Windows XP Professional workstation, enabling your family to access the website and add content via FTP. You create the site, register its name, and enable Internet Connection Firewall (ICF). Later, you receive reports that your family can access the web page without problems, but no one can upload their files. What can you do to resolve the issue? (Check all correct answers.)

　❑　A. Ensure that the FTP box on the Services tab of the Advanced Settings page of the ICF properties is checked and 20 is the number in the External Port box.

　❑　B. Ensure that the FTP box on the Services tab of the Advanced Settings page of the ICF properties is cleared and 21 is the number in the Internal Port box.

　❑　C. Ensure that the FTP box on the Services tab of the Advanced Settings page of the ICF properties is checked and 21 is the number in the Internal Port box.

　❑　D. Ensure that the FTP box on the Services tab of the Advanced Settings page of the ICF properties is cleared and 20 is the number in the External Port box.

43. You have a Windows XP Professional computer, XPM1, that is a member of the CORP.com domain. You want to use Internet Connection Sharing (ICS) on the computer to provide Internet access for your corporate clients. You also want to provide security and thus decide to enable Internet Connection Firewall (ICF) to protect your network from hackers. You enable ICS, but cannot enable ICF. What should you do?

   ○ A. Ensure that you are using a VPN connection for the ICS configuration.

   ○ B. Ensure that the network bridge is established.

   ○ C. Ensure that you are attempting to configure ICF on the proper interface.

   ○ D. Remove XPM1 from the domain.

44. You are the administrator for a national bank, and you will be installing 300 Windows XP Professional computers. During the installation, you want to ensure that you have the most current drivers and files available. Which of the following should you use to accomplish your task?

   ○ A. Dynamic Update

   ○ B. Windows Update

   ○ C. Automatic Update

   ○ D. Winnt /update

45. You are migrating a user's settings from her Windows 98 computer to a new Windows XP computer. You want to use the User State Migration Tool to ensure that the settings are migrated correctly. Which command should you use first?

   ○ A. Scanstate

   ○ B. Loadstate

   ○ C. Update

   ○ D. Miguser

46. You are the administrator for a national bank and you have bought new Windows XP Professional computers for your department. You need to transfer data as well as other settings. You want to create a customized solution to migrate all users' settings as quickly as possible with the least amount of administrative effort. What should you use?

   ○ A. ADMT

   ○ B. USMT

   ○ C. File and Settings Transfer Wizard

   ○ D. Lap Link

47. You are the administrator for a national bank and your current protocol requires that you use Smart Cards for both local and remote user logons. You want the remote users to be able to use the Internet while connected to the corporate LAN. What must you do to ensure the successful connection of your clients? (Check all correct answers.)

   ❑   A. Install a computer certificate on the remote access router.

   ❑   B. Configure remote access on the remote access router.

   ❑   C. Enable a Smart Card logon process for the domain.

   ❑   D. Enable the Extensible Authentication Protocol (EAP) and configure the Smart Card or other certificate (TLS) EAP type on the remote access router computer.

48. You are the CIO of a startup Internet company. You want to provide VPN connectivity to your clients. You have strict requirements, which require that both the IP header traffic and the packets are encrypted. You want to use L2TP with IPSec for the encryption method it offers. You have enabled RAS on a server in your Windows 2000 domain. You are concerned with security, so you enable NAT. When a client tries to connect, he receives the following error message: The remote computer does not support the required data encryption type. What should you do to resolve the issue?

   ○   A. Remove NAT from your server.

   ○   B. Remove IPSec.

   ○   C. Change L2TP to PPTP.

   ○   D. Enable the Extensible Authentication Protocol (EAP).

49. You want to ensure that the correct protocols are being used in your VPN configuration. You are using IPSec for packet filtering, and you also require encrypted transmissions. What authentication protocol should you use?

   ○   A. PPTP

   ○   B. L2TP

   ○   C. EFS

   ○   D. EAP

50. You are a Microsoft Certified Partner and you are concerned with Windows Product Activation. You change hardware frequently in your office. You want to be able to activate your copies of Windows XP Professional without having to call Microsoft frequently to activate the same copy because of the hardware changes. What should you do?

   ○   A. Do nothing. Use the Volume License Key that comes with your copy of the software.

   ○   B. Change only the RAM.

   ○   C. Make an image of the computer you will change and reapply the image after the hardware change.

   ○   D. You must activate every time.

Answers to Practice Exam I

1. A	**18.** C	**35.** D
2. D	**19.** A, C, E	**36.** B
3. A	**20.** B	**37.** A
4. D	**21.** A	**38.** A
5. C	**22.** C	**39.** B
6. C, D	**23.** B	**40.** C
7. A	**24.** A	**41.** B
8. B	**25.** B	**42.** A, C
9. C	**26.** A	**43.** C
10. D	**27.** A	**44.** A
11. B, E	**28.** B	**45.** A
12. A	**29.** A	**46.** B
13. B	**30.** A, B, C	**47.** A, B, C, D
14. B	**31.** B	**48.** A
15. D	**32.** A	**49.** B
16. B	**33.** C	**50.** A
17. A	**34.** A	

Question 1

Answer A is correct. By setting the processor affinity for applications, you can increase performance by distributing processing load. Answer B is wrong because database applications are processor intensive more than they are memory intensive. Answer C is incorrect because increasing the size of your pagefile will not increase performance when it is indicated that lack of performance is due to processing power. Answer D is incorrect because processors must be put in pairs and Windows XP Professional supports only up to two processors.

Question 2

Answer D is correct. In Windows XP, EFS does support file sharing between multiple users on a single file. After selecting the Advanced Properties of an encrypted file, Bob may be added by selecting the Details button. Answer A is incorrect because EFS does support file sharing between multiple users on a single file. Answer B is incorrect because support for the use of groups on encrypted files is not provided in Windows XP. Answer C is incorrect because support for multiple users on folders is not provided in Windows XP.

Question 3

Answer A is correct. A volume mount point must be placed in any empty folder of the host NTFS volume. The volume must be formatted with NTFS. Answer B is incorrect because although the host volume must be formatted with NTFS, the volume to be mounted can be formatted in any Windows XP-accessible file system, including NTFS, FAT16, FAT32, CDFS, or UDF. Answer C is incorrect because a mounted drive can exist on either a dynamic disk or a basic disk. Answer D is incorrect because answers B and C are incorrect. Answer E is incorrect because answer A is correct.

Question 4

Answer D is correct. Because Bob is a member of groups that have at least write permission to the folder, it must be that Bob has a Deny permission to the folder. Therefore, the permission should be changed to Modify. Answer A is incorrect because the Engineering group would grant no more rights to Bob's account. Answer B is incorrect because making Bob a member of the Administrators group would be conferring excessive rights to his account. Answer C is incorrect because removing his account would take rights away.

Question 5

Answer C is correct. Enabling auditing and selecting Object Access will log when a user tries to read or otherwise make changes to any object you select to audit. Answer A is incorrect because Account Management will monitor when a user account property changes and not when an object is accessed. Answer B is incorrect because Directory Service Access auditing will not inform you when a folder or file is accessed. Answer D is incorrect because Network Monitor will allow you to see packets on the network, but not allow you to see who is accessing a folder or file with the least amount of administrative effort.

Question 6

Answers C and D are correct. By default, the built-in support account is disabled and locked out of access to the local computer. The account must be enabled and allowed to connect to the computer across the network and given the right to log on locally to the computer.

Question 7

Answer A is correct. Windows XP Professional can accept a maximum of only 10 concurrent connections. In the scenario given, occasionally, too many people are trying to print and are not able to connect to the printer. You need to install a server. Answer B is incorrect because the same issue would be encountered with too many concurrent connections. Answer C is incorrect because NetBEUI is not a protocol offered natively on Windows XP Professional. Answer D is incorrect because Active Directory requires Windows 2000 Server or Windows .NET Server.

Question 8

Answer B is correct. MSCONFIG enables you to change the Boot.ini file and select which services you want to start from one window. Answer A is incorrect because SYSEDIT will not allow you to do either task. Answer C is incorrect because although modifying Boot.ini manually will accomplish what you need, it does not do it with the least amount of administrative effort. Answer D is incorrect because DXDIAG does not help you accomplish either task.

Question 9

Answer C is correct. Windows XP enables you to add support for languages without the need for installing language versions of the software. In Control Panel, click Regional Settings and add the languages desired. Answers A and B are incorrect because neither accomplishes the task with the least amount of administrative effort. Answer D is incorrect because simply connecting a foreign language keyboard will not add support for foreign languages.

Question 10

Answer D is correct. StickyKeys enables persons who have problems holding down two keys at once to perform this action by simply touching the specified key and then touching the combination key that is desired. Answer A is incorrect because High Contrast is for persons who have sight disabilities. Answer B is incorrect because FilterKeys is an option that instructs the keyboard to ignore brief or repeated keystrokes, which helps people who have problems touching one key at a time. Answer C is incorrect because MouseKeys is an option to enable persons who have problems using a mouse or other pointing device to use the keyboard instead.

Question 11

Answers B and E are correct. Automatic Caching makes every file that someone opens from your shared folder available to them offline. However, this setting does not make every file in your shared folder available to them offline—only those files that are opened. Files that are not opened are not available offline. Therefore, you should open the files you desire the next time you are connected to the server. Answer A is incorrect because Manual Caching of Documents provides offline access only to those files that someone using your shared folder specifically (manually) identifies. This caching option is ideal for a shared network folder containing files that are to be accessed and modified by several people. This is the default option when you set up a shared folder to be used offline. Answer C is incorrect because this option provides offline access to shared folders containing files that are not to be changed. This caching option is ideal for making files (DLL and EXE) available offline that are read, referenced, or run, but that are not changed in the process. Answer D is incorrect because it does not resolve the issue with the least amount of administrative effort.

Question 12

Answer A is correct. The File and Settings Transfer Wizard is useful in a corporate network environment for employees who get a new computer and need to migrate their own files and settings without the support of an IT department or help desk. Answer B is incorrect because the Active Directory Migration Tool (ADMT) is the tool that simplifies the process of migrating users, computers, and groups to new domains. It is not used to migrate files and desktop settings. Answer C is incorrect because although the files may be backed up, the setting will not be. Answer D is incorrect because the ASR utility is only for reinstalling Windows XP with all its previous settings. Answer E is incorrect because it does not accomplish the task with the least amount of administrative effort.

Question 13

Answer B is correct. When you update a driver, a copy of the previous driver package is automatically saved in a special subdirectory of the system files. If the new driver does not work properly, you can restore the previous driver by accessing the Driver tab for the device in the Device Manager and clicking Roll Back Driver. Driver Rollback permits only one level of rollback (only one prior driver version can be saved at a time); this feature is available for all device classes, except printers. Answer A is incorrect because it does not accomplish the task with the least amount of administrative effort. Answer C is incorrect because after you have successfully logged on, the Last Known Good Configuration no longer contains the previous configuration data. Using it would do no good. Answer D is incorrect because although you can accomplish the same result, it does not accomplish the task with the least amount of administrative effort; Rollback Driver is faster and easier.

Question 14

Answer B is correct. The Signature Verification Tool (Sigverif.exe) determines whether a file has been assigned a digital signature and whether that file has been modified after being assigned that digital signature. You should check the list of unsigned drivers and then check whether the driver manufacturer has an updated driver that is digitally signed. Answer A is incorrect because although you can use the Hfnetchk.exe tool to assess the patch status for the Windows XP operating system, it will not help resolve the issue of system instability. Answer C is incorrect because the Eventtriggers.exe utility causes an action to occur based on specific events logged by the Event Viewer, but this does not resolve the issue of system instability. Answer D is incorrect because although booting into Safe Mode may help in giving an environment in which to work, it does not help resolve the issue of system instability.

Question 15

Answer D is correct. The Fax service is not installed by default, as is the case with Windows 2000 Professional; you must install it separately. Answer A is incorrect because the Fax service is not installed by default. Answer B is incorrect because you do not need to purchase a third-party solution for faxing under Windows XP Professional. Answer C is incorrect because the Fax service is not installed by default; therefore, the Fax service is not present until you install it separately or as an optional component during the Windows XP Professional installation routine.

Question 16

Answer B is correct. Although it takes longer to bring your computer out of Hibernate than out of Standby, you should put your computer into Hibernate mode. The Hibernate feature saves everything in memory onto disk, turns off your monitor and hard disk, and then turns off your computer. When you restart your computer, your desktop is restored exactly as you left it. Answer A is incorrect. Although Standby is particularly useful for conserving battery power in portable computers, Standby does not save your desktop state to disk; a power failure while on Standby can cause you to lose unsaved information. Answer C is incorrect because although the information is saved, it will not return you to the last state you were in when you shut down. Answer D is incorrect because a Restart is the same as a shutdown: essentially saving information, but not returning you to the last state you were in when you shut down.

Question 17

Answer A is correct. A hardware profile is a set of instructions that tells Windows which devices to start when you start your computer or which settings to use for each device. By default, every device that is installed on your computer at the time you install Windows is enabled in the Profile 1 hardware profile. You would disable the NIC, create a profile, and name it something different, thus providing two profiles. Answer B is incorrect because by disabling the NIC for Profile 1, the computer would never be able to access network resources when the computer is using the docking station. Answer C is incorrect because booting into Safe Mode may disable other necessary drivers. Answer D is incorrect because booting into Safe Mode with Networking will cause the system to load the NIC driver, and that will cause the errors again.

Question 18

Answer C is correct. The FTP Server service is not installed by default when you install IIS 5.1. Answer A is incorrect because the FTP Server feature is available for Windows XP Professional. Answer B is incorrect because the FTP Server service is not installed by default when you install IIS 5.1, so the FTP service does not get installed by default. Therefore, it would not be listed as a currently installed service. Answer D is incorrect because the FTP Server service is not available in the Plus! Pack nor in the Windows XP Resource Kit; the Resource Kit for Windows XP Professional contains only documentation, not software utilities or add-ons.

Question 19

Answers A, C, and E are correct. Windows XP Professional does not support fault-tolerant volumes. You will need to format the disk, install Windows 2000 Server, convert the disks from basic to dynamic, and then implement disk striping with parity. Answer B is incorrect because disk spanning is not fault tolerant. Answer D is incorrect because disk mirroring is not available in Windows XP Professional, and it doesn't protect in the event that the third disk fails.

Question 20

Answer B is correct. Although Windows XP Professional supports EFS, EFS requires NTFS, and converting the partition to NTFS will accomplish the task. Answer A is incorrect because if you were to format the drive, you would lose all information contained on the drive. Answer C is incorrect because Windows XP Professional is already installed, and it is a more recent version of Windows than Windows 2000. Answer D is incorrect because the drive needs to have the NTFS file system, and running the CIPHER command will yield no results.

Question 21

Answer A is correct. Members of the Domain Administrators group, by default, have an unlimited quota. If User5 were a member of the Domain

Administrators group, he would have an unlimited quota. Answer B is incorrect because had User5 been a member of the Server Operators group, the quota would have an effect on him. Answer C is incorrect because the capability to set quotas would not have been available under the FAT or FAT32 file system. Answer D is incorrect because making a quota entry for User5 would not have been possible if the user were not already a member of the domain.

Question 22

Answer C is correct. To back up *only* the system files and create a floppy disk to recover your system, you will need to select Advanced Mode from the Backup or Restore Wizard window and then select Automatic System Recovery (ASR). Answer A is incorrect because this option will back up *all* files on the computer, not just the system files. Answer B is incorrect because although you can back up just the system files, the option to create a recovery disk is not available. Answer D is incorrect because this option will just back up the Documents and Settings folders of all the users, not the system files. Nor will this option enable you to create a recovery disk.

Question 23

Answer B is correct. When restoring from a backup, the backup program checks for files with the same name. You must then choose what happens when the program encounters a file with the same name. You have three options: Do Not Replace the File on My Computer, Replace the File on Disk Only if the File on Disk Is Older, and Always Replace the File on My Computer. In this case, because the previous build worked, you should replace the file. Answer A is incorrect because you should replace whatever file(s) caused the system to become unstable. Answer C is incorrect because it is just for the current build that you want to replace the file(s). Answer D is incorrect because if you do not choose one of the three options, the restore process cannot proceed.

Question 24

Answer A is correct. System Restore automatically creates restore points every 24 hours and every time that you install a new application. Answer B is incorrect because even though you can disable devices and services from the Recovery Console, doing so takes much more effort than performing a system restore. Answer C is incorrect for the reason that answer B is incorrect, because this also applies to Safe Mode. Answer D is incorrect because the existing settings become the Last Known Good Configuration after you successfully log on to the computer.

Question 25

Answer B is correct. The Performance Logs and Alerts snap-in enables you to track or chart specific system performance metrics over a period of time. Answer A is incorrect because the Task Manager displays only real-time performance data, and you cannot create a history file from Task Manager. Answer C is incorrect because System Monitor either displays system performance counters in real-time or displays the results of a log file created by the Performance Logs and Alerts snap-in—it does not create a history file on its own. Answer D is incorrect because enabling auditing enables you only to track successes and/or failures of specific events—it does not track performance history using performance counters.

Question 26

Answer A is correct. By disabling the floppy in the hardware profile, you prevent your users from copying information to a floppy, and by deleting the default (or original) profile, the users do not have a choice of hardware profiles to choose from at bootup. Answer B is incorrect because the users do not always log on to the domain. Thus they will not get the policy and will not have access to their floppy drive. Answer C is incorrect because although System Policies are written to the Registry, they are designed for down-level clients such as Windows NT and 9X, not Windows 2000 or XP. There is no certainty that the Registry change will be consistent across platforms. Answer D is incorrect because the users will still have access to their floppy drive.

Question 27

Answer A is correct. The message that you would receive states that unless the target location is local to the user, the user will not receive the roaming profile. You should use the universal naming convention (UNC) format to specify the location. Answer B is incorrect because the name of the share will not ensure that users receive their roaming profile. Answer C is incorrect because the issue of the target folder still keeps users from accessing their roaming profiles. Answer D is incorrect because if you proceed through the message, the users' machines will look for the X:\users share. If it doesn't exist, users will be given an error message that states their roaming profile cannot be located.

Question 28

Answer B is correct. The capability to connect remotely using Remote Desktop requires explicit permission. You must allow users to connect remotely using Remote Desktop before they will be able to do so. Answer A is incorrect because putting Bob in the Domain Admins group will not ensure that Bob has permission to use Remote Desktop. Answer C is incorrect because it would give Bob unnecessary rights for the enterprise, and it would not ensure that he could use Remote Desktop. Answer D is incorrect because although Bob would have rights to log on locally, he still lacks permission to use Remote Desktop.

Question 29

Answer A is correct. This problem can occur because Remote Desktop was not designed to communicate with APM services. To work around this behavior, you should disable APM on the laptop. Answer B is incorrect because changing the operating system will not change the behavior of the Remote Desktop services. If the laptop is an older system, the hardware may be the limiting factor because it might support only APM. Answer C is incorrect because disabling PPP might prohibit the laptop from connecting to the network via dial-up. If you can't connect to the remote network, you will not be able to connect to the remote desktop. Answer D is incorrect because the problem is not NIC related. Changing the NIC will result in having the same connectivity problem.

Question 30

Answers A, B, and C are correct. Remote Assistance enables a user to share control of his or her computer with someone on a network or the Internet. An administrator or friend can view the user's screen and control the pointer and keyboard to help solve a technical problem. The fastest way to use Remote Assistance is via Windows Messenger. You can also initiate Remote Assistance sessions via email, by launching the email client directly from the Remote Assistance Invitation Wizard. Alternatively, you can fill out a form and save it as a file. The file can be emailed, shared, or hand-delivered to the desktop support personnel. Answer D is incorrect because you cannot send an invitation to someone for Remote Assistance through IE.

Question 31

Answer B is correct. After the invitation has expired, the request is void. The person who made the request must resend the invitation for assistance. Answer A is incorrect because after the invitation has expired, the request is void. You cannot change the expiration of an invitation. Answer C is incorrect because unless you have permission to connect to the remote computer, you will not be able to connect via Remote Desktop. Answer D is incorrect because this could cause other applications or invitations to behave incorrectly.

Question 32

Answer A is correct. With Exchange in place, you can establish the Instant Messaging service to function as your internal account service. This will allow communication internally, without having an Internet connection. Answer B is incorrect because DNS is not needed for Remote Assistance to work. Answer C is incorrect because this is possible only with an Internet connection in place. Answer D is incorrect because Remote Desktop is a feature of Windows XP and not a necessary service for Remote Assistance to function.

Question 33

Answer C is correct. The answer files are kept in the \RemoteInstall directory, and setting it to Everyone READ will ensure that none of it gets changed. Answer A is incorrect because although the template from which you make the answer files is read-only, it has no effect on the answer files that are created from it. You will need to change the permissions of the answer files themselves. Answer B is incorrect because not everyone should have Read access to all answer files. Answer D is incorrect because changing the permissions of the %systemroot% directory to Everyone READ could cause serious damage and problems to your system. The system itself will not be able to write to it, and your system may become unstable.

Question 34

Answer A is correct. Giving Bob the Create All Child Objects permission will give him the necessary rights to complete the task you gave him without giving him unnecessary rights. Answer B is incorrect because making Bob an Enterprise admin would definitely be giving him unnecessary rights. Answer

C is incorrect because giving Bob Full Control permission in the Delegation of Control Wizard of an OU gives him too much latitude. All he needs to do is create computer objects and nothing more. Answer D is incorrect because making Bob a Domain administrator is giving him unnecessary rights.

Question 35

Answer D is correct. When the RIPrep Wizard is run, a new directory is created where the image file is uploaded, and the answer file is located there. Because this happens automatically, there is nothing you should do. Answer A is incorrect because moving the answer file will result in a failed installation, and placing it in the Sysvol directory would not help the installation. Answer B is incorrect because moving the answer file from its default location will result in a failed installation, and placing it in the \RemoteInstall directory for RIPrep would not suffice either. Answer C is incorrect because moving the file from its default location will result in a failed installation, and moving it into the system32 folder would not help the installation.

Question 36

Answer B is correct. Although RIPrep supports different hardware between the source computer used to create the RIPrep-based OS image and the destination computer that will install the image, the HAL must still be the same or a stop error will occur. Running RIPrep from each vendor's computer will ensure the proper HAL for the remaining installations. Answer A is incorrect because simply copying the Hal.dll file to the \i386 directory will result in the same problem. Answer C is incorrect because running an answer file with a UDF for all 300 computers would be time consuming and would not require the least amount of effort. Answer D is incorrect because only one UDF is needed for all computers.

Question 37

Answer A is correct. The RIPrep utility supports only a single disk with a single partition (C: drive); therefore, the applications must be installed on the C partition. Answer B is incorrect because the RIPrep utility supports only a single disk with a single partition. Answer C is incorrect because this process would be very time consuming. Answer D is incorrect because it does not resolve the issue in the least amount of time.

Question 38

Answer A is correct. The Sysprep tool has new switches, one of them is -reseal. The -reseal switch clears the Event Viewer logs and prepares the computer for delivery to the customer. Answer B is incorrect because the -factory switch restarts the computer in Factory mode, which allows the installation of additional drivers and applications after the reboot that follows Sysprep.exe. It will not clear the event log. Answer C is incorrect because the -pnp switch forces Plug and Play to refresh the next time that the computer is restarted. It will not clear the event log. Answer D is incorrect because the -quiet switch runs Sysprep without displaying the onscreen messages; it will not clear the event log.

Question 39

Answer B is correct. Because you no longer use NetBIOS name resolution in your environment, you should disable the NetBIOS binding for the WINS client (TCP/IP). Answer A is incorrect because Active Directory and the computers in the enterprise depend on DNS to function correctly. Disabling DNS will bring your network down. Answer C is incorrect because the network clients are using DHCP to obtain the IP address to communicate on the network. Answer D is incorrect because TCP/IP is the protocol required for an Active Directory–based domain.

Question 40

Answer C is correct. Tom cannot connect to Srv1 because the information on his client contains cached information that is no longer valid. After he flushes this information and receives new information from the DNS server, he will be able to connect. Answer A is incorrect because this will release only IP information, not DNS cache information. Answer B is incorrect because the information is correct in DNS and the problem is with the client, not the DNS server. Answer D is incorrect because the issue is a name resolution issue and not an IP addressing issue.

Question 41

Answer B is correct. Microsoft Passport delivers the following two services: Passport Single Sign-In and Passport Express Purchase. The Passport Single

Sign-In service offers an authentication service that allows Passport users to use a single username and password for authenticated access to any website that employs Passport authentication. Answer A is incorrect because although cookies may help you log in to a site, you will still need to authenticate to the site when you return. Answer C is incorrect because disabling cookies will make it more difficult to authenticate with a site and will not fix the reauthentication issue. Answer D is incorrect because the security setting does not aid you in authenticating with a site, but may allow malicious users to abuse your system.

Question 42

Answers A and C are correct. Any service that you want to provide for remote clients must be enabled on the Services tab of the Advanced Setting page on the ICF VPN properties sheet. Both ports 20 and 21 need to be checked for the FTP communication to be successful. Answer B is incorrect because the FTP service option must be checked, not cleared. Answer D is incorrect because the option needs to be checked, not cleared.

Question 43

Answer C is correct. The public interface is the only interface that can be configured with ICF if you are using it in conjunction with ICS. Answer A is incorrect because either a VPN or dial-up connection is sufficient when using ICS. Answer B is incorrect because the network bridge would not solve this problem with regard to ICF not working. Answer C is incorrect because the computer can be in the domain and support both ICS and ICF.

Question 44

Answer A is correct. Dynamic Update ensures that the operating system files are up to date. Before the installation occurs, there needs to be a server configured with the latest updates from Microsoft's website. Answer B is incorrect because Windows Update contains compatibility updates, new device drivers, and other updates released for Windows XP Professional as they become available on the Windows Update website, not during installation. Answer C is incorrect because Automatic Update is an option for updating your computer without interrupting your web experience. These downloads are throttled to minimize impact to network responsiveness and are automatically resumed if the system is disconnected before an update is fully downloaded. After the update has been downloaded to the PC, the user can then choose to install it. This does not happen during installation. Answer D is incorrect because the Winnt /update command is used to slip-stream service packs into an installation of Windows XP. It does not ensure that the latest drivers are being installed.

Question 45

Answer A is correct. The User State Migration Tool consists of two executables (Scanstate.exe and Loadstate.exe) and four migration rule information files (Migapp.inf, Migsys.inf, Miguser.inf, and Sysfiles.inf). Scanstate.exe is the command that collects user data and settings. Answer B is incorrect because Loadstate.exe is used to deposit the information on the new Windows XP computer. Answer C is incorrect because it is not a part of the USMT, but rather the command for installing a service pack. Answer D is incorrect because it is one of the INF files used for the migration of the settings, not the command itself.

Question 46

Answer B is correct. The USMT is an excellent tool for customizing the migration of user settings in an efficient manner. With this option, you will be able to script the migration, as well as customize the migration files that determine which files, settings, and configurations are migrated. Answer A is incorrect because the Active Directory Migration Tool (ADMT) is the tool that simplifies the process of migrating users, computers, and groups to new domains. It is not used to migrate files and desktop settings. Answer C is incorrect because the File and Settings Transfer Wizard is useful in a corporate network environment for employees who get a new computer and need to migrate their own files and settings without the support of an IT department or help desk. Answer D is incorrect because it does not accomplish the task with the least amount of administrative effort.

Question 47

All answers are correct. Answer A is correct because you must install a computer certificate on the remote access router because you are using Smart Cards. Answer B is correct because you must also configure remote access on the remote access router that remote clients can connect to. Answer C is correct because the remote clients need to be able to connect to the domain. Answer D is correct because EAP is the authentication protocol necessary for Smart Card use.

Question 48

Answer A is correct. IPSec does not work with NAT; therefore, you will receive the error message. You will need to remove NAT. Answer B is incorrect because your requirements are that you have packet filtering; therefore, you must not remove IPSec. Answer C is incorrect because your requirements are that the IP headers be encrypted, and PPTP does not do this. Answer D is incorrect because EAP is the protocol used for Smart Cards.

Question 49

Answer B is correct. L2TP is an IETF draft specification for encapsulating and transmitting non-IP traffic through TCP/IP networks. L2TP uses IPSec for encrypted transmission. Answer A is incorrect because PPTP will not encrypt IP traffic. Answer C is incorrect because EFS (Encrypting File System) is used to encrypt files, not IP traffic. Answer D is incorrect because EAP is the authentication protocol for Smart Cards.

Question 50

Answer A is correct. Microsoft Certified Partners and CTECs receive a special Volume License Key (VLK) that enables them to activate a copy of the software as many times as needed, without having to call Microsoft. Only by using the VLK is this an option. Answer B is incorrect because it is not feasible to change only the RAM. You may have to change the hard drive or system board. Answer C is incorrect because a change in hardware may cause system instability if you make and try to apply an image on the machine. Answer D is incorrect because by using VLK, you will not have to do this.

Practice Exam II

1. You are the network administrator for a bank, and all their workstations have just been upgraded to Windows XP SP2. The bank's managers are very concerned about the confidentiality and privacy of the
bank's customers. What can you do to guard against data theft when so
many employees and customers now carry around ultra-portable USB
2.0 "flash" drives?

   ○ A. Disable the USB Mass Storage device driver on all workstations, except
   for those users' computers who really need to use USB storage.

   ○ B. Configure the `WriteProtect` value setting in the Registry and set its
   value data to 0.

   ○ C. Configure the `StorageDevicePolicies` value setting in the Registry and
   set its value data to 1.

   ○ D. Configure the `WriteProtect` value setting in the Registry and set its
   value data to 1.

2. You are the network administrator for Magazine Publishers, Inc. All
workstation computers have Windows XP SP2 installed. Management
does not want anyone to use WebDAV over unencrypted connections,
such as port 80, to publicly available websites on the Internet. How do
you turn off basic authentication?

○ A. Create a new DWORD value in the Windows XP SP2 Registry under `HKEY_LOCAL_MACHINE\System\CurrentControlSet\Services\WebClient\Parameters`. Name the new DWORD value `DisableBasicOverClearChannel` and set its value data to 1.

○ B. Create a new DWORD value in the Windows XP SP2 Registry under `HKEY_CURRENT_USER\Software\Microsoft\Windows\CurrentVersion\Internet Settings`. Name the new DWORD value `UseBasicAuth` and set its value data to 1.

○ C. Create a new DWORD value in the Windows XP SP2 Registry under `HKEY_CURRENT_USER\Software\Microsoft\Windows\CurrentVersion\Internet Settings`. Name the new DWORD value `DisableBasicOverClearChannel` and set its value data to 0.

○ D. Create a new DWORD value in the Windows XP SP2 Registry under `HKEY_CURRENT_USER\Software\Microsoft\Windows\CurrentVersion\Internet Settings`. Name the new DWORD value `DisableBasicOverClearChannel` and set its value data to 1.

3. You are the system administrator for a restaurant supply company. Your network comprises about 300 workstations. Some of the workstations are still running Windows 95, some are running Windows 98SE, others are running Windows 2000 Professional, and the newer machines are running Windows XP SP2. All Windows 95 computers have Internet Explorer (IE) 3.0 installed, the Windows 98SE PCs have IE 4.0 installed, and all Windows 2000 and Windows XP SP2 computers have IE 6.0 installed. Management likes the idea of installing the Remote Desktop Web Connection on the new servers that the company has purchased. The new servers are equipped with Windows Server 2003 and Internet Information Services (IIS) 6.0. Which of the company's workstations can successfully connect to the new servers using the Remote Desktop Web Connection feature?

○ A. All of the company's workstations.

○ B. All of the company's workstations except the Windows 95 and the Windows 98SE computers.

○ C. All of the company's workstations except the Windows 95 computers.

○ D. Only the Windows XP computers.

4. As the network administrator for a small retail store, you need to make sure that certain Windows XP computers can connect to the existing Novell NetWare servers using the Client Services for NetWare (CSNW) feature. The entire facility is wired using Category 5e Ethernet cabling. Which of the following network protocols and frame types must you install and configure on the Windows XP computers to enable them to communicate with your NetWare 5.x servers?

○ A. IPX/SPX using frame type 802.3.

○ B. IPX/SPX using frame type 802.2.

○ C. IPX/SPX using frame type 802.5

○ D. TCP/IP with no frame type needed.

5. You are the new help desk technician at ACME Toy Company. One of the sales reps, John, asks you to take a look at his computer. He tells you that "all of a sudden" he cannot connect to the Internet. He thinks that perhaps the company's T1 line is down or maybe he has some bad spyware on his machine. No one else has complained about their Internet access this morning, so it's probably not the T1 circuit. You go to his computer and view his Network Connection Details window, as shown in Figure 12.1. Based on the figure, what do you think is the problem with John's Internet connectivity?

Figure 12.1   The Network Connection Details window for John's workstation.

○ A. The TCP/IP subnet mask is incorrect.

○ B. The IP addresses for the WINS servers are missing.

○ C. The IP addresses for the DNS servers are incorrect because they are private, nonroutable addresses.

○ D. The Default Gateway IP address is incorrect.

6. You are the Lead Help Desk Associate and as you review the trouble tickets that have been assigned to you, you receive a message that the VP of Sales is having trouble with his notebook computer connecting to the corporate LAN. He tells you that he changed the IP settings last night when he took the PC home. You look at his TCP/IP settings on his Windows XP machine and you see that his computer has an Alternate Configuration set up with the correct user-configured IP settings for the corporate network. Because the company is small, DHCP is not used on the corporate network; each PC is manually configured for TCP/IP. What is the fastest thing that you can do, without changing IP settings, so that the user's computer will connect to the corporate network?

○ A. On the Internet Protocol (TCP/IP) Properties dialog box, configure the Alternate Configuration to obtain an IP address automatically.

○ B. On the Internet Protocol (TCP/IP) Properties dialog box, configure his notebook PC to obtain an IP address automatically on the General tab.

○ C. On the Internet Protocol (TCP/IP) Properties dialog box, set the Alternate Configuration to Automatic Private IP Address.

○ D. On the Internet Protocol (TCP/IP) Properties dialog box, change the Preferred and Alternate DNS server IP addresses to match the corporate network settings.

7. You are the network administrator for a rapidly growing company. You have to design private, nonroutable IP schemes for the company's various offices around the world. Which of the following IP addresses are reserved as nonroutable over the Internet?

❑ A. 192.168.122.100

❑ B. 191.168.122.100

❑ C. 10.33.254.252

❑ D. 172.31.254.252

❑ E. 172.16.254.252

❑ F. 10.15.31.254

❑ G. All of the above

8. You are the network administrator for an international clothing manufacturer. You are researching the new features for Windows XP SP2 so that you can report back this information to your IT managers. Which of the following statements are *not* true about the Windows Firewall (WF)? Choose two.

❑ A. WF monitors and blocks incoming and outgoing Internet traffic.

❑ B. WF allows you to create exceptions to the traffic that is configured to be blocked.

❑ C. You can control WF settings via local and group policy.

❑ D. WF is turned off by default under the domain profile.

❑ E. WF is turned off by default under the standard profile.

❑ F. WF applies to all network interface cards (NICs)installed on a computer; you cannot enable or disable WF separately for individual NICs.

9. You are the senior network administrator for All Cities Rent-A-Wreck, Inc. All computers in the company have been upgraded to Windows XP Professional Service Pack 2. You notice that one of the workstations in the accounting department is receiving the Event ID 4226 in its System Event Log. What does this error message mean?

○ A. Too many inbound connections are overwhelming the Windows Firewall.

○ B. TCP/IP Raw Sockets are timing out because of the new security restrictions in SP2.

○ C. Too many TCP/IP outbound connection requests have been generated; therefore, an outbound connection queue has been created.

○ D. The Microsoft Distributed Transaction Coordinator (MSDTC) is blocking unauthenticated network RPC requests.

10. You are the IT manager for an automobile manufacturer. You are trying to understand the tighter security controls that Microsoft has placed on DCOM programs and services as compared to COM programs and services. Which of the following are the major differences in permissions for COM versus DCOM under SP2? Choose two.

❑ A. Local RPC services (COM) may be launched and activated only by authenticated users.

❑ B. Network RPC services (DCOM) may be launched and activated only by authenticated users.

❑ C. Network RPC services (DCOM) may be launched and activated only by members of the Administrators group.

❑ D. Local RPC services (COM) may be launched and activated by authenticated and unauthenticated users.

❑ E. The Local Launch permission and the Local Activation permission for COM-based programs and services are allowed for the Everyone group by default.

11. As the IT administrator for Nuts 'R' US, Inc., you are concerned about viruses, trojans, worms, spyware, and other malware infiltrating your network and your systems. After you upgrade your workstations to Windows XP SP2, what are the default startup values for the Alerter service and the Messenger service? Choose two.

❑ A. Messenger service = Automatic.

❑ B. Messenger service = Manual.

❑ C. Alerter service = Automatic.

❑ D. Alerter service = Manual.

❑ E. Messenger service = Disabled.

❑ F. Alerter service = Disabled.

12. As the IT Manager for a mid-sized accounting firm, you've heard that Windows XP SP2 changes several default settings compared to the original RTM (Release to Manufacturing) and SP1 versions. Which of the following statements is true regarding Internet Connection Sharing under SP2?

○ A. ICS has been renamed WIS—Windows Internet Sharing.

○ B. Internet Connection Sharing is turned on by default.

○ C. ICS uses NAT only for its DHCP allocator service.

○ D. ICS has been replaced by the Windows Firewall.

13. Alexis is the IT administrator for a locally well-known mortgage broker. Because they store confidential identification information, management is extremely concerned with security; they are equally concerned about potential data theft that could lead to identity theft of their clients and potential data destruction that could occur because of an infiltration of malware on their network. Brett, the president of the company, has heard that Windows XP SP2 offers some type of extended protection from rogue applications. Which of the following statements are true about Data Execution Prevention (DEP) under SP2? Choose two.

- ❑ A. DEP is enabled only on 64-bit systems.
- ❑ B. DEP monitors only essential operating system programs and services.
- ❑ C. DEP is available on systems equipped with AMD processors.
- ❑ D. DEP is enabled only on 32-bit systems.
- ❑ E. DEP can monitor all programs and services.
- ❑ F. You can exclude specific programs from being monitored by DEP.
- ❑ G. DEP is disabled on systems equipped with Intel processors.

14. You are the lead IT associate in your company. One of the power users in the company just installed an "updated" printer driver on his Windows XP computer, and now he reports that he cannot print. Which of the following procedures will result in reestablishing the user's previous configuration so that he can once again print?

- ○ A. Use Driver Rollback.
- ○ B. Use the System Restore feature to restore the computer to an earlier time when the proper printer driver was installed and working.
- ○ C. Restore the computer's data backup media set from the previous night.
- ○ D. Create a manual system restore point.

15. You are the network administrator for a used car dealer. Alison, one of the salespeople, reports that she is experiencing various problems with her brand new computer. You review some basic aspects of her PC, and when you open Device Manager on her machine, you see the display as shown in Figure 12.2. Based on the Device Manager display, what exactly are the issues, if any, on Alison's Windows XP Professional computer? Choose two.

- ❑ A. Her wireless network card is disabled.
- ❑ B. Her USB Mass Storage device is disabled.
- ❑ C. Her wireless network card is not functioning.
- ❑ D. Her USB Mass Storage device is not functioning.
- ❑ E. Her FireWire (1394) network adapter is not functioning.
- ❑ F. Her FireWire (1394) mass storage device is disabled.

16. Service Pack 2 (SP2) for Windows XP introduces some new features for wireless networking. Which of the following wireless networking features are available under SP2 that were previously not available prior to SP2? Choose three.

- ❑ A. Native support for Wi-Fi Protected Access (WPA) encryption.
- ❑ B. Wireless Provisioning Services (WPS).
- ❑ C. The Wireless Network Setup Wizard.
- ❑ D. Support for the 802.11g standard.
- ❑ E. Support for the 802.11a standard.
- ❑ F. Native support for Wired Equivalent Privacy (WEP) encryption.

17. You are the help desk technician for an accounting firm. You have been researching the differences between Windows XP SP2 and pre-SP2 releases. When you click the Windows Update button on the Hardware tab of the System Properties dialog box, which of the following options can you choose from under Windows XP SP2? Choose two.

- ❑ A. Ask Me to Search Windows Update Every Time I Connect a New Device
- ❑ B. Download Updates for Me, but Let Me Choose When to Install Them
- ❑ C. Notify Me but Don't Automatically Download or Install Them
- ❑ D. Turn Off Automatic Updates
- ❑ E. If My Device Needs a Driver, Go to Windows Update Without Asking Me

18. As the network administrator for 21ˢᵗ Century Architects, Inc., you need to design the software configuration for 30 new dual-processor computers, which will be running the 64-bit version of Windows XP Professional. The new computers will replace the older single-processor workstations for the firm's architects who use computer-aided-design (CAD) software applications extensively. Each new PC will be equipped with 2GB of RAM and will have four SATA hard disks installed, configured as follows:

> ➤ Disk 0—10GB running at 5400RPM set up as the System partition

> ➤ Disk 1—20GB running at 7200RPM set up as the boot partition

> ➤ Disk 2—80GB running at 7200RPM set up as the programs partition

> ➤ Disk 3—80GB running at 7200RPM set up as the data partition

To optimize these new computers for performance, following Microsoft best practices, how should you configure the paging file settings?

- ○ A. Set up four paging files of approximately 750MB each. Place one paging file on each of the four disks.
- ○ B. Set up two paging files of approximately 1.5GB each and place one on Disk 2 and one on Disk 3.
- ○ C. Set up one paging file of approximately 3GB and place it on Disk 3.
- ○ D. Set up one paging file of approximately 3GB and place it on Disk 1.
- ○ E. Set up two paging files of approximately 1.5GB each and place one on Disk 1 and one on Disk 3

19. You are the IT administrator for the local branch of a national bank. The bank is purchasing new computers for all managers at the branch. Each new system will be equipped with a Pentium 4 CPU running at 2.6GHz, 1GB of RAM, and a 100GB SATA hard drive. Once a month, the bank managers need to run a custom application that runs better when CPU settings in Task Manager are increased for this application. In Task Manager, from the Processes tab, when you right-click the application's process, which of the following options can you select to improve the application's performance on a temporary, per incident basis?

- ○ A. Set Priority, Low
- ○ B. Set Priority, Realtime
- ○ C. Set Affinity, select a CPU
- ○ D. Set Affinity, High
- ○ E. Set Priority, AboveNormal

20. Tim is an IT consultant working on an installation of new workstations at a CPA firm. All workstations are being installed with Windows XP Professional SP2. Tim wants to make sure that the in-house system administrators will be able to copy valuable client data onto removable media in the event of a serious problem with one of the workstations assigned to the partners of the company. Tim installs the Recovery Console onto each of the new computers. What other steps does he need to take to allow data files to be copied from each of the Windows XP computers onto removable media when using the Recovery Console? Choose two.

   ❑ A. Enable the local policy named Recovery Console: Allow Floppy Copy and Access to All Drives and All Folders found in `Computer Configuration\Windows Settings\Security Settings\Local Policies`.

   ❑ B. At the Recovery Console command prompt, type `Set AllowRemovableMedia = TRUE` and press Enter.

   ❑ C. Disable the local policy named Recovery Console: Allow Floppy Copy and Access to All Drives and All Folders found in `Computer Configuration\Windows Settings\Security Settings\Local Policies`.

   ❑ D. At the Recovery Console command prompt, type `Set AllowRemovableMedia = FALSE` and press Enter.

   ❑ E. Leave all local policy settings at their default settings for the Recovery Console.

21. You are a trainer for new help-desk personnel at a law firm that has offices throughout the United States. As part of the curriculum that you need to teach your students, you must demonstrate in your classes how to use the WebDAV protocol to save Microsoft Word documents to the law firm's web servers that exist at each office and that are all connected via the firm's secure intranet. How can you demonstrate saving documents using WebDAV in Microsoft Office Word 2003?

   ○ A. Click File, Save as Web Page, click the Save In drop-down list box, select FTP Locations, type a filename for the document into the File Name box, and then click Save.

   ○ B. Click File, Save As, type the full UNC path and filename for the document into the File Name box (for example, `\\webserver\sharename\doc1.doc`), and then click Save.

   ○ C. Click File, Save As, type the full path and filename for the document into the File Name box (for example, `ftp://webserver/sharename/doc1.doc`), and then click Save.

   ○ D. Click File, Save As, type the full path and filename for the document into the File Name box (for example, `http://webserver/sharename/doc1.doc`), and then click Save.

22. You are the network administrator for a utility company and you need to plan out the hard disk configuration for new desktop and notebook computers that will be delivered in the next four weeks. Some of the new desktop and notebook computers will have Windows XP Home Edition installed. These PCs are earmarked for employees who will be telecommuting; these employees will be working remotely over a secure VPN tunnel from their homes. Some of the new computers will be notebook PCs for the managers who travel a great deal. The balance of the computers will be desktop machines running Windows XP Professional that will be used in-house. Each new desktop and notebook computer comes equipped with two physical hard drives installed. Ideally, management would like you to configure the two disks on each computer as a single large spanned volume. On which of the following new Windows XP computers can you set up such a configuration?

❏ A. On the Windows XP Home desktop computers.

❏ B. On the Windows XP Professional desktop computers.

❏ C. On the Windows XP Professional SP2 notebook computers.

❏ D. On the Windows XP Home SP2 notebook computers.

❏ E. On the Windows XP Professional dual-processor desktop computers.

❏ F. On the Windows XP Professional notebook computers using external FireWire (IEEE 1394) drives.

23. You've just been hired as the new network administrator for the Watertight Plumbing Company, Inc. Amy, who works in the accounting department, notifies you that her Windows XP Professional computer "just stopped working." You look at her PC and you find that Amy is correct; it won't even boot. As the first step in troubleshooting the problem, you want try to boot into the Recovery Console. How can you attempt to run the Recovery Console on Amy's computer since it does not even start?

○ A. Boot the PC from the Windows XP Professional CD-ROM and choose the first repair option presented.

○ B. Boot the computer to a command prompt and run the command `<CD-ROM Drive>\:winnt32.exe /cmdcons`.

○ C. Boot the PC from the Windows XP Professional CD-ROM and choose the second repair option presented.

○ D. Restart the computer, press the F8 key as computer is booting, and select Safe Mode Using Recovery Console from the Advanced Startup Menu options.

24. As the IT manager for an international cosmetics corporation, your enterprise spans the world with an assorted array of desktop operating systems. Your corporate standard is Windows XP Professional; however, hundreds of systems still run the original RTM version, hundreds of other systems have SP1 installed, and several hundred other systems are running SP2. Which of the following features can you use across all Windows XP computers throughout the enterprise? Choose three.

- ❑ A. IPSec
- ❑ B. ICS
- ❑ C. Enabling and disabling firewall settings per NIC
- ❑ D. `netsh` command
- ❑ E. Native firewall turned on by default
- ❑ F. Restricting outbound TCP traffic over Raw Sockets

25. You are a network administrator for your company and you have just installed SP2 for Windows XP on 25 computers. Unfortunately, one of the 25 computers does not boot properly under SP2. This "problem child" PC can only boot into the Recovery Console. Can you uninstall SP2 and return the computer back to its old self again?

- ○ A. No, you cannot uninstall SP2 unless you can boot into Windows and go to the Add/Remove Programs icon in the Control Panel.
- ○ B. Yes, you can uninstall SP2 by booting into the Recovery Console, logging on to the computer, and running the `spuninst.exe` program from the `%systemroot%\$NTServicePackUninstall$\spuninst` folder.
- ○ C. Yes, you can uninstall SP2 by booting into the Recovery Console, logging on to the computer, and running the `spuninst.exe` program from the `%systemroot%\System32\$NTServicePackUninstall$` folder.
- ○ D. Yes, you can uninstall SP2 by booting into the Recovery Console, logging on to the computer, and running the `spuninst.exe` program from the `%systemroot%\$NTServicePackUninstall$` folder.

26. You are the network administrator for a hospital running a Windows 2000 domain. You need to protect the patients' personal information because of increased public concerns about the privacy of medical records for individuals. You implement System and Group Policy to ensure a standard environment for your users, who work with various client operating systems. You have remote salespeople who sell hospital services that use Windows XP Professional on their laptops. Although the users' laptops are configured to use a VPN connection, the salespeople do not always log on to the domain. To ensure that no confidential information is copied to the floppy drive, how should you accomplish this task?

- ○ A. On each of the laptops, copy the default hardware profile and rename it **DISABLE FLOPPY**. Configure the profile to disable the floppy drive. Then delete the default hardware profile.
- ○ B. Create a global group called SALES and then put it in an OU called SALES. Create a Group Policy that disables the floppy drives for users in the SALES OU.
- ○ C. Create a local group called Remote Users on each laptop and then create a System Policy that disables the floppy drive for everyone that logs on to the laptop.
- ○ D. Run the `cipher` command on the remote users' hard drives.

27. You are the network administrator for TriColor, Inc. The network consists of a single Windows 2000 Active Directory domain that contains 50 Windows 2000 Servers, 270 Windows 2000 Professional workstations, 100 Windows XP Professional workstations, and 50 Windows 98 computers. You have a fileserver named FILESRV1. In Computer Management you designate a drive the letter of Y and create a folder for your users called USERS. You share the folder as USERS. You have implemented roaming user profiles and you want to use GPOs to manage the roaming profiles. You create a policy and specify the target location as `Y:\folders`. You receive an error message. What should you do?

   O A. Modify the target location to point to `\\FILESRV1\users`.

   O B. Right-click the USERS folder, select Sharing and Security, select Share This Folder and type **PROFILE**. Click OK twice.

   O C. Cut the USERS folder from its location and paste it to the SYSVOL drive and share it as `%systemroot%\USERS`.

   O D. Do nothing. Select OK and proceed.

28. You are the system administrator for a Food and Beverage company. Your network comprises several Windows 2000 Active Directory domains. Each domain contains a single domain administrator. You are a member of the Enterprise Admins group. One of your co-workers, Sally, is the domain administrator in one of the child domains. Sally tries to log on using Remote Desktop to a remote Windows XP Professional computer, which is a member of her domain, but the logon is unsuccessful. What should you do to ensure that Sally can log on using Remote Desktop without giving her unnecessary rights?

   O A. Delete Sally's account. Re-create it and add her account to the Enterprise Admins global group.

   O B. In the local security policy, grant Sally's user account the capability to access the server from the network.

   O C. Create a duplicate account for Sally and add the account to the Enterprise Administrators group.

   O D. In the local security policy, grant Sally's user account the capability to access the server interactively.

29. You are a sales representative for a shoe manufacturer. You use Windows 98 on your laptop. To connect to your company's private network, you use a dial-up connection and Remote Desktop to your Windows XP desktop computer at your office. You infrequently get disconnected from your RDP session with your Windows XP computer. You sometimes are not able to reestablish a connection. What should you do?

   O A. Disable APM on the laptop.

   O B. Uninstall Windows 98 and install Windows XP on the laptop.

   O C. Disable PPP.

   O D. Reinstall the driver for the network interface card.

30. You have been recently hired in a company that has a Windows 2000 Active Directory domain, which has all new Windows XP Professional clients. Your position is the Lead Desktop Associate. To streamline efficiency, you will use Remote Assistance to resolve many of the problem tickets that are generated in your company. What Remote Assistance options will your users have to use when they need to request assistance? (Check all correct answers.)

❑ A. Outlook

❑ B. Instant Messaging

❑ C. Transmitting documents

❑ D. Web browser

31. You are the Lead Help Desk Associate. As you review the trouble tickets that have been assigned to you, you receive a message that the invitation for Remote Assistance has expired. The request came from an officer of the company and you need to help this person. How should you resolve this as quickly as possible?

○ A. Open the request and alter the expiration date. Then connect to the remote computer.

○ B. Send a request to the originator of the request to resend the invitation.

○ C. Using Remote Desktop, simply connect to the remote computer.

○ D. Change your system time on the remote computer and open the invitation again.

32. You are the network administrator for a rapidly growing company. You currently address user issues using a custom line of business application. You need to develop a way to assist your users' issues in a more efficient manner. Currently your company network environment does not have an Internet connection. You would like to use Remote Assistance in conjunction with Windows Messenger to accomplish this task. What other service must be in place before your solution will function properly?

○ A. SMTP

○ B. DNS

○ C. Single Sign-On

○ D. Remote Desktop

33. You are the network administrator for an international manufacturing company with locations in three countries: USA, Ireland, and Brazil. You have a Windows 2000 domain with three child domains named AMS, IRL, and BRZ. You have created an answer file template for each location because of the differences in configuration at each location. You need to deploy several Windows XP Professional computers using Remote Installation Services (RIS). What should you do to accomplish the task with the least amount of administrative effort while ensuring that each answer file remains unaltered?

○ A. Change the NTFS permissions on the template to Authenticated Users READ.

○ B. Create new SIF answer files for each location and set the NTFS permissions on each file to Everyone READ.

○ C. Set NTFS permissions on the \RemoteInstall directory to Everyone READ.

○ D. Set NTFS permissions C:\winnt to Everyone READ.

34. You are the system administrator of a network that has a single Windows 2000 Active Directory domain. You have several OUs in the domain. To help with the administration of the domains, you want to give Steve, one of your assistants, the capability to add computers, users, and groups to OUs. What should you do to allow your assistant to accomplish the tasks with the least amount of administrative effort and without giving Steve unnecessary rights?

○ A. Use the Delegation of Control Wizard to give your assistant the Create All Child Objects permission.

○ B. Add Steve's user account to the Enterprise Administrators group.

○ C. Use the Delegation of Control Wizard to give your assistant Full Control permission.

○ D. Add Steve's user account to the Domain Administrators group.

35. You are the IT manager for an automobile manufacturer that is opening a new branch in Los Angeles. You want to use RIPrep and create an answer file. You want to ensure that the answer file is placed in the correct location after running RIPrep. What should you do?

○ A. Copy all the pertinent files to the Sysvol directory.

○ B. Place the answer file in the \RemoteInstall directory.

○ C. Copy all the pertinent files to the %systemroot%\system32 directory.

○ D. Everything is in the correct place. Do nothing.

36. Your company has opened a new office in Phoenix. You have informed your vendor that you need to purchase 300 more computers. Your vendor replies that the manufacturer is upgrading the motherboard specs on the models that you ordered. You receive 100 computers that contain the older specification and 200 with the newer specification. You image one system, run RIPrep, and then attempt to apply this image to the rest of the systems. When you do this, 200 machines get a stop error. What should you do to accomplish the task of imaging all 300 machines with the least amount of administrative effort?

○ A. Place the Hal.dll file from the source machine in the \i386 directory of the target machine.

○ B. Run RIPrep on one machine of each vendor and use the corresponding image on the target computers.

○ C. Run an unattended installation and use the /udf parameter on each of the target computers.

○ D. Run an unattended installation and use the /udf parameter on one computer for each vendor.

37. You have several client computers that need Windows XP Professional and various applications. The computers have a single 80GB hard drive. Each drive is partitioned into two partitions: C and D. You install the operating system on partition C and the applications on partition D. After installation of Windows XP Professional and the applications, you run RIPrep. When you attempt to run RIPrep and restore the image to a target computer, none of the applications are installed and you receive several error messages. How should you resolve this issue in the least amount of time?

   O A. After reinstalling the applications on the C partition, rerun RIPrep on the source computer.

   O B. On each target computer, run RIPrep on the C partition.

   O C. On each target machine, create a D partition, run RIPrep on the D partition, and install the applications.

   O D. Run an unattended installation using the /udf parameter.

38. The training center where you work holds technical classes every week.Every week you need to reimage the computers for the next class that will be training the following week. Currently you use a SYSPREP image that has Windows XP Professional. This image is used on all computers and then the appropriate applications are installed depending on the class. In one of the classes, the students are reviewing the system log and report strange entries. Which parameter with the Sysprep command should you use?

   O A. -reseal

   O B. --verbose

   O C. -factory

   O D. -pnp

   O E. -quiet

39. You are the lead IT associate in your company. A mandate has come to optimize the network by upgrading to a purely Windows 2000 network infrastructure. You upgrade all file servers, DNS servers, and DHCP servers to Windows 2000 Advanced Server. You decommission all your WINS servers and upgrade all applications and services to use DNS name resolution only. What should you do next to optimize the network?

   O A. Disable the DNS server service on all your servers.

   O B. Disable NetBIOS over TCP on your servers.

   O C. Disable the DHCP service on all your servers.

   O D. Disable TCP/IP on your servers.

40. You are the network administrator for a water company. You have several teams, some of which are spread out over Canada. Tom, your assistant in Toronto, has a file server called Canuck1 whose IP address is 206.109.180.10. Canuck1 is relocated to Houston and a new IP address is assigned, which is 206.109.50.18. You manually change this information in DNS. Later, Tom reports that he cannot connect to Canuck1. You check DNS and everything appears to be in order. What should you do next?

   - ○ A. Run IPCONFIG /renew and then IPCONFIG /release.
   - ○ B. Restart TCP/IP.
   - ○ C. Run IPCONFIG /flushdns.
   - ○ D. Disable NetBIOS over TCP.

41. You recently bought a retail copy of Windows XP Professional for your own personal home use. You enjoy using it and are learning new features. As you surf the Web, you notice that you have to authenticate and reauthenticate at several sites. What can you do so that you might not have to authenticate and reauthenticate at different websites?

   - ○ A. Disable cookies in your browser.
   - ○ B. Sign up for .NET Passport services.
   - ○ C. Enable ActiveX scripting in your browser.
   - ○ D. Install Single Sign-On on your computer.

42. You want to host a family website from your home on your Windows XP Professional workstation, enabling your family to access the website and add content via FTP. You create the site, register its name, and enable Internet Connection Firewall (ICF). Later, you receive reports that your family can access the web page without problem, but no one can upload their files. What can you do to resolve the issue? (Check all correct answers.)

   - ❏ A. Ensure that the FTP box on the Services tab of the Advanced Settings page of the ICF properties is checked and 20 is the number in the External Port box.
   - ❏ B. Ensure that the HTTP box on the Services tab of the Advanced Settings page of the ICF properties is cleared and 80 is the number in the Internal Port box.
   - ❏ C. Ensure that the FTP box on the Services tab of the Advanced Settings page of the ICF properties is checked and 21 is the number in the Internal Port box.
   - ❏ D. Ensure that the HTTP box on the Services tab of the Advanced Settings page of the ICF properties is cleared and 80 is the number in the External Port box.

43. You have a Windows XP Professional computer, XPM1, that is a member of the CORP.com domain. You want to use Internet Connection Sharing (ICS) on the computer to provide Internet access for your corporate clients. You also want to provide security and thus decide to enable Internet Connection Firewall (ICF) to protect your network from hackers. You enable ICS, but cannot enable ICF. What should you do?

   ○ A. Ensure that you are using a VPN connection for the ICS configuration.

   ○ B. Ensure that ICF permissions are set to Everyone Full Control.

   ○ C. Ensure that you are attempting to configure ICF on the proper interface.

   ○ D. Ensure that you are using a VPN connection for the ICF configuration.

44. You are the administrator for a national bank and you will be installing 300 Windows XP Professional computers. During the installation, you want to ensure that you have the most current drivers and files available. Which of the following should you use to accomplish your task?

   ○ A. Dynamic Update

   ○ B. Software Update

   ○ C. Windows Update

   ○ D. Automatic Update

45. You are migrating a user's settings from her Windows 98 computer to a new Windows XP computer. You want to use the User State Migration tool to ensure the settings are migrated correctly. Which command should you use first?

   ○ A. Scanstate

   ○ B. Loadstate

   ○ C. Savestate

   ○ D. Miguser

46. You are the administrator for a national bank and you have bought new Windows XP Professional computers for your department. You need to transfer data as well as other settings. You want create a customized solution to migrate all users' settings as quickly as possible with the least amount of administrative effort. What should you use?

   ○ A. LDAP

   ○ B. USMT

   ○ C. GPMC

   ○ D. MMC

47. You are the administrator for a national bank and your current protocol requires that you use smart cards for both local and remote user logons. You want the remote users to be able to use the Internet while connected to the corporate LAN. You use a multihomed Windows 2003 Server as your router. What must you do to ensure the successful connection of your clients? (Check all correct answers.)

❑ A. Install a computer certificate on the remote access router.

❑ B. Enable Routing and Remote Access on the remote access router.

❑ C. Activate smart card logon process for the domain.

❑ D. Enable the Extensible Authentication Protocol (EAP) and configure the smart card or other certificate (TLS) EAP type on the remote access router computer.

48. You are the CIO of a startup Internet company. You want to provide VPN connectivity to your clients. You have strict requirements that both the IP header traffic and the packets are encrypted. You want to use L2TP with IPSec for the encryption method it offers. You have enabled RAS on a server in your Windows 2000 domain. You are concerned with security so you enable NAT. When a client tries to connect, he receives the following error message: The remote computer does not support the required data encryption type. What should you do to resolve the issue?

○ A. Disable NAT.

○ B. Uninstall IPSec.

○ C. Change L2TP to EAP.

○ D. Disable encryption.

49. You want to ensure the correct protocols are being used in your VPN configuration. You are using IPSec for packet filtering, and you also require encrypted transmissions. What authentication protocol should you use?

○ A. PPTP

○ B. L2TP

○ C. EFS

○ D. EAP

50. You are a Microsoft Certified Partner and you are concerned with Windows Product Activation. You change hardware frequently in your office. You want to be able to activate your copies of Windows XP Professional without having to call Microsoft frequently to activate the same copy because of the hardware changes. What should you do?

○ A. Do nothing. Use the Volume License Key that comes with your copy of the software.

○ B. Make hardware changes only to the RAM.

○ C. Change the system clock before activation.

○ D. You must activate every time.

Answers to Practice Exam II

1. D
2. D
3. C
4. B
5. D
6. B
7. A, C, D, E, F
8. A, F
9. C
10. B, C
11. E, F
12. C
13. C, E, F
14. B
15. A, D
16. A, B, C
17. A, E

18. B
19. E
20. A, B
21. D
22. B, E
23. A
24. A, B, D
25. B
26. A
27. A
28. B
29. A
30. A, B, C
31. B
32. A
33. C
34. A

35. D
36. B
37. D
38. A
39. B
40. C
41. B
42. A, C
43. C
44. A
45. A
46. B
47. A, B, C, D
48. A
49. B
50. A

Question 1

Answer D is correct because 1 is the proper value data for the WriteProtect Registry value in the StorageDevicePolicies subkey to make USB storage devices read-only under SP2. Answer A is incorrect because disabling the USB Mass Storage driver only for certain users' computers would not be very secure; users could go to the other computers that still had the driver installed to copy confidential information. Answer B is incorrect because the value data setting of 0 disables the USB WriteProtect feature. Answer C is incorrect because StorageDevicePolicies is the Registry subkey, not a value, that you must first create before you create the WriteProtect value setting to enable the WriteProtect feature.

Question 2

Answer D is correct. Under SP2, when you create the DWORD value `DisableBasicOverClearChannel` and set it equal to 1 for the Registry path `HKEY_CURRENT_USER\Software\Microsoft\Windows\CurrentVersion\Internet Settings`, you turn OFF basic authentication over unencrypted connections. Answer A is incorrect because the DWORD value `DisableBasicOver ClearChannel` does not belong under the `HKEY_LOCAL_MACHINE\System\ CurrentControlSet\Services\WebClient\Parameters` Registry key. Answer B is incorrect because the DWORD value `UseBasicAuth` does not belong under the `HKEY_CURRENT_USER\Software\Microsoft\Windows\CurrentVersion\ Internet Settings` Registry key. Answer C is incorrect because by setting the `DisableBasicOverClearChannel` value data to 0, you turn ON basic authentication over unencrypted connections, which is already the default setting under SP2.

Question 3

The correct answer is C. Because all of the company's workstations are installed with IE 4.0 or later, except for the Windows 95 computers, only the Windows 95 PCs cannot use the Remote Desktop Web Connection feature. Answer A is incorrect because the Windows 95 computers have IE 3.0 installed; you must use IE 4.0 or later to connect using the Remote Desktop Web Connection feature. Answer B is incorrect because even though the Windows 95 computers have only IE 3.0 installed, the Windows 98SE computers have IE 4.0 installed, so the Windows 98SE machines can use the Remote Desktop Web Connection feature. Answer D is incorrect because the

Windows 98SE computers, the Windows 2000 computers, and the Windows XP computers all have IE 4.0 or later installed; therefore, the Windows XP computers are not the only ones that can take advantage of the Remote Desktop Web Connection feature.

Question 4

The correct answer is B. For servers running NetWare versions 3.12 and later, you need to use the 802.2 frame type. Answer A is incorrect because the 802.3 frame type is for NetWare versions 2.x through 3.11. Answer C is incorrect because frame type 802.5 is reserved for Token Ring networks. Answer D is incorrect because the CSNW feature works only over the native NetWare IPX/SPX network protocol; it does not work over TCP/IP.

Question 5

The correct answer is D. In Figure 12.1, the Default Gateway IP address is the same as the IP address of the workstation, which is not the proper setting. The Default Gateway IP address should point to the proper router or firewall that connects to the Internet. Answer A is incorrect because the subnet mask appears to be correct for a private, nonroutable subnet of 192.168.x.y. Answer B is incorrect because WINS servers map NETBIOS names to IP addresses and vice versa; DNS servers map hostnames to IP addresses and vice versa. DNS is used on the Internet, not WINS. Answer C is incorrect because DNS servers can use either private, nonroutable IP addresses or public, routable IP addresses.

Question 6

Answer B is correct. The Alternate Configuration for TCP/IP does not take effect unless the Obtain an IP Address Automatically option is selected on the General tab. Answer A is incorrect because there is no option to obtain an IP address automatically on the Alternate Configuration tab for the TCP/IP Properties dialog box. Answer C is incorrect because selecting the option for Automatic Private IP Address removes any manually configured IP settings for the Alternate Configuration. Answer D is incorrect because both the Preferred and Alternate DNS server IP addresses can get assigned via the Alternate Configuration settings; also, changing the DNS server settings does not correct the other improper IP settings for this computer.

Question 7

Answers A, C, D, E, and F are all correct. The IP address schemes 192.168.x.y, 172.16.0.0 to 172.31.255.255, and 10.0.x.y are reserved as private and nonroutable by the bodies that govern the Internet. Each IP address listed in answers A, C, D, E, and F fall within the reserved ranges. Answers B and G are incorrect because the IP address scheme that starts with 191 is not reserved as nonroutable; therefore, B is incorrect and G is incorrect because not all answers listed are correct.

Question 8

Answers A and F are correct. WF does not block outgoing traffic, only incoming traffic; WF applies to all NICs by default; however, you can individually enable or disable WF for each NIC installed in a Windows XP SP2 computer. Answer B is incorrect because WF does allow you to create exceptions to WF traffic-blocking rules. Answer C is incorrect because you can control WF settings by using local and group policy settings. Answers D and E are both incorrect because WF is turned on by default under both the standard and the domain profiles.

Question 9

Answer C is correct. When TCP/IP outbound connections exceed the hard-coded (and unchangeable) threshold under SP2, an outbound connection queue is created and the outbound connections are resolved at an undocumented rate of speed. Answer A is incorrect because Event ID 4226 is not associated with an excessive number of inbound TCP/IP connections. Answer B is incorrect because Event ID 4226 is not associated with TCP/IP Raw Socket connections. Answer D is incorrect because Event ID 4226 is not associated with the behavior of the MSDTC.

Question 10

Answers B and C are correct. The biggest difference between COM and DCOM under SP2 (as compared to pre-SP2) is that Network RPC services (DCOM) may be launched and activated only by authenticated users; this means that only the local Administrators group has Allow permissions for

Remote Launch and Remote Activation of DCOM-based programs and services. Answer A is incorrect because COM-based programs and services may be launched and activated by both authenticated and unauthenticated users. Answer D is incorrect because Local RPC services (COM) could be launched and activated by both authenticated and unauthenticated users prior to SP2. Answer C is incorrect because the Local Launch permission and the Local Activation permission for COM-based programs and services were also allowed for the Everyone group by default prior to SP2.

Question 11

Answers E and F are correct. Both the Messenger service and the Alerter service have their startup values set to disabled under SP2. Answers A, B, C, and D are incorrect because both the Messenger service and the Alerter service have their startup values set to disabled under SP2.

Question 12

The correct answer is C. Internet Connection Sharing (ICS) uses only Network Address Translation (NAT) for its DHCP allocator service and for its IP range of 192.168.0.2 through 192.168.0.254. Answer A is incorrect because ICS has not been renamed at all under SP2. Answer B is incorrect because ICS, unlike WF, is not turned on by default. Answer D is incorrect because ICS has not been replaced by the WF.

Question 13

Answers C, E, and F are all correct. DEP is available on systems equipped with AMD processors as well as Intel processors. DEP can monitor all programs and services as an option. If you enable DEP to monitor all programs and services, you can exclude specific programs from being monitored by DEP. Answer A is incorrect because DEP is automatically enabled on both 64-bit and 32-bit systems. Answer B is incorrect because DEP can be configured to monitor all programs and services. Answer D is incorrect because DEP is automatically enabled on both 32-bit and 64-bit systems. Answer G is incorrect because DEP is not disabled on systems equipped with Intel processors.

Question 14

Answer B is correct. The System Restore feature automatically creates its own system restore point every 24 hours of continuous use. After you restore the computer to an earlier time, the system's settings will revert to what they were previously when the proper printer driver was installed and working. Answer A is incorrect because the Driver Rollback feature does not support printer drivers. Answer C is incorrect because restoring the computer's data from a backup media set will not reinstall the previous printer driver. Answer D is incorrect because creating a manual restore point allows you to restore, some time in the future, the current system configuration; this option does not help you to retrieve earlier settings that you want to reapply now.

Question 15

The correct answers are A and D. According to the Device Manager displayed in Figure 12.2, Alison's wireless network adapter card is currently disabled as indicated by the red X. Alison's USB Mass Storage device is currently not functioning as indicated by the yellow exclamation point(!). Answer B is incorrect because there is no red X next to the USB Mass Storage device to indicate that it is disabled. Answer C is incorrect because there is no yellow ! next to the wireless network card entry to indicate that it is not functioning, as opposed to being disabled. Answer E also is incorrect because there is no yellow ! next to the FireWire (1394) network adapter entry to indicate that it is not functioning, as opposed to being disabled. Answer F is incorrect because there is no FireWire (1394) mass storage device listed in the Device Manager screenshot displayed.

Question 16

Answers A, B, and C are all correct. Windows XP SP2 adds wireless networking support for native Wi-Fi Protected Access (WPA) encryption and Wireless Provisioning Services (WPS) as well as introducing the Wireless Network Setup Wizard. Answers C, D, and E are all incorrect. Releases of Windows XP prior to SP2 already supported the 802.11g wireless networking standard, the 802.11a wireless networking standard, and natively supported Wired Equivalent Privacy (WEP) encryption.

Question 17

Answers A and E are correct. Answer A is correct because Ask Me to Search Windows Update Every Time I Connect a New Device is one of the available options from the Connect to Windows Update dialog box. Answer E is correct because If My Device Needs a Driver, Go to Windows Update Without Asking Me is also one of the available options to choose from the Connect to Windows Update dialog box. Answer B is incorrect because the option Download Updates for Me, but Let Me Choose When to Install Them is an option for Automatic Updates, but not for Windows Update. Answer C is incorrect because the option Notify Me but Don't Automatically Download or Install Them is also one of the options for Automatic Updates, but not for searching for device drivers under Windows Update. Answer D is incorrect because the options for configuring Automatic Updates are listed on the Automatic Updates tab of the System Properties dialog box, not on the Connect to Windows Update dialog box.

Question 18

The correct answer is B. By using two separate paging files, spread across two separate physical disks, you are load balancing the input/output (I/O) between two fast disks, neither of which contain the system partition nor the boot partition. This is following best practices. Answer A is incorrect because by setting up four paging files, each of those paging files would reside on either the system or the boot partitions. Also, Disk 0 is a slower device because its speed is 5400RPM. Answer C is incorrect because by placing only one large paging file on Disk 3, you lose the advantages of both fault tolerance (in case Disk 3 fails) and load balancing across more than one physical disk. Answer D is incorrect for the same reasons as answer C, and Disk 1 also stores the boot partition with the Windows operating system files. Answer E is incorrect because even though you are spreading the paging files across two physical drives, Disk 1 holds the boot partition and has a capacity of only 20GB—Disks 2 and 3 each have capacities of 80GB, which allows for extra "headroom" for defragmentation purposes and allows for more files to be stored on the disks before they reach their maximum capacities.

Question 19

The correct answer is E. When you right-click an application's process from the Processes tab in Task Manager, you have the option to select Set Priority and then you can choose the priority level. From the set of answers listed, Set Priority, AboveNormal is the best available answer compared to the default setting of Set Priority, Normal. Answer A is incorrect because Set Priority, Low allocates fewer CPU cycles to the application, which tends to degrade performance. Answer B is incorrect because selecting Set Priority, Realtime is not a recommended setting because it may destabilize the operating system and require that you reboot the computer. Answer C is incorrect because the computer must have more than one processor installed or it must have a hyperthreaded CPU installed for the Set Affinity option to be available; the question does not state that the processor is hyperthreaded, nor does it state that more than one Pentium 4 processor is installed. Answer D is incorrect for the same reasons as Answer C, and a High setting does not exist for the Set Affinity option.

Question 20

The correct answers are A and B. Two configuration settings must be made in order to copy files from the local hard drive(s) under the Windows XP Recovery Console environment; you must enable the Allow Floppy Copy and Access to All Drives and All Folders local policy settings in advance, before booting into the Recovery console. You must also type **Set AllowRemovableMedia = TRUE** and press Enter at the Recovery Console command prompt to enable this feature. Answer C is incorrect because disabling the Allow Floppy Copy setting retains the default setting and disallows copying files to removable media. Answer D is incorrect because if you type **Set AllowRemovableMedia = FALSE** and press Enter at the Recovery Console command prompt, you retain the default setting and therefore cannot copy files to removable media. Answer E is incorrect because the default setting for the Recovery Console is to disallow files to be copied *from the hard disk(s)* to any type of removable media. You are allowed, however, to copy files from removable media to the hard disk(s) by default in the Recovery Console.

Question 21

The correct answer is D. The WebDAV protocol enables users to access files using the Hypertext Transfer Protocol (HTTP), which uses TCP port 80 as its network transport mechanism. Therefore, to use WebDAV, you must specify http:// as the protocol and then specify the remote path and filename. Answer A is incorrect because saving a Word document as a web page is not the same thing as saving it using the WebDAV protocol over HTTP. Answer B is incorrect because WebDAV does not recognize Uniform Naming Convention (UNC) paths; a UNC path uses the Server Message Block (SMB) protocol, not HTTP. Answer C is incorrect because the File Transfer Protocol (FTP) uses port 21 by default, not port 80.

Question 22

The correct answers are B and E. Spanned volumes can exist only on disks that have been converted from basic to dynamic. Only Windows XP Professional supports dynamic disks; both single-processor and dual-processor systems support dynamic disks under Windows XP Professional. Answer A is incorrect because Windows XP Home Edition does not support dynamic disks. Answer C is incorrect because portable computers do not support dynamic disks, even under SP2. Answer D is incorrect because Windows XP Home Edition does not support dynamic disks, even under SP2. Answer F is incorrect because portable computers do not support dynamic disks and neither do FireWire nor USB drives.

Question 23

Answer A is correct. When you boot a computer from the Windows XP Professional CD-ROM, you are initially presented with two options: To Set Up Windows XP Now, Press Enter or To Repair a Windows XP Installation Using Recovery Console, Press R. Answer B is incorrect because you cannot run the Recovery Console from a command prompt only session (or from MS-DOS). The command `<CD-ROM Drive>\:winnt32.exe /cmdcons` is for installing the Recovery Console, not for running it. Answer C is incorrect because when you boot a computer that already has Windows XP installed from the Windows XP Professional CD-ROM, the second repair option presented to you (after you initially select To Set Up Windows XP Now, Press Enter) is to perform a repair installation. Answer D is incorrect because the option Safe Mode Using Recovery Console is not one of the available selections from the Advanced Startup menu after you press the F8 key.

Chapter 13

Question 24

The correct answers are A, B, and D. IPSec has always been available under Windows XP. ICS (Internet Connection Sharing) has also been available under the RTM, SP1, and SP2 versions of Windows XP. Even the netsh command has been around since the RTM version, although SP2 adds some new functionality to this tool. Answer C is incorrect because the capability to enable or disable the Windows Firewall is available only under SP2. Answer E is incorrect because the Internet Connection Firewall (ICF) is turned off by default under the RTM and SP1 versions. Finally, answer F is incorrect because the restriction on outbound TCP traffic over Raw Sockets was introduced under SP2.

Question 25

Answer B is correct. You can uninstall SP2 for Windows XP from the Recovery Console by executing the spuninst.exe program that is located in the %systemroot%\$NTServicePackUninstall$\spuninst folder. Answer A is incorrect because you can uninstall SP2 from the command line or from the Recovery Console. Answer C is incorrect because the spuninst.exe program is not located in the %systemroot%\System32\$NTServicePackUninstall$ folder. Answer D is incorrect because the spuninst.exe program is also not located in the %systemroot%\$NTServicePackUninstall$ folder.

Question 26

The correct answer is A. You want to prevent your users from copying information to a floppy, which means you have to disable the floppy drive. You can do this by using a hardware profile. You will also need to prevent the users from having a choice when the machine boots up, so you will need to delete the default (or original) profile. Answer B is incorrect. Because users will not always log on to the domain, they may not get the policy and will have access to their floppy drive. Answer C is incorrect because System Policies are written for down-level clients such as Windows NT and 9X, not Windows 2000 or XP, and the remote users are using Windows XP. Answer D is incorrect because the cipher command has no effect on whether users will still have access to their floppy drive.

Question 27

The correct answer is A. The error message that you would receive refers to the target location not being local to the user. Because the location is a network drive, the user will not receive the roaming profile. You should use the universal naming convention (UNC) format to specify the location. Answer B is incorrect because this action will share the folder only with the name Profile. Answer C is incorrect because this will not ensure that the users will receive their roaming profile and cannot be shared with that name. Answer D is incorrect because when a user tries to log on, the user's machine will look for the Y: drive on the local machine. If it doesn't exist, the user will be given an error message that states the roaming profile cannot be located.

Question 28

The correct answer is B. For a user to connect using Remote Desktop, the administrator must explicitly give permission to that user. Answer A is incorrect because even Enterprise Admins are not given permission by default to access a server via Remote Desktop; in addition, it would give Sally excessive rights. Answer C is incorrect because even Enterprise Admins are not given permission by default to access a server via Remote Desktop; in addition, it would give Sally excessive rights. Answer D is incorrect because Sally needs access to Remote Desktop, and not local access. Sally needs to have access given to her explicitly or to be added to the Remote Desktop Users group.

Question 29

The correct answer is A. Although APM was designed for laptop battery performance, using APM in conjunction with Remote Desktop causes problems because Remote Desktop was not designed to communicate with APM services. To work around this behavior, you should disable APM on the laptop. Answer B is incorrect because the APM issue with Remote Desktop is irrespective of the operating system or the use of the laptop. Answer C is incorrect because dialing up to your network and disabling PPP will prevent the laptop from connecting to the network via dial-up. Answer D is incorrect because you are dialing in and the NIC is not used.

Question 30

The correct answers are A, B, and C. Remote Assistance is a convenient way for an administrator to connect to your computer from another computer. There are three ways an administrator can use Remote Assistance. One is via Windows Messenger. Another is by initiating an invitation via email directly from the Remote Assistance Invitation Wizard. The last way is by filling out a form and saving it as a file. The file can be emailed, shared, or hand delivered to the desktop support personnel. Answer D is incorrect because you cannot send an invitation to someone for Remote Assistance through IE.

Question 31

The correct answer is B. You cannot connect to someone's computer via Remote Assistance if the invitation has expired. The person who made the request must resend the invitation for assistance. Answer A is incorrect because you cannot connect to someone's computer via Remote Assistance if the invitation has expired. You cannot change the expiration of an invitation. Answer C is incorrect because you aren't sure that you would be able to connect to the user's computer. Answer D is incorrect because this could cause other applications or invitations to behave incorrectly.

Question 32

The correct answer is A. You must have an SMTP server so that the Instant Messaging service can function as your internal account service. This will allow communication internally, without having an Internet connection. Answer B is incorrect because DNS is not needed for Remote Assistance to work. Answer C is incorrect because Single Sign-On is not necessary for Remote Assistance to function. Answer D is incorrect because Remote Desktop is a feature of Windows XP Professional and not a necessary service for Remote Assistance to function.

Question 33

The correct answer is C. The answer files are kept in the \RemoteInstall directory, and setting the permissions to Everyone READ ensures that no one will be able to alter the file. Answer A is incorrect because although the template is read-only, it has no effect on the answer files that are created from it. You will need to change the permissions of the answer files themselves. Answer B is incorrect because it is not the least amount of administrative effort. Answer D is incorrect because changing the permissions of the %systemroot% directory to Everyone READ will cause your system to destabilize. The system needs to be able to write to certain files. This action could cause serious damage and problems to your system.

Question 34

The correct answer is A. Giving Steve the Create All Child Objects permission will give him the necessary rights to complete the task you gave him without giving him unnecessary rights. Answer B is incorrect because making Bob an Enterprise Admin would be giving him excessive rights. Answer C is incorrect because giving Steve Full Control permission in the Delegation of Control Wizard of an OU gives him excessive permissions. All he needs to do is create computer objects and nothing more. Answer D is incorrect because making Steve a domain administrator is giving him excessive rights.

Question 35

The correct answer is D. When the RIPrep Wizard is run, a new directory is created where the image file is uploaded, and the answer file is located there. This will happen automatically and there is nothing more you should do. Answer A is incorrect because moving the answer to the Sysvol directory will do nothing for the unattended installation. The installation will fail because the file is in the wrong directory. Answer B is incorrect because the RIPrep Wizard places the file in the correct directory, and moving the answer file from its default location will result in a failed installation. Answer C is incorrect because moving the file from its default location will result in a failed installation.

Question 36

The correct answer is B. Because RIPrep produces an image of the computer, if any piece of the hardware is different and an incompatible image is installed on it, a stop error will occur. Running RIPrep from each vendor's computer will ensure the proper HAL for the remaining installations.

Answer A is incorrect because simply copying the Hal.dll file to the \i386 directory will result in the same problem. Each machine with a different HAL must be imaged. Answer C is incorrect because it requires the most amount of effort. Running an answer file with a UDF for all 300 computers would be time consuming. Answer D is incorrect because only one UDF is needed for all computers.

Question 37

The correct answer is D. The RIPrep utility supports only a single disk with a single partition (C: drive); therefore, the applications must be installed on the C partition. Answer B is incorrect because the RIPrep utility supports only a single disk with a single partition. Answer C is incorrect because this process would be very time consuming. Answer A is incorrect because it does not resolve the issue in the least amount of time.

Question 38

The correct answer is A. The -reseal switch clears the Event Viewer logs. If you do not use this switch, the event logs will be imaged on all machines using the image. Answer B is incorrect because it will not clear the event log. The -factory switch restarts the computer in factory mode, which allows the installation of additional drivers and applications after the reboot that follows Sysprep.exe. Answer C is incorrect because the -pnp switch forces Plug and Play to refresh the next time that the computer is restarted. It will not clear the event log. Answer D is incorrect because the -quiet switch runs Sysprep without displaying the onscreen messages; it will not clear the event log.

Question 39

The correct answer is B. Because you no longer use NetBIOS name resolution in your environment, to ensure that your servers are using solely DNS, you should disable the NetBIOS binding for the WINS client (TCP/IP). Answer A is incorrect because the Active Directory service depends on DNS to function correctly. Disabling DNS will disable Active Directory and prevent it from functioning. Answer C is incorrect because servers and clients that are not configured with a static IP address will not be able to connect to resources. Answer D is incorrect because TCP/IP is the protocol required for an Active Directory–based domain.

Question 40

The correct answer is C. Tom cannot connect to Srv1 because the information in his TCP/IP cache is no longer valid. After he flushes this information and receives new information from the DNS server, he will be able to connect. Answer A is incorrect because although this may give him new TCP/IP information, it will not change the information in his cache. Answer B is incorrect because the problem is with the client, not the DNS server. Answer D is incorrect because the issue is not a NETBIOS name resolution issue, but a DNS issue.

Question 41

The correct answer is B. Using the Microsoft Passport service Passport Single Sign On will allow a user to use a single username and password for authenticated access to any website that employs Passport authentication. Answer A is incorrect because even if you were to enable cookies, cookies are session based or time based. You will still need to authenticate to the site when you return or at some date in the future. Disabling cookies will make it more difficult to authenticate with a site and will not fix the reauthentication issue. Answer C is incorrect because Active X scripting has nothing to do with reauthenticating you to a website. Answer D is incorrect because the Single Sign On service on the machine refers to authentication on that particular computer, not on a website.

Question 42

The correct answers are A and C. First, both ports 20 and 21 need to be checked in order for the FTP communication to be successful, and because your family can browse the web page, port 80 is already open. Answer B is incorrect because clearing the check box will disable the web server. Answer D is incorrect because clearing the check box will disable the web server.

Question 43

The correct answer is C. To use ICF, you must use the public interface as it is the only interface that can be configured with ICF if you are using it in conjunction with ICS. Answer A is incorrect because ICS requires either a

VPN or dial-up to function properly. Answer B is incorrect because changing permissions will not make ICS work. Answer D is incorrect because ICS requires either a VPN or dial-up to function properly and ICF is not required.

Question 44

The correct answer is A. Dynamic Update ensures that the operating system files are up to date. Before the installation occurs, a server must be configured with the latest updates from Microsoft's website. Answer C is incorrect because Windows Update contains compatibility updates, new device drivers, and other updates released for Windows XP Professional as they become available on the Windows Update website, not during installation. Answer D is incorrect because Automatic Update is an option for updating your computer without interrupting your web experience. These downloads are throttled to minimize impact to network responsiveness and are automatically resumed if the system is disconnected before an update is fully downloaded. After the update has been downloaded to the PC, the user can then choose to install it. This does not happen during installation. Answer B is incorrect because Software updates refer only to updates to applications installed on the computer.

Question 45

The correct answer is A. The User State Migration Tool consists of two executables (`Scanstate.exe` and `Loadstate.exe`) and four migration rule information files (`Migapp.inf`, `Migsys.inf`, `Miguser.inf`, and `Sysfiles.inf`). `Scanstate.exe` is the command that collects user data and settings. Answer B is incorrect because `Loadstate.exe` is used to deposit the information on the new Windows XP computer. Answer C is incorrect because Savestate is the command for installing a service pack. Answer D is incorrect because it is one of the INF files used for the migration of the settings, not the command itself.

Question 46

The correct answer is B. The USMT is an excellent tool for customizing the migration of user settings in an efficient manner. With this option, you will be able to script the migration as well as customize the migration files that determine which files, settings, and configurations are migrated. Answer A is incorrect because LDAP is the primary way the Operating System accesses the Active Directory database. It is not used to migrate files and desktop settings. Answer C is incorrect because GPMC is a Microsoft Management Console (MMC) snap-in for managing Group Policy and is not used to migrate files and desktop settings. Answer D is incorrect because the MMC is not used to migrate files and desktop settings.

Question 47

All answers are correct. Answer A is correct because you must install a computer certificate on the remote access router, because you are using smart cards. Answer B is correct because you must also configure remote access on the remote access router that remote clients can connect to. Answer C is correct because the remote clients need to be able to connect to the domain. Answer D is correct because EAP is the authentication protocol necessary for smart card use.

Question 48

The correct answer is A. IPSec does not work with NAT; therefore, you will receive the error message. You will need to remove NAT. Answer B is incorrect because if you must encrypt both the IP header traffic and the packets, you must not remove IPSec. Answer C is incorrect because your requirements are that the IP headers be encrypted, and PPTP does not do this. Answer D is incorrect—you are not implementing smart cards.

Question 49

The correct answer is B. L2TP is used for encapsulating and transmitting non-IP traffic through TCP/IP networks. L2TP uses IPSec for encrypted transmission. Answer A is incorrect because although PPTP will encrypt the header information, it will not encrypt IP traffic. Answer C is incorrect because EFS (Encrypting File System) is used to encrypt files, not IP traffic. Answer D is incorrect because you are not implementing smart cards.

Question 50

The correct answer is A. Microsoft Certified Partners and CLPSs receive a special Volume License Key (VLK) that enables them to activate a copy of the software as many times as needed without having to call Microsoft. Only by using the VLK is this an option. Answer B is incorrect because you may change a motherboard or even the whole system. Answer C is incorrect because changing the clock will not change the activation status. Answer D is incorrect because by using VLK, you will not have to do this.

CD Contents and Installation Instructions

The CD features an innovative practice test engine powered by MeasureUp, giving you yet another effective tool to assess your readiness for the exam.

Multiple Test Modes

MeasureUp practice tests are available in Study, Certification, Custom, Adaptive, Missed Question, and Non-Duplicate question modes.

Study Mode

Tests administered in Study Mode enable you to request the correct answer(s) and explanation to each question during the test. These tests are not timed. You can modify the testing environment *during* the test by selecting the Options button.

Certification Mode

Tests administered in Certification Mode closely simulate the actual testing environment you will encounter when taking a certification exam. These tests do not allow you to request the answer(s) and/or explanation to each question until after the exam.

Custom Mode

Custom Mode enables you to specify your preferred testing environment. Use this mode to specify the objectives you want to include in your test, the timer length, and other test properties. You can also modify the testing environment *during* the test by selecting the Options button.

Adaptive Mode

Tests administered in Adaptive Mode closely simulate the actual testing environment you will encounter taking an Adaptive exam. After answering a question, you are not allowed to go back; you are allowed only to move forward during the exam.

Missed Question Mode

Missed Question Mode enables you to take a test containing only the questions you have missed previously.

Non-Duplicate Mode

Non-Duplicate Mode enables you to take a test containing only questions not displayed previously.

Question Types

The practice question types simulate the real exam experience. For a complete description of each question type, visit http://www.microsoft.com/learning/mcpexams/faq/innovations.asp.

➤ Create a Tree Type
➤ Select and Place
➤ Drop and Connect
➤ Build List
➤ Reorder List
➤ Build and Reorder List
➤ Single Hotspot
➤ Multiple Hotspots
➤ Live Screen
➤ Command Line
➤ Hot Area

Random Questions and Order of Answers

This feature helps you learn the material without memorizing questions and answers. Each time you take a practice test, the questions and answers appear in a different randomized order.

Detailed Explanations of Correct and Incorrect Answers

You'll receive automatic feedback on all correct and incorrect answers. The detailed explanations are a superb learning tool in their own right.

Attention to Exam Objectives

MeasureUp practice tests are designed to appropriately balance the questions over each technical area covered by a specific exam.

Installing the CD

The minimum system requirements for the CD-ROM are the following:

➤ Windows 95, 98, ME, NT4, 2000, or XP

➤ 7MB disk space for testing engine

➤ An average of 1MB disk space for each test

To install the CD-ROM, follow these instructions:

 NOTE If you need technical support, please contact MeasureUp at 678-356-5050 or email support@measureup.com. Additionally, you'll find Frequently Asked Questions (FAQs) at www.measureup.com.

1. Close all applications before beginning this installation.

2. Insert the CD into your CD-ROM drive. If the setup starts automatically, go to step 6. If the setup does not start automatically, continue with step 3.

3. From the Start menu, select Run.

4. Click Browse to locate the MeasureUp CD. In the Browse dialog box, from the Look In drop-down list, select the CD-ROM drive.

5. In the Browse dialog box, double-click `Setup.exe`. In the Run dialog box, click OK to begin the installation.

6. On the Welcome Screen, click MeasureUp Practice Questions to begin installation.

7. Follow the Certification Prep Wizard by clicking Next.

8. To agree to the Software License Agreement, click Yes.

9. On the Choose Destination Location screen, click Next to install the software to `C:\Program Files\Certification Preparation`.

 If you cannot locate MeasureUp Practice Tests through the Start menu, see the section titled "Creating a Shortcut to the MeasureUp Practice Tests" later in this appendix.

10. On the Setup Type screen, select Typical Setup. Click Next to continue.

11. In the Select Program Folder screen, you can name the program folder your tests will be in. To select the default, click Next and the installation will continue.

12. After the installation is complete, verify that Yes, I Want to Restart My Computer Now is selected. If you select No, I Will Restart My Computer Later, you will not be able to use the program until you restart your computer.

13. Click Finish.

14. After restarting your computer, choose Start, Programs, MeasureUp, MeasureUp Practice Tests.

15. On the MeasureUp Welcome Screen, click Create User Profile.

16. In the User Profile dialog box, complete the mandatory fields and click Create Profile.

17. Select the practice test you want to access and click Start Test.

Creating a Shortcut to the MeasureUp Practice Tests

To create a shortcut to the MeasureUp Practice Tests, follow these steps:

1. Right-click your desktop.

2. From the shortcut menu select New, Shortcut.

3. Browse to C:\Program Files\MeasureUp Practice Tests and select the MeasureUpCertification.exe or Localware.exe file.

4. Click OK.

5. Click Next.

6. Rename the shortcut MeasureUp.

7. Click Finish.

After you have completed step 7, use the MeasureUp shortcut on your desktop to access the MeasureUp products you ordered.

Technical Support

If you encounter problems with the MeasureUp test engine on the CD-ROM, contact MeasureUp at 678-356-5050 or by email at support@measureup.com. Technical support hours are from 8 a.m. to 5 p.m. EST Monday through Friday. Additionally, you'll find Frequently Asked Questions (FAQs) at www.measureup.com.

If you'd like to purchase additional MeasureUp products, telephone 678-356-5050 or 800-649-1MUP (1687) or visit www.measureup.com.

Glossary

A (address) resource record

A resource record used to map a Domain Name System (DNS) domain name to a host Internet Protocol (IP) address on the network.

Accelerated Graphics Port (AGP)

An interface specification (released in August 1997) developed by Intel. AGP is based on the Peripheral Connection Interface (PCI), but is designed especially for the throughput demands of 3D graphics. Rather than using the PCI bus for graphics data, AGP introduces a dedicated point-to-point channel so that the graphics controller can directly access main memory. The AGP channel is 32 bits wide and runs at 66MHz. This translates into a total bandwidth of 266Mbps, as opposed to the PCI bandwidth of 133Mbps. AGP also supports two optional faster modes, with throughputs of 533Mbps and 1.07Gbps. In addition, AGP allows 3D textures to be stored in main memory rather than in video memory. AGP has a few important system requirements: The chipset must support AGP, and the motherboard must be equipped with an AGP bus slot or must have an integrated AGP graphics system.

access control entry (ACE)

An element in an object's discretionary access control list (DACL). Each ACE controls or monitors access to an object by a specified trustee. An ACE is also an entry in an object's system access control list (SACL) that specifies the security events to be audited for a user or group.

account lockout

A Windows XP security feature that locks a user account if a certain number of failed logon attempts occur within a specified amount of time, based on security policy lockout settings. Locked accounts cannot log on.

Active Directory

The directory service included with Windows 2000 Server. It is based on the X.500 standards and those of its predecessor, the Lightweight Directory Access Protocol (LDAP). It stores information about objects on a network and makes this information available to users and network administrators. Active Directory gives network users access to permitted resources anywhere on the network using a single logon process. It provides network administrators with a hierarchical view of the network and a single point of administration for all network objects.

Active Directory Users and Computers snap-in

An administrative tool designed to perform daily Active Directory administration tasks. These tasks include creating, deleting, modifying, moving, and setting permissions on objects stored in the directory. These objects include organizational units (OUs), users, contacts, groups, computers, printers, and shared file objects.

Address Resolution Protocol (ARP)

A Transmission Control Protocol/Internet Protocol (TCP/IP) that translates an Internet Protocol (IP) address into a physical address, such as a Media Access Control (MAC) address (hardware address). A computer that wants to obtain a physical address sends an ARP broadcast request onto the TCP/IP network. The computer on the network that has the IP address in the request then replies with its physical hardware address.

Advanced Configuration and Power Interface (ACPI)

A power management specification developed by Intel, Microsoft, and Toshiba. ACPI enables Windows XP to control the amount of power given to each device attached to the computer. With ACPI, the operating system can turn off peripheral devices, such as CD-ROM players, when they are not in use. As another example, ACPI enables manufacturers to produce computers that automatically power up as soon as you touch the keyboard.

Advanced Power Management (APM)

An application programming interface (API) developed by Intel and Microsoft that enables developers to include power management in basic input/output systems (BIOSs). APM defines a layer between the hardware and the operating system that effectively shields programmers from hardware details. Advanced Configuration and Power Interface (ACPI) will gradually replace APM.

ARPANET

A large wide area network (WAN) created in the 1960s by the U.S. Department of Defense (DoD) Advanced Research Projects

Agency for the free exchange of information between universities and research organizations.

Asynchronous Transfer Mode (ATM)

A networking technology that transfers data in cells (data packets of a fixed size). Cells used with ATM are relatively small compared to packets used with older technologies. The small, constant cell size enables ATM hardware to transmit video images, audio, and computer data over the same network and ensures that no single type of data consumes all the connection's available bandwidth. Current implementations of ATM support data transfer rates from 25Mbps to 622Mbps. Most Ethernet-based networks run at 100Mbps or below.

attribute

A single property that describes an object; for example, the make, model, or color that describes a car. In the context of directories, an attribute is the main component of an entry in a directory, such as an email address.

auditing

The process that tracks the activities of users by recording selected types of events in the security log of a server or workstation.

authentication ticket

A permission to indirectly access resources that a Kerberos Key Distribution Center (KDC) grants to clients and applications.

authorize

To register the Remote Installation Services (RIS) server or the Dynamic Host Configuration Protocol (DHCP) server with Active Directory.

Automatic Private IP Addressing (APIPA)

A client-side feature of Windows 98, 2000, and XP Dynamic Host Configuration Protocol (DHCP) clients. If the client's attempt to negotiate with a DHCP server fails, the client automatically receives an Internet Protocol (IP) address from the 169.254.0.0 Class B range.

automatic update

A service that checks with the Windows Update website for critical updates and automates the process of downloading and installing the critical updates.

backup domain controller (BDC)

In Windows NT Server 4, a server that receives a copy of the domain's directory database (which contains all the account and security policy information for the domain). BDCs can continue to participate in a Windows 2000 domain when the domain is configured in mixed mode.

Bandwidth Allocation Protocol (BAP)

A protocol that dynamically controls the use of multilinked lines. BAP eliminates excess bandwidth by allocating lines only when they are required. You can control dynamic links with remote access policies, which are based on the percentage of line utilization and the length of time the bandwidth is reduced.

baselining

The process of measuring system performance so that you can ascertain a standard or an expected level of performance.

basic disk

A Windows XP term that indicates a physical disk, which can have primary and extended partitions. A basic disk can contain up to three primary partitions and one extended partition, or four primary partitions. A basic disk can also have a single extended partition with logical drives. You *cannot* extend a basic disk.

Basic Input/Output System (BIOS)

Built-in software that determines what a computer can do without accessing programs from a disk. On PCs, the BIOS contains all the code required to control the keyboard, display screen, disk drives, serial communications, and a number of miscellaneous functions. A BIOS that can handle Plug and Play devices is known as a Plug and Play BIOS. A Plug and Play BIOS is always implemented with flash memory rather than read-only memory (ROM). Windows XP benefits if your machine has the latest Advanced Configuration and Power Interface (ACPI)-compliant BIOS.

boot partition

The partition that contains the Windows XP operating system and its support files.

CD-R

A recordable CD-ROM technology using a disc that can be written to only once.

CD-RW

A rewritable CD-ROM technology. CD-RW drives can also be used to write CD-R discs, and they can read CD-ROMs. Initially known as CD-E (for CD-Erasable), a CD-RW disc can be rewritten hundreds of times.

Challenge Handshake Authentication Protocol (CHAP)

An authentication protocol used by Microsoft Remote Access as well as network and dial-up connections. Using CHAP, a remote access client can send its authentication credentials to a remote access server in a secure form. Microsoft has created several variations of CHAP that are Windows-specific, such as Microsoft Challenge Handshake Authentication Protocol (MSCHAP) and MSCHAP 2.

client-side caching (CSC)

See offline file.

compression

The process of making individual files and folders occupy less disk space with the NT File System (NTFS) 5 file system in Windows XP. Compressed files can be read and written to by any Windows- or

DOS-based program *without* having to be decompressed first. They decompress when opened and recompress when closed. The NTFS 5 file system handles this entire process. Compression is a file attribute that you can apply to any file or folder stored on an NTFS 5 partition.

computer account
An account that a domain administrator creates and that uniquely identifies the computer on the domain. The Windows XP computer account matches the name of the computer that joins the domain.

container
An object in the directory that contains other objects.

counter
A metric that provides information about particular aspects of system performance.

daily backup
A backup of files that have changed today but are not marked as backed up.

Data Recovery Agent (DRA)
A Windows XP administrator who has been issued a public key certificate for the express purpose of recovering user-encrypted data files that have been encrypted with Encrypting File System (EFS). Data recovery refers to the process of decrypting a file without having the private key of the user who encrypted the file. A DRA may

become necessary if a user loses his or her private key for decrypting files or if a user leaves an organization without decrypting important files that other users need.

default gateway
An address that serves an important role in Transmission Control Protocol/Internet Protocol (TCP/IP) networking by providing a default route for TCP/IP hosts to use when communicating with other hosts on remote networks. A router (either a dedicated router or a computer that connects two or more network segments) generally acts as the default gateway for TCP/IP hosts. The router maintains its own routing table of other networks within an Internetwork. The routing table maps the routes required to reach the remote hosts that reside on those other networks.

Device Manager
The primary tool in Windows XP used to configure and manage hardware devices and their settings.

dial-up access
When a remote client uses the public telephone line or an integrated services digital network (ISDN) line to create a connection to a Windows XP remote access server.

differential backup
A backup that copies files created or changed since the last normal or incremental backup. It does *not* mark files as having been backed up

(in other words, the archive attribute is not cleared). If you are performing a combination of normal and differential backups, restoring files and folders requires that you have the last normal backup as well as the last differential backup.

digital signature
The use of public key cryptography to authenticate the integrity and originator of a communication.

digital versatile disc or digital video disc (DVD)
A type of CD-ROM that holds a minimum of 4.7GB, enough for a full-length movie. The DVD specification supports discs with capacities from 4.7 to 17GB and access rates of 600Kbps to 1.3Mbps. One of the best features of DVD drives is that they are backward compatible with CD-ROMs. This means that DVD players can play old CD-ROMs, CD-I discs, video CDs, and new DVD-ROMs. Newer DVD players can also read CD-R discs. DVD technology uses Moving Picture Experts Group (MPEG)-2 to compress video data.

Direct Memory Access (DMA)
A technique for transferring data from main memory to a device without passing it through the CPU. Computers that have DMA channels can transfer data to and from devices much more quickly than can computers without a DMA channel. This is useful for making quick backups and for real-time applications. Some expansion

boards, such as CD-ROM cards, can access the computer's DMA channel. When you install the board, you must specify the DMA channel to be used, which sometimes involves setting a jumper or dual inline package (DIP) switch.

discretionary access control list (DACL)
A list of access control entries (ACEs) that lets administrators set permissions for users and groups at the object and attribute levels. This list represents part of an object's security descriptor that allows or denies permissions to specific users and groups.

disk group
A Windows XP term for multiple dynamic disks that are managed as a collection. All dynamic disks in a computer are members of the same disk group. Each disk in a disk group stores replicas of the same configuration data. This configuration data is stored in a 1MB region at the end of each dynamic disk.

Disk Management
A Windows XP MMC snap-in that you use to perform all disk maintenance tasks, such as formatting, creating partitions, deleting partitions, and converting a basic disk to a dynamic disk.

disk quota
A control used in Windows XP to limit the amount of hard disk space available for all users or an individual user. You can apply a quota on a per-user, per-volume basis only.

domain

The fundamental administrative unit of Active Directory. A domain stores information about objects in the domain's partition of Active Directory. You can give user and group accounts in a domain privileges and permissions to resources on any system that belongs to the domain.

domain controller

A computer running Windows 2000 Server that hosts Active Directory and manages user access to a network, which includes logging on, authentication, and access to the directory and shared resources.

domain forest

A collection of one or more Windows 2000 domains in a non-contiguous DNS namespace that share a common schema, configuration, and Global Catalog and that are linked with two-way transitive trusts.

Domain Name System (DNS)

The standard by which hosts on the Internet have both domain name addresses (for example, rapport.com) and numerical Internet Protocol (IP) addresses (for example, 192.33.2.8). DNS is a service that you use primarily for resolving fully qualified domain names (FQDNs) to IP addresses.

domain tree

A set of domains that forms a contiguous DNS namespace through a set of hierarchical relationships.

driver signing

A method for marking or identifying driver files that meet certain specifications or standards. Windows XP uses a driver signing process to make sure that drivers have been certified to work correctly with the Windows Driver Model (WDM) in Windows XP.

DVD-R

A write-once optical disk used to master DVD-Video and DVD-ROM discs. DVD-Rs are the DVD counterpart to CD-Rs and use the same recording technology to "burn" the disc.

DVD-RAM

A rewritable DVD technology best used for data storage. Recorded movies cannot be played on most consumer DVD players.

DVD-RW

A rewritable DVD technology. Information can be written and erased multiple times. DVD-RW primarily is used for movies and is compatible with most of the DVD players on the market.

DVD+RW

A rewritable DVD technology. Data can be written and erased multiple times. DVD+RW can be used for both data and movies and is compatible with most of the DVD players on the market.

dynamic disk

A physical disk in a Windows XP computer that does not use partitions or logical drives. It has dynamic volumes that you create using the Disk Management console. A dynamic disk can contain any of five types of volumes. In addition, you can extend a volume on a dynamic disk. Dynamic disks can contain an unlimited number of volumes, so you are not restricted to four volumes per disk as you are with a basic disk.

Dynamic Host Configuration Protocol (DHCP) server
A Windows 2000 server that dynamically assigns Internet Protocol (IP) addresses to clients. Along with the assignment of IP addresses, it can provide direction toward routers, Windows Internet Naming Service (WINS) servers, and Domain Name System (DNS) servers.

Dynamic Update
Works with Windows Update to download critical fixes and drivers needed during the setup process. Dynamic Update provides important updates to files required for Setup to minimize difficulties during setup.

dynamic volume
The only type of volume you can create on dynamic disks. The five types of dynamic volumes are simple, spanned, mirrored, striped, and RAID-5. Only computers running Windows XP can directly access dynamic volumes. Windows XP Professional machines *cannot* host, but *can* access, mirrored and RAID-5 dynamic volumes that are on remote Windows 2000 servers.

emergency repair process (or repair process)
A feature that helps you repair problems with system files, your startup environment (if you have a dual-boot or multiple-boot system), and the partition boot sector on your boot volume. Before you use the emergency repair process to repair your system, you must create an Emergency Repair Disk (ERD). You can do this using the Backup utility. Even if you have not created an ERD, you can still try to use the emergency repair process; however, any changes you have made to your system (for example, service pack updates) may be lost and might need to be reinstalled.

Encrypting File System (EFS)
A subsystem of NT File System (NTFS) that uses public keys and private keys to provide encryption for files and folders on computers using Windows XP. Only the user who initially encrypted the file and a recovery agent can decrypt encrypted files and folders.

Extensible Authentication Protocol (EAP)
An extension of Point-to-Point Protocol (PPP) that provides remote access user authentication by means of other security devices. You may add support for a number of authentication schemes, including token cards; dial-up; the Kerberos v5 protocol; one-time passwords; and public key authentication using smart cards,

certificates, and others. EAP works with dial-up, Point-to-Point Tunneling Protocol (PPTP), and Layer 2 Tunneling Protocol (L2TP) clients. EAP is a critical technology component for secure Virtual Private Networks (VPNs) because it offers more security against brute force or dictionary attacks (where all possible combinations of characters are attempted) and password guessing than other authentication methods, such as Challenge Handshake Authentication Protocol (CHAP).

fault tolerance

The capability of a computer or operating system to ensure data integrity when hardware failures occur. Within Windows 2000 Server, Advanced Server, and Datacenter Server, mirrored volumes and redundant array of independent disks (RAID)-5 volumes are fault tolerant.

file allocation table (FAT) or FAT16

A 16-bit table that many operating systems use to locate files on disk. The FAT keeps track of all the pieces of a file. The FAT file system for older versions of Windows 95 is called the virtual file allocation table (VFAT); the one for Windows 95 (OEM Service Release 2, or OSR 2) and 98 is called FAT32. Windows XP can use the FAT file system; however, it is not often used on Windows XP, 2000, and NT machines because of its larger cluster sizes and inability to scale to larger volume sizes. The FAT file system has no local security.

file allocation table (FAT32)

A newer, 32-bit version of FAT available in Windows 95 OEM Service Release (OSR) 2 and 98. FAT32 increases the number of bits used to address clusters and reduces the size of each cluster. The result is that it can support larger disks (up to 2TB) and provide better storage efficiency (less slack space) than the earlier version of FAT. The FAT32 file system has no local security. Windows XP can use and format partitions as FAT, FAT32, or NT File System (NTFS).

FireWire or Institute of Electrical and Electronics Engineers (IEEE) 1394

A new, very fast external bus standard that supports data transfer rates of up to 400Mbps. Products that support the 1394 standard go under different names, depending on the company. Apple originally developed the technology and uses the trademarked name FireWire. You can use a single 1394 port to connect up to 63 external devices. In addition to its high speed, 1394 supports time-dependent data, delivering data at a guaranteed rate. This makes it ideal for devices that need to transfer high levels of data, such as video devices, in real-time. Although extremely fast and flexible, 1394 is expensive. Like Universal Serial Bus (USB), 1394 supports both Plug and Play and hot plugging and provides power to peripheral devices. The main difference between 1394 and USB is that 1394 supports faster data transfer rates and is more expensive. For these reasons, it is used mostly for devices that require large throughputs, such as video cameras, whereas USB is used to connect most other peripheral devices.

forward lookup

In Domain Name System (DNS), a query process in which the friendly DNS domain name of a host computer is searched to find its Internet Protocol (IP) address.

forward lookup zone

A Domain Name System (DNS) zone that provides hostname to Transmission Control Protocol/Internet Protocol (TCP/IP) address resolution. In DNS Manager, forward lookup zones are based on DNS domain names and typically hold host (A) address resource records.

Frame Relay Permanent Virtual Circuit (PVC)

A protocol where messages are divided into packets before they are sent. Each packet is then transmitted individually and can even follow different routes to its destination. After all the packets that form a message arrive at the destination, they are recompiled into the original message. Several wide area network (WAN) protocols, including Frame Relay, are

based on packet-switching technologies. Ordinary telephone service is based on a circuit-switching technology where a dedicated line is allocated for transmission between two parties. Circuit switching is best suited for data that must be transmitted quickly and must arrive in the same order in which it is sent. Most real-time data, such as live audio and video, requires circuit-switching technology. Packet switching is more efficient and robust for data that can withstand some delays (latency) in transmission, such as email messages and Web content.

global group

A group that can be granted rights and permissions and can become a member of local groups in its own domain and trusting domains. However, a global group can contain user accounts from its own domain only. Global groups provide a way to create sets of users from inside the domain that are available for use both in and out of the domain.

Group Policy

The mechanism for managing change and configuration of systems, security, applications, and user environments in an Active Directory domain.

Group Policy Editor (GPE)

A Windows XP snap-in that enables customers to create custom profiles for groups of users and computers.

Group Policy Object (GPO)

An object created by the Group Policy Editor (GPE) snap-in to hold information about a specific group's association with selected directory objects, such as sites, domains, or organizational units (OUs).

Hardware Abstraction Layer (HAL)

A component of an operating system that functions something like an application programming interface (API). In strict technical architecture, HALs reside at the device level, a layer below the standard API level. HAL enables programmers to write applications and game titles with all the device-independent advantages of writing to an API, but without the large processing overhead that APIs normally demand.

hardware profile

A profile that stores configuration settings for a collection of devices and services. Windows XP can store different hardware profiles so that users' needs can be met even though their computer may frequently require different device and service settings, depending on circumstances. The best example is a laptop or portable computer used in an office while in a docking station and then undocked so that the user can travel with it. The two environments require different power management settings, possibly different network settings, and various other configuration changes.

Hash Message Authentication Code (HMAC) Message Digest 5 (MD5)

A hash algorithm that produces a 128-bit hash of the authenticated payload.

hibernation

A power option in Windows XP Professional portable computers that helps to conserve battery power. Hibernation is a complete power down while maintaining the state of open programs and connected hardware. When you bring your computer out of hibernation, your desktop is restored exactly as you left it, in less time than it takes for a complete system restart. However, it takes longer to bring your computer out of Hibernate mode than out of Standby mode. Put your computer in hibernation when you will be away from the computer for an extended time or overnight.

home directory

A location for a user or group of users to store files on a network server. This provides a central location for files that users can access and back up.

HOSTS file

A local text file in the same format as the 4.3 Berkeley Software Distribution (BSD) Unix /etc/hosts file. This file maps hostnames to Internet Protocol (IP) addresses. In Windows XP, this file is stored in the \%SystemRoot%\System32\Drivers\Etc folder.

incremental backup

A backup that backs up only those files created or changed since the last normal or incremental backup. It marks files as having been backed up (in other words, the archive attribute is cleared). If you use a combination of normal and incremental backups, you need to have the last normal backup set as well as all incremental backup sets to restore your data.

Infrared Data Association (IrDA) device

A device that exchanges data over infrared waves. Infrared technology lets devices "beam" information to each other in the same way that your remote control tells the TV to change the channel. You could, for example, beam a document to a printer or another computer instead of having to connect a cable. The IrDA standard has been widely adopted by PC and consumer electronics manufacturers. Windows XP supports the IrDA standard.

input locale

The specification of the language you want to type in.

input/output (I/O) port

Any socket in the back, front, or side of a computer that you use to connect to another piece of hardware.

integrated services digital network (ISDN)

An international communications standard for sending voice, video, and data over digital telephone lines or normal telephone wires.

ISDN supports data transfer rates of 64Kbps. Most ISDN lines offered by telephone companies give you two lines at once, called B channels. You can use one line for voice and the other for data, or you can use both lines for data, giving you data rates of 128Kbps.

integrated zone storage

Storage of zone information in an Active Directory database rather than in a text file.

Internet Connection Firewall (ICF)

A built-in service that monitors all aspects of the traffic that crosses the network interface, which includes inspecting the source and destination addresses, for further control.

Internet Connection Sharing (ICS)

A feature that is intended for use in a small office or home office in which the network configuration and the Internet connection are managed by the computer running Windows XP where the shared connection resides. ICS can use a dial-up connection, such as modem or an integrated services digital network (ISDN) connection to the Internet, or it can use a dedicated connection such as a cable modem or digital subscriber line (DSL). It is assumed that the ICS computer is the only Internet connection, the only gateway to the Internet, and that it sets up all internal network addresses.

Internet Printing Protocol (IPP)

A standard that allows network clients the option of entering a Uniform Resource Locator (URL) to connect to network printers and manage their network print jobs using a Hypertext Transfer Protocol (HTTP) connection in a web browser. In Windows XP, IPP is fully supported. The print server is either a Windows 2000 server running Internet Information Services (IIS) 5 or a Windows XP Professional system running Personal Web Server (PWS). PWS is the "junior" version of IIS. All shared IPP printers can be viewed at http://servername/printers (for example, http://Server2/printers).

Internet Protocol (IP)

One of the protocols of the Transmission Control Protocol/ Internet Protocol (TCP/IP) suite. IP is responsible for determining if a packet is for the local network or a remote network. If the packet is for a remote network, IP finds a route for it.

Internet Protocol (IP) address

A 32-bit binary address used to identify a host's network and host ID. The network portion can contain either a network ID or a network ID and a subnet ID.

Internet Protocol Security (IPSec)

A Transmission Control Protocol/Internet Protocol (TCP/IP) security mechanism. IPSec provides machine-level authentication, as well as data encryption, for Virtual Private Network (VPN) connections that use Layer 2 Tunneling Protocol (L2TP). IPSec negotiates between your computer and its remote tunnel server before an L2TP connection is established, which secures both passwords and data.

Interrupt Request (IRQ)

A hardware line over which a device or devices can send interrupt signals to the microprocessor. When you add a new device to a PC, you sometimes need to set its IRQ number. IRQ conflicts used to be a common problem when you were adding expansion boards, but the Plug and Play and Advanced Configuration and Power Interface (ACPI) specifications have helped to remove this headache in many cases.

ipconfig

A command that enables you to view, renegotiate, and configure Internet Protocol (IP) address information for a Windows NT, 2000, or XP computer.

Kerberos v5

A distributed authentication and privacy protocol that protects information on a network between devices and enables Single Sign-On (SSO). Kerberos v5 is used in the Windows XP security model.

language group

A Regional Options configuration that allows you to type and read documents composed in languages of that group (for example, Western Europe and United States, Japanese, and Hebrew).

Last Known Good Configuration

Starts Windows XP using the Registry information that Windows saved at the last shutdown. Use this only in cases when you have incorrectly configured a device or driver. Last Known Good Configuration does not solve problems caused by corrupted or missing drivers or files. Also, you will lose any changes you made since the last successful startup.

Layer 2 Tunneling Protocol (L2TP)

An industry-standard Internet tunneling protocol. Unlike Point-to-Point Tunneling Protocol (PPTP), L2TP does not require Internet Protocol (IP) connectivity between the client workstation and the server. L2TP requires only that the tunnel medium provide packet-oriented point-to-point connectivity. You can use the protocol over media such as Asynchronous Transfer Mode (ATM), Frame Relay, and X.25. L2TP provides the same functionality as PPTP.

local group

A group account that is stored in the Security Accounts Manager (SAM) of a single system. You can give a local group access to resources only on that system.

local user

A user account that is stored in the Security Accounts Manager (SAM) of a single system. A local user can belong only to local groups on the same system and can be given access to resources only on that system.

logical drive

A simple volume or partition, indicated by a drive letter, that resides on a Windows XP basic disk.

logon script

A file that you can assign to user accounts. Typically a batch file, a logon script runs automatically every time the user logs on. You can use it to configure a user's working environment at every logon, and it allows an administrator to influence a user's environment without managing all aspects of it. You can assign a logon script to one or more user accounts.

Microsoft Challenge Handshake Authentication Protocol (MSCHAP) 1

A special version of Challenge Handshake Authentication Protocol (CHAP) that Microsoft uses. The encryption is still two-way and consists of a challenge from the server to the client that is made up of a session ID. The client uses a Message Digest 4 (MD4) hash to return the username to the server.

Microsoft Management Console (MMC)

A set of Windows XP utilities that allows authorized administrators to manage the directory remotely. The MMC provides a framework for hosting administrative tools, called consoles.

mirrored volume

A fault-tolerant set of two physical disks that contain an exact replica of each other's data within the mirrored portion of each disk. It is supported only on Windows 2000 Server versions.

mixed-mode domain

A migration concept that provides maximum backward compatibility with earlier versions of Windows NT. In a mixed-mode domain, domain controllers that have been upgraded to Active Directory services allow servers running Windows NT versions 4 and earlier to exist within the domain.

mounted drive, mount point, or mounted volume

A pointer from one partition to another. Mounted drives are useful for increasing a drive's "size" without disturbing it. For example, you could create a mount point to drive E as c:\CompanyData. Doing so makes it seem that you have increased the size available on the C partition, specifically allowing you to store more data in c:\CompanyData than you would otherwise be able to.

Moving Picture Experts Group (MPEG)

A family of digital video compression standards and file formats. MPEG generally produces better-quality video than competing formats. MPEG files can be decoded by special hardware or by software. MPEG achieves a high compression rate by storing only the changes from one frame to another, instead of each entire frame. There are two major MPEG standards: MPEG-1 and MPEG-2. The MPEG-1 standard provides a video resolution of 352×240 at 30 frames per second (fps), which is

video quality slightly below that of conventional VCR videos. A newer standard, MPEG-2, offers resolutions of 720×480 and 1,280×720 at 60 fps, with full CD-quality audio. This is sufficient for all the major TV standards, including NTSC and even HDTV. DVD-ROMs use MPEG-2. MPEG-2 can compress a two-hour video into a few gigabytes. Currently, work is being done on a new version of MPEG called MPEG-4 (there is no MPEG-3). MPEG-4 will be based on the QuickTime file format.

Multilink

An extension of Point-to-Point Protocol (PPP) that enables you to combine multiple physical connections between two points into a single logical connection. For example, you can combine two 33.6Kbps modems into one logical 67.2Kbps connection. The combined connections, called *bundles*, provide greater bandwidth than a single connection.

Multiple Processor Support (MPS)-compliant

Windows XP provides support for single or multiple CPUs. If you originally installed Windows XP on a computer with a single CPU, you must update the Hardware Abstraction Layer (HAL) on your computer so that it can recognize and use multiple CPUs.

name resolution

The process of translating a name into an Internet Protocol (IP) address. This could be either a fully qualified domain name (FQDN) or a NetBIOS name.

namespace

The method or conventions by which objects in a group of cooperating directories or databases are hierarchically structured and named.

native mode domain

A migration concept in which all domain controllers are running Windows 2000. The domain uses only Active Directory services multimaster replication between domain controllers, and no Windows NT domain controllers can participate in the domain through single-master replication.

network directory

A file or database from which users or applications can get reference information about objects on the network.

network interface card (NIC) or network adapter

A piece of computer hardware called an adapter card that physically connects a computer to a network cable.

normal backup

A backup that copies all files and marks those files as having been backed up (in other words, clears the archive attribute). It is the most complete form of backup.

NT File System (NTFS) 5

An advanced file system designed for use specifically within the Windows XP operating system. It supports file system recovery, extremely large storage media, and long file names.

NT File System (NTFS) permission

A rule associated with a folder, file, or printer to regulate which users can gain access to the object and in what manner. The object's owner allows or denies permissions. The most restrictive permissions take effect between share permissions and NTFS permissions on an object.

object

In the context of performance monitoring and optimization, a system component that has numerous counters associated with it. Objects include Processor, Memory, System, Logical Disk, and Pagefile.

offline file

A new feature of Windows XP that enables users to continue to work with network files and programs even when they are not connected to the network. When a network connection is restored or when users dock their mobile computers, any changes that were made while users were working offline are updated to the network. When more than one user on the network has made changes to the same file, users are given the option of saving their specific version of the file to the network, keeping the other version, or saving both.

Open Systems Interconnect (OSI) model

A layer architecture developed by the International Organization for Standardization (ISO) that standardizes levels of service and types of interaction for computers that are exchanging information through a communications network. The OSI model separates computer-to-computer communications into seven layers or levels, each building on the standards contained in the levels below it.

optimization

The process of tuning performance for a particular system component.

organizational unit (OU)

A type of container object used within the Lightweight Directory Access Protocol (LDAP)/X.500 information model to group other objects and classes together for easier administration.

Packet Internet Groper (Ping) utility

A utility that determines whether a specific Internet Protocol (IP) address for a network device is reachable from an individual computer. It works by sending a data packet to the specified address and waiting for a reply. You use it to troubleshoot network connections in the Transmission Control Protocol/Internet Protocol (TCP/IP) network protocol.

paging file

Formerly called the swap file or virtual memory file, an extension of memory space stored on the disk drive as a kind of virtual memory.

partition

The information area beginning at a branch of a directory tree and continuing to the bottom of that tree and/or to the edges of new partitions controlled by subordinate Directory System Agents (DSAs).

Password Authentication Protocol (PAP)

The protocol that allows clear-text authentication.

Peripheral Connection Interface (PCI)

A local bus standard developed by Intel. Most modern PCs include a PCI bus in addition to a more general Industry Standard Architecture (ISA) expansion bus. Many analysts, however, believe that PCI will eventually replace ISA entirely. PCI is a 64-bit bus, although it is usually implemented as a 32-bit bus. It can run at clock speeds of 33 or 66MHz. Although Intel developed it, PCI is not tied to any particular family of microprocessors.

Personal Computer Memory Card International Association (PCMCIA)

An organization of some 500 companies that developed a standard for small, credit-card–sized devices called PC Cards. Originally designed for adding memory to portable computers, the PCMCIA standard has been expanded several times and is suitable for many types of devices. There are in fact three types of PCMCIA cards, along with three types of PC slots the cards fit into: Type I, II, and III, respectively.

Plug and Play

A standard developed by Microsoft, Intel, and other industry leaders to simplify the process of adding hardware to PCs by having the operating system automatically detect devices. The standard's intention is to conceal unpleasant details, such as Interrupt Requests (IRQs) and Direct Memory Access (DMA) channels, from people who want to add a new hardware device to their system. A Plug and Play monitor, for example, can communicate with both Windows XP and the graphics adapter to automatically set itself at the maximum refresh rate supported for a chosen resolution. Plug and Play compliance also ensures that devices will not be driven beyond their capabilities.

Point-to-Point Protocol (PPP)

A method of connecting a computer to a network or to the Internet. PPP is more stable than the older Serial Line Internet Protocol (SLIP) and provides error-checking features. Windows XP Professional is a PPP client when dialing into any network.

Point-to-Point Tunneling Protocol (PPTP)

A communication protocol that tunnels through another connection, encapsulating PPP packets. The encapsulated packets are Internet Protocol (IP) datagrams that can be transmitted over IP-based networks, such as the Internet.

policy

A configuration or setting that is specified for one or more systems or users. Policies are refreshed at startup, at logon, and after a refresh interval, so if a setting is manually changed, the policy refreshes the setting automatically. Policies provide for centralized management of change and configuration.

primary domain controller (PDC)

In a Windows NT Server 4 or earlier domain, the computer running Windows NT Server that authenticates domain logons and maintains the directory database for a domain. The PDC tracks changes made to accounts of all computers on a domain. It is the only computer to receive these changes directly. A domain has only one PDC.

primary master

An authoritative Domain Name System (DNS) server for a zone that you can use as a point of update for the zone. Only primary masters can be updated directly to process zone updates, which include adding, removing, or modifying resource records that are stored as zone data. Primary masters are also used as the first sources for replicating the zone to other DNS servers.

primary monitor

The monitor designated as the one that displays the logon dialog box when you start your computer. Most programs display their window on the primary monitor when you first open them. A Windows XP computer can support multiple monitors or displays.

privilege

The capability to perform a system behavior, such as changing the system time, backing up or restoring files, or formatting the hard drive. A privilege used to be, and often still is, referred to as a user right.

public key cryptography

An asymmetric encryption scheme that uses a pair of keys to code data. The public key encrypts data, and a corresponding secret key decrypts it. For digital signatures, the sender uses the private key to create a unique electronic number that can be read by anyone who has the corresponding public key, thus verifying that the message is truly from the sender.

Recovery Console

A command-line interface (CLI) that provides a limited set of administrative commands that are useful for repairing a computer. For example, you can use the Recovery Console to start and stop services, read and write data on a local drive (including drives formatted to use NT File System— NTFS), repair a master boot record (MBR), and format drives.

You can start the Recovery Console from the Windows XP CD or by using the `winnt32.exe` command with the `/cmdcons` switch.

redundant array of independent disks (RAID)-5 (or striped set with parity) volume

A fault-tolerant collection of equal-sized partitions on at least three physical disks, where the data is striped and includes parity data. The parity data is used to help recover a member of the striped set if one of its members fails. Windows XP Professional cannot host a RAID-5 volume, but Windows 2000 Server versions can.

Remote Assistance

A built-in service that enables another user, typically a help desk or IT employee, to remotely help the end user with an issue that they are experiencing on their Windows XP Professional computer.

Remote Authentication Dial-In User Service (RADIUS)

A protocol used by Internet Authentication Services (IAS) to enable the communication of authentication, authorization, and accounting to the homogeneous and heterogeneous dial-up or Virtual Private Network (VPN) equipment in the enterprise.

Remote Desktop

A built-in service that enables you to access a session that is running on your computer while you are sitting at another computer. This will be extremely useful for employees who want to work from home, but need to access their computer at work.

Remote Installation Service (RIS)

An RIS server provides Windows XP Professional operating system image(s) that can be downloaded and installed by network clients using network adapters that comply with the Pre-Boot Execution Environment (PXE) boot read-only memory (ROM) specifications. RIS requires Active Directory, Dynamic Host Configuration Protocol (DHCP), and Domain Name System (DNS) to serve clients.

Removable Storage

Allows applications to access and share the same media resources. This service is used for managing removable media. Different types of media include floppy disks, Zip disks, CD-ROMs, CD-Rs, CD-RWs, DVD media, and tape backup devices. Some include removable hard drives as removable storage.

Resulting Set of Policies (RSoP)

A term for the resulting group policies that are applied to a computer and user. With multiple group policies at sites, domains, and OUs, it is very complex to determine the final, resulting policies that are applied.

reverse lookup zone

A Domain Name System (DNS) zone that provides Transmission Control Protocol/Internet Protocol (TCP/IP) address to hostname resolution.

route

A Windows XP command-line utility that manipulates Transmission Control Protocol/Internet Protocol (TCP/IP) routing tables for the local computer.

Safe Mode startup options

The options you get at startup when you press the F8 function key. Safe Mode helps you to diagnose problems. When started in Safe Mode, Windows XP uses only basic files and drivers (mouse, monitor, keyboard, mass storage, base video, and default system services, but no network connections). You can choose the Safe Mode with Networking option, which loads all the previously listed files and drivers plus the essential services and drivers to start networking. Or you can choose the Safe Mode with Command Prompt option, which is the same as Safe Mode except that a command prompt is started instead of Windows XP. You can also choose Last Known Good Configuration, which starts your computer using the Registry information that Windows XP saved at the last shutdown. If a symptom does not reappear when you start in Safe Mode, you can eliminate the default settings and minimum device drivers as possible causes. If a newly added device or a changed driver is causing problems, you can use Safe Mode to remove the device or reverse the change. In some circumstances, such as when

Windows system files required to start the system are corrupted or damaged, Safe Mode cannot help you. In this case, the Emergency Repair Disk (ERD) may be of use.

sampling (or update) interval

The frequency with which a performance counter is logged. A shorter interval provides more detailed information but generates a larger log.

scalability

A measure of how well a computer, service, or application can grow to meet increasing performance demands.

Security Accounts Manager (SAM)

The database of local user and local group accounts on a Windows 2000 member server or Windows XP Professional system.

Security Identifier (SID)

A unique number that represents a security principal, such as a user or group. You can change the name of a user or group account without affecting the account's permissions and privileges, because the SID is what is granted user rights and resource access.

Serial Line Internet Protocol (SLIP)

An older remote access communication protocol used in Windows XP for outbound communication only.

service (SRV) record

A resource record used in a zone to register and locate well-known Transmission Control Protocol/Internet Protocol (TCP/IP) services. The SRV resource record is specified in Request for Comments (RFC) 2052 and is used in Windows 2000 or later to locate domain controllers for Active Directory Service.

Setup Manager

Used to create answer files for Windows XP unattended installations. Setup Manager can create answer files for unattended, Sysprep, or RIS installations.

share permission

A rule associated with a folder, to regulate which users can gain access to the object over the network and in what manner.

Shiva Password Authentication Protocol (SPAP)

A protocol that third-party clients and servers typically use. The encryption for the protocol is two-way, but it is not as good as that for Challenge Handshake Authentication Protocol (CHAP).

simple volume

In Windows XP, the disk space on a single physical disk. It can consist of a single area on a disk or multiple areas on the same disk that are linked together. You can extend a simple volume within the same disk or among multiple disks. If you extend a simple volume across multiple disks, it becomes a spanned volume.

slipstreaming
The process of integrating a Windows XP service pack into an existing Windows XP installation share. Subsequent installations of Windows XP will then include the service pack that you have slipstreamed into the installation share.

Smart Card
A credit-card–sized device used to securely store public and private keys, passwords, and other types of personal information. To use a Smart Card, you need a Smart Card reader attached to the computer and a personal identification number (PIN) for the Smart Card. In Windows XP, you can use Smart Cards to enable certificate-based authentication and Single Sign-On (SSO) to the enterprise.

Smart Card reader
A small external or internal device, or even a built-in slot, into which you insert a Smart Card so that it can be read.

spanned volume
In Windows XP, the disk space on more than one physical disk. You can add more space to a spanned volume by extending it at any time. In NT 4 and earlier, a spanned volume was called a volume set.

spooler service
The primary Windows XP service that controls printing functionality.

standard zone storage
Storage of zone information in a text file rather than in an Active Directory database.

Standby mode
A power-saving option in Windows XP. Your computer switches to a low-power state where devices, such as the monitor and hard disks, turn off and your computer uses less power. When you want to use the computer again, it comes out of Standby quickly, and your desktop is restored exactly as you left it. Standby is useful for conserving battery power in portable computers. Standby does not save your desktop state to disk; if you experience a power failure while on Standby, you can lose unsaved information. If there is an interruption in power, information in memory is lost.

static pool
A range of Internet Protocol (IP) addresses configured on the remote access server that enables the server to allocate IP addresses to the remote access clients.

striped volume
A volume that stores data in stripes on two or more physical disks. Data in a striped volume is allocated alternately and evenly (in stripes) to the disks of the striped volume. Striped volumes are *not* fault tolerant. Striped volumes can substantially improve the speed of access to your data on disk. Striped volumes with parity, also known as

RAID-5 volumes, can be created *only* on Windows 2000 Server machines. In NT 4 and earlier, a striped volume was called a striped set.

subnet mask

A filter used to determine which network segment, or subnet, an Internet Protocol (IP) address belongs to. An IP address has two components: the network address and the host (computer name) address. For example, if the IP address 209.15.17.8 is part of a Class C network, the first three numbers (209.15.17) represent the Class C network address, and the last number (8) identifies a specific host (computer) on this network. By implementing subnetting, network administrators can further divide the host part of the address into two or more subnets.

Suspend mode

A deep-sleep power-saving option that still uses some power.

symmetric multiprocessing (SMP)

A computer architecture that provides fast performance by making multiple CPUs available to complete individual processes simultaneously (multiprocessing). Unlike with asymmetric processing, you can assign any idle processor any task as well as add additional CPUs to improve performance and handle increased loads. A variety of specialized operating systems and hardware arrangements support

SMP. Specific applications can benefit from SMP if their code allows multithreading. SMP uses a single operating system and shares common memory and disk input/output (I/O) resources. Windows XP supports SMP.

Sysprep

A tool that prepares a Windows XP computer to be imaged using third-party disk image software. It does this by removing unique identifiers such as computer name and Security Identifiers (SIDs). Sysprep adds a service to the image that generates a unique local domain SID after the image has been applied.

system state

In Backup, a collection of system-specific data that you can back up and restore. For all Windows 2000 and XP operating systems, the system state data includes the Registry, the Component Object Model (COM)+ Class Registration database, and the system boot files. For Windows 2000 Server, the system state data also includes the Certificate Services database (if the server is operating as a certificate server). If the server is a domain controller, the system state data also includes the Active Directory services database and the Sysvol directory.

Sysvol

A shared directory that stores the server copy of the domain's public files, which are replicated among all domain controllers in the domain.

ticket

A feature of the Kerberos security model by which clients are granted access to objects and resources only indirectly, through services. Application servers use the service ticket to impersonate the client and look up its user or group Security Identifiers (SIDs).

tracert

A Windows XP command-line utility that follows that path of a data packet from a local computer to a host (computer) somewhere on the network (or Internetwork). It shows how many hops the packet requires to reach the host and how long each hop takes. You can use tracert to figure out where the longest delays are occurring for connecting to various computers.

universal group

A security or distribution group that you can use anywhere in the domain tree or forest. A universal group can have members from any Windows 2000 domain in the domain tree or forest. It can also include other universal groups, global groups, and accounts from any domain in the domain tree or forest. Universal groups can be members of domain local groups and other universal groups but cannot be members of global groups. Universal groups appear in the Global Catalog and should contain primarily global groups.

Universal Serial Bus (USB)

An external bus standard (released in 1996) that supports data transfer rates of 12Mbps. You can use a single USB port to connect up to 127 peripheral devices, such as mice, modems, and keyboards. USB also supports Plug and Play installation and hot plugging. It is expected to completely replace serial and parallel ports.

User Datagram Protocol (UDP)

A connectionless protocol that runs on top of Internet Protocol (IP) networks. Unlike Transmission Control Protocol/Internet Protocol (TCP/IP), UDP/IP provides very few error recovery services and does not guarantee delivery of data. UDP is a direct way to send and receive datagrams over an IP network. It's used primarily for sending broadcast messages over an IP network.

user locale

Controls the date, time, currency, and numbers on a per-user basis. These settings are used by all applications and can be configured via the Regional Options applet in the Control Panel folder.

user profile

The collection of desktop and environmental settings that define the work area of a local computer.

user right

See privilege.

User State Migration Tool (USMT)

A command-line interface set of tools that stores user data and settings for an upgrade or reinstallation of the computer. The tools include scanstate and loadstate, which extract and restore the information, respectively.

video adapter

The electronic component that generates the video signal sent through a cable to a video display. The video adapter is usually located on the computer's main system board or on an expansion board.

Virtual Private Network (VPN)

A private network of computers that is at least partially connected using public channels or lines, such as the Internet. A good example would be a private-office local area network (LAN) that enables users to log in remotely over the Internet (an open, public system). VPNs use encryption and secure protocols such as Point-to-Point Tunneling Protocol (PPTP) and Layer 2 Tunneling Protocol (L2TP) to ensure that unauthorized parties do not intercept data transmissions.

Volume Shadow Copy Technology (VSCT)

A volume that represents a duplicate of the original volume taken at the time the copy began.

Windows Backup

A Windows XP utility that helps you plan for and recover from data loss by enabling you to create backup copies of data as well as restore files, folders, and system state data (which includes the Registry) manually or on a schedule. The Windows XP Backup program enables you to back up data to a variety of media types, not just tape.

Windows Installer Packages

Files with the .msi extension that install applications. These files contain summary and installation instructions as well as the actual installation files. You can install Windows Installer Packages locally or remotely through Group Policies.

Windows Internet Naming Service (WINS)

A service that dynamically maps NetBIOS names to Internet Protocol (IP) addresses.

Windows Management Instrumentation (WMI)

An initiative supported in Windows XP that establishes architecture to support the management of an enterprise across the Internet. WMI offers universal access to management information for enterprises by providing a consistent view of the managed environment. This management uniformity enables you to manage your entire business rather than just its components. You can obtain more detailed information regarding the WMI Software Development Kit (SDK) from the Microsoft Developer Network (MSDN).

Windows Messenger

The new application built into the OS that allows for chatting, notifications, voice communication, file transfer, and sharing of applications.

Windows or Win32 Driver Model (WDM)

A 32-bit layered architecture for device drivers; it allows for drivers that Windows XP, 2000, NT, and 98 can use. It provides common input/output (I/O) services that all operating systems understand. It also supports Plug and Play; Universal Serial Bus (USB); Institute of Electrical and Electronics Engineers (IEEE) 1394 bus; and various devices, including input, communication, imaging, and digital versatile disc or digital video disc (DVD) devices.

Windows Update

Offers device driver support that supplements the extensive library of drivers available on the installation CD. Windows Update is an online extension, providing a central location for product enhancements.

winnt32 /cmdcons

The command and switch used to install the Recovery Console onto a Windows XP computer. This command uses winnt32 on the installation media or in the distribution source.

workgroup

A peer-to-peer network in which user accounts are decentralized and stored on each individual system.

X.25 Virtual Circuit (VC)

A connection between two devices that acts as though it's a direct connection, although it may physically take different routes. X.25 connections involve at least two hosts in a packet-switching network. With X.25 VCs, two hosts can communicate as though they have a dedicated connection, although the data packets might actually travel very different routes before arriving at their destinations. VCs can be either permanent or temporary.

ZAP

A file that you use to allow applications without an MSI file to be deployed via Group Policy.

zone

In Domain Name System (DNS) standards, the namespace partition formed by each domain within the global namespace or within an enterprise namespace. Each zone is controlled by an authoritative DNS server, or in the case of Active Directory services, by a group of domain controllers.

zone transfer

Copying of Domain Name System (DNS) database information from one DNS server to another.

Index

NUMBERS

802.1x standard, 195
1394 devices, 203

A

access
    encrypted files, 247-249
    NTFS volumes, 48-50
        advanced permissions, 53-55
        basic permissions, 53
        built-in security principals, 50-51
        conflicts, 57
        default permissions, 56-57
        Deny permission, assigning, 62-64
        local accounts versus domain
            accounts, 59
        optimizing, 64
        permissions versus rights, 59-60
        Read-Only permission, assigning,
            60-62
    offline files and folders, 137
    remote access
        authentication protocols, 330-333
        encryption, 333-334
        setting up connections, 334-337
    shared folders. See shared folders
    USB devices, 67-68, 251-252
access control entries (ACEs), 52
access control lists (ACLs), 52
Accessibility Option applet, 160-163
accessibility options, 160
    Accessibility Options applet, 160-163
    Accessibility Wizard, 163

accessing with Utility Manager, 163-164
    Magnifier, 163
    Narrator, 163
    On-Screen Keyboard, 163
Accessibility Wizard, 163
Account Lockout Duration account policy,
    111
Account Lockout Threshold account policy,
    111
Account Management audit policy, 111
account policies, 110-111
accounts. See also group accounts; user
    accounts
    built-in, 96-98
    configuring properties, 99-100
    creating, 98-99, 106
    deleting, 102, 107
    passwords, 103-104
    renaming, 101
    User Accounts tool, 102
ACEs (access control entries), 52
ACLs (access control lists), 52
ACPI (Advanced Configuration and Power
    Interface), 2, 206-207
activating Windows XP Professional, 30-31
Active Directory, 59
    backing up, 295-296
    Sites and Services Console, 108
    Users and Computers snap-in, 106-107
ad-hoc wireless networks, 196
adapters
    compatibility with Windows XP
        Professional, 2
    network, 194
    PC Card, 203, 209
    video, 197

How can we make this index more useful? Email us at indexes@quepublishing.com

Adaptive Mode (MeasureUp), 432
Add Hardware applet, 178
  installing
    modems, 189
    network adapters, 194
    non-PnP devices, 178
    optical media, 191
    Smart Card readers, 209
    tape devices, 201
    video adapters, 197
  troubleshooting hardware, 180, 184
Add Hardware Wizard, 178
  accessing, 179
  device conflicts, troubleshooting, 184
  IrDA devices, installing, 194
  modems, installing, 189
Add Printer Wizard, 80-82
Add/Remove Programs applet, 6
Address Resolution Protocol (ARP), 269
Address toolbar, 142
ADMIN$ hidden share, 43
Administrative Options option (Accessibility
  Options applet), 163
administrative shares, 42-43
Administrator account, 49, 96
  compared with Limited account, 102
Administrators group, 49, 97
Administrators permission, 57
Advanced Configuration and Power
  Interface (ACPI), 2, 206-207
advanced NTFS permissions, 53-55
Advanced Power Management (APM),
  206-207
Advanced tab
  Customize Start Menu dialog box, 141
  printer Properties dialog box, 84-85
  Regional and Language Options dialog
    box, 157
Alerter service, 352
alternate DNS servers, 267
Anonymous Logon group, 98
Anonymous Logon security principal, 51
/:answer switch (winnt.exe), 11
answer files, creating, 8-10
APIPA (Automatic Private IP Addressing),
  261, 271
APM (Advanced Power Management),
  206-207
Appearance tab (Display applet), 139
AppHelp.sdb file, 146
AppleTalk protocol, 274
applications. *See also* software
  assigning, 152
  compatibility support, 145-148
  installing, 148-153
  managing performance, 321

Archives tab (Fax Properties window), 166
ARP (Address Resolution Protocol), 269
ASR (Automated System Recovery),
  309-310
assigning
  applications, 152
  drive letters, 239-240
  NTFS permissions, 60-64
audio
  Sounds and Audio Devices applet, 139
  Speech applet, 140
auditing, 68-72
  audit policies, 111-112
  Audit option (Sysprep), 14
Authenticated Users group, 98
Authenticated Users security principal, 51
authentication, 105
  disabling over clear channels, 78
  EAP-TLS protocol, 209
  enabling for WebDAV, 77
  remote access protocols, 330-333
Automatic Private IP Addressing (APIPA),
  261, 271
Automatic Reset option (Accessibility
  Options applet), 162
Automatic Updates, 28-29, 180-181
Available Bytes counter, 316

B

Backup Operators group, 49, 97
backups, 292
  Automated System Recovery, 309-310
  backup markers, 293
  configuring, 295
  IIS metabase, 74
  permissions, 293
  restoring files and folders, 298-299
  scheduling, 296-297
  strategies, 294-295
  System State data, 295-296
  types of, 293-294
  Volume Shadow Copy Service, 298
BAP (Bandwidth Allocation Protocol),
  332-333
baselines, creating, 314-315
Basic Collection, 154
basic disks, 218
  compared to dynamic disks, 220-221
  converting dynamic disks to, 224
  upgrading to dynamic disks, 221-224
basic partitions, 225
  creating, 226
  deleting, 226-227
  extending, 226
BIOS, 2
boot files, backing up, 295-296

boot partition, 218
boot.ini file, 218
    editing, 144-145
bridges, 274-275
built-in security principals, 50-51

C

C$ hidden share, 43
Cachemov.exe utility, 46
caching
    configuring shared folders, 45-46
    deleting cache files, 235
canceling print jobs, 82
card services, 209
CardBus standard, 209
CD devices, 191-192
CD-ROMs
    Windows XP Professional installation, 7
    with this book, 431-435
CDFS (Compact Disc File System), 191
certificate rules, 118
certification, 431-435
Change Journal, 293
Change permission, 48
Change Permissions permission, 55
chkdsk utility, 234
chkntfs utility, 234
Chkupgrd.exe, 4
CIDR (Classless Interdomain Routing),
    265-266
Classful IP addressing, 264
Clean option (Sysprep), 14
Clear the Virtual Memory Pagefile When
    the System Shuts Down policy, 110
ClearType, 164
clients
    Client Service for NetWare, 273
    Client-Side Caching. See Offline Files
    RIS clients, configuring, 19
    Restrictions for Unauthenticated RPC
        Clients policy, 352-353
    RestrictRemoteClients Registry key, 352
cold docking/undocking, 203
color schemes, customizing, 139
COM settings, administering restricted, 355
Compact Disc File System (CDFS), 191
CompatAdmin tool, 147
Compatws.inf security template, 117
Complex Script Collection, 154
Compressed (Zipped) Folders, 243
compression, 4-5, 243-245
Computer Scope option (RSoP), 114
configuring
    account properties, 99-100
    application compatibility settings, 147
    backups, 295

desktop settings, 137-143
driving-signing options, 186-188
Fax service, 165-166
hardware profiles, 204
Internet Connection Sharing, 348-349
logon scripts, 127
Multilink, 190
multiple-monitor support, 197-200
Offline Files, 45-46, 131-133
optical media devices, 191
Performance Logs and Alerts, 312-314
printer properties, 83-86
Remote Desktop, 277-278
Remote Installation Services, 16-17
roaming user profiles, 128-129
System Monitor, 311-312
system settings, 143-145
TCP/IP, 266-268
wireless networking, 196
connections
    dial-up. See dial-up connections
    ICS (Internet Connection Sharing),
        348-350
    intranet connections, troubleshooting,
        79
    network printers, 81-82
    Novell NetWare, 272-274
    Remote Desktop, 278-279
    to shared resources, 43-45
    Unix, 274
Control Panel applets, 137-138
    Accessibility Options, 160-163
    Add Hardware. See Add Hardware
        applet
    Display, 138-139, 198-199
    Keyboard, 138
    Mouse, 139
    Power Options, 206-208
    Regional and Language Options,
        154-157
    Scanners and Cameras, 139, 188-189
    Sounds and Audio Devices, 139
    Speech, 140
    Taskbar and Start Menu, 140-143
converting
    basic disks to dynamic disks, 221-224
    dynamic disks to basic disks, 224
copy backups, 294
copying
    compressed files and folders, 244-245
    encrypted files, 249
    NTFS files and folders, 64-65
counter logs, 313-314
counters
    disk, 318-319
    memory, 315-316
    network, 319

objects to monitor, 315
Performance Logs and Alerts, 312-314
processor, 319-320
System Monitor, 310-312
CPUs
multiple, upgrading to, 201-203
performance, managing, 319-320
Create Files/Write Data permission, 55
Create Folder/Append Data permission, 55
Create Partition Wizard, 226
Creator Group security principal, 51
Creator Owner group, 98
Creator Owner permission, 57
Creator Owner security principal, 51
critical updates, 28-30
CSC (Client-Side Caching). *See* Offline
Files
CSPs (Cryptographic Service Providers),
209
Cursor Options (Accessibility Options
applet), 162
Custom Mode (MeasureUp), 432
custom modes, compatibility support, 147
Customize Start Menu dialog box, 141

D

D$ hidden share, 43
daily backups, 294-295
daisy-chaining USB devices, 193
data compression. *See* compression
data encryption. *See* EFS; encryption
Data Execution Prevention (DEP), 119,
322-323
Data Link Control (DLC) protocol, 83, 274
data recovery agents (DRAs), 247-248
DCOM, administering restricted settings,
355
Debugging Mode startup option, 301
default
FTP site, 76
gateway, 267
local groups, 49-50
local users, 49
NTFS permissions, 56-57, 239
share permissions, 48
defrag.exe, 235
defragmenting hard disks, 234-235
Delete permission, 55
Delete Subfolders and Files permission, 55
deleting
accounts, 102
cache files, 235
disk quotas, 242
group accounts, 102
partitions, 226-227
program files, 235

temporary files, 235
user accounts, 102, 107
Deny permissions
assigning, 62-64
precedence, 58
DEP (Data Execution Prevention), 119,
322-323
boot.ini switches, 145
dependency failures, 32
deploying. *See* installing
Desktop tab (Display applet), 138
Desktop toolbar, 143
desktop, configuring, 137-138
Display applet, 138-139
Keyboard applet, 138
Mouse applet, 139
Scanners and Cameras applet, 139
Sounds and Audio Devices applet, 139
Speech applet, 140
Taskbar and Start Menu applet, 140-143
user profiles. *See* user profiles
device drivers, 176
reverting to previous drivers, 184
signing, 185-188
updating, 180-183
Device Manager
hardware problems, troubleshooting,
232
hardware profiles, enabling/disabling,
204
modem operation, verifying, 190
multiple CPU support, installing, 202
status icons, 185
tape devices, managing, 201
USB devices, troubleshooting, 194
USB hub power allocation, viewing, 193
Devices tab (Fax Properties window), 166
DHCP (Dynamic Host Configuration
Protocol), 260, 266, 271-272
diagnostic tools, TCP/IP, 269
dial-up connections
authentication protocols, 330-333
connecting to remote access servers,
334-335
encryption, 333-334
installing modems, 189
multilinking modems, 189-190
troubleshooting modems, 190
Dial-up group, 98
Dialup security principal, 51
differential backups, 294-295
digital cameras, 188
installing, 188
testing, 188-189
Directory Services Restore Mode startup
option, 301

disabling
    authentication over clear channels, 78
    Fast User Switching, 130
    receiving files via IrDA connections, 195
    Simple File Sharing, 40
    user accounts, 101, 107
disallowed software restriction policies, 118
Disk Cleanup Wizard, 235
Disk Defragmenter, 234-235
disk groups, 219
Disk Management snap-in
    basic disks, upgrading to dynamic disks,
        221-222
    drive letters, assigning/changing/
        removing, 239
    dynamic disks, converting to basic disks,
        224
    extending volumes, 229
    missing/offline disks, reactivating, 225
    mounted drives, creating, 240-241
    moving disks to another computer,
        224-225
    partitions, creating/deleting, 226
    simple volumes, creating, 228
    spanned volumes, creating, 228
    striped volumes, creating, 230
disk quotas, 241-243
disk-imaging software, 12
diskpart.exe, 222-223
    converting basic disks to dynamic disks,
        222
    extending partitions, 226
Diskperf.exe, 233
Display tab (Accessibility Options applet),
    161-162
displays
    accessibility options, 161-162
    ClearType, 164
    Display applet, 138-139
    Dualview, 165
    multiple-monitor support, 197-200
    refresh frequency, 200
    troubleshooting, 139, 200
distributed servers, Windows XP
    Professional installation, 7-8
DLC (Data Link Control) protocol, 83, 274
DLLs (dynamic link libraries), 4
DNS servers, 261, 267
Do Not Display Last Username in Logon
    Screen policy, 110
Domain Local groups, 100
domain user accounts, 106-107
domains
    joining, 20-21
    linking to GPOs, 108
    security, 59
    troubleshooting, 32

dotted-decimal notation, 263
DRAs (data recovery agents), 247-248
Driver Rollback, 184
Driver Verifier utility, 182
Driver.cab file, 180
drivers. *See* device drivers
Dualview, 165
/dudisable switch (winnt32.exe), 11
/duprepare:*pathname* switch (winnt32.exe),
    11
/dushare:*pathname* switch (winnt32.exe), 11
DVD devices, 191-192
DVD-RAM disks, FAT32 support, 241
dynamic disks, 219-220
    compared to basic disks, 220-221
    converting to basic disks, 224
    limitations, 220, 230-232
    moving to another computer, 224-225
    reactivating, 225
    reverting back to basic disks, 223
    upgrading basic disks to, 221-224
Dynamic Host Configuration Protocol
    (DHCP), 260, 266, 271
dynamic link libraries (DLLs), 4
Dynamic Update, 29-30
dynamic volumes, 227
    formatting, 220
    limitations, 230-232
    mirrored, 219, 230
    RAID-5, 219, 230
    simple, 228
    spanned, 228-229
    striped, 229-230

E

E$ hidden share, 43
EAP (Extensible Authentication Protocol),
    331
EAP-TLS protocol, 209
East Asian Collection, 154
EFS (Encrypting File System), 245
    accessing encrypted files, 247-248
    encrypting files and folders, 246
    moving and copying encrypted files, 249
    sharing access to encrypted files,
        249-251
El-Torito No Emulation, 7
Enable Boot Logging startup option, 300
Enable VGA Mode option (Windows
    Advanced Options menu), 197
Enable VGA Mode startup option, 301
enabling
    auditing, 68-70
    Fast User Switching, 130
    printer pooling, 80
    receiving files via IrDA connections, 195

user accounts, 101
WebDAV authentication, 77
encryption, 245-251
accessing encrypted files, 247-248
encrypting files and folders, 246
moving and copying encrypted files, 249
remote network connections, 333-334
sharing access to encrypted files,
249-251
Web Folders, 77
WebDAV protocol, 77
end-user modes, compatibility support, 146
Enforce Password History account policy,
111
Error-Checking tool, 234
errors
disk, 234
STOP, 32
event logs, 321
Event Viewer
accessing, 71
Security Log, 68, 71-72
Eventtriggers.exe, 321
Everyone group, 98
Everyone permission, 57
Everyone security principal, 51
extended partitions, 218
creating, 226
deleting, 226-227
extending partitions, 219
basic partitions, 226
simple volumes, 229
spanned volumes, 229
Extensible Authentication Protocol (EAP),
331

F

Factory option (Sysprep), 14
Fast User Switching, 104, 130
FAST Wizard, 22-23, 157-159
Fastwiz.exe, 22
FAT and FAT32 file systems, 236
converting partitions to NTFS, 238-239
DVD-RAM disk support for, 241
upgrading to Windows XP Professional,
4-5
fault-tolerant volumes, 219, 226
Fax Configuration Wizard, 165-166
Fax Console, 165-168
Fax Properties window, 166-167
Fax Security tab (Fax Properties window),
167
Fax service, 165-168

file systems, 236-237. *See also specific file
systems*
converting from one to another, 237-239
errors, 234
upgrading to Windows XP
Professional, 5
FileList.xml file, 307
files
auditing, enabling, 70-71
compatibility database files, 145-146
compressing, 243-245
copying
compressed files, 244-245
encrypted files, 249
NTFS files, 64-65
data encryption, 245-251
migrating using USMT, 21-25, 157-159
moving
compressed files, 244-245
encrypted files, 249
offline. *See* Offline Files
ownership, taking, 66-67
updating system files, 183
Files and Settings Transfer (FAST) Wizard,
22-23, 157-159
FilterKeys, 161
Finger utility, 268
firewalls. *See* Windows Firewall
FireWire devices, 203
flash drives, 194
folders
auditing, enabing, 70-71
compressing, 243-245
copying, 64-65
data encryption, 245-251
migrating using USMT, 21-25, 157-159
offline. *See* Offline Files
ownership, taking, 66-67
shared. *See* shared folders
font schemes, customizing, 139
Forgotten Password Wizard, 104
format.exe, 220
Found New Hardware Wizard, 178
FTP (File Transfer Protocol), 263, 268
default site, administering, 76
Full Control permission, 48, 53-54

G

Gateway Service for NetWare (GSNW),
273
gateway, default, 267
General tab
Accessibility Options applet, 162-163
Fax Properties window, 166
printer Properties dialog box, 83
System Configuration Utility, 144

GPMC (Group Policy Management Console), 108-109
GPOs (Group Policy Objects), 108-109
publishing MSI files, 150-151
Resultant Set of Policy, 112-115
SP2 changes, 112
gpresult command, 113
gpupdate command, 114
group accounts
built-in, 97-98
creating, 98-99
default local groups, 49-50
deleting, 102
domain security, 59
managing membership, 100
permissions
Deny, assigning, 62-64
Read-Only, assigning, 60-62
viewing, 65
renaming, 101
system groups, 98
user rights assignment, 109-110
workgroup security, 59
Group Policy, 107
account policies, 110-111
audit policies, 111-112
deploying service packs via, 25
driver-signing options, modifying, 187-188
Local Group Policies, 107-108
security options, 110
user profiles, managing, 129-130
user rights assignment, 109-110
Group Policy Editor, 108
Group Policy Management Console (GPMC), 108-109
Group Policy Objects. *See* GPOs
Group Policy Result tool, 113
Group Policy Update tool, 114
grouping taskbar buttons, 142
GSNW (Gateway Service for NetWare), 273
Guest account, 49, 96
enabling, 101
Guests group, 49, 97

H

hard disks, 218
basic, 218-219
defragmenting, 234-235
disk quotas, 241-243
drive letters, assigning/changing/removing, 239-240
dynamic, 219-220
images, creating, 12-19

mounted drives, 240-241
moving to another computer, 224-225
performance, monitoring, 233, 318-319
reactivating, 225
troubleshooting, 232-235
upgrading, 221-224
hardware
compatibility, 4
device drivers. *See* device drivers
HCL (Hardware Compatibility List), 2
installing, 178-179
profiles, 204
requirements for Windows XP installation, 2
setup disks, 3
troubleshooting, 180
Hardware tab (System Properties dialog box), 179
hardware-based volumes, 226
hash rules, 118
HCL (Hardware Compatibility List), 2
HelpAssistant account, 49, 96
HelpServicesGroup local group, 49-50
Hibernate mode, 139, 208
hidden shares, 42-43
High Contrast option (Accessibility Options applet), 161
High Performance File System (HPFS), 236
Hisecws.inf security template, 117
home folders, 127
HOSTNAME utility, 269
HOSTS file, 73
hot docking/undocking, 203
hotfixes, installing, 27-28
HPFS (High Performance File System), 236
hubs, USB, 192-193

I

ICS (Internet Connection Sharing), 348
setting up, 348-349
troubleshooting, 349-350
IEEE 1394 devices, 203
IEEE 802.1x standard, 195
IIS (Internet Information Services), 72
Console
default FTP site, administering, 76
default website, administering, 74-76
launching, 73
FTP. *See* FTP
installing, 72-73
metabase backups, 74
Remote Desktop web connections, 279
SMTP, 263
troubleshooting, 78-79
World Wide Web service, 263

image devices, 139
images (disk), creating
  with Riprep.exe, 18-19
  with Risetup.exe, 16-17
  with Sysprep.exe, 12-14
incremental backups, 294-295
Infrared Data Association (IrDA) devices,
  194-195
infrastructure wireless network connections,
  196
Install New Modem dialog box, 189
installing
  CD-ROM with this book, 433-434
  digital cameras, 188
  Fax service, 165
  hardware, 178-179
  hotfixes, 27-28
  IIS (Internet Information Services),
    72-73
  modems, 189
  MSI files, 149-150
  network adapters, 194
  RIS (Remote Installation Services),
    15-16
  scanners, 188
  service packs, 25-26
  Smart Card readers, 209
  Windows XP Professional
    activating installations, 30-31
    adapter compatibility, 2
    additional information, 38
    answer files, creating, 8-10
    CD-ROM installations, 7
    distributed servers, 7-8
    hardware requirements, 2
    migrating user settings, 21-25
    RIS (Remote Installation Services),
      14-19
    setup disks, 3
    Sysprep, 12-14
    troubleshooting, 31-32
    winnt.exe switches, 11
    winnt32.exe switches, 11-12
Interactive group, 98
interactive logons, 105
Interactive security principal, 51
Internet Connection Sharing (ICS),
  348-350
Internet Explorer shortcut, 143
Internet Information Services. See IIS
Internet Printing Protocol (IPP), 86
intranet website connections,
  troubleshooting, 79
invitations (Remote Assistance), 280-281

IP addresses
  APIPA (Automatic Private IP
    Addressing), 261, 271
  CIDR (Classless Interdomain Routing),
    265-266
  Class IP addressing, 264
  default gateway, 267
  dotted-decimal notation, 263
  ICS (Internet Connection Sharing),
    348-350
  loopback, 264, 270
  network broadcasts, 263
  nonroutable, 264
  subnet masks, 266
    configuration settings, 269
    variable-length, 264-265
  TCP/IP profiles, 271-272
IPC$ hidden share, 43
ipconfig command, 269-271
IPP (Internet Printing Protocol), 86
IPSec, 262, 331
IPX/SPX protocol, 272-273
IrDA devices, 194-195

J - K

joining
  domains, 20-21, 32
  workgroups, 19
Joliet standard, 191
jump drives, 194
  write access, controlling, 67-68, 251-252

Keyboard applet, 138
Keyboard tab (Accessibility Options),
  160-161
keychain drives, 194
  write access, controlling, 67-68, 251-252

L

L2TP (Layer 2 Tunneling Protocol), 262,
  332
Languages tab (Regional and Language
  Options dialog box), 156
languages. See multiple-language support
Last Known Good Configuration option,
  197, 301
Layer 2 Tunneling Protocol (L2TP), 262,
  332
legacy application support, 145-148
Limited account, 102
Line Printer Daemon (LPD), 268, 274
Line Printer Remote (LPR) ports, 268, 274
Links toolbar, 142

List Folder Contents permission, 53
List Folder/Read Data permission, 55
LMHOSTS file, 73
Local Group Policy, 107-108
local printers, adding, 80-81
Local Security Policy, 107-108
Local Security Settings Console, 68-69
Local Security Settings snap-in, 68-70
Local Settings folder, 126
local user accounts
    creating, 98-99
    deleting, 102
    disabling, 101
    enabling, 101
    naming, 98
    passwords, 99
    renaming, 101
local user profiles, 126-127
Local Users and Groups snap-in, 96
locales, 154-157
locking taskbar, 142
logging mode (RSoP), 115
logical drives
    creating on basic disks, 226
    deleting, 226-227
LogicalDisk performance counters, 318-319
Logon Events audit policy, 111
logon scripts, 127
logons
    Group Policy account policies, 110-111
    interactive, 105
    remote, 105
loopback address, 264, 270
LPD (Line Printer Daemon), 268, 274
LPQ utility, 269
LPR (Line Printer Remote) ports, 268, 274
LPR utility, 268

M

Magnifier, 163
/makelocalsource switch (winnt32.exe), 11
master boot record (MBR), 219
master file table (MFT), 235
Maximum Password Age account policy,
    110
MBR (master boot record), 219
MD5-CHAP, 331
MeasureUp test engine, 431-435
media pools, 200-201
memory
    performance, managing, 315-316
    RIS partition requirements, 15
    virtual. *See* virtual memory
    Windows XP Professional SP2
      requirements, 2

Messenger service, 352
MFT (master file table), 235
Microsoft Passport, 119, 276
MigDB.inf file, 145
migration DLLs, 4
Minimum Password Age account policy, 111
Minimum Password Length account policy,
    110
mirrored volumes, 219, 230
Missed Question Mode (MeasureUp), 432
missing disks, reactivating, 225
mobile computing, 203
    power management, 206-208
modems
    installing, 189
    multilinking, 189-190
    troubleshooting, 190
Modify permission, 53
monitoring performance, 233-234
    baselines, creating, 314-315
    disk counters, 318-319
    Eventtriggers.exe, 321
    memory counters, 315-316
    network packets, 319
    paging files, 316-318
    Performance Logs and Alerts, 312-314
    processor counters, 319-320
    System Monitor, 310-312
    Task Manager, 320-321
monitors. *See* displays
mounted drives, 240-241
Mouse applet, 139
Mouse tab (Accessibility Options applet),
    162
MouseKeys, 162
moving
    compressed files, 244-245
    encrypted files, 249
MSCONFIG.EXE utility, 143-145
MSDTC (Microsoft Distributed
    Transaction Coordinator), 353-354
MSI files
    installing, 149-150
    publishing, 150-151
    repairing, 152-153
MSIEXEC.exe, 152-153
MUI (Multilingual User Interface) Pack,
    153
Multilink, 190
multiple-device dialing, 189-190
multiple-language support, 153-157
multiple-monitor support, 197-200
My Computer, 41
My Documents, 126-128
My Network Places, 44

N

name resolution
 DNS servers, 261, 267
 NetBIOS, 267
 WINS, 261, 267
naming user accounts, 98
Narrator, 163
NAT-T, 337
NBTSTAT utility, 269
.NET Passport, 119, 276
Net Share command, 44-45
Net Use command, 45, 82
NetBEUI protocol, 274
NetBIOS
 current connections, listing, 269
 IP address name resolution, 261, 267
 NWLink, 272-273
Netcap.exe, 319
netsh firewall command, 339
NETSTAT utility, 269
NetWare connectivity, 272-274
network adapters, installing, 194
Network Configuration Operators group,
 49-50, 98
Network group, 98
Network Monitor Driver, 319
network printers, connecting to, 81-82
Network security principal, 51
networks
 bridges, 274-275
 domains, joining, 20-21
 installing Windows XP Professional
 over, 7-8
 answer files, creating, 8-10
 RIS (Remote Installation Services),
 14-19
 Sysprep.exe, 12-14
 winnt.exe switches, 11
 winnt32.exe switches, 11-12
 logons, 105
 Novell NetWare connectivity, 272-274
 performance, managing, 319
 shared folders. See shared folders
 Unix connectivity, 274
 wireless. See wireless networking
 workgroups
 joining, 19-20
 security, 59
New Connection Wizard, 334
New Toolbar toolbar, 143
New Volume Wizard, 228-230
Non-Duplicate Mode (MeasureUp), 432
nonroutable IP addresses, 264
normal backups, 294-295
Nosidgen option (Sysprep), 14
Notification option (Accessibility Options
 applet), 162

Novell NetWare connectivity, 272-274
NTBackup.exe, 292. *See also* backups
 configuring backups, 295
 permissions, 293
 optical media not supported by, 201, 295
 restoring files and folders, 298-299
 scheduling backups, 296-297
 System State data backups, 295-296
 Volume Shadow Copy Service (VSS),
 298
NTCompat.inf file, 145
ntdetect.com file, 218
NTFS (NT File System), 237
 data compression, 243-245
 data encryption, 245-251
 default permissions, reapplying, 239
 disk quotas, 241-243
 errors, detecting and repairing, 234
 master file table (MFT), 235
 permissions
 ACEs (access control entries), 52
 ACLs (access control lists), 52
 advanced, 53-55
 basic, 53
 changing, 56
 conflicts, 57-58
 copying files and folders, 64-65
 cumulative nature of, 56
 default, 56-57
 Deny, assigning, 62-64
 optimizing access to files and folders,
 64
 Read-Only, assigning, 60-62
 users and groups, 49-50, 59
 versus share permissions, 58-59
 viewing, 65
 upgrading to Windows XP Professional,
 4-5
ntldr, 218
Number of Previous Logons to Cache
 policy, 110
NWLink, 272-273

O

Object Access audit policy, 112
offline disks, reactivating, 225
Offline Files, 203
 accessing offline files/folders, 137
 configuring, 45-46, 131-133
 making files/folders available offline,
 133-134
 managing offline files/folders, 137
 storage location, default, 46
 synchronizing offline files/folders,
 135-136
 viewing offline files/folders, 134

On-Screen Keyboard, 163
optical media devices, 191-192
  Backup utility and, 201
optimizing performance. *See* performance, monitoring and optimizing
OUs (organizational units) linking to GPOs, 108
ownership of files and folders, 66-67

P

paged pool, 322
Pages/sec counter, 315
paging files
  clearing, 110
  managing, 316-318
partitions
  on basic disks, 218-219
  boot, 218
  compressing, 243
  extending, 219
  system, 218
Password Reset Disks, 104
passwords, 103-104
  forgotten, 104
  Group Policy account policies, 110-111
  Remote Assistance, 282
Passwords Must Meet Complexity Requirements account policy, 111
path rules, 118
pausing print jobs, 82
PC Card adapters, 203, 209
performance, monitoring and optimizing, 233-234
  baselines, creating, 314-315
  disk counters, 318-319
  Eventtriggers.exe, 321
  memory counters, 315-316
  network packets, 319
  paging files, 316-318
  processor counters, 319-320
  System Monitor, 310-312
  Task Manager, 320-321
Performance Logs and Alerts, 233, 312-314
Performance snap-in, 233-234
permissions
  for backing up files, 293
  network share permissions, 47-48, 58
  NTFS permissions, 52
    ACEs (access control entries), 52
    ACLs (access control lists), 52
    advanced, 53-55
    basic, 53
    changing, 56
    conflicts, 57-58
    copying files and folders, 64-65

cumulative nature of, 56
  default, 56-57, 239
  Deny, assigning, 62-64
  optimizing access to files and folders, 64
  Read-Only, assigning, 60-62
  users and groups, 49-50, 59
  versus share permissions, 58-59
  viewing, 65
  printer permissions, configuring, 85
  versus user rights, 59-60
pfirewall.log file, 347
PhysicalDisk performance counters, 318-319
ping command, 269-270
PKZip, 243
planning mode (RSoP), 115
PnP (Plug and Play) devices, 176
  installing, 178
  power management during installation, 208
  troubleshooting, 180
  UPnP (Universal PnP), 177
  Windows XP Pro installation and, 2
Point-to-Point Protocol (PPP), 262
Point-to-Point Tunneling Protocol (PPTP), 262
Ports tab (printer Properties dialog box), 84
power management, 206
  ACPI (Advanced Configuration and Power Interface), 207
  allocations for USB hubs, viewing, 193
  APM (Advanced Power Management), 206-207
  and PnP device installation, 208
  portable computers, 208
  power schemes, 207-208
Power Options applet, 139, 206-208
Power Users group, 49-50, 97
PPP (Point-to-Point Protocol), 262
PPTP (Point-to-Point Tunneling Protocol), 262
preferred DNS servers, 267
primary partitions, 218
  creating, 226-227
print servers
  configuring, 83-86
  definition of, 79
Print Services for Unix, 274
print$ hidden share, 43
Printers and Faxes folder, 79
  adding printers, 80-82
  configuring printer properties, 83-86
  managing print jobs, 82-83
printing
  IPP (Internet Printing Protocol), 86
  local printers, adding, 80-81

managing print jobs, 82-83
network printers, adding, 81-82
pooling printers, 80
Print Services for Unix, 274
printer properties, configuring, 83-86
terminology overview, 79-80
Privilege Use audit policy, 112
privileges. *See* user rights
processors
multiple, upgrading to, 201-203
performance, managing, 319-320
profiles
hardware, 204
TCP/IP, 271-272
Program Compatibility Wizard, 146-147
program files
compressing, 243
deleting, 235
publishing MSI packages, 150-153

Q - R

Qchain.exe, 28
Quick Launch toolbar, 143
quotas, disk, 241-243

RADIUS, 332
RAID-5 volumes, 219, 230
raw sockets, restrictions, 351
rbfg.exe, 19
RCP utility, 268
RDP (Remote Desktop Protocol), 277, 280
reactivating dynamic disks, 225
Read & Execute permission, 53
Read Attributes permission, 55
Read Extended Attributes permission, 55
Read permission, 48, 53-55
Read-Only permission, 60-62
Readiness Analyzer, 4
Reboot startup option, 301
recovering system settings, 302-303
Recovery Console, 304-307
refresh frequency, 200
Regional and Language Options applet, 154-157
regional options, 154-157
Registry
authentication, 77-78
backing up, 295-296
remote access, 105
authentication protocols, 330-333
connections, setting up, 334-337
encryption, 333-334
Remote Assistance, 280-283
Remote Desktop, 277-279
Remote Desktop Protocol (RDP), 277, 280
Remote Desktop Users group, 49-50, 98

Remote Installation Services. *See* RIS
Remote Interactive Logon security
principal, 51
removable storage, 200-201
removing. *See also* uninstalling
drive letters, 239-240
shared folders, 41-44
Windows XP Professional, 5-6
renaming accounts, 101
Replicator local group, 49-50
Reseal option (Sysprep), 14
Reset Account Lockout Counter After
account policy, 111
restoring files and folders, 298-299
ASR (Automated System Recovery), 310
restore points, 308
Restrictions for Unauthenticated RPC
Clients policy, 352-353
RestrictRemoteClients Registry key, 352
Resultant Set of Policy. *See* RSoP
Return to the OS Choices Menu startup
option, 301
REXEC utility, 268
Riprep.exe, 18-19
RIS (Remote Installation Services), 14-15
client connections, 19
configuring, 16-17
creating additional images, 17-18
downloading images, 19
installing, 15-16
requirements, 15
risetup.exe, 16
roaming user profiles, 126-129
Roboxopy.exe, 65
ROUTE utility, 269
RPCs (Remote Procedure Calls)
restrictions, 352-353
RPC Endpoint Mapper, 353
RSH service, 268
RSHSVC.EXE, 268
RSoP (Resultant Set of Policy), 112-113
Group Policy Result tool, 113
Group Policy Update tool, 114
RSoP snap-in, 114-115

S

/s:sourcepath switch (winnt.exe), 11
Safe Mode, 299-300
Safe Mode option (Windows Advanced
Options menu), 197
Safe Mode with Command Prompt startup
option, 300
Safe Mode with Networking startup option,
300
scanners, 139, 188
installing, 188
testing, 188-189

Scanners and Cameras applet, 139, 188-189
Scheduled Tasks folder, 168-170
    creating tasks, 168-169
    troubleshooting tasks, 170
Scopy.exe, 65
Screen Saver tab (Display applet), 139
secedit command, 116, 239
sectors, bad, 234
Securews.inf security template, 117
security
    authentication. *See* authentication
    built-in security principals, 50-51
    Data Execution Prevention (DEP), 119,
        322-323
    domain security, 59
    faxes, 167
    Group Policy settings, 110
    NTFS, 49, 52
        advanced permissions, 53-56
        basic permissions, 53
        default permissions, 56-57
        domain security, 59
        permission conflicts, 57-58
        viewing permissions, 65
        workgroup security, 59
    printer settings, 85
    Remote Assistance, 283
    Security Center, 120
    Security Configuration and Analysis
        snap-in, 115-116
    software restriction policies, 117-118
    SP2 enhancements, 350-355
    templates, 116-117
    Windows Security Center, 343-344
    workgroup security, 59
Security Center, 120, 343-344
Security Configuration and Analysis
    snap-in, 115-117
Security dialog box, 105
Security Log, 68, 71-72
    audit policies, 111-112
Security Options node (Group Policy), 110
Send Fax Wizard, 166-167
Serial Line Internet Protocol (SLIP), 262
SerialKey Devices option (Accessibility
    Options applet), 162
servers
    distributed, 7-8
    DNS, 261, 267
    print, 79, 83-86
service packs. *See* SPs
session pool, 322
SETPASS.EXE, 273
sets. *See* volumes
Settings tab (Display applet), 139
setup disks, 3

Setupcl.exe, 13
SFU (Services for Unix), 274
Shared Documents folder, 40
shared folders
    connecting to shared network resources,
        43-45
    controlling access, 45-48
    creating
        for dynamic updates, 30
        from command line, 44-45
        from My Computer, 41
        from Shared Folders MMC snap-in,
            41-42
        from Windows Explorer, 41
    hidden shares, 42-43
    permissions, 47-48, 58
    removing, 41-42, 44
    Web Folders, 76-77
Shared Folders snap-in, 41-42
Shared Music folder, 40
Shared Pictures folder, 40
Sharing tab
    Fax Properties window, 166
    printer Properties dialog box, 84
Show Desktop shortcut, 143
ShowSounds, 161
SID (Security Identifier), 101-102
Signature Verification tool, 185-186
signing device drivers, 185-188
Simple File Sharing, 40
Simple Mail Transfer Protocol (SMTP),
    263
simple volumes, 228-229
sites, linking to GPOs, 108
SLIP (Serial Line Internet Protocol), 262
slipstreaming service packs, 25-26
Smart Cards, 209, 331
SMP (symmetric multiprocessing), 201
SMTP (Simple Mail Transfer Protocol),
    263
software. *See also* applications
    compatibility, 4
    device drivers. *See* device drivers
    identification rules, 118
    restriction policies, 117-118
Software Update Services (SUS), 25
software-based volumes, 226
Sound tab (Accessibility Options applet),
    161
Sounds and Audio Devices applet, 139
SoundSentry, 161
spanned volumes, 228-229
Speech applet, 140
Speech Properties dialog box, 140
SPs (service packs), 25-27
spuninst.exe, 27

How can we make this index more useful? Email us at indexes@quepublishing.com

Standby mode, 139, 207-208
Start menu, customizing, 140-141
Start Windows Normally startup option, 301
startup options, 299-301
StickyKeys, 160
STOP errors, during installation, 32
striped volumes, 229-230
Study Mode (MeasureUp), 431
subnet masks, 266
    configuration settings, 269
    variable-length, 264-265
SUS (Software Update Services), 25
symmetric multiprocessing (SMP), 201
synchronizing offline files and folders, 46, 135-136
SysMain.sdb file, 146
Sysprep, 12-14
System Configuration Utility, 143-145
system files
    backing up, 295-296
    updating, 183
system groups, 98
system modes, compatibility support, 147
System Monitor, 233, 310-312
system partition, 218
System permission, 57
System Preparation tool, 12-14
System Restore, 307-309
System Restore Wizard, 308-309
system settings
    configuring, 143-145
    recovering, 302-303
        actions, 302-303
        Automated System Recovery, 309-310
        Recovery Console, 304-307
        System Restore, 307-309
System State data, backing up, 295-296
System.ini file, editing, 144

raw sockets, restrictions, 351
    troubleshooting, 268-271
technical support, MeasureUp test engine, 435
Telnet, 268
template user accounts, creating, 106
templates, security, 116-117
temporary files, deleting, 235
Terminal Server User security principal, 50-51
Themes tab (Display applet), 138
thumb drives, 194
TLS (Transport Level Security), 331
ToggleKeys, 161
toolbars, adding to taskbar, 142-143
trace logs, 313-314
TRACERT utility, 269
Tracking tab (Fax Properties window), 166
Transport Level Security (TLS), 331
Traverse Folder/Execute File permission, 55
troubleshooting
    disks, 232-235
    displays, 200
    hardware devices, 180
    ICS, 349-350
    IIS, 78-79
    modems, 190
    scheduled tasks, 170
    TCP/IP, 268-271
    USB devices, 193-194
    volumes, 232-235
    Windows XP Professional systems
        Automated System Recovery, 309-310
        installations, 31-32
        recovery actions, 302-303
        Recovery Console, 304-307
        startup options, 299-301
        System Restore, 307-309
Trust for Delegation setting, 246

T

Take Ownership permission, 55
tape devices, 201
Task Manager, 320-321
taskbar customization options, 142-143
Taskbar and Start Menu applet, 140-143
Taskbar and Start Menu Properties dialog box, 140-143
TCP/IP, 260
    addresses, 263. *See also* IP addresses
    components and services included, 260-263
    configuring, 266-268
    outbound connection limits, 351-352
    profiles, 271-272

U

/udf:id switch (winnt.exe), 11
UDF (Universal Disk Format), 191, 241
Udfs.sys driver, 191
/unattend switch (winnt32.exe), 11
Unattend.txt file, 8
uninstalling
    service packs, 27
    Windows XP Professional, 5-6
Universal Disk Format (UDF), 191, 241
Universal groups, 100
Universal Plug and Play (UPnP), 177
Universal Serial Bus. *See* USB devices
Unix connectivity, 274
unrestricted software restriction policies, 118

Update.msi file, 26
updates
　Automatic Updates, 28-29, 180-181
　device drivers, 180-183
　Dynamic Update, 29-30
　system files, 183
　Update Hardware Wizard, 201-202
　update packs, 4
　update.exe, 26
upgrading
　basic disks to dynamic disks, 221-224
　to multiple processors, 201-203
　to Windows XP Pro, 3-6, 68
UPN (User Principal Name), 105
UPnP (Universal Plug and Play), 177
USB devices, 192-194
　daisy-chaining, 193
　troubleshooting, 193-194
　write access, controlling, 67-68, 251-252
USB host controllers, 192-193
USB hubs, 192-193
user accounts
　built-in, 96
　configuring properties, 99-100
　creating, 98-101, 106
　deleting, 102, 107
　disabling, 101, 107
　domain security, 59
　enabling, 101
　naming, 98
　passwords, 99, 103-104
　permissions, 60-65
　renaming, 101
　switching between, 104, 130
　workgroup security, 59
User Accounts tool, 102
User Principal Name (UPN), 105
user profiles, 126
　Fast User Switching, 130
　Group Policy settings, 129-130
　home folders, 127
　local, 126-127
　logon scripts, 127
　roaming, 126, 128-129
user rights, 109-110
　versus permissions, 59-60
User Scope option (RSoP), 114
User State Migration Tool. See USMT
users
　authentication, 105
　default local users, 49
　migrating settings, 21-25, 157-159
Users group, 49-50, 97
Users permission, 57

USMT (User State Migration Tool), 21-22
　command-line options, 23-25
　Files and Settings Transfer Wizard,
　　22-23, 157-159
Utility Manager, 163-164

V

variable-length subnet masks (VLSMs),
　264-265
Verifier.exe, 182
video adapters, 197
Video Display Troubleshooter, 139
virtual memory
　clearing pagefiles, 110
　managing pagefiles, 316-318
virus scan software, 5
VLSMs (variable-length subnet masks),
　264-265
Volume Shadow Copy Service (VSS), 298
volumes
　boot, 218
　compressing, 243
　disk quotas, 241-243
　dynamic, 227
　　extending, 229
　　formatting, 220
　　limitations, 230-232
　　mirrored, 219, 230
　　RAID-5, 219, 230
　　simple, 228
　　spanned, 228
　　striped, 229-230
　fault-tolerant, 219, 226
　mounted, 240-241
　system, 218
　troubleshooting, 232-235
VPNs (virtual private networks)
　authentication protocols, 330-333
　encryption, 333-334
　setting up connections, 336-337
VSS (Volume Shadow Copy Service), 298

W

wake events, ACPI-compliant devices, 208
Web Folders, 76-77
WebDAV protocol, 77-78
WF. See Windows Firewall
Win.ini file, editing, 144
Windows 98, reverting to from Windows
　XP Professional, 5-6
Windows 9x, upgrading to Windows XP
　Professional, 5
Windows 2000, upgrading to Windows XP
　Professional, 5

Windows 2000 Professional, migrating data to Windows XP Professional, 231-232
Windows Catalog, 176
Windows Explorer, creating shared folders, 41
Windows Firewall, 337-347
    exceptions, configuring, 345-346
    logging, 347
    Windows Security Center, 343-344
Windows Installer Service, 148-153
    installing MSI packages, 149-150
    publishing MSI packages, 150-153
Windows Internet Naming Service. *See* WINS
Windows ME, reverting to from Windows XP Professional, 5-6
Windows Media Player, 191
Windows Media shortcut, 143
Windows Messenger, 275-277
Windows NT
    migrating data to Windows XP Professional, 231
    upgrading to Windows XP Professional, 5
Windows Product Activation (WPA), 31
Windows Security Center, 343-344
Windows Update
    drivers, searching for automatically, 182-183
    system files, updating, 183
Windows XP Professional
    activating, 30-31
    installing
        adapter compatibility, 2
        additional information, 38
        answer files, creating, 8-10
        CD-ROM installations, 7
        distributed servers, 7-8
        hardware requirements, 2
        migrating user settings, 21-25
        RIS, 14-19
        setup disks, 3
        System Preparation, 12-14
        troubleshooting, 31-32
        winnt.exe switches, 11
        winnt32.exe switches, 11-12

startup options, 299-301
uninstalling, 5-6
upgrading to, 3-6
    file sharing and, 68
    file system considerations, 5
    pre-upgrade checklist, 3-5
winnt.exe, 11
winnt32.exe, 7-8, 11-12
WINS (Windows Internet Naming Service), 261
    server addresses, obtaining, 267
WinZip, 243
Wireless Network Setup Wizard, 143, 196
wireless networking
    configuring, 196
    IEEE 802.1x standard, 195
    SP2 enhancements, 196
Wireless Provisioning Services (WPS), 196
workgroups
    joining, 19-20
    security, 59
WPA (Windows Product Activation), 31
WPS (Wireless Provisioning Services), 196
Write Attributes permission, 55
Write Extended Attributes permission, 55
Write permission, 53
WriteProtect storage device policy, 67-68, 251-252
WWW (World Wide Web) publishing service, 263

X - Z

Xcopy.exe, 65
Xpsp2.exe, 26

ZAP files, 150
ZIP files, 243-244
zone rules, 118